D0117834

SMB CONSULTING
BEST PRACTICES

Harry Brelsford

Shoryn
HARA
PUBLISHING
Seattle, Washington

SMB Nation Press
P.O. Box 10179
Bainbridge Island, WA 98110-0179
206-842-1127
Fax: 425-488-3646

ISBN: 0-974858-06-04
Library of Congress Number: 2003110685

Printed in USA
10 9 8 7 6 5 4 3

Editor: Vicki McCown
Design & Production: Lisa Delaney

Dedication

To my father, Harry Gregg Brelsford, who left us during the writing of this book and is now practicing law in the sky!

Contents

PART ONE: PAINTING THE SMB CONSULTING PICTURE

CHAPTER 1

SO YOU WANT TO BE AN SMB CONSULTANT?!?!

CHAPTER 2

SMB CONSULTING BUSINESS PLAN

PART TWO: FINDER

CHAPTER 5
SMB MARKETING

CHAPTER 6
SMB CONSULTING SALES 6-1

CHAPTER 7

xiv

PART THREE: MINDER

CHAPTER 8
CRM: CLIENT RELATIONSHIP MANAGEMENT 8-1

CHAPTER 10

PART FOUR: GRINDER

CHAPTER 12
SMB CONSULTING NICHES

Appendix A

Appendix B

Appendix C

Foreword

To live free, make an impact, enjoy your work, and make a profit. Those are the primary life goals of most any SMB consultant you are likely to meet. The trick is that an SMB consultant can't get too hung up on any one of those four issues, because the secret to happiness is to balance those often conflicting needs, rather than letting any one of them dominate at the expense of the other three.

Of course, this is all much easier said than done, so it takes an extraordinary individual to be a successful SMB consultant. Unlike their mercurial customers, the SMB entrepreneur needs to combine patience with business insight to help guide their customers through a labyrinth of technology choices that can easily aggravate a class of customers who are keenly aware "time is money."

The simple truth is the SMB owner is the most challenging customer in the IT industry because, more often than not, their business can flourish or expire thanks to the right or wrong technology decision. Alas, nothing in this industry is ever as straightforward as it seems, so a nervous SMB owner who is typically worried about making payroll can easily be led astray. And once that happens, a torrent of frustration and recrimination is quickly unleashed squarely on the head of the SMB consultant.

All too frequently this leads to the tarring of all SMB consultants in the same way a few bad lawyers or journalists can cast aspersions on an entire profession. Of course, there are times when the misstep of a consultant does lead to some debacle, but the root cause of that disaster is usually ignorance rather than malfeasance. All told, the vast majority of SMB consultants are a credit to the industry.

Whether an SMB consultant created their practice as a deliberate act to advance their careers or as an unintended consequence derived from events beyond their control, everybody needs a helping hand. So we at *CRN* applaud the publishing of a book that seeks to increase the number of savvy SMB consultants in the world, which will reduce the number of failed IT projects and consulting practices while simultaneously increasing the value proposition of technology itself.

It's important to remember that the technology industry as a whole would not exist as we know it today if it were not for the SMB consultants serving as its evangelists for countless products. More often than not, it is the SMB market leading the way in terms of bringing new technology innovations to market. That becomes even more apparent when you consider the challenges of the SMB owner. With fewer resources and people, the SMB owner frequently needs to compete for business against larger rivals by being more adroit. And in the absence of larger rivals, there's always the need to be more efficient, because the cardinal rule of business is "Revenue drives growth."

The only way to achieve those twin goals is to reduce the steps it takes to execute a business process and increase revenue per employee. And the quickest way to do that is to maximize a technological edge before any one else does.

Of course, most SMB owners are not technological gurus. So they turn to trusted SMB consultants to get them through the all-too-often daunting tasks associated with investing in technology. For the industry as whole, this means the SMB consultant is the primary way the word gets out about which products work and which don't. Without the guidance of the SMB consultant, billions of dollars spent on technology marketing would fall on the deaf ears of SMB owners too busy to appreciate the lasting impact any given technology can have on their business.

So here's a salute to the SMB consultant. For the most part, they make a good living and enjoy being masters of their own domain. But more often than not, they are typically underappreciated and undervalued by vendors who are more focused on the name on the check than the actual person who got them the deal.

We can only hope that with the publishing of more books such as this one, it will become easier for a larger number of people to form their own SMB consulting practices. Lest we forget, it is the SMB consultant who truly forms the bulwark of this industry and, as such, we are invested in their success.

Yours very truly,
Michael Vizard,
Editor In Chief, *CRN*

Michael Vizard joined CMP Mediaπs CRN, the newsweekly for builders of technology solutions, as editor in chief in August 2002. In this role, Mr. Vizard is responsible for the strategic vision of the newsweekly, ensuring editorial coverage goals are met by evolving the reporting and editorial beats to accommodate readers' information needs.

Mr. Vizard has more than 15 years of computer technology and publishing experience. In 2001 and 2002, Mr. Vizard was voted one of the Top 30 Most Influential Technology Journalists by Technology Marketing. He was also named one of the Top 15 media influencers in the trade press category. Prior to joining CRN, Mr. Vizard spent seven years as editor in chief of InfoWorld Media Group, where he was responsible for managing strategic editorial partnerships, the day-to-day management of InfoWorld's editorial department, and leading the content of InfoWorld Online.

Prior to joining InfoWorld, Mr. Vizard had been an editor at PC Week, Computerworld, Digital Review, and ebn.

Mr. Vizard holds a degree in journalism from Boston University.

About the Author

Seasoned SMB consultant and Bainbridge Island, Washington, author Harry Brelsford actively serves a portfolio of business clients each and every day in his Small Business Server (SBS) niche. The author of ten technology books, including *Small Business Server 2003 Best Practices*, Harry is a long-time trainer and lecturer on all matters related to SMB technologies and frequently speaks at domestic US and international events. He is the founder of SMB Nation, a conference series dedicated to small and medium business technology solutions (www.smbnation.com). He publishes the biweekly *Small Business Best Practices* newsletter that speaks to SMB and SBS technologies, with over 5,000 readers worldwide. Though he has earned an alphabet soup of certifications (MCSE, MCT, CNE, etc.) and an MBA, Harry welcomes the opportunity to learn from and share information with colleagues in the industry. He can be reached at harryb@nethealthmon.com.

Preface

Welcome to *SMB Consulting Best Practices*, a book that addresses an important need in the small and medium business technology community: how to use your technical skill set to make good money and have fun as a successful SMB consultant. With a focus on best business practices, you will learn the all-important business side of consulting to balance out the technical "bits" side you've already mastered (and will read about in other books, such as *Small Business Server 2003 Best Practices*). For some readers of this book, being a successful SMB consultant means making a lot of money. Others are seeking professional fulfillment, client service opportunities, and perhaps self-employment. Some want it all. This book is for all parties.

What This Book Is About

This book focuses on the business side of being an SMB consultant and running a professional services practice. I use the popular finder (sales), minder (management), and grinder (work) model of professional services to present my SMB consulting wisdom. My words to you are based on my real-world experiences as a long-time and still-active SMB consultant. And as you'll see when you turn the pages, I have interjected stories of other SMB consultants so you receive complete, well-rounded, and balanced business information for you to process.

More important, this book tells it like it is. I speak to the good, which is making six-figure incomes—without the nuisance of a boss and with the freedom of setting your own work schedule (within reason)—but I don't shy away from the bad, such as forcing you to honestly assess your fitness as an SMB consultant and your ability to weather long hours and client tirades. The big dollars and big fun don't come cheaply. I think you'll find my honesty to be refreshing, and I hope it lends credibility to the words in this tome. While this book won't always make you feel good about the world of SMB consulting, it will serve and protect you in your professional SMB consulting career.

Perhaps following the advice in this book will allow you to exceed the financial compensation numbers for IT professionals you read about in different trade journals such as *CRN* and *Microsoft Certified Professional Magazine*. Or perhaps you may find this book leads you to a different decision—to keep your existing salaried staff job and not to endeavor to excel as an SMB consultant. Thus I think you'll feel the money spent on this book to be well-allocated and returned several times over. I'd like everyone who buys the book to become a successful SMB consultant, but if that goal can't be reached at this time, I'd like this book to prevent people from becoming an unsuccessful SMB consultant.

In this book, I never leave the practical and pragmatic real world of SMB consulting for the comfort of the training classroom for more than a paragraph. That would be inappropriate. But I've brought over one practice from my time as a college adjunct instructor and Microsoft Certified Trainer (MCT) in the education realm: Brelsford's Dozen. In nearly every chapter of this book, you will find a Brelsford's Dozen. By consistently applying an easily understood framework to complex, real-world SMB consulting matters, you can see how the advice applies to you, the SMB consultant seeking to do a better job, without feeling like you're being told to do what I say and do myself. A Brelsford's Dozen is a way for me to give you a key checklist for the topic at hand, such as giving out one business card per week (or a dozen business cards per fiscal quarter). I believe you'll find my insights via Brelsford's Dozen to be both enlightening and enjoyable. I also throw in reader mail as part of Brelsford's Mailbox to provide even more real-world perspective.

I also sprinkle in tidbits of technical information where appropriate. This book certainly isn't a rewrite of the online help system or product resource manuals, a common reader complaint posted with online book resellers for technical books. Nor does the limited technical discussion in any way replace technical texts. Rather, I attempt to present billable opportunities to you. For example, Small Business Server installations are a tremendous SMB consulting opportunity. It is in that spirit I present targeted technical discussion.

Another interesting aspect to my take on this subject is my use of third-party applications. My belief is this book should mirror the real-world of SMB consulting as closely as possible. In order to accomplish that, I break away from the strict Microsoft mindset of using only Microsoft solutions. Instead, I look at how I run my SMB consulting practice and with what software tools. I find I use software solutions from a wide range of independent software vendors (ISVs). That's why you'll find me singing the praises of GFI's Network Security Scanner, ConnectWise PSA, QuickBooks, and Timeslips. I also think you'll find between these covers a book with an appropriate Microsoft focus that honors the SMB consulting community we live in.

SMB consultants work in a competitive business environment. In many parts of this book I put on my MBA hat and present competent strengths, weakness, opportunities, and threats analysis. For example, my competitive analysis speaks to the types of competitors you'll likely encounter.

Who Should Read This Book

Several masters are served by this book, including:

- **Those considering an SMB consulting career** — If you are a potential SMB consultant, you are clearly among the largest audience for this book. Hopefully, you'll read this book with interest from cover to cover as you make the professional decision to become an SMB consultant. This book has been written as a one-stop resource for your occupational research undertaking.

- **Existing SMB consultants seeking higher professional performance levels** — I have heard time and time again that while the SMB consulting field is a great profession, individual performances can be improved. If you are an existing SMB consultant who strives to deliver better customer service, to pick better clients, and to select better technology solutions, you will benefit from this book.

- **Consulting managers** — Perhaps you've traded the TechNet technical library for life behind the desk as an SMB consulting firm manager or owner. This book can improve your effectiveness in this role by not only speaking directly to you and your issues, but also by educating you on what your consulting staff does. When I incorporated this thinking into my text, I drew on my time as an SMB consultant working for a regional accounting firm. If only I had had a book like this at the time to hand to the CPAs and say, "Read this— this is what I do," my life would have been much more pleasant.

- **Salespeople** — The members of the sales force are important people in many larger SMB consulting organizations. They get the work for SMB consultants. This book can make the lives of those in the professional services business development field much easier. By knowing more about what they're selling (your SMB consulting services), the salespeople can be more successful. And that can only make you more successful. Take my friendly advice and buy an extra copy of this book to give to the salespeople at your consulting firm.

- **Microsoft Windows Small Business Server 2003 fans** — This book provides a sneak peek at Microsoft Windows Small Business Server 2003 (SBS). It was written late in the development cycle of SBS 2003, and I was allowed to discuss it and display screenshots. If you're still using SBS 2000, fear not, as much of the book speaks to both SBS 2000 and 2003.

- **Stakeholders: Spouses, partners, parents, and siblings** — I certainly plan to give copies of this book to my wife, folks, brothers, sister, kids, and in-laws. Hopefully, the book can save me a lot of time having to explain what I do for a living and why I work long hours.

How This Book Is Organized

Simply stated, this book is organized into sections that honor the finder, minder, and grinder consulting practice business model.

1. Painting the SMB Consulting Picture

2. Finder

3. Minder

4. Grinder

5. Appendixes

Part I: Painting the SMB Consulting Picture

Before getting into the details, I spend some time providing foundational knowledge about running a business, writing a business plan, and defining professional services consulting.

Part II: Finder

Clearly, you have to get the business in the door to stay in business, so accordingly the finder role is explored over several chapters. By the end of this part, you'll have a newfound appreciation for business development.

Part III: Minder

You'll find early on in your career that managing the business is as important as getting the work and doing the work. I speak to management issues in this part. And if management isn't your gig, I also speak to outsourcing some business functions, such as accounting, so you can focus on your strengths and not become bogged down by your weaknesses.

Part IV: Grinder

"Ah, time for the *good stuff*," as many SMB consultants have remarked to me. In this part of the book, I speak to providing appropriate solutions for your beloved clients. I cover a wide range of solutions, such as security consulting to business advisory services, but I primarily focus on Microsoft Windows Small Business Server 2003.

Appendixes

In the back part of this book, you'll find many goodies, including lots of SMB consulting resources, a recap of the Brelsford's Dozen presented in the book, and a quick-and-dirty SMB consulting success kit (trinkets of wisdom in a short form).

Acknowledgments

Even though I live on an island, it took a lot of people living on the mainland to make this book happen. All books are an exercise in synergy, with the sum of everyone's contributions exceeding what any one person could accomplish.

First and foremost, I want to acknowledge my clients and fellow SMB consultants who have taught me more about business and technology than I can find words to express.

The team at Hara Publishing has kept me true and focused on getting this book out the door. A tip of the hat to Sheryn Hara, and fellow island dwellers Vicki McCown and Lisa Delaney.

Additionally, the good people at HP/Compaq who loaned me test servers need a serious round of applause from me. Here it is.

Finally, I acknowledge my modern influences in the business community who have gotten me where I am today, including Anton Krucky.

Forward!

I started this front matter with a Foreword and I end it with a Forward! It's now time to read the book. Afterward, your next steps are to consider the following actions:

- **Go forth and be a successful SMB consultant!** By the final pages of this book, you'll be well equipped to go out and do it. Be the SMB consultant you're capable of being.

- **Subscribe to my free *Small Business Best Practices* newsletter.** This is how I effectively update this book and communicate with you on a biweekly basis. Subscribe by visiting my Web site: www.nethealthmon.com

- **Read my other SMB and SBS books.** Another next step would be to read some of my other books such as Small Business Server 2003 Best Practices (November 2003).

- **Attend SMB Nation.** So you want to go to the next level and be a leader in the SMB consulting movement? Then attend this ongoing conference, which I produce. Visit www.smbnation.com

So it's time to stop talking to you and let you read. All the best to you, mates!

Harry Brelsford
Author, Consultant, Trainer
Bainbridge Island, WA, USA

Part One

PAINTING
THE SMB CONSULTING
PICTURE

Chapter One
So You Want to Be an SMB Consultant?!?!

Chapter Two
SMB Consulting Business Plan

Chapter Three
Foundation for SMB Consulting

Chapter 1
So You Want to Be an SMB Consultant?!?!

In This Chapter

- Reasons to be an SMB consultant

- Enjoying the financial and professional rewards of SMB consulting

- Observing an average work week of an SMB consultant

- Appreciating the success factors affecting SMB consulting

- Understanding failure factors affecting SMB consultation

So you want to be an SMB consultant? And not just any SMB consultant, but a profitable and content SMB consultant? Congratulations. This is the starting point in your journey to become a successful SMB consultant! Savor this moment, because your professional life will change from this point forward. Another reason to savor the moment is to firmly establish your humbleness baseline from which you'll draw your modesty later when success beckons. That is, you'll want to remember where you came from once you've graduated and moved a long way from this space.

Moving forward, the pace quickens from this moment for the balance of your SMB consulting career. Believe it or not, starting with these introductory paragraphs, you've launched yourself as an SMB consultant (albeit a relatively new one).

As I've traveled the world preaching about Microsoft Small Business Server, I have seen time and time again that many, many good people *want* to become SMB consultants. However, few of these people truly accomplish that wonderful yet challenging goal. For most people, their SMB consulting plans never progress beyond idle bar-be-cue banter with neighbors, shooting the breeze over the grill on a sunny summer weekend when such talk is especially cheap. Others get part of the way through the process before things like family matters preclude them from reaching the promised land of SMB consulting. Others become SMB consultants, but not truly profitable in their work, remaining content to eek out a living, receive no client referrals, but otherwise enjoy their professional lives. Finally, a select class will not only enjoy being an SMB consultant but will thrive financially along the way and be able to look back many years hence and agree it was all worth it.

I'm going try my best to get you to that place — and you've taken the all-important first step by not only purchasing this book, but actually starting to read it! You'd be amazed how many folks buy books and then never use them. So onward, one paragraph at a time, as we journey together through this book and reach the lofty heights of successful SMB consulting.

You've likely concluded that the goal of this book is to better your professional life. I assert that achieving this goal will lead to a better personal life. Properly done, SMB consulting can get you there. Poorly done, SMB consulting can become a professional and personal nightmare, with what seems like hostile clients converging from all sides. This chapter sets the foundation for making the best decision for you as you consider a career in SMB consulting.

Why Be an SMB Consultant?

In the SMB consulting community, there are both common and dissimilar reasons for becoming SMB consultants. My motivations may or may not be the same as yours. That's okay, as there is room for all of us in the vast field of SMB consulting. In this section, I explore the most frequent motivations for becoming an SMB consultant.

Working for yourself

As an SMB consultant, a trainer, and an author, I have observed that the number one reason people make the break and become SMB consultants is their desire to be self-employed. Working for yourself has different meanings and motivations for different people. For me, it means having flex time and not riding the Bainbridge to Seattle ferry with the eight-to-five crowd each day. For you, it might be a way to rebel against authority and not be beholden to corporate bosses. For many, it is a way to follow the family tradition of self-employment. Some folks just come out of the womb with an independent streak and, like those on the family farms of America, would only be happy if they worked for themselves.

One additional thought on authority figures and problems working for them: I've witnessed very successful SMB consultants who weren't good employees (that's the "e" word) when they were under a boss (or, more important, a boss's thumb!). These people didn't like taking directions and orders from higher-ups. In fact, they would stage outright rebellion. But, fast forward to that point when they have finally blossomed into a self-employed SMB consultants. Often that rebelliousness is under control and they actually thrive as successful SMB consultants.

> BEST PRACTICE: Becoming an SMB consultant doesn't necessarily or always mean being self-employed. Many SMB consultants work for consulting firms ranging from large computer resellers (such as Gateway) to local contract houses and temporary agencies. It's true that you can work your magic and practice your craft as a salaried (or W2) SMB consultant for a firm (read "employer") and find that many of the same SMB consulting dynamics — such as billing for your time and enjoying the high degree of freedom that SMB consultants love — exist no matter where, how, or for whom you work.

Variety is the spice of life and this is a theme that holds true for SMB consultants. There is this notion that by becoming an SMB consultant, you are escaping the day-to-day drudgery that many employees feel in their cubicles. This could be epitomized by an evil coworker, a difficult boss, or the rote and routine of life as a network administrator. Escapism works for me and perhaps you too.

Making money

Second to the motivation of enjoying relative freedom as a self-employed SMB consultant is the incentive to make money. SMB consulting promises the opportunity to make great money, albeit you will earn each and every one of those dollars (to which the next couple hundred pages of this book will attest). There are no free goods, free lunches, or windfalls here, my fellow SMB consultant. That said, I routinely hear from SMB consultants who are making more than the salaries earned at their previous jobs. And even when I hear from SMB consultants who have simply maintained the same salary they had before, typically they exclaim with excitement that they get paid for doing what they now love: SMB consulting!

> BEST PRACTICE: A cautionary few words of wisdom. If your primary motivation for becoming an SMB consultant is to make money, you're probably not going to last for the long term. Money is great, but if you're ill-equipped in other departments, such as managing clients or enjoying the actual hands-on work, your enduring wanderlust will overcome your desire for dough. Trust me on that, as I've seen it happen many times.
>
> Need more proof for this theorem? Let me cite the observation offered to me by a small business client, a lady who has been and remains the president of a successful real estate firm. She said that in her after-hours role as the chairperson of the local chamber of commerce, she'd seen many a flash-in-the-pan volunteer sign up for chamber duties in the hopes of quickly scoring lucrative business contacts (and thus make some fast money). When these same volunteers — more often than not assigned to newbie duties like managing the membership committee — realized they faced a lot of hard work with any payoff long down the road, they promptly ran out the door, never to be seen at a chamber function again.
>
> The lesson is that money is a great, but not your one and only, motivator to become an SMB consultant.

A final thought on the money thing. Clients don't write a check just because you parade around as an SMB consultant. You've got to go out, get the work, manage the work and do the work before you ever get paid. All along the way, you've got to keep your eyes focused on the bottom line of profitability. It's harder than it looks, and I've seen many an SMB consultant find, mind, and grind out the work only to be star-struck by the top line of their financial statements (gross revenues), leading them to believe they'd enjoy a huge profit—but actually recording a loss. In short, because they spend everything they earn, they're really not making any money. The middle sections of this book will keep you keenly focused on profitability. You have my word on it.

Serving and helping others

Many SMB consultants enjoy working with people and make the break from other jobs exactly so they can do more of that. As you know, many "regular" SMB jobs, such as network administrator positions, offer limited opportunities to interact with diverse groups of people. It has been my observation that the extroverts amongst us in the SMB consulting crowd are in it as much to work with people as to make money. True, that's not to say an introvert personality type can't help people too, because many do. But truth be told, when it comes to outgoing human interaction, extroverted types find that dialogue and communications with clients come more naturally than introverted types. Just calling it like I see it!

Perhaps you've seen what I've seen, as illustrated in this next example. A liberal arts major from college enters the technology field and, by all accounts, enjoys the people more than the technology. And these same folks might value the relationships they build over the big bucks of technology consulting. These are SMB consultants who work with not-for-profit organizations, who are hobbyists (having made their millions at Microsoft or the neighborhood dot-com startup before the dot-gone crash), or who are "true" trainers. In short, some members of the SMB consulting community truly like helping people.

Variety

Some of us carry childhood disorders into our adult lives, often without knowing it. Many years ago, I learned that my grade school teachers were absolutely correct in their assessment of my hyperactivity. Not only do I need variety, but that variety must be engaging. My specialty clearly wasn't routine administration, which can often be mindless. My life as an SMB consultant has proven to be a true lifesaver, given my need for variety. That is, SMB consulting has provided both the variety and technical challenges I crave.

I'm not alone in this need for variety in applying technical solutions. Not too long ago I had lunch in Redmond at Microsoft with a member of Microsoft's TechNet team. This gentleman felt dissatisfied with his desk job and sought advice on becoming a technology consultant. His job at Microsoft had such a narrow scope as to be dull and boring. And while he was entertaining the possibility of becoming an enterprise-level consultant instead of working at the SMB level, the underpinnings of his cry for help were the same. He couldn't focus on his work while sitting at his desk each day, because he hungered for variety.

Becoming an SMB consultant allows you to do what many of you love best: apply technical solutions to a variety of clients. In the "A Week in the Life of an SMB Consultant" section later in this chapter, I provide a glimpse of the variety of technical solutions an SMB consultant can be expected to apply in any given week.

Sunk costs

Some SMB consultants pressure themselves or feel spousal pressure to go out and make some money with the technical skill set they spent so many years acquiring. A common refrain is "You took five years of evenings and weekends to master this software product, you for damn sure better go make some money now!" While that sense of duty or guilt over hours invested in your skill set might not be the best foundation for launching your SMB consulting career, there's no doubt it's a decision-making factor for many of us. If you recall the "sunk costs" lecture from Economics 101 in college, you'd know that basing future decisions on past outlays is typically a poor strategy. That said, we SMB consultants are only human, and sometimes we make slightly irrational decisions, like listening to sunk costs.

A Week in the Life of an SMB Consultant

At this point, you've been exposed to some of the factors that motivate someone to become an SMB consultant. Now let me drop down to the day-to-day level and attempt to further manage your expectations on what it's like to live and breathe the life of an SMB consultant.

Contrary to popular belief, the SMB consultant's week doesn't commence with dawn on Monday and end with sunset on Friday. I'll show you why that is in Table 1-1. Note this was taken from one of my actual weeks in early 2003.

Table 1-1
SMB Consultant's Typical Week

Day	Task
Monday	Morning: Returned to office after two-week holiday. Replied to e-mail and returned telephone calls all morning. Wrote my monthly column for Microsoft Press (a marketing approach I use to generate business).
	Afternoon: More deskwork and made two sales calls: John O, the attorney, and John S, the CPA. Extensive telephone conversations with both prospects followed by e-mails.
	Evening: Drove 2 hours north to Bellingham, WA, and checked into Holiday Inn Hotel. Had dinner with Microsoft TS2 instructor.
Tuesday	Morning: Attend Microsoft TS2 event and was introduced to crowd as Small Business Server specialist. Spoke with individual attendees during breaks. Made sales contacts. Returned to Seattle in late AM.
	Afternoon: Stopped by two clients. At the property management firm, I added a new PC to the Small Business Server (SBS) network by configuring the firewall client, IE browser proxy settings, mapped drives, adding the users to the local administrator group, and fully configuring the Outlook profiles for e-mail. I stopped by another client (CPA firm) to pick up a night key to perform some after hours work on Wednesday evening.
	Evening: Caught up on e-mails, participated in SBS Yahoo! user group matters and planned for travel to a San Francisco cardiology clinic later in the week.
Wednesday	Morning: Answered e-mail and created time slips to bill clients. Went to bank to deposit checks received from clients from December billings. Faxed accounting information to bookkeeper and reviewed with follow-up telephone call. Went to post office to

Table 1-1, cont.

	ship a copy of my Small Business Server 2000 Best Practices book to a winner of an eBay auction.
	Afternoon: Deskwork and outlined new book (yes – the SMB Consulting Best Practices book). Talked with a second client in San Francisco, a manufacturing firm, who would like to use my services later in the week when I travel.
	Evening: Went to CPA firm and added new hard disk for more space, added new virus detector, read client memo on restoring data from tape, added modem to use Shared Fax Service in SBS 2000. Attempted to restore client data but didn't have Veritas Backup Exec password. Left client a site report and departed at midnight.
Thursday	Morning: Stopped by CPA client site (from last night) at 7:00am on the way to airport. Attempted to restore data again using some older passwords I found. Proceeded to Seattle airport to fly to two client sites in San Francisco.
	Afternoon: Landed in San Francisco and rented car. Proceeded to first client site (manufacturer) and installed SBS Service Pack 1. Answered numerous questions client had (e.g., using Windows NT 4.0 Workstation clients, user profiles, etc.). Departed this client site in late afternoon and proceeded to second client site (cardiology clinic).
	Evening: Arrived cardiology clinic in early evening. Shut down SBS server machine and added second network adapter card. Implemented ISA Server-based firewall protection. Installed backup program and engaged in security hardening (e.g., use of Security event log to audit logons and deleted files). Arrived at hotel at 10:00pm.
Friday	Morning: Returned to cardiology clinic at 9:00am and added SBS client-side components (e.g., Firewall Client) to each workstation.

Table 1-1, cont.

	Configured server for POP3 Connector in Exchange 2000 to retrieve existing POP-based e-mail and deliver inside of Exchange IS. Numerous other tasks, including restoring SQL Server-based database. Implemented Shared Fax Services and tested. Configured intrusion detection in ISA Server 2000. Afternoon: Completed outstanding action items at cardiology clinic and proceeded to airport to fly back to Seattle. Evening: Arrived in Seattle at 8:00pm. Proceeded to CPA office to complete data restore from tape. Received call from lead CPA and worked with him to perfect VPN connectivity from his Vashon Island, WA, home. Left CPA firm at 11:30pm and arrived home at 1:00am (Saturday morning).
Saturday	Woke early to drive kids to ski resort for Nordic and alpine ski schools. Spoke with lead cardiologist from cardiology clinic from car cellular telephone while driving to ski resort.
Sunday	Spoke several times with cardiologist at cardiology clinic advising him on how to correctly implement Shared Modem Service at each desktop on his SBS 2000 network.

So, what's the point to showing you this table? You are able to witness how, through the course of a week, I engaged in the three major areas of SMB consulting: finder, minder, and grinder — my quick description for getting the business, managing the business, and performing the actual work. These three areas of SMB consultant activities reflect the premise of this book. I also had a busy, booked, and billable week (if we could always have such problems!). In this week, I billed over $3,000 USD of time! Many months hence, when you're up and running as a successful SMB consultant, you'll naturally engage in these three work areas without much thought. It'll be automatic.

Business Planning

Part of my mission with this book is to put the "B" — as in "business" — back in SMB! This book isn't written to simply be a technical how-to by any stretch. Woven into this book is something that's frequently overlooked in the real world of SMB consulting and completely absent in many courses taught at Microsoft Certified Technical Education Centers: business planning.

Business planning applies to the SMB consultant on two fronts:

First, there is the business of running a business. An SMB consultant must possess sound business skills. You can't make it on technical skills alone.

Second, SMB consultants are increasingly participating in a client's business decisions and interacting more and more with business people. This occurs because, at SMB client sites, you are the technical resource. It's unlikely you will enjoy the opportunity to interact with a large IT staff. Instead, the only people you will interact with at the client site will be business people, who will look to you for your technical expertise and how it relates to their business. Ergo – you are drawn into business planning at the client site whether you like it or not.

> BEST PRACTICE: Remember that SBS provides a great SMB consulting opportunity for you to be butcher, baker, and candlestick maker. Not only are you delivering a small business network for SMB clients, but you can help them recast operations along the way. For example, a landscaping company that I've advised in years past on SBS decided to create an e-mail newsletter announcing spring sales and the like. This would replace advertisements that were mailed via the post office (and save postage). In this example, the SBS technology capabilities helped to lower sales and marketing expenses.

SMB Consulting Success Factors

Many of the following observations are my firsthand experiences, confirmed time and time again in the SMB consulting trenches.

- **Communication skills** — Hardly a day goes by that I don't hear the following: An SMB consultant, largely working alone and out of view from his business clients, scores a major technical success with Small Business Server. But the SMB consultant fails to communicate this coup to the client, who, being unaware of the new technical capability, neither congratulates the SMB consultant on a job well done nor takes advantage of the new capability. An example of this would be implementing the send fax capability of the Shared Fax Service in SBS. Perhaps the client has enjoyed the receive fax capability for some time but didn't know that he could easily send faxes from the desktop as well, saving precious time. SMB consultants, often armed with abundant technical aptitude, need to constantly tell themselves to be a communicator as well (more on this in future chapters).

- **Technical skills** — It's assumed an SMB consultant has the technical skills to solve technical problems (the old "merchant of the trade" assumption in the Uniform Commercial Code legal treatise); however, such is not always the case. Many people are technically unqualified to work on networking solutions such as SBS. Clients pay for bona fide technical solutions when they retain an SMB consultant and expect you to quickly achieve an acceptable technology outcome. I've seen clients become frustrated at some SMB consultants who are great communicators but can't make SBS budge. Bottom line, while all the other SMB consulting success factors are important, you still have to produce favorable technical results.

- **Business acumen** — Do you know how to work efficiently and effectively? Can you schedule and budget your time? Do you show up on time for your appointments? I have witnessed brilliant SMB consultants who have been very poor business people. And by poor business people, I mean both incompetent and unprofitable.

- **Business-development activities** — You are the master of your craft and are doing everything right technically. People think you're a great SMB guru, but you have little or no business activity. Why? Because you aren't gaining new accounts. After spending a couple years in the profession, many SMB consultants come to realize how much selling they must do. A successful SMB consultant is always developing business.

- **Ability to deal with confusion and chaos** — SMB consultants are subject to rapidly shifting small business technology solutions from Microsoft, not to mention rapidly shifting client priorities. Many of the best SMB consultants thrive in this volatile professional environment. As SMB consultants like to say with pride: "Every day is different in my job!"

- **Successful track record** — A key indicator of a successful SMB consulting career can be found in your professional track record. Many star performers who hold in-house positions as competent network administrators make great SMB consultants. Past performance is usually the best predictor of the future outcomes concerning achievement in professional services.

- **Countless variables** — If any of us knew the true predictors of what makes a successful SMB consultant, we'd bottle such a formula. And before we knew it, Bill Gates would be shining our shoes. The point is that your unique gifts may make you a successful SMB consultant where others have tried and failed. Because you're providing professional services, there is a huge human element here that isn't easy to quantify, cannot be taught, and to which no one holds the patent.

Who Shouldn't Be an SMB Consultant

Truth be told, some people simply shouldn't be SMB consultants. Hopefully, they'll arrive at that decision before hurting themselves, a client, a computer system, or the SMB consulting field as a whole. Please carefully review this short list of those who might not thrive in an SMB consulting environment:

- **Process-oriented types** — It has been my experience that SMB consultants who like to come to the same job, office, desk, and chair each and every day make poor consultants. These folks are typically happiest with established routines.

- **Preference for clarity and not ambiguity** — Individuals who admittedly don't tolerate change or are frustrated by the constant technical learning curve confronting SMB consultants should consider keeping their day jobs.

- **Introverted individuals**— Many SMB consultants are introverted because the technology realm naturally attracts those types. While that shyness is a fact of life, it shouldn't be put on display at client sites. A true SMB consultant must have, at a minimum, the ability to shift between his or her introverted side of performing technical work to the extroverted side when speaking with clients. This point is in no way intended to violate the letter or the spirit of the American Disabilities Act (ADA), a United States Congressional mandate that suggests reasonable accommodations must be made for people with disabilities. Introvertism is not a disability by any stretch of the imagination. Rather, such shyness can be a big hurdle to earning the six-figure incomes possible in the world of SMB consulting. To be brutally honest, the client in a consulting relationship has the expectation of constant and consistent communication. Extroverted SMB consultants just don't have to work as hard to meet this client expectation.

- **Mistake-prone individuals** — Some people are born with that special touch when it comes to computers; others never will attain it. Take the example of a young child growing up in Seattle where Boeing is based. Such a Seattle native could close his or her eyes and identify the model of a Boeing jet flying overhead just by the noise of the airplanes engines. These people often become superior Boeing engineers later in life. You get the point. Back to SMB consultants. While some people are "naturals" when it comes to computers, others create more problems than solutions. If you're blessed with being mistake-prone when dealing with computers and software, consider a software-testing career instead. Why? Because software testers are paid to break things and make mistakes. It's a job requirement!

- **Fundamentally angry individuals** — You've likely seen them — I know I certainly have: the tense, always on edge, overly controlling type who loses it and becomes angry at the system or the client. If you lose your temper or your patience often or easily, you're not going to be a successful SMB consultant no matter what your technical skill set. And if you have an anger management problem, take a deep breath, count to ten, and seek professional help. Hey, if a macho guy like Tony Soprano (from HBO's hit cable TV crime show *The Sopranos*), can do it, so can you.

- **Goofy guys and gals** — Perhaps you're the class clown who never grew up. Perhaps you're a part-time comedian who can't keep your act straight in business situations. Fair enough, but your challenge in making it as an SMB consultant might be your ability to inspire trust in your clients and, when appropriate, lend an air of suitable business presence.

- **Those otherwise unemployable** — The old joke is that a consultant is really just an unemployed job-seeker in disguise. Plying your trade as an SMB consultant because you can't make it in business or technology any other way isn't the firmest foundation from which to launch and operate.

Wrapping up this section on who shouldn't be an SMB consultant, I want to ease the day-to-day downside of SMB consulting by suggesting that the price you paid for this book was value well received if it helps you avoid making a mistake. Perhaps the grass isn't greener on the other — read "SMB consulting" — side for everyone. In other words, don't give up your day job just yet (or at least until you complete reading this book from cover-to-cover!). Over the years, I have received e-mails and notes from readers of my other books who commented that they've decided not to go into consulting based on what they've read about it. These people concluded camping out in their corporate cubicle wasn't so bad after all!

Summary

This is only the first chapter of an entire book dedicated to making you a successful SMB consultant. As such, it has cast a broad vision of the SMB consulting profession with the details to follow in the chapters to come. Please read on before marching up to your boss's office and tendering your resignation.

This chapter introduced the world of SMB consulting from a realistic perspective. Why realistic? Because while great riches and happiness await you as a successful SMB consultant, so does a lot of hard work, worry, and heartache. I also didn't pull any punches when it came to managing your expectations about what life as an SMB consultant is all about. Let's face it. You'll be managing the expectations of your clients each and every day, so in a similar view, I'll manage your expectations in each and every chapter. The process started here by presenting reasons for SMB consulting failure. Don't get me wrong. The world needs great SMB consultants, but like any professional services field, we don't need misfits, malcontents, and incompetent professionals. Wouldn't you agree?

But at the end of the day, the gains clearly outweigh the pain if SMB consulting is indeed your calling. Bottom line? The chapter set the stage for making the best career decision for you when it comes to considering a career as an SMB consultant. While this professional path may not be for everyone, those who are competent SMB consultants do very well.

Major points discussed included:

- Suggested reasons for being an SMB consultant

- The good side of SMB consulting, with a focus on financial and professional success

- Success factors, as well as factors that configure to failure

- The bad and ugly side of SMB consulting, providing a balanced view of the SMB consulting career path

Chapter 2
SMB Consulting Business Plan

In This Chapter

- Defining a business plan

- Considerations when organizing your consulting practice

- Understanding your consulting space and the markets you serve

- Addressing promotion, marketing, management topics

- Surrounding yourself with business advisors

- Making the final decision to become an SMB consultant

Minimizing regrets is a big part of being in business. You can be successful often by trying things out and not regretting later that you let an opportunity slip by. But, that's not to say you should take risks willy-nilly. Indeed your business risks should be well-analyzed and documented. To do that you need a business plan.

With a business plan, you can lay out the game plan for your business and understand both the risks and returns associated with the endeavor. A business plan is a dynamic road map the SMB consultant follows, updating frequently as conditions change. Better yet, consider your business plan to be the Global Positioning System (GPS) device that guides your SMB consulting practice.

Once you accept the importance of a business plan, take it seriously. I regret, in my younger days, not ascribing credibility to a business plan that crossed my desk for a start-up game company in Seattle. I even had the opportunity to get involved if I so desired. I didn't participate and several years later I read about this game-maker having hit the big time with its "Magic – The Gathering" card game.

This chapter defines and presents the mechanics of a business plan. You will literally use the remainder of this book to fill in the blanks on forms, finish sentences in documents, and complete cells in spreadsheets as you prepare to become an SMB consultant. On nearly every page, the wisdom will all be pointing to things you should consider including in your business plan as you refine your business model. As an example of how you will do this, in the second section of this book, dedicated to the "finder" activities of business development, marketing, and promotion, you'll find the tools and information necessary to complete the marketing section of your SMB consulting business plan. By the last page of this book, if you've followed along correctly, you will have successfully completed your SMB consulting business plan.

How to Write a Business Plan

I enjoy writing business plans, and I've even discovered that writing business plans for others can be a profitable element of my own SMB consulting practice. But for many, writing business plans is akin to the drudgery of completing an annual tax return. Because it doesn't rank high on the list of preferred activities, many SMB consultants never complete a business plan, which means they're steering their career without a rudder.

One goal of this book is to get you excited about completing a business plan because the business plan is *your* business plan. You'll develop a vested interest in seeing it through to completion. It'll be used to convince both yourself and your stakeholders (spouse, partner, banker, landlord) that you're making the right business decisions and are headed in the right direction. A business plan provides an opportunity to validate your business model much sooner rather than much later.

Business plan length

Great debates exist in the business writing community on how long a business plan should be. It can range anywhere from 10 pages to over 100 pages, depending on the depth of the subject presented, the complexity of the business model, and the writing skills of the business plan writer. However, don't focus on business plan length at this point. Rather, simply get the show on the road and start creating a business plan.

BEST PRACTICE: At this time, turn on your computer, launch your word processor, such as Microsoft Word, and save the blank document as "BusinessPlan.doc" to My Documents. Type that all-critical first sentence and leave the document open so you can return to it and type more thoughts as you proceed through this chapter and book. Trust me, just having that ability to instantly capture a thought for your SMB consulting business plan is tremendously helpful.

My best practice aside, truth be told, the business plan doesn't have to be written on a computer. Countless success stories abound whereby business plans were sketched out on napkins over lunch or on air-sickness bags on long plane flights. Let's face it—if you have a business plan at all, you're miles (or kilometers, for my beloved Australian friends) ahead of your competition. There are many good resources to help you complete your business plan listed at the end of this chapter.

Only the start

Here's something important to note. A business plan isn't an end in the business planning process, but rather the start of a lifelong business planning process. Typically you write the business plan and tweak it along the SMB consulting journey. Once a year you might get away and have a "think week," much like Bill Gates does each year at his family's long-time vacation compound in Union, Washington, USA. Larger SMB consultant practices might hold an annual planning session. You get the point. Keep at it and don't let the plan gather dust after its first draft.

An ongoing business planning process means that you will be surrounding yourself with advisors. This could be your trusted bookkeeper or CPA who holds vast knowledge about what is working for small entrepreneurs and what isn't. You'll likely have a legal relationship and perhaps even a therapist to help you deal with the stress of being an SMB consultant!

BEST PRACTICE: In all seriousness, look at your existing clients and see what type of advisors they surround themselves with. This will show you in part how these clients actually became successful business people. Imitating your successful clients can be a terrifically helpful tool.

Another ongoing business planning exercise is to constantly assess and evaluate whether it is in your best interests to work in the SMB consulting field. I'm not suggesting here that you throw in the towel after a bad day (of which there can be many), but periodically look out to sea and determine if sailing on the good ship "SMB Consulting" is the best place for you to be. It's healthy.

Hear me out on this next point: You want to use your time and efforts to their highest and best use. Adhering to basic economic principles, you should be efficient and profitable in your chosen profession. Much like in real estate, where you attempt to place land in its highest and best use, your life as an SMB consultant should represent your highest and best use of professional time. The business planning process can help you discover that being an SMB consultant is your highest and best use of time. In Figure 2-1, the business planning process is presented graphically.

Figure 2-1:
The business planning process

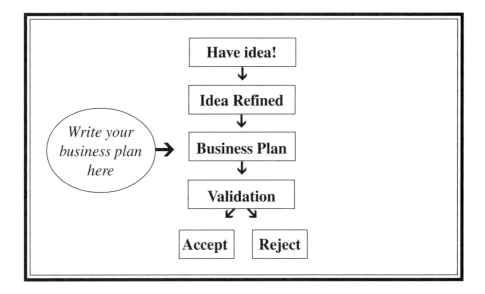

Business plan food chain explored

Time for the nuts and bolts of business plan content. This section will demystify what a business plan is and is not. It's a top-down process starting with the "Why are we here?" style questions and ending with specific implementation tasks. As an SMB consultant, you should have some guiding principles that get you up each morning to go serve your clients. It should also be what motivates you to stay up late at night solving technical SBS problems, completing your invoices, and paying your bills. It all begins with the mission statement, where you effectively put words to your guiding principles.

Mission statement

Believe it or not, the mission statement is typically the last part of the business plan to be written, even though it appears first when the business plan is read. Clearly this sounds backwards and perhaps works against some of my assertions in the last section on guiding principles and the like. I'll try to explain.

It's easy to sit down and create a slogan such as "Quality is Job #1," call it a mission statement, and move on. However, the slogan or phrase you initially select in haste is unlikely to be the mission statement with which you'll end up. As you go through the business planning process, learn about yourself, your services, your market, your competition, and so on, you're likely to find your original mission statement to be out of alignment with where you find yourself as an SMB consultant. And your mission statement definitely needs to be in alignment with your SMB consulting practice. Otherwise, you'll not only suffer from an identity crisis, but you'll also spend an inordinate amount of valuable time sitting around asking and trying to answer the following questions well after the business plan has been created — and likely well beyond when you should be working (and earning money) as an SMB consultant.

The following list of questions represents the appropriate framework for selecting a mission statement that works for you, the SMB consultant, as you launch your professional services practice. While pondering these high-level questions, just be glad you're not paying $30,000 per year as an MBA student at Harvard to hear the same lecture (my book costing significantly less):

- Why are we here?

- Who are we?

- What line of work are we in?

- What do we want to be known for?

BEST PRACTICE: Here the old adage "a means to an end" really rings true. It is important to respect the process of asking these high-level questions, but after a reasonable amount of iterations, your mission statement should be acceptable and you should move on. If you find yourself asking these same questions three months, six months, nine months down the road, it suggests your mission statement is irrelevant and your business plan may be less than useful. In other words, sitting around day after day as an SMB consultant asking "Who are we?" is a serious organizational warning sign that things aren't going well. And that kind of bench time for an SMB consultant isn't billable!

Here are a half-dozen sample mission statements you might consider for now, subject to refinement as you develop your own SMB consulting business plan.

- To implement technology solutions that make a positive difference for the clients I serve

- To use technology solutions to create wealth for my clients and myself

- To enjoy the trust and respect of my clients

- To provide excellent technical solutions in our Small Business Server niche while maintaining superior client relations

- To build a well-respected SMB consulting practice

- To take pride in my SMB consulting efforts each day, knowing I made the best decisions possible, given the information available at the time

Chapter 3 will help you prepare your mission statement with its 50,000-foot view of the world of consulting and its consulting fundamentals discussion.

Goals

Goals are derived from the mission statement. Not surprisingly, following our walk down the business plan food chain, goals are more detailed than a mission statement. Goals might include statements relating to:

- growth by referrals

- increasing profitability each year

- shedding day-to-day management responsibilities by recruiting a management team

- acquiring key competitors via buy out or merger to solidify our market position

Objectives

Objectives follow after goals and are even more specific. Typically, objectives are stated in greater detail than goals and offer some measure of accountability. For example, an objective might be to start your firm by June 30th of this year or to enjoy an after-tax return on your equity of at least 12 percent.

Objectives are often what you're measured by in a traditional job, working for an employer from 8AM to 5PM five days per week. But they are also a useful way to measure your success as an SMB consultant, assuming you'll be working for yourself. The point is that you need to be accountable to someone, even if that someone is yourself. Or as we say in business, "Everyone has a boss!" Objectives offer this accountability and comprise a common business management approach called "Management by Objectives" (MBO). There are many good business books that expand on this principle. Just look in the business reference section of airport bookstores the next time you are waiting to board a plane. (For example, see business books by author James Champy,).

Tactics

Simply stated, tactics are how you get there. Once you are armed with objectives, you have to make choices about how to attain those objectives. Those methods you select come from various tactics. In day-to-day SMB consulting life, your tactics may well be your entries in your Outlook 2000 Tasks List. It's really that clear-cut and simple.

Services explained

Business plans have a major section that defines products and services, and your SMB consulting business plan is no exception. It is here that you will list the specific services (and perhaps products) you intend to offer.

As you write this section, ask the question "Exactly what do I do?" and see if you can answer it in a fairly succinct manner. If you can't answer that question for yourself, you risk your practice being aimless. Might I suggest that you consider focusing on providing SBS services as an SMB consultant? You'll hear that from me many more times across these pages. In a few chapters, I also talk about providing services that are general or specific in nature.

Structuring your SMB consulting practice

There are two critical issues to discuss in your SMB business plan when it comes to structuring your consulting practice: substance and form.

Substance

Each and every day, how do you, as an SMB consultant, operate? Consider the following questions:

- Do you answer your telephone calls via a cellular telephone while at clients' sites? Or do you let the calls go to voicemail to be returned later during a block of time you've reserved each day for that activity? Also, what are your concerns with speaking to one client will at another client's location?

- Do you recruit and manage staff so that you can better leverage your time as an SMB consultant? That is, do you have clerical help that is attentive to the nuts and bolts of running a business so you can focus on SMB consulting?

- Do you have a physical office location or a home office? Do you have no office and simply roam around with your cellular telephone turned on all day, receiving calls hither and yon?

- What is the reality of making your SMB consulting practice function like a business (billing, collections, paying bills, and so on)? This question is separate from the one above that deals with staffing, because even if you have some staff support, you still have to be engaged in the process of running a business. This is covered more in the Minder section of the book.

The substance of organizing and maintaining your SMB consulting practice is making your SMB consulting dreams happen daily. It's implementing a business and management infrastructure to deal with the hundreds of little details that crop up in a given month. At worst, you want your business planning process and the resulting business plan to produce a functional organizational structure. At best, the outcome of writing a clear, substantive organizational section to your consulting practice's business plan could result in a practice that other SMB consultants would envy. In a traditional business plan, the operations section outlines the organizational structure you desire.

BEST PRACTICE: I guess now is as good a time as any to give the "practice what you preach" lecture. Look closely at how you run your SMB consulting practice or intend to in the future. If you're advising clients on leveraging technology to run their businesses better, then you best do the same as an example. Don't fall into the trap of the "car mechanic's car" whereby your server-based infrastructure is in the worst shape because you spend all day working on clients' servers and are too burned out at night to maintain your own. What kind of example is that?

I speak from experience on this topic. A few months prior to writing these words, I had to STOP running so hard and devote an entire weekend to rebuilding my server infrastructure. My server, running SBS 2000, was five years old and had been upgraded for RAM and storage more than once. It was running out of space and I elected to proactively retire the server rather than have the server reactively retire on me unexpectedly. Needless to say it took all weekend for little old me to migrate to a super-server running SBS 2000. It was a humbling experience, but I sure feel better about myself as an SMB consultant!

Form

In your SMB consulting business plan, you will want to spend a few minutes discussing the form of your consulting practice. Is it a sole proprietorship with you and only you at the helm steering the ship? Have you retained a tax attorney or certified public accountant to help you organize your practice as a legal entity, such as a Professional Limited Liability Company (PLLC)?

Financial considerations

Let's call a spade "a spade." One of the key reasons for becoming an SMB consultant is to make money. While some would say they are "entitled" to make good money as an SMB consultant, the more realistic attitude is that they have the "opportunity" to make as much money as they'd like.

If you choose to become an SMB consultant, rest assured you will have to earn all of the money you make. But that said, I encourage you to go forward with gusto. For some SMB consultants, their financial goal is to make a decent living free of an immediate supervisor. For others, a financial goal might be the big payoff that typically comes after long—and I mean really long—hours of work. The choice is yours. Either way, the financial section of your SMB business plan is critical. We're talking money right here and right now!

What to charge

Let's start with the good part: revenue. As an SMB consultant, one of the key questions is what to charge. Few other financial variables will have a greater impact on your financial position as an SMB consultant. Billing rates are a function of locality, expertise, specialty, luck, and ability to negotiate. Your SMB consulting business plan must include discussion and analysis of the revenues you intend to generate.

Incurred costs

Next up is costs, the second most important financial variable after determining your SMB consulting bill. I've witnessed many technically competent SMB consultants who enjoy an overwhelming volume of business actually report underwhelming financial results because they couldn't control costs. Leasing a flashy minivan with a company logo on it before your financial resources can justify such an expenditure is an example of letting your costs get out in front of your revenues. Your SMB consulting business plan must include discussion and analysis of the costs you will likely incur. The highway to SMB consulting success is littered with road kills of smart

SMB consultants who busted the bank (not to mention wrecking the company minivan!) before making their mint.

Pro forma financial information

In a business plan, the financial analysis section typically results in pro forma financial information. A couple of thoughts for you to consider:

- **Zero-based cost budgeting** — Believe it or not, as a budding SMB consultant, you can more easily estimate your costs than your revenues. With some legwork and elbow grease, you can surf the Internet or call around and get estimates for nearly all the costs you'll incur. For example, suppose you're considering leasing a small office for your SMB consulting practice. By calling a few real estate leasing agents, you could easily determine how much per square foot per month you will be paying. Other costs, such as equipment outlays and fees for services, can be estimated in a similar manner.

- **Break-even analysis** — If you are just starting your SMB consulting practice without a track record, it has been my experience that the only type of valid pro forma budget is one based on break-even analysis. Here you are looking at how much business you have to bring in to make it. This should include the salary you will pay yourself. The only exceptions for using other budgeting techniques, such as percentage of growth, are 1) when you have signed long-term consulting contracts as part of your SMB consulting practice launch, and 2) when, after months or years of hard work, you have developed a business track record.

- **Extrapolation as budgeting** — This is the easiest form of budgeting, one that most anyone can perform. That's the good news. The bad news is that you need some historical data to start with. That's because an extrapolated budget is typically built by taking an existing budget (or historical financial accounting statements), then simply adding a growth rate, say 5 percent, and badda boom badda bing! You have next year's budget. It's that simple. Of course, the simplicity has a way of masking the inherit inaccuracies with the method.

Your specific marketplace

Up to this point in your business plan, you've determined why you're here with your mission statement, set goals, and defined objectives to attain those goals. You know what services you intend to provide and how your SMB consulting practice will be organized. You've even cast your eyes toward profitability via growing revenues and cost control in the financial analysis section.

Now it's time to see if the marketplace agrees with your planning. You will define what your markets are, based on segments and geographic location.

Markets via segmentation

Your SMB consulting business plan should include thoughtful analysis about the market you serve based on segment. A market segment is an identifiable group or niche. You could also think of it as a discreet territory. For some, this will amount to serving only law firms or some other specific industry. This is common in professional services. You might take a slightly broader view as an SMB consultant and say that you intend to serve only services firms, because they best suit your background and personality. Indeed, you might use this section of your SMB business plan to list types of businesses with which you won't do business. An example of this for me is construction firms. I have had negative SMB consulting experiences in the rough-and-tumble world of construction. Worst of all, some of my invoices have gone unpaid by construction firms with plenty of money but a penchant for treating service providers with disregard. And if things don't get better soon with a couple of accounts, the next revision of this book might add law firms to this list. While I've got a couple of great law firm accounts, I've got two law firms that aren't acting like Class A clients right now!

In this book, I've effectively created a segment for you based on business size. The focus of this book is SMB, not enterprise. And you'll probably conclude, as you continue to read, that I tend to emphasize "small" most of all. If you prefer the enterprise world, don't fret, as many of the points presented in this book relate to technology consulting in general, and you're sure to find some knowledge nuggets in these pages. The important point to catch in this section is that you need to know your market(s) and communicate such understanding in your SMB business plan.

Local

For most SMB consultants, all engagements are local. Your clients are the same people that you see at the Parent Teacher Organization (PTO) meetings at your local school, in line at the movie house in your town, or in the case of Australia, sitting across the pub from ya. Local markets—which could be defined as those within a seventy-five -mile radius—are the best fit for SMB consultants. Why? Because relationships tend to run deeper in the SMB arena. When you keep your engagements local, the founder and business owner you deal with could very well be a long-time friend, not some stranger in a distant corporate head office, and maintaining that personal relationship serves both you and your client.

Necessity also causes SMB consultants to gravitate to keeping engagements local. SMB engagements aren't typically rich enough to justify extensive travel and associated expenses, such as lodging. And some technology consultants go into SMB consulting specifically so they don't have to travel, but can arrange their schedule to include attending their kids' soccer games and so on.

Regional

If you envision a wider scope for your SMB consulting business, consider regional markets. "Regional" is an imprecise word, meaning different things to different people. In my world of the Pacific Northwest, I consider regional to be the four-state region of Washington, Idaho, Oregon, and Alaska. Not surprisingly, many medium-sized firms that operate in the Pacific Northwest have a main office in Seattle with branch offices dispersed across these four states. If my business plan targets regional clients, I've now defined my market and what type of medium-sized firms might appeal to me.

A similar scenario applies for my friend Wayne Small in Sydney, NSW, Australia. Wayne, a Microsoft SBS MVP and leader of Correct Solutions (see more at www.sbsfaq.com), has some medium-sized clients that necessitate his boarding regional flights in Eastern Australia to deliver his services.

National

So perhaps you aspire to be one of those SMB consultants who want the recognition and all the other accolades that accrue when you're a nationally respected consultant. You may or may not be able to develop a national-level

SMB consulting practice as an individual. Andy Goodman, the SBS forum moderator at Microsoft Certified Professional Magazine (www.mcpmag.com), has successfully accomplished this feat. Andy lives on the East Coast of the US but has clients scattered about, including way across the country on the West Coast.

I've enjoyed the opportunity to serve clients across the US and even in Canada whom I've met as a result of my publishing and speaking activities. It's been an enriching experience to observe how folks in other lands seek to implement SMB-level technology.

The introduction of a host of remote management tools in SBS 2000 and SBS 2003 have made it possible for you to cultivate clients far from home. With the terminal services capability of remote server management, you can perform nearly all SBS server management tasks without having to go on-site. Other SBS tools, like the Server Status Report and Health Monitor, further allow you to support long-distance client relationships.

Notes:

But there is another take on the national market segment you might not know about. Firms like Gateway and Dell have developed nationwide service and support networks in the US. Each has a slightly different model. Gateway attempts to leverage off its hundreds of Gateway stores located in communities all across the US, as seen in Figure 2-2.

Figure 2-2:

Gateway stores are located in nearly every major US

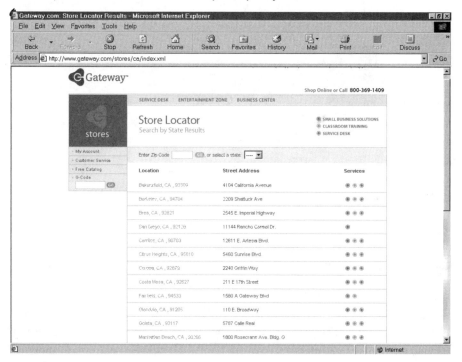

Each Gateway store has a Network Service Provider (NSP), which is a local SMB consulting firm that performs actual work at client sites. The Gateway store stays focused on selling hardware, software, and services, but then outsources the actual work to an NSP. Gateway then takes a cut of the NSP's revenues (this was 15 percent last time I heard, but it could have changed since then). The NSP program is referenced in Figure 2-3.

Figure 2-3:
Gateway NSPs are part of Gateway's service delivery approach.

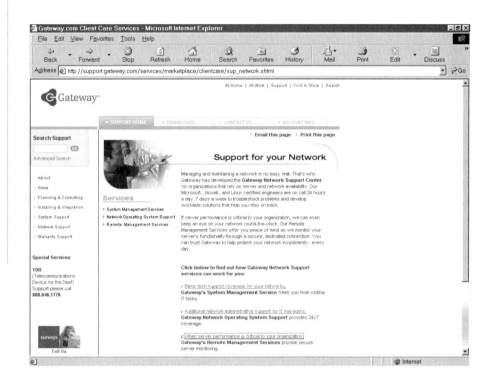

Dell has no stores but has built a nationwide network of service partners similar to Gateway's NSPs. Dell dispatches its partners to client sites needing service and support. A recent CRN article on Dell's SMB program is shown in Figure 2-4. This can be viewed at www.channelweb.com/sections/ Newscenters/Article.asp?newscenterID=32&ArticleID=39037).

Notes:

Figure 2-4:

Dell's SMB service delivery has three approaches: network design, installation, and business professional training.

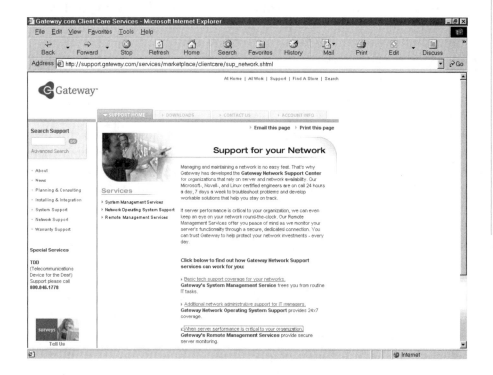

There are several benefits to the Gateway and Dell SMB support models. One such benefit is that they allow the customer to benefit from a unified deployment approach. SMB consultants who participate in the Gateway or Dell programs are trained and certified in the respective hardware vendor's products, deployment, and service methodologies. Another benefit of the Gateway and Dell partner programs is that they provide opportunities for SMB consultants to gain referrals. I discuss these vendor programs more in the Finder section of this book.

BEST PRACTICE: The following applies to US readers. At your next reading break, and definitely before you get to the Finder section of the book, drop by a Gateway store and ask some preliminary questions about how to become a Gateway NSP. This initial research will be beneficial when you reach the Finder section of this book.

Your SMB consulting business plan should at least make mention of national markets and your willingness or unwillingness to serve those markets.

International

There are a couple of interesting points to mention in the International segment. First of all, you might be engaging in internationalism right in your own neighborhood. For example, some SMB consultants I know in San Diego not only serve a diverse client base that speaks multiple languages, but they are located right at the US/Mexico international border, opening up additional SMB consulting opportunities. I've found myself helping some SMB clients in Vancouver, BC, Canada due to my living in the Seattle area and the close proximity to this marketplace.

BEST PRACTICE: Be sure to take the following point seriously. Consider going to night school at the local college to learn a foreign language. In the US, it's worth your time to learn Spanish, given the macro demographic trend whereby the Hispanic population will dominate the US population composition within a generation. You might shy away from less popular languages in order to get the biggest bang for your SMB consulting practice dollar!

A second interesting point is how the SMB arena seems to have a stronger foothold in overseas markets compared to the US. It's the worst kept secret in Redmond, Washington, home of Microsoft, that SBS sells dramatically better overseas than in the US. In fact, Australia has sold as many copies of SBS as the US, even though the US is 15 times larger in population and even larger when measured by gross domestic product (GDP).

This can be attributed to several factors. The SBS message overseas has been better-received than in the US. Overseas markets are, in general, comprised of smaller firms while the US has a stronger enterprise, Fortune 500 orientation. If you go to a US city, the technology consulting opportunity might be more skewed toward enterprise (say a corporate headquarters or the branch office of a large, US company) than SMB, while overseas, the opportunity is just the opposite. You get the picture and it's something you should consider if you have the flexibility to relocate when you plan to launch your SMB consulting practice. For example, a US military member might just as soon start an SMB consultant practice upon his or her honorable discharge at an overseas location (e.g., Germany) instead of returning to the US.

Overseas markets learned about SBS later in its life, which meant they did not suffer through the difficult SBS 4.x era, when the product was immature and still finding its feet. Because of this late introduction to SBS, SMB consultants located overseas who did not have to experience the program's growing pains are generally happy with it.

The bottom line is that knowing your market(s) is a smart business practice for anyone.

Promotion/marketing/advertising

With basic identification of markets behind you, it's time to shift your thinking about how you will go out and get the business. Any worthy business plan demands a bona fide marketing section that details how you plan to solicit business. In this section, it's important to step outside your own world with your own biases and try to look objectively at promotion, marketing, and advertising. Remember that an excellent mission statement doesn't mean much if you have no sales. You need an effective marketing plan that isn't so costly that you end up being unprofitable.

That last point is very important. Many eager SMB consultants print good-looking color brochures and business cards and buy expensive telephone book advertising before they've earned one dollar.

In the Finder section of the book, I'll point you to a wealth of free marketing avenues, such as press releases and existing client referrals.

Competition

In the business of writing a business plan, the fastest way to lose credibility is to proclaim "I don't have competition!" That simply isn't so. Not only are you fooling yourself, but you won't be taken seriously if your business plan is being used to impress other stakeholders, such as a spouse, lender, or landlord.

Competition is typically discussed in a business plan as primary and secondary competition. Don't ignore this section.

Primary competition

The primary competition includes the other entities against which you are most likely to bid. This might be other individuals providing similar SMB consulting services, often people you know. Your primary competition should receive your greatest attention, both in your SMB business plan and your day-to-day operations.

> BEST PRACTICE: Be sure to bookmark your primary competitors' Web sites and have a Favorites folder titled COMPETITION. Revisit these sites frequently to monitor what services your primary competitors are offering, what marketing message they are communicating, and what rates are being charged.

> Another time-tested trick to monitor your competition is to walk the show floor at tradeshows. Visit the booths of your competition. You'll see what other SMB consultants are doing and what emerging industry trends are.

Secondary competition

This broader category of competitors can potentially range from the high school student who works in technology at a fraction of your billing rate to the big consulting firms that are testing the SMB consulting space. Firms like IBM will periodically try SMB consulting and charge significantly more per hour than most SMB consultants. Be sure to include a list of secondary competitors in your SMB consulting business plan so that these other forms of competitors remain uppermost in your mind. If you don't think that's necessary, then you may go the way of the once-popular railroads, which would have been smart to consider secondary forms of competition, such as road and air travel.

Repositioning yourself

Once you've identified and zeroed in on your competition, you need to think about how you will reposition your SMB consulting practice to thwart these competitive threats. For example, you may find that your competitors don't have after-hours services. You might want to consider keeping your cellular telephone on at all times, making you reachable 24 hours a day, seven days a week.

Repositioning your SMB consulting practice means refining your service offerings to fill holes in the marketplace. It's the old zigzag theory. When your competitors "zig," then you "zag." You get the picture.

More tips on writing the competition section of your SMB consulting business plan are coming up in the Finder section of this book.

Presenting the management team

Time to think positively. The management section will contain your résumé with a narrative profile that presents your SMB consulting skills in the most positive light possible. You should also include the résumés of coworkers and job descriptions of positions you intend to fill.

I discuss the management area in greater detail in the Minder section of this book.

Risks

All businesses have risk factors and your SMB consulting practice is no exception. Your SMB consulting business plan should discuss business risks to which you are susceptible, including the following:

- **Obsolescence** — What happens if you don't stay current with your skill set? Worse, what happens if you stay current but Microsoft stops producing SBS or other SMB product offerings? Don't laugh too hard at that statement as such a decision could be made as part of its antitrust settlement down the road. If such an event happened, where Microsoft stopped selling your niche software product, the skills you've worked hard to develop might be in far less demand.

- **Economy** — When I wrote several books on SBS and consulting in the late 1990s, I was able to proclaim that times were very good in the technology consulting world. That was a true and honest statement before April of 2000, when the NASDQ stock market, top-heavy in technology issues, begin its slow descent (okay, call it a "crash"). With the middle of the first decade in the 21st century fast approaching, you and I both have the benefit of 20/20 hindsight. Whereas technology consulting, including the SMB sector, was unbelievably lucrative in the late 1990s, today we have to work keenly to earn our profits. When assessing economic risks, be sure to insert commentary as to how both boom time and recessions might impact your plans to launch a successful SMB consulting practice.

- **Key person** — What happens if, as a key person, you are unavailable to deliver your services? I'm not so much implying you'll be going to the SMB consulting practice in the sky before your time, but you might suffer an accident and be sidelined for a few months. Do you have enough cash in the bank to survive downtime?

Resources to Assist With Your Business Plan

Whether you live in the US or not, the Small Business Administration (SBA), located at www.sba.gov, provides significant business planning resources. Not only will you find business plan templates and articles of interest, but in many US cities, the SBA offers a program called SCORE. SCORE is a group of volunteer business executives who will assist you in constructing your business plan. People who have engaged SCORE report it's been a good use of time, and they benefited from the objective feedback.

Notes:

Figure 2-5:

The SBA is a tremendous resource for constructing your SMB consulting business plan.

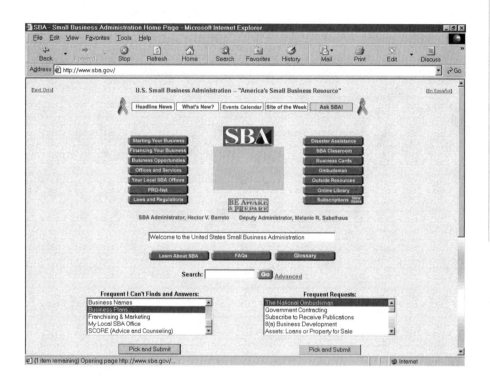

Your first step in taking advantage of the SBA's business planning resources is to click the "Starting Your Business" button in the upper left. Notice in the lower left, there is a selection box titled "Frequent I Can't Finds and Answers" where business plans and SCORE are specific selection options. The information presented at the SBA site is typically free, and I've found it to be worthy. However, there are business plan software programs on the market which can be found by searching on the term "business plan" at your favorite software reseller. From such a search, I discovered Palo Alto Software (www.paloaltosoftware.com) and its offerings as shown in Figure 2-6.

Figure 2-6:

Palo Alto Software's business planning and marketing software provide professional templates to guide the creation of your SMB business plan.

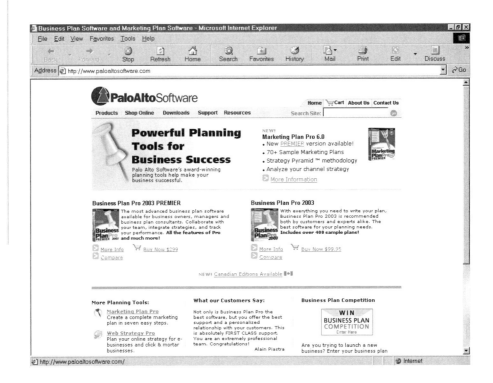

Another example is PlanWare (www.planware.org), where you can download EXL-PLAN Super 2.1, a shareware business planning template designed to work with Microsoft Excel and Word. The Excel spreadsheet component is shown in Figure 2-7 and the Word document component is shown in Figure 2-8. One positive for PlanWare is that, because it's located in Ireland, the tools it offers would likely have more of an international flavor for overseas readers of this book.

Figure 2-7:
The spreadsheet-side of EXL-PLAN Super.

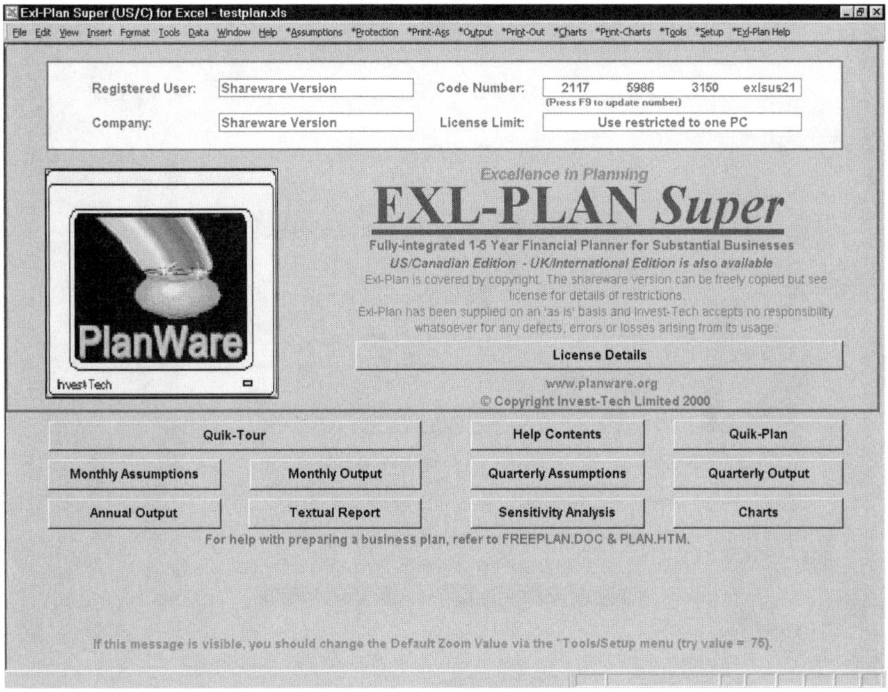

Notes:

Figure 2-8:
The document-side of EXL-PLAN Super.

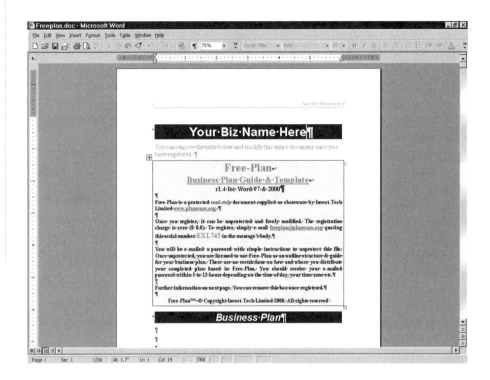

Perhaps you're really not a writer and it's not in the cards to complete your own business plan. There are professionals waiting to assist you, but be advised that a professional business plan can cost as much as $10,000 to create. You can find the names of business plan writing firms from local accountants and business attorneys. In fact, as shown in Figure 2-9, many accounting firms are in the business of writing business plans.

Notes:

Figure 2-9:

CFO2Go is representative of accounting firms that will write your business plan.

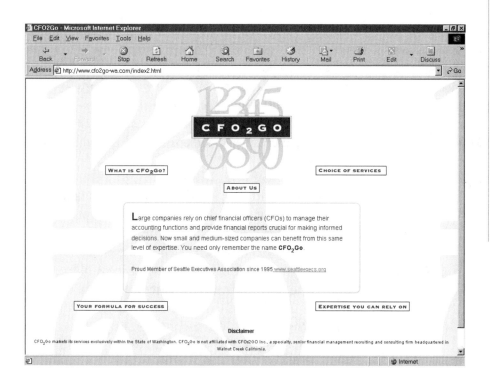

BEST PRACTICE: When it was time to write my own business plan, I engaged CFO2Go in a trade-out of services to write my business plan. CFO2Go needed assistance implementing SBS, and I felt that I really needed the independent analysis of an accounting firm to write my business plan, interview me, bring forth concrete suggestions for profitability, etc.

I share this with you to make two points. First, I received a professional business plan for my SMB consulting practice on the cheap via a client trade-out and encourage you find similar opportunities. This allows you to lower your start-up costs while still completing the all-important business plan. Second, even though I'm a writer,

> I didn't want to consume all of my hours writing an SMB consulting firm business plan. Rather, I wanted someone else who wasn't emotionally involved to write it for me and allow me to make edits.

Something else to think about is approaching the business department of your local business college and having a student who is pursuing a master's degree in business administration (MBA) or an upper-level student in the undergraduate program write your business plan while working for you on an internship basis. In my community, Seattle Pacific University (www.spu.edu) requires business students to complete internships as part of earning their degrees. This is a common requirement and perhaps used at a college located in your area.

> BEST PRACTICE: It's been said that it's easier to write someone else's business plan than your own. There is some truth to that statement, as someone on the outside can see things the business owner doesn't. The point is, you might assist another business person in gathering together and writing his or her business plan so you can gain some experience before you write your own. And who knows? Perhaps your calling is to be a management consultant, in addition to an SMB consultant in technology. Maybe you'll be earning part of you're living as a business plan writer. Hey – no harm, no foul if that's the direction you go to add this to your portfolio of services.

Required Paperwork

Part of your SMB business plan should speak to identifying and obtaining the proper business licenses, permits, and certificates necessary to conduct business in your particular area. I can't hope to identify what those requirements are, given the thousands of distinct and separate municipalities that exist in the United States alone. However, I can cast some general thoughts your way that will guide you in this area.

At the US federal level, you typically need to acquire a tax identification number, which can be an Employer Identification Number (EIN) or a social security number. Otherwise, there are few federal permits, licenses, or certificates required to operate as an SMB consultant. One fact of life in the

United States is that you will need to file a federal tax return. In my case, with my SMB consulting activities, this has historically taken the form of a Schedule C filing that is attached to my 1040 federal tax return. However, everyone's tax situation is different.

> Best Practice: It is up to you to research what is required in the way of licenses, permits, and certificates. These requirements can differ by location and change over time. A certified public accountant is usually a good source for helping you complete the required paperwork to start as an SMB consultant.

Many states have business licenses and tax assessments. This clearly varies by state, but in Washington State, you need a business license and a registered business name, and you must file a business and occupation tax return.

At the local level, you may need another business license. Some municipalities also impose occupancy taxes on businesses. One other consideration at the local level is special assessment districts. These are often legally binding organizations of merchants and business people who have banded together and taxed themselves to accomplish some feat. Often, retailers will form a special business improvement district to hire private security details to improve the general atmosphere of the neighborhood (such as driving drug dealers out).

> BEST PRACTICE: The SBA site at www.sba.gov has tons of discussion on permits and licenses. Use it!

Business Advisors

Perhaps you've observed that many successful business people owe much of their success to having surrounded themselves with the right people. These business people let their common sense rule, not their ego. You've likely witnessed egocentric business people who operate under the mistaken assumption that they don't need outside advice or help. More pragmatic business people understand it isn't how hard you work, but how smart you work, and they understand the importance of developing a team of business advisors.

You might consider retaining the following business advisors as your needs and financial resources warrant:

- **Other SMB consultants** — There's nothing quite like running ideas by a valued peer group. Fellow SMB consultants whom you know and trust might be a tremendous source of business advice for you. It's why fellow SMB consultants are first on my list today.

- **CPA/accountant** — Not only should you enlist qualified accounting help to assist in setting up your accounting system and engage in yearly tax preparation, but before you know it, you may seek tax planning advice. It's nice to have such problems as an SMB consultant, because when you need tax planning help, you're making big money!

- **Bookkeeper** — Early on, after an accountant creates your accounting system, you'll want to use a bookkeeper regularly to assist in your billings, collections, and general financial statement preparation. Trust me! These are dollars wisely spent, as a bookkeeper is typically much cheaper than an accountant and can perform the tasks outlined herein. And you may remember my story earlier in this chapter, whereby CFO2Go did a trade-out of professional services with me to obtain an SBS network (and I received a professional business plan for my SMB consulting practice). Well, I have an update. On an ongoing basis, CFO2Go provides my monthly bookkeeping and accounting services, while I provide SBS consulting and remote network monitoring services for them.

- **Business consultant** — Perhaps you're a true tech-head with limited business wisdom. And while you're financially successful, you could be missing out on some tremendous business opportunities. I've always been impressed by technical types who accept their business limitations and hire a business consultant to guide them. In fact, you might find your best use of time and money to be hiring a business consultant to complete your SMB consulting business plan.

- **Lawyer** — Initially, a lawyer may well be retained to assist you in organizing your SMB consulting practice. For example, quickly on you may elect to incorporate. As your SMB consulting practice becomes more sophisticated, you may seek legal review of business contracts. Two thoughts here: First, don't try to be your own lawyer. Second, hire a good lawyer who specializes in the needs you have. A general practitioner lawyer probably doesn't even know what an SMB consultant is.

- **Banker** — Bankers review many business plans in the course of their finance work. It is the job of a banker to cast a leery eye toward all schemes. So if you really want to get a thorough and revealing check on the validity of your SMB consulting business plan, have it critically reviewed by your banker. A banker will point out weaknesses you might not otherwise have seen.

- **Spouse and other family members.** By far your toughest critics will be your spouse and family members. This group of business advisors can most likely be counted on for offering frank and brutally honest feedback. If that's not enough, have your friends take a look as well. Ouch!

Your Decision Point

Following the advice found in this chapter and the remainder of this book to write a business plan is one thing. Actually throwing caution to the wind and launching your practice is an entirely different matter. At some point, however, you'll need to make the decision to either go for it or decline the opportunity to launch an SMB consulting practice. Understand that, while I prefer and hope you give SMB consulting a chance, deciding that SMB consulting isn't for you is an entirely acceptable outcome from this exercise. I'd rather have you take a hard look at SMB consulting and know with certainty whether the profession is—or is not—for you. If your only investment is the price of this book, hopefully you will consider it to be money well spent.

Ongoing Business Planning

Moving forward, let's assume you've made the decision to become an SMB consultant. The business planning process doesn't stop here. On an annual basis, you should be getting away from your practice for a few days to reflect on the past year and to engage in some strategic planning. A framework you can use for strategic planning is SWOT analysis, which stands for Strengths, Weaknesses, Opportunities, and Threats. Strengths and weaknesses are internal variables used to look at the pluses and minuses of your SMB consulting practice. Opportunities and threats are external variables used to examine the competitive and economic landscape affecting your SMB consulting practice. Simply sit down with a pad of paper and create your own SWOT analysis as the starting point for your annual planning process. As a follow-up to that, touch base with your key business advisors periodically to assess whether you're still on track to becoming and remaining a profitable SMB consultant!

Brelsford's Mailbox

Across the pages of this book, I intend to insert authentic e-mails I've received from loyal readers. I hope you'll find the replies I offer to my dear readers provide a real-world perspective on SMB consulting.

From: Bob D
To: Harry Brelsford
Subject: Business Plan

I currently work for a consulting firm, and I am responsible for the networking side of the house. Like other people, I can't seem to type those first words when it comes to writing a business plan. I need help on how to start one.

Where to go from here?

Thanks,

Bob D

Hi Bob—

Thanks for the e-mail and sorry for the delay in replying...been a tad busy this past week. Aside from using the resources highlighted in my SMB Consulting Best Practices book, such as the US Small Business Administration (SBA) at www.sba.gov, consider the following:

- *Troll your lure at www.microsoft.com/partner. (The partner materials include tons of helper tools.)*

- *Attend a TS2 event in your area. Visit www.ts2.com. (Business resources are located at this site too.)*

- *Search on business plans and other like keywords at Google and MSN. You'll see an abundance of resources.*

Keep in touch...all the best mate...harrybbbb

Summary

This chapter has covered the basics for your SMB consulting business plan. You'll spend the balance of the book discovering the answers you need to complete your SMB consulting business plan. Major points covered in this chapter included:

- Defining what a business plan is

- Launching your SMB consulting business plan

- What to consider in organizing an SMB consulting practice

- Learning how to define and understand your consulting space and the markets you will serve

- Developing the promotion, marketing, and management sections in your SMB business plan

- Surrounding yourself with business advisors

- Understanding there is a point at which you will be making the final decision to become an SMB consultant

Chapter 3
Foundation for SMB Consulting

In This Chapter

- Presenting SMB consulting fundamentals

- Learn about key cornerstone concepts to successful SMB consulting

- Introducing Brelsford's Dozen

Let's face it. All successful SMB consulting practices are built on solid foundations. These bedrock basics are typically core values that define the consultant and the SMB consulting practice. This chapter presents SMB consulting fundamentals that are crucial tenets for your budding consulting practice. The intent of this chapter is to start from the ground up, laying a solid SMB consulting foundation before entering the wonderful and profitable world of SMB consulting.

Gain Trust

When you get right down to it, what we really sell as SMB consultants is trust. New SBS versions are released with incremental improvements. Software feature sets come and go. Technologies shift with the introduction of new products. Technological change can occur rapidly, sometimes in a matter of months. Because we live in the super fast-forward world of small and medium technology, appropriately called "Internet time," you can't hope to master more than a small fraction of the actual technology being introduced and used. If you think otherwise, you aren't being honest with yourself.

Given you're only one product release away from obsolescence and because there's no sure way to know what features will be included in future technology products one or two releases down the road, I recommend you stake your SMB consulting claim on trust, not technology.

If your efforts are properly directed toward gaining and retaining the trust of your clients, you'll have the political capital necessary to survive technical mistakes you're bound to make and weather the learning curve inherent in new product introductions. In a strong trusting client relationship, I've even found that I can bill for much of my research time with a client as I learn how to deploy new product releases. And no, I'm not duping the client; these people trust my judgment and agree some time spent on learning is fair in the delivery of my professional services.

With trust as the basis for your client relationships, you'll find yourself thriving even during tough economic times. Why? Because gaining trust as a practice in business survives the ups and downs of economic cycles.

> BEST PRACTICE: Go easy on yourself in the trust department. It takes time. I've worked for years to build up trust with my clients. It's an ongoing function; trust must be earned over the long haul, sometimes time and time again. It's one of the reasons that I'll emphasize long-term relationships many times in this book. So, if you're not quite there yet with your clients, don't be discouraged. Be patient and keep at it. You'll get there.

Let's do a 180-degree shift and consider a relationship where trust is absent. Here you are, truly only one SBS reboot away from being fired by the client. (And in the SBS 4.x era, we all had one too many reboots!) If the client doesn't fully trust you, every move you perform is questioned. SMB consulting relationships lacking in trust tend to have high consultant turnover, as measured by the consultants who parade through these "Class C" client sites-"Class C" clients being least desirable and "Class A" most desirable. And I'm definitely not referring to IP address classes!

So, to sum up the trust discussion: You won't make it as an SMB consultant if you can't get trust, and you can't help but be successful if you've got trust. Admittedly, "trust" is difficult to measure, but it is definitely recognizable. The best explanation I can give to describe trust comes from the US Supreme Court on one of its landmark rulings: "You know it when you see it."

So just how do SMB consultants consistently gain the trust of their clients? Some SMB consultants gain client trust because of safe, conservative technology and sound business decision-making that keeps the client site up and running while minimizing downtime. (This last point has become much easier with SBS 2000 compared to prior versions.) Other SMB consultants earn trust as pompous guru know-it-alls who are ascribed credibility simply because of their vast knowledge. This is a risky strategy that assumes you can keep current with and master a wide range of constantly changing technologies.

One of the easiest ways I've observed for SMB consultants to gain client trust is by being on time to appointments, returning telephone calls, billing in a timely manner, and communicating clearly and consistently. SMB consultants who use better business practices consistently inspire client trust. You can take a bow and affirm you've made it in the "trust" department as an SMB consultant when the client would trade a family member before getting rid of you. Dramatic, yes—but you get the point.

Practice Expectation Management

Second only to the trust issue is the matter of "expectation management." Inexperienced or immature SMB consultants often fall into the trap of trying to please everybody. This people-pleasing behavior can look like the following:

- **It'll only cost this much** — Have you every knowingly or unknowingly underquoted the true costs of an engagement?

- **Next release syndrome** — Have you ever tried to duck and dodge a technical problem by promising it will be fixed in the next release (whether you know this to be true or not)?

- **Overpromising and underdelivering** — Have you ever found yourself saying, "Oh yeah, Small Business Server 2003 can do that," when you've never successfully implemented that particular feature?

- **Staff capabilities** — Have you ever said, "We've got someone who can do that," when you don't?

- **The client is always right syndrome** — Have you ever been bullied by a client into committing to a technology solution that isn't feasible?

All of these examples underscore the importance of expectation management.

Any of these instances can falsely raise a client's expectations so high that there's no chance to be successful as his SMB consultant. Many technically adept, well-meaning SMB consultants engage in self-defeating behavior with clients by not managing the client's expectations well.

Expectation management strikes at the heart of what an SMB consultant is all about. In my opinion, an SMB consultant differs from a straight technician (tech head) in this aspect of the professional services relationship. Such an association requires relationship management, and to manage the relationship, the consultant has to manage expectations.

No matter what line of work you are currently in, I'm sure you've seen situations where expectations weren't managed well. Based on your experiences, it probably wouldn't be hard for you to develop your own example of how best to manage expectations.

> BEST PRACTICE: Avoid surprises. That is one valuable fundamental you can incorporate from this page forward. And nowhere is this basic principle more important than in client billings. Not only should you carefully delineate what charges are within and outside of the project scope, but you might communicate to the client in advance (say, by e-mail or voicemail) that the invoice is on the way and these are the charges to expect. Hear me now that avoiding billing surprises is one of the best expectation management tricks around!

Overcommunicate

Good communication is vital to your doing well in your SMB role and keeping your clients happy, and in theory it appears so easy to do. And what I call over communicating is even better where you impress the client with your communication skills and ability to articulate technical concepts in business speak. Yet for some reason, technology consultants, including those in the SMB sector, have a hard time communicating well. My practice has grown by gaining many good clients who were frustrated with past consultants who just didn't communicate enough. Sure warning signs of undercommunication include:

- **SMB consultant shyness** — Many SMB consultants are introverted, a fact of life within the technology field as a whole. This introversion can often take the form of shyness in social interactions, such as talking to clients. It's important to know that being a consultant is as much about communication as technical competency. The chronically shy are likely to be severely challenged to make it big as an SMB consultant, because their communications skills can hold them back. On the other hand, these same individuals can be very successful as software developers, where communication isn't as large a success factor as other skills (say mathematics).

- **SMB consultant arrogance** — On the opposite end of the spectrum to the chronically shy is the arrogant SMB consultant. A consultant who acts like he knows everything by sharing nothing with others (including sharing important system information with clients) will not only anger the client, but will completely leave the client out of the communication loop. Please don't be the type of technology consultant who marches in, completes the technical work, and leaves having barely uttered a word to anyone.

- **ESL — English as a second language** — Many SMB clients are alarmed and frustrated by the communication problems that can result from working with SMB consultants who are unable to speak the English language well (assuming the client is English-speaking). In all fairness, I suspect those of us who speak English as a primary language would face the same communication challenge if we were to work overseas in a country where English was a secondary language.

- **Incompetence** — Some SMB consultants either don't know better about good communications, don't care to communicate, or are incompetent. Whatever the reason, a lack of communication between the SMB consultant and client is a bad thing.

Here are a few pointers about communicating with your clients: Tell them in advance what you're going to do; do what you said you would do; and then tell them what you did.

- **Tell the client in advance what you're going to do.** Take a few moments to explain what your plan is to the client. You might use e-mail to communicate this if face-to-face communication isn't possible.

- **Do the work you said you would do.** Make sure you deliver the work you promised. If, for some reason, your game plan changes along the way, communicate this immediately to the client. How many times have you intended to add hardware to a machine only to find the device driver software doesn't work? Have you ever had to ship a piece of hardware back to the reseller for this very reason? Whenever I'm caught by such a surprise, I communicate this information to the client immediately and seek advice. Clients can handle the truth; it just needs to come sooner rather than later.

- **Tell the client what you did.** I typically leave a short "site report" on e-mail to the client explaining the work that was accomplished and how much I billed for it (say 2.5 hours at $125 per hour to accomplish the six tasks). If possible, it's even better to communicate this stuff face-to-face and then follow-up with an e-mail site report. However, I find my clients have typically left work by the time I complete my duties.

BEST PRACTICE: Hail to the babblers. When in doubt, overcommunicate with your client. While I've seen SMB consultants excused from a site for not being a communicator, I've not seen an SMB consultant terminated for being too talkative. This even includes the chatty chap I knew who, when asked what time it is, replied in great detail about how to build a watch. He was agony to work with, but I'd rather put up with such an overcommunicator than an undercommunicator. And if you are a babbler, kindly keep your eyes open for visual cues from your client that it's time to shut up!

Last, I share with you the "roger" syndrome. In radio communications and some sports, like sailboat racing, a communication acknowledgement is issued. When speaking on a radio system, such as in a military operation, the recipient will typically answer "roger" to let the communicator know the message was received. In sailing, the crew always repeats the skipper's command as a form of acknowledgement. For example, the skipper orders,

"Raise the sail," and the crew repeats, "Raise the sail." Both parties know the message was received and understood. I guess another example would be the TCP/IP three-way handshake, where there is an ACK packet that confirms receipt of the packet. The point is this: As an SMB consultant, when you receive a phone message or e-mail from a client, you should reply immediately, saying, "I received your message. Thanks." This will put the client at ease and him know you are on top of the situation.

Be Willing to Wear Many Hats

Truth of the matter is that SMB consultants aren't just pretty faces and SBS heavyweights. Clients are bound to request additional services from you. These can range from making espresso coffee to lifting heavy equipment to running to the computer shop for a part. More likely, you'll be brought into business meetings where you find yourself participating in a marketing discussion, etc. On the one hand you can chalk it up to all in a day's work and consider these tasks all part of the job. On the other hand, you have to be careful about offering advice on areas where you might do more harm than good. For me, that boundary typically comes in the accounting software area. I'm happy to provide the SBS infrastructure needed to support an accounting system, but I do not work on the accounting software system myself.

Your work is not made up of just bits and bytes when you're an SMB consultant. Often it's about putting on an analytical hat and helping plan the strategic direction of the client's information infrastructure. Wearing many hats as a professional has often gone by another phrase: "Doing whatever it takes."

On the technical discussion side, remember that a product like SBS requires you to be a jack of all trades. SBS, being a product suite in the Microsoft "BackOffice" tradition, contains components that are typically consulting niches in and of themselves. For example, there are people in this world who make a great six-figure living from just mastering and consulting on Microsoft Exchange. Yet this robust e-mail application is but one of many pieces in SBS. So if you're an SMB consultant who works with SBS, you will by default wear many technical hats, let me tell you!

I'll leave more technical discussion on SBS until the last section of the book: Grinder.

Become a Business Advisor

Microsoft got it with its Go To Market (GTM) framework for business development for it certified partners. GTM is about how to incorporate business-thinking into Microsoft products so you deliver the "total solution" instead of simply installing software. I'll discuss GTM much more in the Finder section of the book. My point is that you need to "get it" as well: The "B" in both SBS and SMB stands for BUSINESS!

As an SMB consultant, you're increasingly being called upon to understand business needs and to implement technology solutions in the context of those needs. No longer is it sufficient just to know the cool tools inside SBS, unless you're shooting for a lower-paying, less value-added job as a technician who can't add bona fide business value to the clients you serve.

An SMB consultant adds value to the client relationship by serving as a business advisor. In fact, some of the most successful SMB consultants I've met have mastered both the computer "BackOffice" and the business boardroom. I've even seen folks with both the MCSE and MBA credentials.

So why the concern about business activity? Whatever happened to good old-fashioned computing consulting? Times have changed and now consultants are expected to integrate business with technology. This trend can be attributed to several factors:

- **Operating system and application maturity** — Basic user needs are being well satisfied with the latest operating systems and applications. Business application suites, such as Microsoft Office, do just about everyhting now that folks want to do. People are literally starting to say they can't imagine what else they'd need technically in some areas.

- **Pressure to be profitable** — Bye-bye "dot-com" business models and hello profits! Businesses are looking for a higher return on investment (ROI) on technology expenditures. Financial types, like the CFO, are looking closely at your SMB consulting rate, which isn't going down the same way hardware and software prices are. If your bill rate remains stable or increases in a period of declining hardware and software prices, you have to do one of two things: boost your productivity by accomplishing more amazing technical feats per billable hour or add more value to the SMB consulting engagement. One example of a value-added feature would be to participate as a business advisor, marrying technology to the client's line of business.

- **Better business practices** — Many clients view technology implementations as a fresh start. That is, they look at SBS as an opportunity to change their work procedures and business habits with tools such as the instant messaging capabilities of Exchange or the public folder-based group calendars in Outlook. The savvy SMB consultant will be able to see business opportunities, given the technology being implemented. Some days you might find yourself acting as a management consultant to your SMB client.

- **Competitive advantage** — The real hard-core business types, the MBAs, are looking to squeeze out every competitive advantage they can in this new, "whacked out and crazy" Web-based world of business (a phrase coined by management guru and author Tom Peters). Think outside the box, buddy!

Some SMB consultants naturally have a brain for business and others don't. Fair enough (or fair dinkum if you're in Australia!). If business issues escape you at first blush, consider attending a business course at your community

Notes:

college. Also, if you monitor popular business periodicals, such as Business Week, you can find free online business courses and Webcasts that might be beneficial to you. An example of this is shown in Figure 3-1.

Figure 3-1:

The Web has many business course offerings if you look around. This is a Web "TV" site from Business Week magazine.

Take a Long-Term View

Imitation is the greatest form of flattery. As an active SMB consultant, I've frequently observed how my successful clients conduct business, hoping some of that good mojo will rub off on me. By emulating successful behaviors, I hope to enjoy the same success as the people I serve with great pride. At the risk of sounding like an airport hotel seminar on the power of positive thinking, I do believe that thinking positively and surrounding yourself with positive, successful people helps you to be successful as well.

My most financially successful client, a real estate brokerage firm, considers long-term relationships to be the cornerstone of its success. This is a firm with generations of service to the Seattle business community working successfully in an industry (real estate) that depends on and counts professional reputation as a critical success factor.

So what can you learn from this section? Developing and maintaining long-term client relationships is critical to your success as an SMB consultant. There aren't enough hours in the day to keep losing and acquiring clients. Such client turnover is not only unprofitable financially, but it also taxes your limited energy unnecessarily. Taking a long-term view focused on client retention is a much better path.

> BEST PRACTICE: Once a client always a client, eh? A client today should be a client tomorrow, regardless of the software releases, technology shifts, and the latest and greatest gizmo. With the pace of technology product upgrades only increasing (or so it seems), it would clearly be unprofitable for you to retain a client for only one product life cycle (e.g., SBS 4.0). Why? Just as you were getting to know a client and that client's information infrastructure, it would be time for you to hit the road. Ouch!

Act as a Client Advocate

The SMB consultant represents his or her client much as a lawyer, CPA, or any other professional service provider does. When it comes to technology matters, such as SBS, you act on behalf of your client. This relationship creates a fiduciary obligation for you to do whatever is in the best interest of the client. Ways that you can act as a client advocate include the following:

- **Represent the client, not the vendor** — Take ordering hardware, software, and services for the client. Remember that you are speaking on behalf of the client, not the wallet in your hip pocket or purse. You might find yourself subcontracting out specialized tasks to your personal financial detriment because it is your fiduciary obligation in the context of your client relationship to do so. That is, there might be some parts of the client's technology project that you aren't qualified to perform. You'll want to strongly consider using outside help to complete those tasks even though, in these discrete cases, it's the outside help doing the billing and not you.

- **Conflict of interest disclosure** — If you have a direct financial interest in a product being recommended to the client, it's your obligation to disclose such conflicts of interest. As an author, I'm often put in a tight spot where I'm recommending my own book to a client who has asked me for "some good computer books." Of course, I'm all too happy to recommend my own tomes, but I usually make the point, via an appropriate dose of humor, that I'll pocket a buck and quarter in royalties from the book purchase. The point is typically well taken by the client, appreciated, and accepted in the spirit in which it was delivered.

- **Practice tough love with honor** — Part of the advocacy role will likely include tough love. An SMB consultant, acting as the client's advocate, is honor-bound to "tell it like it is." Inevitability, you'll have to tactfully tell your client something he doesn't want to hear. If the client has junk machines, you have to let him know. You might encounter this with SBS when it comes to line of business (LOB) applications or terminal services (TS) running in application-sharing mode. LOB applications and TS in application-sharing mode can be great reasons to introduce a second server (typically acting as a member server) onto the network. If you deliver such a message based on fact and sincerity, in all likelihood you will prevail and the client will purchase a member server for the company's network.

Mentor Your Clients

There is one law of consulting you should learn sooner rather than later: A great consultant is one who works his way out of his job. That is, if you're doing your job correctly as an SMB consultant, the client shouldn't need you around forever. It's a noble goal and one that keeps you focused on providing exceptional customer service while you're there.

However, the reality is different from the theory-in a good way. Rather than truly working yourself out of the SMB consulting business, as you might conclude from the first paragraph, the opposite usually occurs. Clients, sensing that you mean well and have their best interests and budget at heart, simply adore you and tend to find more work for you to complete. But then a really good thing happens. These same clients become great referral sources, sending more business your way than you can reasonably handle! So who's complaining?

There is another angle on the "working your way out of a consulting gig" theme. Perhaps at your client site one of the staff members is really keen on computers. This person tends to shadow you when you're working on-site so he can learn more about the system. Over time, you slowly allow this person to start performing simple maintenance tasks. Later on, he'll often add basic technology management responsibilities to his job role. I've found mentoring someone on staff makes for great client relations.

Provide Pro Bono Services

Have you every wondered what made one professional service firm last over one hundred years while others come and go? One key to longevity that will span generations is community involvement. These firms typically have stellar track records of volunteerism, which is essentially what "pro bono" means in Latin. Many professionals view this as a good way to give back to the community that's given so much to them. SMB consultants should think no differently. More important, I've found you can earn tons of "karma dollars" by being a giver of your time.

So what type of pro bono services can you provide as an SMB consultant? I've seen the following services provided without charge:

- Wiring a local school for networking

- Teaching an "Introduction to Computers" class at the senior citizen center

- Donating computer equipment to the local library

In many communities, you can associate yourself with a not-for-profit

Notes:

organization that coordinates technology volunteers to help others. One group is NPower (www.npower.org). See in Figure 3-2. NPower has recently increased its scope to be national in the US.

Figure 3-2:

For many years, NPower has coordinated technology volunteers in the Seattle area. It now has several nationwide US affiliates.

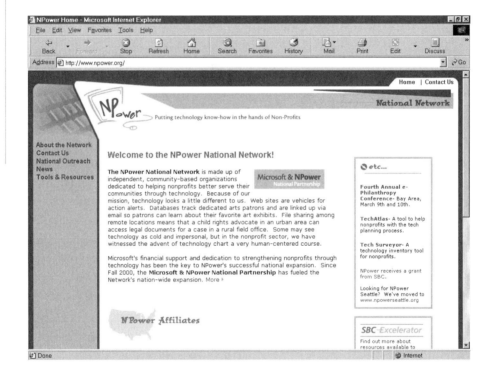

Live By Referrals

Something long-time SMB consultants who are consistently profitable know is that you must live by referrals in this business. You can't make it in the long run if you have to go out and educate each prospect with a lengthy sales cycle. Rather, you need "Class A" clients to be dropped right into your lap. That is part of the SMB consulting foundation. I discuss referrals much more in the Finder section of this book.

Always Operate Under NDA

Always think of yourself as operating under a nondisclosure agreement. When you read a war story in this book, it's only because I've received permission to share it with you from my client. It's incumbent upon you to keep secrets closely held and not be showing your hand at every card table in town. Clients expect your professionalism to include confidentiality. Heck, you've likely got the keys to the kingdom with the administrator password for your client sites. You're probably going to see things like Excel spreadsheets with the owner's net worth listed and other confidential matters. No owner would appreciate you babbling around town how much he makes, would he?

Notes:

First, Do No Harm

Lastly, it should be should be said, a key SMB consulting fundamental is to leave a system in the same or better shape than you found it. No, we're not doctors, nor do we play them on TV, but following their sacred oath is always a good practice for SMBers. Enough said!

Introducing Brelsford's Dozen

This chapter presents the foundation for your consulting career. But it's not the last you will hear about foundation-level issues in this book. In each chapter, I'll present pragmatic and practical SMB consulting rules, titled "Brelsford's Dozen," that layer right on top of the foundation you've built in this chapter. For example, in the Finder section of the book, I share with you some Brelsford's Dozen rules for getting more business. And it should not be lost on you that the following rules, presented as the body of this chapter, were your first exposure to Brelsford's Dozen:

1. GainTrust
2. Practice Expectation Management
3. Overcommunicate
4. Be Willing to Wear Many Hats
5. Become a Business Advisor
6. Take a Long-term View
7. Act as a Client Advocate
8. Mentor Your Clients
9. Provide Pro Bono Services
10. Live By Referrals
11. Always Operate Under NDA
12. First, Do No Harm

Brelsford's Mailbox

Harry:

How are you?

I have a question for you: What is the best way to go about starting a consulting practice focusing on Small Business Server? I have been in IT for 19+ years and have had my own company (Client/Server Systems, Inc.) for about 11, previously focused on consulting to large federal clients (through the EDS's, SAIC's and generally large government prime contractors).

Over the last year or so I have noticed the trend toward the SMB market (anywhere from the home office worker to the 1-10/100 employee businesses). I am an MCSE and my company is an MS Certified Partner.

Since this is a different direction for me (i.e., marketing to a small business owner is VERY DIFFERENT than marketing to a govt. prime!), if you could point me in the direction of some "best practices" it would be very helpful.

Thanks,
David
C/SS Inc.

Hi, David—

Thanks for the e-mail. I agree with what you say. The SMB market is getting much more attention in recent times than the past. In fact, leading journals like CRN have dedicated SMB sections now (CRN has a monthly supplement titled Selling Small Business). And you've got it right that selling to small businesses would be very different from selling to government prime contractors.

So first things first. Take a long weekend to sketch out an SMB consulting business plan. It's important to validate your entry into this field. If you can do that via a written business plan, you're well on your way to being a successful SMB consultant. I suspect the business planning process will allow you to think through the SMB sales process and find an SMB consulting niche that will be very profitable for you.

Next, I'd encourage you to hole up in a room with a broadband connection to the Internet and spend days surfing through the ready-made "Go To Market" marketing materials on the Partners site at Microsoft (http:// www.microsoft.com/partner). Because you are an MS Certified Partner, you'll have access to some of the great restricted content (read "the good stuff") that isn't available to the general public and non-partners.

Please write again and let me know how it goes for you!

All the best....harrybbbbbb

Summary

This chapter closes the important introductory section of this book. Having commenced your business plan in Chapter 2 and discovered the fundamentals of SMB consulting in this chapter, the door has been opened to the next section, where you'll learn to go out and get the business. In this chapter you:

- Learned about SMB consulting fundamentals

- Reviewed key SMB consulting concepts to help you be successful

- Were introduced to Brelsford's Dozen rules for SMB consultants

Part Two

FINDER

Chapter Four
Planting Seeds and Growing an SMB Consulting Practice

Chapter Five
SMB Marketing

Chapter Six
SMB Consulting Sales

Chapter Seven
Be the SMB Rainmaker

Chapter 4
Planting Seeds and Growing
an SMB Consulting Practice

In This Chapter

- How to plant SMB consulting seeds

- Understanding the SMB business development life cycle

- Brelsford's Dozen: Cash-on-hand and Client Rejection Ratio

- Prelaunch interim measures to take

- The first client has landed!

- SMB consulting transition plans

- Online auctions are your friend

- Good client selection and firing bad clients

Because of the low barrier to entry when becoming a SMB consultant, you can enter this profession via many different paths. That said, most SMB consultants break into this business as lone rangers. Each day, you are accountable only to yourself and the comings and goings of the free marketplace. If you're self-reliant, this is tremendously exciting and a new adventure awaits you around each corner. However, if you prefer to work for someone else, or harbor deep fears of failure, or lack self-confidence, breaking out on your own might just be too intimidating. And most of us know intuitively that a fine line exists between excitement and intimidation, success and failure, pain and pleasure.

This chapter is about growing your SMB consulting business. This primary focus will be a sole proprietorship, but many points raised herein can be applied to larger SMB consulting organizations and the employees within those larger organizations.

Plant the Seeds

Prior to that first day you open for business, you will have put in many months of planning. Not only will you will have completely read this book, you will no doubt have written a few drafts of your SMB consulting business plan and performed other foundational tasks. That's planting the seeds. And hopefully you've helped those seeds germinate by bringing a mentor on board, someone to add a little fertilizer and cheer you on. Along the way, I assume you've started to put the word out in your community that you'll be an SMB consultant soon.

Then, you awaken one morning and you realize it's time to grow your business. Let me share a couple of thoughts about that first day of business as an SMB consultant.

First, you might find it difficult to circle a specific day on a calendar wherein you declared you were open for business. Seriously, how many times have you listened to other technology consultants say that initially they just tinkered with computers, helping friends and answering queries on newsgroups, etc., and suddenly one day they looked up and realized that they had been technology consultants for as long as they could remember. To paraphrase John Lennon, becoming a technology consultant is often what happens when you're busy making other plans—even for people who didn't plan to be in this line of work!

Another point is, assuming you can truly identify the day you became an SMB consultant, I suspect you'll look back at it as anticlimactic. You'll probably recall the anticipation you felt building up to the launch of your SMB consulting practice, but you may also remember feelings of loneliness. It's unlikely you will initially have a full book of business to fondly recollect. It's much more probable that you'll reminisce about the time you devoted to tedious clerical tasks, such as ordering business cards and stationery. I spent my first day as an officially self-employed SMB consultant deciphering competing wireless plans for cellular telephone service. I felt relatively unproductive, but nonetheless I had launched myself into the wild and whacky world of SMB consulting.

Life Cycle for Developing Business

Another point to substantiate my initial claim about the lower barriers to entry in the SMB consulting field is the fact that you will enjoy a shorter sales cycle than other technology consultants. Whereas an enterprise-level technology consultant might spend well over a year consummating a seven-figure consulting engagement, your SMB consulting road is shorter. Granted, there is a business development cycle in SMB consulting, but it is shorter than other disciplines. And understand that at this juncture, your initial entry into SMB consulting, the business development cycle will be at its longest. I suggest that you plan for an initial business development cycle in the neighborhood of six months. Add another month to perform the work which you've won plus another month for the accounting billing cycle, and it's possible that you can expect eight months to pass between making the initial contact and actually getting cash in your hand.

Why does the SMB business development cycle take six months or more? Don't calls come in from clients desperately asking you to start working immediately? Sure, there are always spot or cash buyers in the market for SMB consulting services. However, not only are these clients the exception, but their panicked call, rife with overwrought urgency may be a good indicator of the type of client they will be. These are the "Class C" clients who are less loyal to their SMB consultant than the blue-chip or high-grade clients you should be cultivating. Many times, the spot buyer of your services has terminated another consultant, and you're just the next victim being lined up for an unsuccessful engagement.

> BEST PRACTICE: When you receive a distress call from a client urgently seeking your services, be sure to ask if there was a previous consultant and, if so, what happened to that consultant. Remember that the same can happen to you. For example, if the client speaks poorly of the former consultant, they could certainly speak so of you. Ask yourself if this is the type of client you want and if this is the type of client that will allow you to earn a profit in the long term.

Again, to make a major point in this chapter, the six-month business development cycle is where you start. Later on, when you have a track record, you can anticipate a sales cycle in the three- to four-month range in

SMB consulting. And be humble, for every client that retains you inside a three-month window, take a moment to reflect and count how many clients took years to win over. Need further humbling? Don't forget to factor in those prospects you "wasted" time on and pursued for months and years who never became clients. Once you amortize these additional efforts into the business development cycle equation, the three-month+ time frame is a reasonable sales-planning horizon. You'll be interested to know that I've confirmed this three-month+ business development cycle in other businesses. Ask an established accountant what the business development cycle is for a tax client. And for a different answer entirely, ask the new accountant what the time frame for landing that first client is (in this second case, the time frame will likely be six months or more). In professions such as commercial real estate leasing, it's not at all uncommon to spend over a year working on a transaction. Of course these transactions come in at six and seven figures, and result in a worthwhile payoff for the realtor.

In Table 4-1 the business development dance that tends to occur between SMB consultant and client is portrayed.

Table 4-1
Sample Business Development Cycle

Time Frame	Status
Month One	Initial contact between SMB consultant and prospective client initiated. Follow-up communications, such as telephone calls and e-mail between parties. The SMB consulting courtship has commenced.
Month Two	Follow-up meeting where SMB consultant learns more about technology needs.
Month Three	Dead zone with no immediate work. The prospective client gets busy running his business. Client doesn't return your call or answer your e-mail because need isn't there. Hang in there and continue client communications (your day will come!).

Month Four	Still no immediate need with client. But the prospective client, cleaning out old e-mails, finally replies to you and suggests another meeting. You delay your family vacation a few days to meet with this client. The meeting occurs.
Month Five	HP and other major hardware manufacturers release new lines of servers for SMB market. Your client sees news article about this and requests another meeting. This meeting results in your submitting a proposal for networking services. The prospective client reads proposal and exchanges e-mail with you to clarify points and lower overall costs. You revise the proposal several times.
Month Six	The prospective client approves your proposal and becomes a bona fide client. However, the signed SMB consulting contract contains several stipulations, including one noting that the work can't start for 60 days because a new release of a narrow vertical market software application won't be available until that time.

The six-month business development cycle for the new SMB consultants is just for business development. The actual work may begin the next day or a couple of months hence. Needless to say, the initial business development cycle for SMB consultants can be surprisingly long and shouldn't be underestimated (even though I've highlighted above and set your expectation that the SMB sales cycle is significantly shorter than at the enterprise level).

The sooner you accept the initial six-month business development cycle as a fact of life, the better. Not only will you start to manage your SMB consulting practice from a visionary point of view, where you're thinking six months out as the time frame to make good things happen, but you may also become a higher-quality SMB consultant. Here is what I mean. Like a fine wine, clients improve with age. You typically don't land blue-chip clients in a short business development cycle. In fact, it may take years to land that icon of commerce and business in your market that every SMB consultant is seeking. Perhaps you'll need to golf, sail, and ski for years with the business owner until you get a crack at the account, and even then you are allowed to bid only because the existing consultant finally lost interest and didn't serve the client well.

And again, I'm focusing here on the six-month development cycle that faces a new SMB consultant. Later on, as you grow into an experienced SMB consultant, it's a safe bet you'll cut your business development time in half. Why, you ask? In part it's because you'll be more skilled at business development and the leads you get will be via referrals, a practice that dramatically shortens the sale cycle.

Brelsford's Dozen:
Have 12 Months' Cash on Hand

All professionals and small business people, yourself included as an SMB consultant, need starting capital. Think about this. Maybe you've witnessed the following scenarios. Perhaps a friend or family member is in some type of commission-based professional capacity and started with a year of cash to initially cover living expenses. Or perhaps you saw a middle-aged, middle-management dude leave his corporate capacity and borrow against his retirement funds to open a hobby shop. Maybe you witnessed the housewife of a dentist start a fabrics store, bankrolled by her husband for the first year of operations. No matter what new business you might jump into, the first year is a total financial bearcat and you need some cash to carry you through!

This area of sufficient start-up capital is so important that I'll state the obvious again: Starting out with enough money is an essential fact of being in business for commission-based salespeople, small business owners, and SMB consultants alike. When you break out on your own, you need a reserve of cash on which to survive until your business efforts yield sustainable cash flow. In real estate sales career seminars, you're advised to have a year of cash for living expenses-although new real estate agents are notorious for running up credit card debt, or begging from family and friends, or otherwise borrowing from Peter to pay Paul to survive the first year. This real estate career advice applies equally well to SMB consultants just starting out.

But I can hear some of you asking why you should have one-year's cash on hand to launch as an SMB consultant. The billing cycle that follows the initial contract, which follows the initial sales cycle, is way out there! Plus I need to preintroduce a concept that I'll explore more in the Minder section of this book: accounting write-downs. Long story short, you'll have some billing write-downs in the SMB consulting field. Write-downs are charges against your billing revenues when a client will not pay your consulting invoice. Accounting rules dictate that you write down doubtful accounts receivable balances after a reasonable period of time. Figure 4-1 displays the 12-month initial cash-on-hand cycle for you.

Figure 4-1:
Proof positive the 12-month supply of cash at launch theorem holds true.

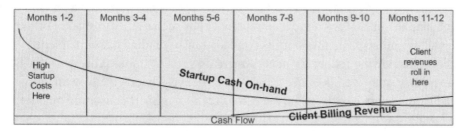

Betcha didn't know that the 12-month rule can even apply to established SMB consulting practices. From the first sales call to the first satisfied invoice (which is cash in hand to you), it's not uncommon for nearly 12 months to have passed. These stark facts about cash-flow timing are only stronger for the newbie SMB consultant.

Bottom line: Your new SMB consulting practice is a startup. It's risky and some of you, bless your hearts, might not be around in a year or two. This sobering reality is all the more reason to have sufficient cash to launch! You'll greatly appreciate having enough money at the ready, let me tell you.

Interim Measures to Accumulate Startup Cash

So you're involved in a family feud and funds from the bloodline aren't coming your way to launch you as an SMB consultant. Your friends flee fast as soon as you request startup cash. What's a new SMB consultant to do? Clearly, you need to look at other financial alternatives. I have seen two strategies used to overcome the cash nest egg problem. These alternatives are (in order of decreasing desirability): working a night job and borrowing money.

Take a night job

Ever been to the retirement party for a titan of industry and commerce? If you don't hear an immigration story of how the person arrived on these domestic shores (à la Ellis Island in New York) with no money, you're likely to hear a story of how the individual went to night school, worked a night job, and the like. Many a great entrepreneur has such a story to share. For the small businessperson, this story is typically one of tending bar or delivering pizzas and are the fodder for many American success stories. You, as an SMB consultant, may well don the "funny" pizza delivery hat on the way up the ladder to generate cash during the early life of your SMB consulting practice.

And while I have nothing against pizza, there are some night shift alternatives that complement what you're trying to accomplish as an SMB consultant in the long term. From the "do as I did department," you could work as an adjunct computer instructor at night at a local vocational-technical or community college. This is exactly how I launched my technology consulting practice! But back to you. In many cases, educational institutions will start an instructor with little or no formal teaching experience. The old adage about teaching—"If you really want to learn a subject, teach it"—applies, plus you make a little pocket change along the way. Better yet, some of my longest SMB consulting client relationships hark back to my adjunct teaching days, because night teaching is a great referral source for SMB consulting engagements.

Another popular swing shift possibility for those with a propensity for technology is software product support. Many companies need to staff their help desks around the clock. This could be a software development firm or a traditional business that has a 24/7 help desk function. Think about it for a minute. Not only can you make some badly needed cash in your startup phase, but this work allows SMB consultants to increase their technical skill sets. Swing shift technical support opportunities exist in the following types of firms:

- **ISVs** — Computers don't care what time it is, and many technology projects occur after hours when users have gone home. Both of these dynamics mean night work for you and others at software development firms!

- **Telcos and ISPs** — Internet service providers and the telecommunications firms that provide communication links experience some of the heaviest activity after hours. Any respectable telco and ISP will provide sufficient, bona fide 24/7 technical support.

- **Fortune 1000 and beyond** — Regardless of where you are, there is probably real technology-based night shift work. In urban areas, the need is apparent with enterprise-level entities on every block. In remote areas, just look down the road at your local call center. And don't forget you can play the time zone game. For example, in the United States, morning on the East Coast is half past the bewitching hour in Alaska (and nearly O'beer-thirty in the UK). More to the point-when considering global firms, part of their appeal is that they have business operations that are nonstop. Glance around your town and see what large firms have distant branch offices and remote locations. These firms likely staff a technology help-desk night shift crew.

- **Traditional night businesses** — Night auditors are standard fare for hotels. Look for businesses that have long engaged in nighttime operations and can avail themselves of your contribution. These firms should receive your résumé seeking a swing shift, technology-based opportunity.

Borrow money

Yes, the "b" word. If you can get a long-gone dot-com entrepreneur to speak with you about how he started out (and not how he flamed out), there is typically a maxed-out credit card somewhere in the equation. You might be an exception to the following point, but to launch yourself as an SMB consultant, there comes a point where you'll probably have to borrow funds during your formative years. In itself and as explained in upper-level corporate finance courses, borrowing isn't a bad thing. Borrowing can be used to provide the working capital you need on that newly landed, enormous consulting contract. I did it myself, borrowing on a credit card to purchase a Macintosh computer that was needed for my first contract as an SMB consultant. It was a lucrative contract that paid on time 30 days later, but I needed the Macintosh in advance. You get the point. And, it's leverage, which is another financial term that essentially means using other people's money. That's called "OPM" in Texas! For non-Texans, that's OTHER PEOPLE'S MONEY, with capitalization for emphasis!

There exist various forms of borrowing, ranging from commercial lines of credit at a bank to pawn shops to loan sharks. Here are the most common forms of borrowing I've seen used by fledgling SMB consultants:

- **Home equity loan** — This debt vehicle is reasonable both in its costs and in your ability to obtain it. You should obtain your funds via this avenue prior to leaving your day job and becoming a full-fledged SMB consultant. It's much easier to get a home equity loan while gainfully employed. In today's environment, a home equity loan is desirable because of the historically low interest rates tied to this form of borrowing. But at any time, under any economic conditions, home equity loans allow you to FEEL that you're investing directly in your SMB consulting business. These strong feelings come from having drawn "foundation" money, such as home equity.

- **Credit cards** — More, but not all, of us can resist the enticing preapproved credit card offers that seemingly multiply in our mailboxes. Granted, this is a high-cost form of debt, but it's so darn easy to acquire. And as stated earlier, credit cards are used at some point by almost every small business person.

- **Friends, family, and in-laws** — Major "ouch" territory, but it's been done before. This form of debt carries the high cost of tension and hurt feelings when things don't go exactly as expected.

Landing Your First Client

Forward march. Time to go land the first client. As with most anything in life, the first time is typically the hardest. This section speaks to you about several strategies to try in landing the first client.

Capitalizing on an existing employer

Perhaps you've seen this. One of the most tried-and-true methods of gaining your first client is turning your existing employer into a client. Consider the following:

- **Changing your status from W-2 to 1099 (applicable in the US) —** Perhaps you can work for your existing employer as a contractor. Not only does the treatment of your income change for tax purposes, but it also absolves you of the employer/employee relationship. As a contractor, you typically have fewer restrictions on additional, outside work, allowing you to build your SMB consulting practice. Be advised that I've been told similar tax status issues exist in other countries such as Australia and the United Kingdom, but I'm not qualified to discuss those matters.

BEST PRACTICE: In fact, some clients for whom you serve as a contractor will demand that you have a diverse client base. Here is what I mean. I serve Microsoft on an occasional basis as a vendor. In order to become a vendor, Microsoft needs to see evidence that I am a real company and have a portfolio of real clients. Microsoft is not interested in having a "perma-temp" relationship with me, where we dupe taxation authorities by their calling me a contractor but really treating me like a full-time employee. You can share this story with an existing employer as a bona fide reason why, upon changing your status to that of contractor, you need to proceed in all haste and land some additional client accounts.

- Shift changes — Many people contract back to their existing employers so that they can work fewer hours. This is common with new moms who must continue to work but want to back off the professional pace a tad. You might consider that same strategy when you make the break as an SMB consultant. Instead of working 40+ hours per week as a salaried or exempt employee, you might elect to work 20 hours per week as a contractor, freeing up the time needed to start your SMB consulting practice.

BEST PRACTICE: Perhaps you've observed that people who return as consultants to their existing employers often do so at a higher billing rate than their previous wage. There are several reasons why this occurs, including the contractor's incurring overhead expenses, such as medical insurance and self-employment taxes. For this and other reasons, employers often have to pay a slightly higher wage for the flexible staffing option that contractors provide. This flexibility includes the ability for employers who are dissatisfied with contractors to terminate the business relationship immediately with little fear of wrongful discharge litigation. By using contractors, employers typically don't have to issue layoff notices.

Volunteering

Another way to land the first client is by offering your services free. That is, you can establish yourself as a legitimate SMB consultant and gain reference letters and referrals by volunteering. Fact of the matter is that there are typically more volunteer opportunities than volunteers, so finding an "unpaid learning opportunity" (a common euphemism for volunteering) to strut your stuff as a competent SMB consultant shouldn't be that hard. Two volunteer organizations that I've seen SMB consultants successfully exploit are not-for-profit organizations and political campaigns.

Not-for-profit organizations

Not-for-profit organizations are chronically short on funds, yet have the same technology needs, both hardware and software, as private sector firms. Pick a cause, and somewhere there is a not-for-profit organization behind it. Give them a call and see how you can help. Better yet, in major cities there are not-for-profit organizations that provide low-cost and no-cost technology consulting services for fellow not-for-profit organizations. In the Pacific Northwest region of the US there is one such group called NPower (www.npower.org). For more information on Npower, refer to Chapter 3 of this book.

If you have a higher calling and aspire to assist in the meaningful implementation of technology across the word, there are two organizations that can benefit from your inherent goodness: GeekCorps and Peace Corps. Late in the writing of this book, I enjoyed a lengthy telephone call with Ana Maria Harkins, Executive Director of GeekCorps (www.geekcorps.org). She sold me on a mission that has technology improving the world, often one small business, government or school at a time. GeekCorps has accepted my offer to have a free booth at my SMB Nation conferences (www.smbnation.com) and tell their story to attendees (and perhaps even recruit a few of you along the way as volunteers). Peace Corps has similar opportunities but typically not as technology oriented. I can say that Peace Corps did select SBS as its worldwide remote site computing platform and that's something you might want to know if you have a volunteer interview with that organization. PeaceCorps can be reached at www.peacecorps.gov.

Political campaigns

Regardless of your political beliefs, there is a campaign out there that needs your SMB consulting services. They just can't pay you. Find a candidate you support and volunteer to run the computer system. Not only is this approach a door-opener for meeting the rich, famous, and politically connected, but you just might help your candidate get elected. And better yet, almost by definition, political campaigns are themselves small businesses (with the few exceptions being national campaigns).

> BEST PRACTICE: Something else to consider. Many technology types are deficient in the ye olde political skills department. Some of us wouldn't know how to be smooth even if we'd been sanded with gentle sandpaper. Working in not-for-profits-environments in which inhabitants are noxiously known for their politicking prowess-will expose you to some smooth movers. Needless to say, working on a political campaign will do the same.
>
> All humor aside, at some point in your SMB career, you'll need a refined political skill set to take your consulting practice to the highest levels. Speaking only for myself, when I was a newbie in the land of SMB consulting, I'd just as soon flee or fight when in a tight spot with a client. Both such reactions didn't bode well for having my invoice paid quickly and with a smile. But, in writing these words, I can reflect on a recent situation where I was able to terminate a problem client and still have my final invoice for $950 paid a month later. Whew! We're talking real money here as a result of being cool and not insulting or alienating the client, even though doing so would have felt so good. Cashing the company's check felt even better.

Working for half price

Properly proposed in such a way that doesn't cheapen yourself, working at a reduced rate can help you acquire those first clients. This approach allows you to recognize your SMB consulting limitations (perhaps your technical skill set) as a new SMB consultant. If you explore this wisely, you'll find that there is no shortage of clients willing to accept a lower rate to pay for your services. It's a fair deal. You get a client, and the client gets work performed at bargain rates.

> BEST PRACTICE: Be careful here. These half-priced clients are seldom long-term fits for your SMB consulting practice. Once a cheap client, always a cheap client. A client that is susceptible to your initial bargain pricing will likely trade you out for the next cut-rate deal that crosses his desk, rather than pay your full consulting rate at a future date. So, if you dance with the half-priced devil, understand it might well be a short dance.

Auctioning yourself as an SMB Consultant

Auction barkers and hucksters have been around forever, dating back to the first ice age. So this section is really presenting nothing new. But hang in there for the twists on being an SMB consultant and using auctions.

Auctions for charity

The following is a true story that was widely reported in US newspapers. A medical doctor donated a vasectomy operation to a local school fundraising auction. Granted, it would hardly be as dramatic, but why couldn't you, as an SMB consultant, donate a day of services to go to the highest bidder? If you look closely, there are charity auctions every week in medium and large cities. It's a cheap and effective way to market yourself. Figure 4-2 shows one such charity auction.

Notes:

Figure 4-2:

Here is an example of a charity auction for a not-for-profit organization.

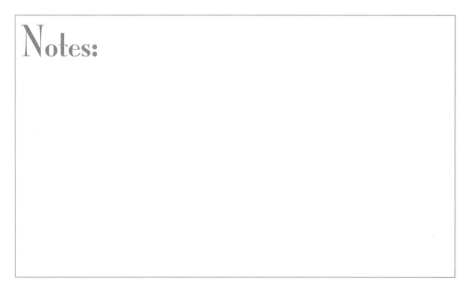

Notes:

Online auction sites

Crafty professionals have made headlines when they auctioned themselves through eBay. Today, the practice doesn't necessarily make headlines, but it still occurs. What have you got to lose by putting your SMB consulting services up for bid at an online auction site? Nothing! Figure 4-3 displays the results of a recent keyword search on "Small Business Server."

Figure 4-3:

Tons of SBS product is sold on eBay but there is a noticeable lack of SMB consulting services being offered. As you read this, consider clicking over and adding your offering to this mix.

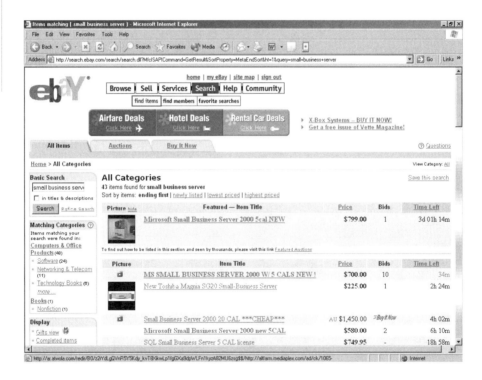

Let me dig deeper into the online auction theme. First, the sheer number of clicks at an online auction site such as eBay is impressive (eBay is one of the most popular sites on the Internet). Second, eBay has signaled to the auction community that it seeks to have more high-end auction items and more services as part of its business model. Third, the eBay auction approach allows you to offer a complete solution for a fixed price. You could package your services with a server machine and the SBS software, with bidding starting at, say, $6,500 US.

> BEST PRACTICE: The operative words above were "complete so-lution." Selling the solution is in alignment with Microsoft's "Go To Market" mantra being espoused upon its certified partners. I can honestly say that "solution selling" is one of the key success factors employed by SMB consultants in Australia. I'll mention this several times in the course of this book, but it's important to know that Australia kicks ass when it comes to SMB consulting. SMB consultants from the land of OZ (an affectionate nickname the land Downunder) have reportedly sold as many copies of SBS as the entire US (even though the US is 15 times larger!). This has been accomplished in large part because of solution selling.

Another benefit from online auction selling of your SMB consulting services is that, even though you'll offer up a fixed bid scenario for your SMB solution (I'm assuming it's based on SBS), you can deftly cover your variable costs for travel, your dining per diem, and your lodging above and beyond the winning bid price. How? This is accomplished by completing the online auction submission to have "shipping and handling" costs determined post-auction between buyer and seller. Here is how that works. The winning bidder alerts you that they've won your SMB consulting services. Let's say it turns out that the winning bidder lives on the other coast. You obtain an airfare quote for $1,250, lodging is quoted at $850, and you calculate your per diem at $50 per day, with an estimated three-day setup making the total per diem $150. Thus, this example of the "shipping and handling" costs presented to the buyer would be $1,250 + $850 + $150 = $2,250.

> BEST PRACTICE: Here again, I inserted operative words that I want to emphasize: "fixed bid." It's only been since SBS 2000 that SMB consultants could seriously consider engaging a client and de-ploying SBS under a fixed bid scenario. In the distant past of SBS, in the SBS 4.x time frame, offering SMB consulting services under fixed bid was financial suicide because the product was unstable and not ready for prime time. But those dark days are behind us and you can now engage in fixed bids for SBS.

One more consideration about fixed bid pricing: Because you have the newfound confidence to deploy SBS under a fixed bid scenario, you should now consider the fact the the OEM installation of SBS will save an hour or so in the multi-hour SBS setup process. When you've locked in your bid price, such savings are now highly desirable to the SMB consulting, eh? And I'm here to say you can pull it off with SBS stability in the modern era.

Before I demonstrate the step-by-step posting of your SMB consulting solution on eBay, there is one final business point to make. In business, there is great value to being paid sooner rather than later. This concept is valid for two reasons: time value of money and risk mitigation. Those with MBAs know exactly what I'm talking about when the topic of time value of money comes up. Here, a dollar received today is more valuable than a dollar received tomorrow, because that dollar can be put to work sooner for you, inflationary pressures exist, risk is always a factor, and so on. And speaking of risk, getting paid upfront on a consulting gig is much better than being paid later. Enough said.

So how does the above financial analysis discussion tie into eBay? Simple. With eBay, the buyer pays for the item (your complete SMB consulting solution plus shipping and handling) at the end of the auction. You then deliver your SMB solutions at a future date.

BEST PRACTICE: Something else to ponder about the eBay payment system. As an experienced SMB consultant, I'm willing to consider a significant discount for my services rendered if said services are paid for in advance. There is great value in the professional services area to having what in effect is a retainer. You know you will get paid! Thus, you might lower the starting bid point for your SMB consulting solution on eBay to reflect the prepayment nature of the business transaction.

Notes:

So, let's get the show on the road and show off an example of posting an eBay listing.

1. You will first launch a browser and click over to the eBay URL of **http://www.eBay.com**. If you like, search on the term "Small Business Server" or something similar in the **What are you looking for?** field and investigate if other SMB consultants are auctioning a similar solution. Look at what they offer and what they charge to help you decied on how to package yourself.
2. Click the **Sell** button.
3. First, click the **Register** button under the **New to eBay** area. Complete the eBay registration process.
4. Create a seller's account by clicking the **Create a seller's account link**. You will need this to become a seller on eBay.

BEST PRACTICE: One consideration in working with online auction sites like eBay is your track record and reputation, much like SMB consulting. You could even extend that thinking further to read that you're only as good as your last transaction. eBay uses a rating system where purchasers of your services are asked to rate you based on a scale that includes positive, neutral, and negative. Potential purchasers look at your ratings to decide whether you are fit to conduct business with.

It behooves you to take some time to build up your positive eBay ratings so that you can be a credible seller of an SMB technology solutions, such as a complete SBS package. I'd recommend you start small and sell a few things on eBay and "get your ratings up." Interestingly, if you sell numerous small items, such as books, and build up high ratings, the eBay system doesn't readily display the comparative value for which those ratings apply. That is, you could sell a bushel of cheap books, build up your positive ratings and then go for the big banana and list a complete SMB technology solutions based on SBS, as you will do in this example.

Taking the above steps is a legitimate way to package yourself so you can successfully present yourself and sell your SMB consulting solution on eBay. FYI, and for your use as a reference point, my eBay ratings are shown in Figure 4-4.

Figure 4-4:
I've used the individual sale of my books to build my eBay ratings so I can credibly sell increasingly larger items on eBay. This is facilitated by accruing positive buyer ratings.

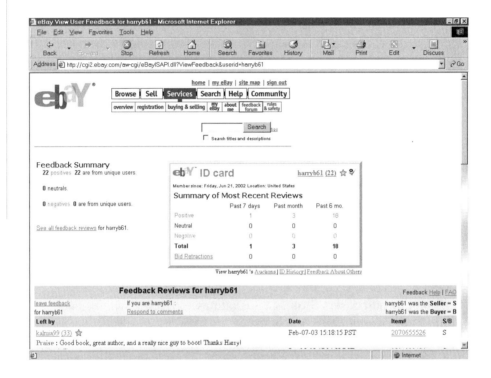

One last thought. A real positive about the eBay rating system is that you need to keep your rating current. As you can see in the above figure, ratings effectively expire. This is a positive step, because sometimes a legitimate seller from the past has somehow become a corrupted and morally bankrupt soul. The eBay rating system will reflect that with its emphasis on the here and now.

5. You are now ready to create an item for sale, in this case, an SMB solution based on SBS. Log in by putting your account name in the **eBay User ID** field and your password in the **Password** field. Click the **Sign In** button.

6. On the **Sell Your Item — Choose Selling Format** screen, select **Sell item at online Auction** and click **Continue**.

BEST PRACTICE: You might consider selling at a fixed price with no bidding if that better fits your business model. Perhaps you've defined your SMB solution and you are interested in providing it for a fair price, no more and no less. The choice is yours.

7. On the **Sell Your Item: Select Category**, I recommend you select a category close to the following: **Computers & Office Products -> Services -> Other.** Do not select a second category. Click **Continue**.

BEST PRACTICE: Two thoughts about eBay categories. The first category is free on eBay, but to add multiple categories costs a nominal charge, something like 20 cents each. Also, I've found categories aren't really very useful, as people I've conducted SBS business with simply search on terms like "Small Business Server." Keyword searches appear to be more effective in this realm on eBay.

8. You will complete the **Sell Your Item: Describe Your Item** screen. Type **Complete Small Business Server Solution** in the **Item title** field. Complete the **Description** field with the following entry and confirm by viewing Figure 2-5. Click **Continue**.

BEST PRACTICE: Consider typing out your description in Microsoft Word first so you can spell-check your document. The Description field on the eBay page does not have spell-check available. After creating the description in Word, simply paste your perfect description in the Description field.

Microsoft Small Business Server (SBS) consultant offers complete, turn-key SBS solution including:

- *Microsoft Small Business Server 2000 (5-user CAL) (NEW, UNUSED)*

- *HP ProLiant ML350 with Intel Xeon processor (2.4 MHZ), 512MB RAM, internal dual-Wide Ultra3 SCSI adapter, two 36GB hard disks (mirrored), two network adapter cards, 20/40GB DAT drive plus one DAT backup tape, 15" color monitor, standard three-year HP warranty. (NEW, UNUSED)*

• *Three days on-site installation and deployment service by skilled, expert Small Business Server consultant.*

• *One-month of remote and telephone-based SBS-specific deployment support. This includes one month of network monitoring. Future and additional work as agreed by all parties. Service limited to specific SBS deployment issues (not line-of-business applications, database creation or maintenance, or end-user support issues on desktop applications or operating systems, etc.).*

Note: Shipping and handling charges calculated after bidding and will constitute the following charges:

• *airfare, hotel and per diem for consultant to travel to customer site to complete on-site installation work.*

• *actual shipping charges for hardware and software to customer site.*

These shipping and handling charges will vary by customer location. SBS consultant located in Seattle, Washington, USA.

Note: Please e-mail if you have questions about this solution. Seller happy to answer all questions promptly and in detail.

Notes:

Figure 4-5:

This is a key step to be taken seriously-describing your SMB solution. Take your time here and use compelling marketing language.

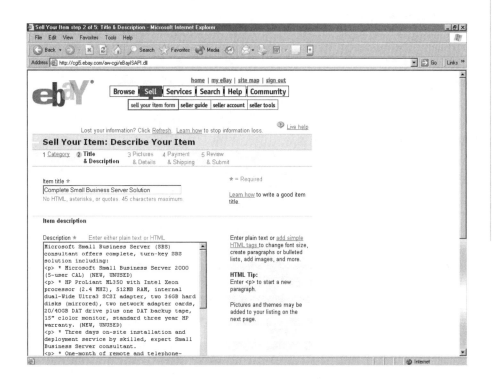

BEST PRACTICE: Not to jump the gun on my hands-on "grinder" topics later in the book, such as how to deploy SBS, I do need to introduce a few granular items in the example herein. For example, to determine what server to include in my SBS turn-key solution on eBay, I visited www.hp.com and specified a suitable SMB server solution. To be honest, this eBay example is best viewed as information for the moment, so please bookmark/dog-ear this page and return to it after you've completely read this book and you're ready to post a "complete SMB solution" on eBay for bidding!

And as you can see in Figure 4-6, I've specified a Microsoft Small Business Server 2000 machine for the HP ProLiant ML350 server.

Figure 4-6:

Select a server machine that you trust to be part of your solution. Because you are offering your turn-key solution on a fixed bid basis, you should select a server machine that you know will work well. I only select name-brand manufacturers such as HP for that very reason. I can't afford to troubleshoot server-side hardware when working under fixed bid!

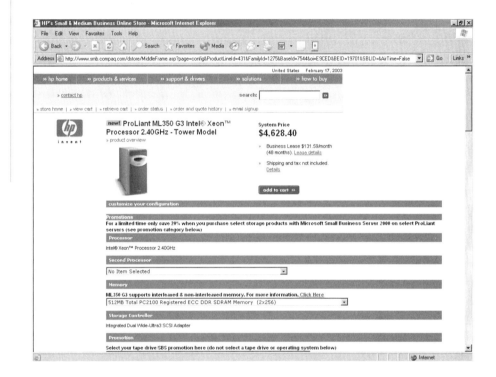

9. On the **Sell Your Item: Provide Pictures and Item Details** page, complete the following fields show in Table 4-2. (Note that I've left some fields found on the Web page intentionally blank as you won't use these fields.) Your efforts should appear similar to Figure 4-7. After completing, click **Continue**.

Table 4-2
Completing Item Details

Field	Value
Duration	7 days
Start Time	Start listing when submitted (free)
Quantity	1
Starting price	$10,000 (note that I've provided this value as an example, but you will need to calculate the starting price for your own solution)
Buy It Now price	$15,000 (again, input a value that makes sense for you)
City/State/Region/Country	Input your location information (e.g., Bainbridge Island, Washington, USA)
Picture1	I'd recommend you consider uploading your photo
Free Page Counter	Green LED (this allows you to see how many people have visited your item page)

Notes:

Figure 4-7:

The **Sell Your Item: Describe Your Item** *page is step 2 of 5 to list your SBS solution on eBay.*

10. Complete the **Sell Your Item: Enter Payment & Shipping** information screen. For this example, I've selected PayPal as my payment approach, that the buyer will pay the shipping costs, and that I'll provide information on the shipping costs later. Under the **Payment instructions** area, I repeated the shipping instructions that I initially posted on the page in Step 8 where I described the item. In the **Ship-to-locations** section, I selected **Will ship to the United States and the following: Canada**. You may select the geographic location(s) of your choice. You may elect your own escrow terms at the bottom of this page. Your screen should look similar to Figure 4-8. Click **Continue**.

Figure 4-8:

Carefully review and complete the payment and shipping information.

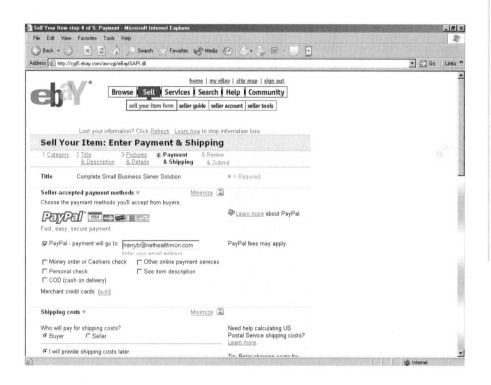

BEST PRACTICE: If you haven't set up a PayPal account, you will need to do so at this time by clicking the **Learn more about PayPal** link. I found creating a PayPal account to take about 30 minutes because I had to find some financial information from my accounting records that had been requested.

11. This next step is important. Carefully review the **Sell Your Item: Review & Submit Listing** page. Once you confirm all the information is correct, click the **Submit Listing** button. Your results should look similar to Figure 4-9.

Figure 4-9:

You're almost there! After this step, your listing will be posted and you, an SMB consultant, will have a listing on eBay for your complete SBS solution.

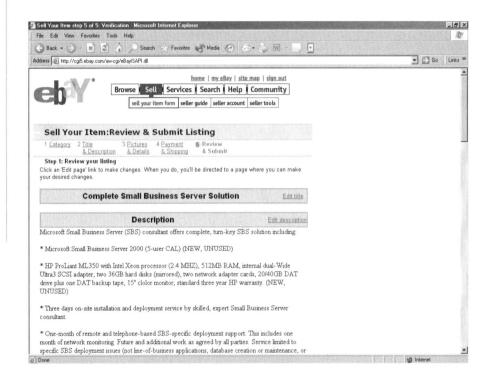

BEST PRACTICE: Be advised that eBay has a listing fee. This is found in **Step 2: Review the fees** section. To be honest, the fee is modest and acceptable (it is a total of $3.35 in the above example). Nonetheless, the fee must be accounted for as a sales expense in your SMB consulting practice, an accounting concept that will be explored in the Minder section of this book.

12. The **Sell Your Item: Congratulations** screen will appear. Review and observe your **Item #** and **URL**. Click the URL link to view the item page (it should look similar to Figure 4-10).

Figure 4-10:

It's live — your listing for the "Complete Small Business Server Solution."

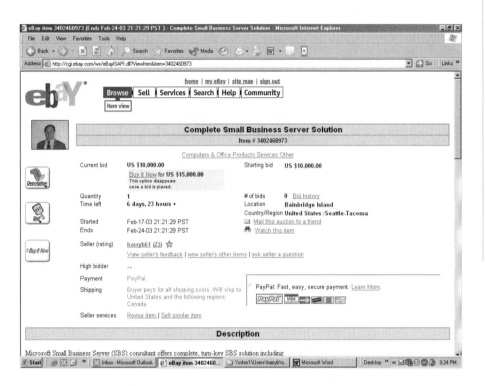

Notes:

Finally, to see your listing listed with all Small Business Server-related listings, simply click the **Search** button and type **Small Business Server** in the **Search** (required) field. The results should look similar to Figure 4-11.

Figure 4-11:
When you post your own Small Business Server solution, it'll be listed similar to the one added in this example.

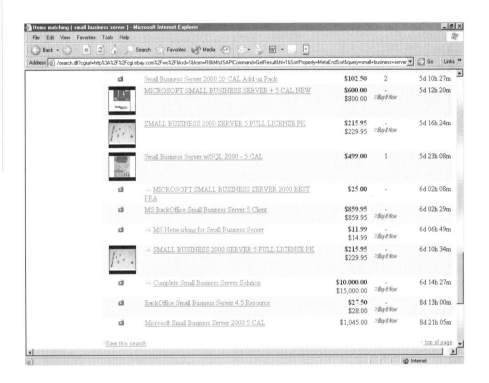

Your SMB Consulting Transition Plans

Any major life change requires a plan if you want to do it right. Becoming an SMB consultant is a significant lifestyle change for many, so a transition plan is in order. This might include transitioning in stages. First, you might be a part-timer earning other revenue by taking odd jobs or part-time work (such as the night jobs discussed earlier in the chapter). As your SMB consulting practice becomes larger and crowds out your other activities, you can completely transition into becoming a bona fide full-time SMB consultant.

Here are a couple of ways to begin and complete that transition. Most important, these examples insert you into applicable work environments, working as a technology consultant while serving a real client.

Temp agencies

Hey, I'm not so full of hubris that I can't tell you I benefited greatly by walking the temporary agency path on the way up. By working as a technology temporary employee, I was exposed to a wide range of client sites, including a summer gig at Microsoft testing Microsoft Excel 3.0 macros in the early 1990s. (Now that seems like a long time ago!)

> BEST PRACTICE: A temporary agency is a great place to gain legitimate consulting experience, and perhaps you can acquire your own clients this way. The temporary agency contract with the client typically won't let you take the client for your own billings. However, such contracts are often silent with respect to third-party referrals you receive from said client. In other words, you work as a temp at a company. You demonstrate superior skills, and an employee at this company gives your name to his spouse who works for another company. The spouse calls you and retains your services as an SMB consultant.

Contract houses

The story is much the same working for contract houses (which are really higher-end temp agencies). You are likely to be placed on longer term and more analytically demanding assignments than the temporary agency offered you. But you'll still gain important technology consulting experience and the possibility of referrals that are outside the scope of the contract house employment and client services agreement. Granted, these are typically higher-end assignments that start at the upper-medium space and quickly become "enterprise" in nature. But such assignments give you the opportunity to learn the fundamentals of consulting and customer service. These are transferable skills that can be applied to the SMB consulting space.

Online employment agencies

Employment agencies have changed with the times and are now bricks and clicks. The "clicks" are online employment agencies, such as Monster.com (seen in Figure 4-12). By registering with a site like Monster.com, you can easily advertise your skills to a much larger audience than your local hometown audience. This is an especially good way to jumpstart your SMB consulting practice if you are willing to travel to distant lands to ply your craft.

Figure 4-12:
Consider registering with online employment services to develop your SMB consulting practice.

Working for another consulting firm initially

If you look at other professions, you'll see the following trend. An accountant who starts an accounting firm first worked for another accounting firm and gained significant experience. Then this person broke away and started her own accounting practice. I've seen the same thing in law and medicine. To start your own SMB consulting practice, it often makes sense first to work in the industry as an SMB consultant with an established consulting firm.

Experience

One of the key reasons to work for another consulting firm before making the break is to gain bona fide experience. It's one thing to read a book on SMB consulting (such as this one), but an entirely different thing to actually do it. By working for another consulting firm as an SMB consultant, you essentially learn on their payroll.

Instant client base

Working for another consulting firm typically provides you with the instant client base you can take with you when you leave. This is seen in the legal and accounting fields all the time. Clients have a relationship with you and follow you when you make your move. Of course, I offer these above thoughts subject to the employment and non-compete agreements you might have entered into. See my next point.

Non-compete agreements

Typically when you are employed by a consulting firm, you'll sign a non-compete agreement on your date of hire. This agreement will spell out how the firm must be compensated if you take existing clients to start your own consulting practice.

> BEST PRACTICE: Read the terms and conditions of any non-compete agreement carefully. These are often written to protect the firm from being unduly raided. The agreement may spell out restrictive terms such as a distance radius (not within 50 miles), a duration (not within six months), or a financial penalty (all future client billings for one year paid to previous employer) under which you will have to operate when you leave the firm. You should consult an attorney on these agreements. The courts have a track record for frowning upon agreements that stifle competition and business growth.

Firing Your Clients

A big part of maturing as an SMB consultant and part of growing your business is about making the right engagement decisions along the way. Accept a bad engagement, and you'll undoubtedly have a few of those, and watch your profit level fall, your energy become depleted, and your good attitude go south.

Identifying bad fits

You can typically identify a bad-fit client without a superfluity of words of wisdom from me. A very basic sign would be that things aren't going well when you're at the client site. Perhaps the environment is consistently tense and the conversations terse. Worst of all, the client isn't paying your invoices in a timely manner. "Face the facts," as the new self-help TV guru Dr. Phil would bellow: You aren't going to get referrals from this client.

> BEST PRACTICE: A point I'll make several times in this book is that your goal is to have each of your clients be referenceable and referable. Clients that are bad fits should be fired.

Terminating a relationship

Each situation is different, but often the easiest way to terminate the client relationship is to explain to the client that you're taking the practice in a "new direction" and you'll be happy to help them line up another consultant. You will often need to dedicate a few hours, usually not billable, to the old client in helping transition the account to this new consultant. Why isn't this work, in reality, billable? A client who's been fired isn't too pleased about paying you for additional work, such as a transition.

> BEST PRACTICE: As usual, timing is everything. Be sure to time the termination of your client so that you have minimal outstanding accounts receivable or monies owed from this entity. You don't want to terminate an account and be out some serious money.

Good Client Selection

The best way to avoid having to fire a client-or worse, being fired by a client—is to do a better job of upfront client selection. A few thoughtful and reflective moments during the business development process can save untold hours of grief during the engagement.

Making the best decision is always critical

No matter how experienced and successful you are as an SMB consultant, you're never that far removed from making a bad client selection decision. You may be susceptible to the friendly demeanor of a client or a poignant tale of woe. The bottom line is that a bad client is always a bad client. It is incumbent upon you to remain as objective as possible at all times when considering a consulting engagement with a prospective client. This is a task that never goes away.

Surviving early growth stages of business

As you build your SMB consulting practice, it is especially important that you make the best client selection decisions possible. At this stage of your consulting practice, you literally can't afford a bad fit. If you were to land a big consulting gig where the client takes an excessive amount of your time and doesn't pay your bills, it could cause your young practice to falter and fail.

Listening to your clients

Something that certainly took me a while to understand was the importance of hearing what my client was saying. If you make it a habit to talk less and listen more when selecting clients, you'll find that many clients will either qualify or disqualify themselves from contention for your services. Here is an example of what I mean, using a scenario where a customer asks for certain business reports but fails to understand the information.

It likely takes a database, such as Microsoft SQL Server, to generate the wanted reports for the customer. And for a database to run properly, you need a network with a network operating system such as Windows 2003 Server. Digging deeper, the client likely wants (but hasn't communicated to you) e-mail and Internet connectivity. Of course, Internet connectivity means a firewall tool, such as Internet Security and Acceleration (ISA) Server, must be considered. You get the point. The client communicates a business need without much knowledge of the technology. You, the SMB consultant, hear the business need and translate it into a technology solution. But if the client can't articulate a bona fide business need, they may, in effect, be disqualifying themselves from your consideration.

Brelsford's Dozen: Client Rejection Ratio

I discovered I needed an SMB consulting guideline to help me stay focused on selecting good clients. When I operated under no such rule, client selection decisions tended to be emotional and political, if not made in occasional desperation. Later, as a successful SMB consultant and after looking over my business development practices, I determined that I was rejecting about half the potential clients that asked for my services. So I devised the following rule for myself:

> On average, reject six out of twelve clients.

Let me shed some light on how this rule works:

- **The long run** — When you first open your doors for business as an SMB consultant, it's probably not practical to say "no" to nearly anyone who wants to hire you. Sometimes you just have to take what you can get. Perhaps you'll reject only the most offensive prospects. To be honest, it took me years to get my practice to where I could comfortably turn away half the business.

- **Natural laws** — To some extent, the marketplace is already performing this winnowing for you. If you count how many sales calls never go past discussing your rate or how many client meetings you've attended where both you and your client discover that the service you provide is different than the one required by the client, then you're probably close to a 50 percent client rejection ratio without even knowing it.

- **Comfort zone** — If you have the confidence that leads will flow to you and being selective is critical to your success, you'll also have the confidence to say "no" when it doesn't feel right between you and a prospective client.

Microsoft's Go To Market Campaign

At the Microsoft Partner conference called FUSION in July of 2002, Microsoft formally rolled out its "Go To Market" mantra. Go To Market (GTM) is a business development and technology deployment methodology that is the "message" for Microsoft partners to be successful. And while much of GTM is oriented toward the enterprise space, there are SMB snippets here and there.

In Figure 4-13, you can see that Microsoft's SBS page for partners typically lists current news (such as the early 2003 rebate program), followed by Figure4-14 which shows the GTM methodology.

Figure 4-13:

Microsoft's partner page for SBS.

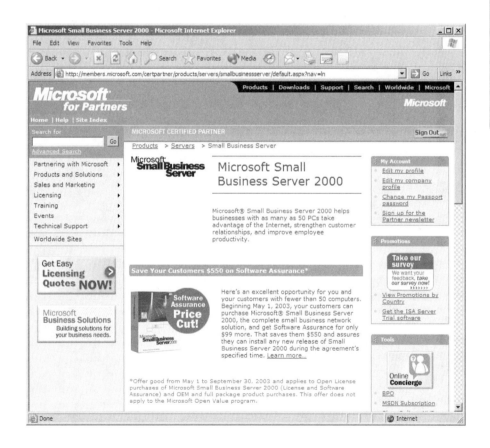

Figure 4-14

The GTM message for SBS (and thus SMB).

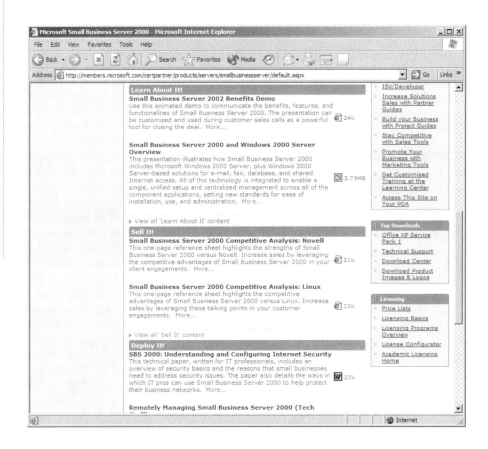

Notes:

While I'll weave GTM into several other chapters that follow, here is the basic 4-step methodology.

1. **Learn About It!** The idea here is to develop technical competencies in a technology niche. Microsoft provides a bevy of educational resources, including a series of worldwide GTM Hands-On Labs (HOT Labs) tours to assist your learning process.

2. **Sell It!** This is the business development or finder function. There's no shortage of marketing resources for you from Microsoft. I cover the "sell it" function over the next few chapters.

3. **Deploy it!** This maps to my Grinder section of the book where you "do it" and implement the technology solutions. This is the nuts, bolts, and bits many of us are most comfortable with. Here, you install the network, install the applications, and make good things happen immediately for the customer. But don't forget this phase would also include project planning, project management, engagement management, and the like (topics covered across this book).

4. **Build on it!** This is Microsoft's newfound appreciation for valuing the long-term customer relationship in a consulting scenario by focusing on solution selling. After the technology infrastructure is in place, it's incumbent on the consultant to continue to add value to the customer by providing solutions that improve business operations. An example of this would be introducing a client to Exchange Server-based Instant Messaging several weeks after successfully rolling out Exchange Server for simple e-mail. Much more on solutions across the balance of this book.

I applaud Microsoft in this case for giving the bits a kick and focusing more on providing bona fide business solutions for customers. It's nice to see the big "M" mature much like watching a protégé work her way up the consulting career ranks. Oh, and did I forget to mention that, at the same FUSION conference referenced above, Steve Ballmer announced Microsoft was pouring over $500 million US into the GTM campaign? That's a lot of pesos, pardner!

If It's Broke, Fix It!

A final comment. Why is it that the human species has lost its way when it comes to migrating and finding new food sources when demand warrants? What made us great was our ancestors' ability to travel great distances over generations when necessary to survive. But as I've been traveling around and presenting technology workshops during the midst of the technology recession of the early 2000s, I've noticed that few people are willing to move for work. So while they sit underemployed in their hometown, they are likely forgoing bona fide technology consulting opportunities in other lands. Must be acceptable for these folks to take a pay cut in their household. It's not in mine. So find your feet, and as a rocker band named "Dan Hicks and His Hot Licks" once sang, "....MOVE IT!"

Brelsford's Mailbox

From: Brian [mailto:Brian@brisysconsulting.com]
Sent: Sunday, March 02, 2003 10:22 AM
To: Harry Brelsford
Subject: Curious about the projected release date of your next book

Hello Harry,

I hope things are going well for you. I am looking forward to attending one of your SBS seminars but nothing ever gets close enough to NJ for me. If I had the budget I would fly out to the closest appearance. Your SBS Best Practices is my bible! lol

In an e-mail to me months ago you mentioned writing a book on small business technology consulting.

Any time line or projected release date for the book? Will it be more than 6 months from now? Just curious, and it is your fault! If you had not made SBS Best Practices so darn good I would not be so impatient.

I have said this before but I cannot help repeating it to you...THANKS! Thanks for allowing me to find my niche and giving me a step-by-step book to guide me through it. It was the lighthouse for me in the storm of techno books.

Before I sign off...I would like to make some suggestions for your next book. These are my biggest troubles so far (one young man, just starting, limited budget) and ones I would love to see addressed in your next book:

1) Handshaking/foot in the door — getting new business, finding it, etc., without an advertising budget.

2) Contracts — finding good sources for technical consulting service contracts. I cannot afford to have an attorney put together multiple variations of contracts for me. I also do not find many attorneys adept at the IT business. I have limited experience in this area and most of the attorneys I have met don't have a clue when it comes to IT either, they convert standard service contracts into IT contracts. I am sure there are major loopholes not being covered.

3) Insurance — what types should an IT consultant have? What is too much? What coverage is needed that your agent may miss? What are the current trends?

4) Employment status — what are some good techniques to get past the problem of being considered an employee by the firm that hires you? I have lost a job because the company would have been obligated to provide health coverage, worker's comp...etc. We need some strategies to get around these obstacles. I am going to be consulting an attorney friend of mine about these issues soon, but would love to get your take on them too.

Thanks again for your eyes and ears and good luck with your next book,

Brian Williams
Brisys Consulting
Brian@brisysconsulting.com

# # #

REPLY:

Hi, Brian!

Thanks for the kind words and permission to use this e-mail in my SMB

Consulting Best Practices book. I appreciate your suggestions and eagerness for this book (BTW — book out in mid-2003 which you would know if you're reading this dialog in the book itself). I've taken your suggestions to heart and will include these topics in the following way. The "finder" section of this book will discuss the first point about handshaking and foot in door (and hopefully not foot in mouth!). Points two and three are covered in the "minder" section of this book. And earlier in this chapter I addressed employment status in a positive spin, but I also return to that topic in passing later in the "minder" section.

All the best to you and happy reading...harrybbbbb

Summary

This chapter was about how to initially build your business as an SMB consultant. People I've observed who make it to this stage and beyond often comment that they didn't realize being an SMB consultant would be such hard work and that so much selling and business development were involved. However, don't lose sight of the financial and other rewards of being an SMB consultant. While it is difficult to build your business, the rewards are out there and will be discussed later. The following points were covered in this chapter:

- How to plant SMB consulting seeds

- Understanding the SMB business development life cycle

- Brelsford's Dozen: Cash on hand and Client Rejection Ratio

- Prelaunch interim measures to take

- The first client has landed!

- SMB consulting transition plans

- Online auctions are your friend

- Good client selection and how to fire bad clients

Chapter 5
SMB Marketing

In This Chapter

- Introduction to the five Ps of SMB consulting

- Defining your product

- Services to offer and type of work to perform

- Addressing "P-distribution" issues

- How to package yourself

- How to price your services

- How to promote your SMB consulting practice

So it's time to get practical and meet the five Ps of marketing. Earlier chapters helped set the SMB consulting practice table. It's now time to hunt and gather to put food on that table. This chapter starts an increasingly hands-on theme in this book to go forth, provide valuable SMB consulting services, and make money.

For the vast majority, making the right decisions and finding opportunities are a combination of timing, smart thinking, luck, and possession of a skill set that is in demand. For some, finding opportunities occurs by a process of elimination and by avoiding mistakes. However you find them, if the opportunities exist, the money is there for you. Let's get started.

The Five Ps of SMB Consulting

Upper-level business school students in the hallowed halls of academia recall all to well the required core course in marketing. In that class, you learned about the five Ps of marketing which also serve as the outline for this chapter.

   a. Product

   b. P-distribution

   c. Packaging

   d. Pricing

   e. Promotion

Each of these elements is discussed next in the following sections.

Product

Granted, you're really providing a "service" versus a "product" as an SMB consultant, but bear with me. One man's product is another man's service. It's basically all the same and allows me to communicate with you in the five Ps marketing construct.

> BEST PRACTICE: When you think about it, the Grinder section at the end of this book is where I really define the nuts and bolts of what your product or service will be. This section on product, in the context of business marketing, is about selecting a service that will have built-in demand for it. The discussion that follows is necessarily business-oriented and not specifically technical in nature.

Service selection

The biggest decision you will make as an SMB consultant is what type of consulting services you will offer and to whom you will offer them. No other decision will have a greater impact on your financial position. In reality, it's the same for nearly everyone in the working world. Choice of occupation has the largest impact on your financial net worth. Period.

What happened to the old "do what you love and the money will follow" mantra? First, people who are doing what they love usually aren't in it for the money. Second, in many professions, money is both the inducement to work and the reward for unpleasantness. The higher you move up in income tax brackets, typically the more work-related stress there is. Of course, this isn't always true, but it has been my observation the following correlations exits: People who have high incomes have high stress levels. Those big dollars are earned, each and every one of them.

> BEST PRACTICE: It is possible to love what you do and make a substantial amount of money along the way. I think SMB consulting is potentially one of these rare rewarding professions. Most SMB consultants whom I know enjoy their jobs, as well as the financial rewards. It can be done and it's being done each and every day.

Call it the "guns and butter" neo-argument for professional success and happiness, but when you like what you're doing *and* making money at it, life is very good. By the way, "guns and butter" is a basic economic concept in the production possibilities frontier area where an economy can either produce guns or butter but typically not both. The translation on that is "you can't have it all" in the its strictest form but when you turn the guns and butter argument around, I'm saying you can possibly have it all!

Words from *CRN*

CRN is a great resource for monitoring SMB trends. It recently posted a hopeful story about demand for IT consulting services and projected double-digit growth. This is shown in Figure 5-1 and can be read in its entirety at: http://www.crn.com/Sections/BreakingNews/breakingnews.asp?ArticleID=40624)

Notes:

Figure 5-1:

This CRN article summarizes research pointing to better times ahead in technology consulting.

In another recent story titled "Hard Facts: IT Spending," *CRN* noted that small businesses have turned cautious about IT spending (*CRN*, page 30, 2-17-03). This is of great importance to the SMB consultant. Witness:

- Both Internet-related and hardware/software-related spending have become lower priorities from late 2002 to early 2003 for SMB.

- The overall drop in Internet-related spending priority was 9 percent.

- The overall drop in hardware/software-related spending priority was 10 percent.

- SMB spending priorities did not increase in any categories (18 Internet and hardware/software categories were surveyed).

CBS/MarketWatch

In an article titled "Technical Difficulties – Many small businesses still catching up on technology" (CBSMarketwatch, 11-19-02), author Keith Girard found that most small businesses are still behind the curve when it comes to using technology. First in his findings for this was that small businesses lack money and expertise to put current technology to work (you can fill the expertise void as an SMB consultant). Also, small firms with less than 100 employees invest a quarter of their capital budget on technology, including computers and communications equipment. However, this capital investment amount still lags behind the amount invested in technology on a "per employee" basis by medium-sized and larger firms (over 500 employees).

So, in the past few pages you've been exposed to a lot of economic factors that can be supportive or restrictive to your efforts to launch a fledging SMB consulting practice. Keep in mind that you need to work hard and have fun where you find it in this business!

Work types

There are different types of work to pursue as an SMB consultant. This includes project and recurring work. Both types of work present different engagement opportunities.

Project work

Many SMB consultants view consulting from a "love 'em and leave 'em" project orientation. That's because consulting has traditionally been pitched as an engagement-to-engagement endeavor. Project work is filled with endless variety; offers the ability to see a beginning, middle, and end to the work; is comprised of complete discrete tasks; and lets you have enough mobility to avoid getting roped into client-side internal politics.

It is the project work that first attracted me to SMB consulting, because by moving from job site to job site, I see more techno scenarios in a month than many in-house network administrators see in year. The variety creates exposure to a wealth of technology solutions.

So far so good. But what are the drawbacks to project work? It can result in erratic cash flow. Months with back-to-back project activity are typically very lucrative. Months in between projects are darn lean, sometimes forcing you to dip into retained earnings or savings. And the constant shifting of assignments doesn't sit well with all personality types. Some prefer a long-term relationship to project work.

Recurring work

There's nothing like the comfort of having a book of clients with whom you have long-term relationships of providing technology support services. You develop site-specific expertise that helps you retain the account (versus a new consultant who would have to relearn the computer system). Much of the work, at least in terms of managing the client, becomes routine. In consulting, a routine process is often a profitable process.

Recurring work also introduces you to the Microsoft mantra of "solution selling." Here the focus is on a technology solution that meets business needs and not necessarily a wham-bam installation project. By its very nature, solution selling is a longer-term viewpoint to building customer relationships.

Both

In reality, your SMB consulting practice will probably have both project and ongoing maintenance work. I encourage this diversity as I enjoy the variety of projects, but really like the familiarity of my steady book of clients. More important, the dips in project work tend to be offset by my ongoing maintenance work.

Work styles

Lord knows there are many different work styles in the delivery of SMB consulting services. Some of us are full-timers, while others are part-timers. Some prefer niches, while others prefer to be generalists. Whatever your situation, this discussion will force confrontation. You will need to determine just who you are at a very core level. Are you an advisor who works best as a generalist? Or are you a specialist who works best with the nuts and bolts of the technology? Choosing between being a generalist or a specialist will have a tremendous impact on the type of work you do, the way you run your SMB consultant business, and how much money you make.

Note in the Grinder section I revisit the discussion on work styles.

Generalists

Being an advisor to kings and queens isn't a bad way to go through your technology consulting career. But to be honest, this is a proven path for the medium and enterprise space. I've found true SMB clients aren't willing to pay tons of money for advisory services. That said, consider the following.

Many people don't have either the skills or the desire to master Microsoft SMB technology solutions at a granular level. These people would prefer to act as business technology advisors, emphasizing their communication skills over hands-on skills. Generalists typically serve as project managers and contract out much of the specialized work.

Specialists

These are the surgeons of the SMB consulting community, specializing in one niche or another. As in the medical profession, both the demand for services and larger financial rewards tend to accrue to specialists. On the downside, specializations, especially in technology, can dry up and disappear. That's a fear that generalists typically don't have to worry about. It has been my experience that many SMB consultants start as generalists and migrate to a specialization after they gain more experience as consultants.

In your SMB consulting practice, you might migrate to a specialization due to a couple of other factors. First, after working with a variety of technologies as a generalist, you may discover where your interests lie. Second, you may develop the bona fide expertise needed by a specialist as you focus on one area. When you bill yourself as a specialist, clients have a right to assume you have real expertise.

> BEST PRACTICE: Let's face it. Some of us are here for the money. That's not a negative statement. If you attend a "how to get rich" seminar titled "The Millionaire Mind," you'll find yourself in a room of several hundred people blessing the rich. But back to business.
>
> There is a great book you should read next titled *The Millionaire Next Door: The Surprising Secrets of America's Wealthy*, by Thomas J. Stanley and William D. Danko (Pocket Books, ISBN: 0671015206). This book demonstrates how one of the true paths to wealth is via specialization. Business people who found a lucrative (but, yes, often boring) niche just sat there and let the money roll in! Sounds good to me! Serve me up SBS in the SMB area as my niche, please.

Full-time vs. part-time

I recently presented a Microsoft "Go To Market" workshop over four days in San Jose, California. One day, during lunch, I met with two eager students who were looking to launch an SMB consulting practice. I was delighted to review their business plan, and as it turns out, temper their enthusiasm a tad. Seems these two intrepid entrepreneurs where looking for SBS to yield upwards of $250,000 in profit to them as a consulting niche. I concluded, given the tough market they were in and their SBS experience level, that SBS might be a great strategic business unit (SBU) for them, but I didn't think it'd deliver that type of profitability to them. In effect, maybe SBS could be a part-time SMB niche, but they'd probably need to do other things as well.

Most of the people reading this book are probably looking at a full-time commitment. That's what it'll take to be successful without a doubt. But there are part-timers in our SMB consulting community who do just fine. I've met a retired Microsoft millionaire who just wanted to dabble with SBS. And then there are a large number of retired military personnel who have a one-person SMB consulting practice while pulling retirement pay. These are the double-dippers of the SMB consulting world.

Microsoft's SMB Product Ladder

The SMB marketing maestros at Microsoft's Redmond campus have come up with an SMB product map. (Kindly note this is current as of spring 2003 and will be updated by Microsoft for future product releases—and it doesn't reflect Small Business Server 2003.) The SMB product map is shown in Figure 5-2 with comments and analysis to follow.

Notes:

Figure 5-2:

Microsoft's SMB Product Map (circa spring 2003)

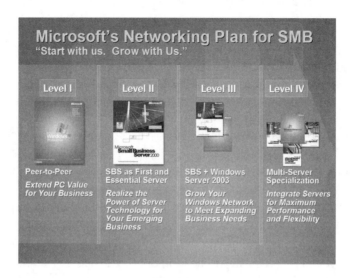

There are two way to interpret the above figure. On the one hand, you could view it as four distinct levels. You might have clients on different levels. Micro-businesses, such as home-based professionals, might have a simple peer-to-peer network with Windows XP Pro. Your larger clients in the medium space might have standalone Windows Server 2003 machines, each dedicated to an important function, such as e-mail, database, and firewall. SBS fits in the middle in two roles: standalone and in conjunction with additional servers.

But I've got another take on this: the tale of two CPAs and a pizza. Try this story on for size. Imagine in a land far away where oil and sunshine are plentiful, a worldwide respected accounting firm took a tumble because if its auditing oversights involving a huge energy trading company. Two CPAs, shown the door on a Friday afternoon, spend the weekend purchasing a laptop computer each, printing business cards and stationery, and soliciting past clients to join their new practice. Follow these career steps for the two CPAs and how it relates to Microsoft's SMB product map.

- **Monday Morning.** The two CPAs use Windows XP peer-to-peer networking just to get the ball rolling. They enjoy basic file sharing, printing, and Internet connectivity. This is Level 1 in Figure 5-2.

- **90 Days Later.** Now that our two CPAs have cash flow, they retain you to deploy SBS. Think about this milestone. It takes the CPAs and an initial 30 days just to do new-client work, then another 30 days to get paid for it, and yet another 30 days to complete a second billing cycle to be able to afford you and SBS! This is Level 2 in Figure 5-2.

- **Nine Months Later.** Happy with SBS all this time, the CPAs contact you again to discuss adding two additional Windows Server 2003 machines to the network. It turns out that tax season has arrived and the accounting staff would like to work their long hours at night from home, connecting to the office network via a broadband-supported VPN connection. Then they'd like to launch a Terminal Services session. At this point, you will install a member server, running Terminal Services in Application Sharing Mode. Oh yeah, the CPAs also ask you to implement an additional server running Windows Server 2003 to host Great Plains Dynamics, a Microsoft business accounting program. This is Level 3 in Figure 5-2.

- **Two Years Later.** Because these CPAs have the Midas touch, they have grown and grown. Now they are about to cross the SBS licensing threshold (in the SBS 2000 time frame) of 50 client computers. So it's time to migrate this client to the full Microsoft Server SKUs via the SBS Migration Kit. This is Level 4 in Figure 5-2.

BEST PRACTICE: There is an important need to glean from Figure 5-2 another message: the repositioning of SBS. In the past, SBS was the black sheep of the family, the distant cousin no one knew growing up. That all changed at FUSION in July 2002, when Microsoft Vice President Bill Vegthe pronounced that SBS would be called the "first and essential server for small business." There have been variations on this theme, with the popular press at one point calling it "My First Server," but the message is clear: SBS now has a full seat at the Windows table. For the first time, there is a direct link to the SBS product Web page from the Microsoft Windows Servers page. In the past, many good SMB consultants and their respective customers didn't even know that SBS existed, but the hyperlinkage from other mainstream Microsoft pages will greatly help this.

SMB Product Proof

So in our hunt for SMB viability, you might be asking for more proof of the pudding. Perhaps you're thinking that, if SMB is so great, why aren't the big boys doing it more? I submit to you the following arguments, taken from a *USA Today* article titled "Software companies cater to small businesses in a big way" (March 10, 2003, page 6B).

- Microsoft redeploys Orlando Ayala to head SMB. Effective July 1, 2003, Orlando Ayala (who was head of worldwide sales and marketing) now leads the new $2 billion US SMB business group that will target retailers, manufacturers, and real estate firms that are increasingly using computers for customer data, payroll and accounting.

- Microsoft expects to see its SMB revenue grow from $2 billion in 2003 to $10 billion in 2010.

- Oracle, which has a small business suite product, sees the entire small business software market growing to $30 billion in 2003 and upwards to $46 billion in 2005.

- Other firms catering to small businesses with specific SMB SKUs include Siebel Systems, SAP America, and PeopleSoft, according to the *USA Today* article.

- Unnamed tech analysts predict "software sales for small- and medium-sized businesses should see double-digit growth rates for the next three years.

- Karen Smith of Aberdeen Group is quoted as saying SMB is where the action is for ISV and solution providers because "there aren't as many multimillion-dollar software contracts (from big companies) as there were during the tech boom a couple of years ago."

Paul Thurrott, well respected author for Windows and .NET Magazine, reported the following from his July 2, 2003 UPDATE newsletter (http://www.winnetmag.com/Articles/Index.cfm?ArticleID=39455&pg=1&show=408)

"…small businesses are a ray of sunshine in an otherwise cloudy business environment. Although sales in most markets that invest in IT are stagnant, sales to small businesses are growing 8 percent to 10 percent annually, according to IDC, and broadband usage in small businesses is growing almost 20 percent."

And CRMDaily.com reporter Kimberly Hill commented in her "SMBs are big spenders" article (July 1, 2003, www.newsfactor.com/perl/story/21832.html) that "While larger enterprises expect to increase their IT spending this year by just over 1 percent, their smaller counterparts will spend 17 percent more on IT products and services in 2003 than in 2002." Hill attributes this information to an interview she conducted with Meredith Child of Forrester Research. This spending will primarily be on applications such as CRM and not plain old infrastructure, according to Hill.

Finally, consider reading an article from yours truly at TechRepublic ("Signs indicated that this is the year of SMB" visit www.techrepublic.com/article.jhtml?id=r00720030711gcn01.htm) where I recast many of the arguments in this chapter for the enterprise and Linux lovin' crowd.

P-distribution

In classic marketing, the term distribution doesn't begin with the letter P, so some wise acre professor put a P in front of the word distribution in order to create the five Ps marketing model. The P is silent in this word.

In the case of SMB consulting, the distribution question equates to your work locations and the channel as a whole. I briefly discuss work locations followed by an exhaustive economic thesis on the SMB channel.

Work Locations

Perhaps you're a good ol' boy who simply wants to serve his local community well as an SMB consultant. This would fit the profile of two leading SBSers in the Carolinas whom I know. Or perhaps you fit the classic consulting mode of getting on a plane and traveling to client sites (this is my own SMB consulting business model in recent times).

Near

In many ways, SMB consulting best lends itself to serving the customer of the community in which you live. SMB consulting relationships tend to be more personal, and because many engagements are smaller, it just makes sense for the customer to use a local resource. It's why some of us are in SMB consulting: a lot less travel to make a living. As I've traveled the lands of the world preaching the SBS gospel, I've seen that most SMB consultants restrict their practices to a specific, local geographic area. Perhaps this would be a 100-mile radius, just enough distance to encompass your metropolitan statistical area, but still allow you to be home in time for dinner.

Far

On the other hand, it's been said you're not a credible consultant until you're at least 100+ miles from your home town. Because familiarity breeds contempt, in consulting you've often got to be the "pro from Dover," and the out-of-town expert to get the customer's attention. It's a well-worn and time tested game in management and technology consulting.

To be honest, being the traveling consultant probably makes more sense in the "M" or medium space in SMB consulting. That's because the gigs are large enough to justify travel and per-diem expenses. Small gigs often don't have that much financial cushion to justify bringing in an outside subject-matter expert.

So just how far is far? It depends on your perspective. Try these two thoughts on for size.

- 300-mile radius. Perhaps you can expand your SMB consulting practice to the regional level to take into account a larger radius, but remain within a day's drive of your home base: 300 miles. If you try this, depending on where you live, you just might be surprised what such mobility will do for your economic opportunities. For example, if you lived in Indianapolis, Indiana, USA, in the Midwest heartland, a 300-mile radius (approximately) includes ten major USA cities as seen in the list below and Figure 5-3.

  o Chicago, IL

  o Detroit, MI (plus Grand Rapids, MI)

o Cleveland, OH

o Cincinnati, OH

o Saint Louis, MO

o Milwaukee, WI

o Columbus OH

o Louisville and Lexington, KY

o Nashville, TN

o Pittsburgh, PA

Figure 5-3:
Indianapolis is known for being at the "center of everything." This is where the first SMB Nation conference was held in part because of its location (visit www.smbnation.com).

- World traveler. Most of Microsoft's SMB sales are overseas in the international community, not in the USA domestic market. So one thing to consider is to possibly map your SMB efforts to mirror those of Microsoft. It's the old "when in Rome, do as the Romans do" thought pattern. I'm in the process of doing exactly that, as I'm trying to drive new SMB-related business overseas in the SBS 2003 time frame.

Home-based vs. rented office space

A quasi-distribution issue is where you'll physically locate your practice. Home-based certainly makes sense early on for convenience and to keep expenses down. In the "Volatility" section, I cite a *USA Today* article that reiterates this point. Rented office space makes more sense when you're a true-blue company with inbound customers and you need the professionalism a real office brings. But, of course, rented office space comes at a price: rent!

A twist on this debate is the office in the car concept. Perhaps your true distribution vehicle is a "vehicle," such as an automobile. Think about it. Often SMB consulting is nothing more than driving from client site to client site. Given that, perhaps a permanent office doesn't make as much sense.

Nationwide SMB consulting practices and franchises

Over the years I've maintained high hopes for Gateway's store concept. The idea here was to make it the IT department for small businesses in nearly every community in the USA. I even saw it as the first attempt to create a nationwide SMB consulting practice.

At one point, Gateway had nearly 300 stores, each with an impressive interior, training room and repair shop. If that concept had taken fire, the idea was the SMB customer could have the same positive experience in any store. Quality control would be maintained, SMB technology deployment methodologies adhered to, and Gateway could enjoy lucrative service revenue to supplement earnings from product sales. Under ideal circumstances, it would sell a server loaded with SBS and then have Gateway Network Solution Providers (NSPs) deliver the deployment consulting services. It looked great on paper but, as of this writing, has not worked as planned. At last check, Gateway was closing many of its stores and selling consumer electronic items (a far cry from traditional SMB consulting that focuses on service delivery, let me tell ya'). You will recall I discussed Gateway and its NSP program in Chapter 2 of this book.

Other efforts to create nationwide SMB consulting practices are emerging. And there are interesting variations on this idea of going national. Take a directory service called www.rentageek.com. Here, a customer could find a local SMB consultant who has registered with RentaGeek by searching "Region," "Needs," etc. But one of the best-known attempts to create a nationwide SMB consulting practice would have to be GeekSquad (www.geeksquad.com). This SMB tech-for-hire firm, which also serves home-based businesses, is full of characters. The consultants carry badges and play up the "special agent" theme. As of this writing, GeekSquad has operations in Chicago, Los Angeles, Minneapolis, and San Francisco.

BEST PRACTICE: Robert Stephens, founder of GeekSquad, reports in a *Kiplinger's* magazine article (December 2002, page 82) that training has been an especially strong source of revenue for his firm. Something to think about as you define your SMB consulting product mix.

There have been numerous SMB consulting franchising attempts. In central Florida, my friend was involved in the opening a franchise field office for Computer Doctors. Her experience didn't work out, not because of the franchising concept, but rather because of an unsavory business partner. The same *Kiplinger's* article from December 2002 found several other SMB consulting franchising attempts:

- Geeks On Call (www.geeksoncall.com) based out of Norwalk, Virginia, has operations in Colorado, Florida, Kansas, Maryland, Missouri, Texas, Virginia, and Washington DC. Geeks On Call intends to continue its nationwide expansion.

- Soft-Temps is a running full-page ads in *PC Magazine* in the spring of 2003 proclaiming you can make Soft-Temps your dream business by purchasing a franchise. An interesting twist on Soft-Temps, as compared to the other franchise models described above, is that Soft-Temps allows you to avoid doing the actual work. You could simply schedule appointments and assign the work to local service providers. Like many traditional franchises in the business community, Soft-Temps promises a turn-key business operation and demand generation. More information may be found at www.soft-temps.com

BEST PRACTICE: You might consider the franchise approach as a vehicle to enter the SMB consulting business. A couple valid points were raised in the last paragraph: turn-key operation, demand generation. These are value-added components and help you overcome the hurdles to starting and operating a thriving SMB consulting practice. However, franchises come at a cost, typically in the form of a sign-up fee and ongoing revenue-sharing with the corporate main office. Combine this with a healthy dose of buyer beware and you should entertain such franchising opportunities objectively and avoid getting duped right out of the gate.

Rural vs. urban

It's a debate as old as the family farm in America, where sons and daughters often head off for the big cities. It's being argued in Australia, where people leave the outback for Sydney's urban opportunities. This debate is rural versus urban lifestyles. Here are a few observations.

- Rural fits the SMB foot print. When you step back and think about it, rural territories are prime for SMB solutions. That's because there are few enterprises in rural regions and the business community is nearly all SMB.

- Urban has SMB too! Of course there are SMB entities in urban areas, and many SMB consultants focused only on urban areas do very well.

- SMB consulting provides a way to live the rural lifestyle. Some people, fed up with urban stresses such as traffic, seek the good life in the country. Whereas your hardcore enterprise-level clustering infrastructure skills might not play well out on the farm, SBS and other Microsoft SMB solutions will. That is, you could make a living in the woods as an SMB consultant and enjoy what you believe might be a higher quality of life. Maybe you've always wanted to live at a ski resort on a professional's salary level!

- Tertiary markets have worked wonders for WalMart and others. Firms such as WalMart have made it part of their respective business models to locate and thrive in rural areas. Remember that rural doesn't necessarily mean poor. If it works for WalMart, it works for me!

- Microsoft Big Day got it right. Microsoft's SMB seminar series for customers called "Big Day" and its TS2 events for consultants are focused more on rural communities than urban for a good reason: SMB is most at home in rural areas.

- An article by Keith Girard on CBSMarketWatch (November 19, 2002) cast an interesting perspective on rural markets. Keith reported that, based on census data, he found America is still a country of small communities served by small businesses. There are just over 36,000 towns incorporated within the USA, of which 90 percent have fewer than 10,000 residents and 51 percent had fewer than 1,000 residents.

- Other business strategies I've seen play out in rural areas include Gateway's Country Store concept located in rural areas and the ITEC technology trade show series in the USA that made a point of visiting more rural communities than urban.

- Finally, rural often offers the opportunity to be a king-maker. If you're the only SBS expert for 100 miles, you've got quite a captive market!

So why am I so partial to rural even though I'm willing to admit that urban areas also offer tremendous SMB consulting opportunities? First, I've really enjoyed the reception by folks in rural regions who have a huge hunger for technology knowledge and solutions. Second, I think many people only assume that they can make a great living in the big city and never give rural markets a second hard look.

Areas of economic demand

The economic demand discussion occurs at the following five levels: general, specific, macro, micro, and countercyclical. Remember that demand, as viewed by economists, concerns the wants and needs of rational purchasers.

General

Perhaps your path into SMB consulting is the following well-worn trail: unemployment. Many SMB consultants have been laid off from declining industries such as dot-com, logging, fishing, and mining. Perhaps you've heard it before (and you'll hear it again): a consultant is really an unemployed professional otherwise seeking a job. Welcome to one form of the SMB consulting club.

When asked to advise young'uns, such as high school graduates as part of a graduation commencement address, I tell them to avoid economic sectors that are in fundamental decline and pursue career opportunities in economic sectors that are expanding. This is common sense, but sometimes people need to sharpen their common sense skills.

Just in case you don't get the point, another take on economic sector analysis is the following. Suppose you come from a long line of family farmers in the heartland of America (or your respective country). Today, you might have to question the viability of family farming as the highest and best use of your working years. History, emotion, and family pressure may try to keep you working the farm and deprive the world of your SMB consulting skill set, but you must ask yourself if that is that the most rational decision you could make. The point is that no one individual can swim against the current of economic sector decline. Better you leave emotion behind and go with the flow to participate in an expanding economic sector, such as the SMB technology community.

Specific

If you're reading this, I assume you've made the rational economic decision to become an SMB consultant. Now you need to hone in on areas of demand that will potentially provide you the greatest return for your time and effort. In economics, this is called being efficient. For SMB consultants, there are numerous opportunities on which to capitalize by being an efficient service provider. In fact, SBS is now designed with SMB consultant efficiency in mind. Witness the efficient setup process that makes deployment of SBS a breeze compared to earlier SBS versions.

Demand for specific SMB consulting skills is often a function of how "bits" are being used as part of an overall business technology solution. For example, just about every business uses e-mail, and among e-mail users, Microsoft Exchange has established a dominant position. This translates into high demand for Microsoft Exchange skills in the SMB area. However, I'd temper your enthusiasm with two small doses of reality. First, many of your competitors know of the demand for Microsoft Exchange skills, so there is potentially a greater supply of service providers with whom you will have to compete. This includes our unemployed enterprise brethren who are butting into the SMB space to pick up a paycheck and will work with Microsoft Exchange on a standalone server or as part of our beloved SBS. As promised, look for more on the "bits" side of specific niche SMB consulting deliverables in the Grinder section of this book.

Regional

Economies vary by region. For example, during the late 1990s, the general economic boom in the United States wasn't evenly distributed. While many regions did well, some did not. Cities that experienced plant closings during that time had people wondering aloud, "What boom?" The same phenomenon occurred in certain regions in the early part of this century, with Seattle and San Francisco down in the doldrums, but some other regions doing pretty well.

Macro

Each and every day you've likely seen the macro economy at work right in front of your eyes. You've seen newly moneyed professionals, many from technology fields, driving late-model foreign cars. That's a picture that was painted as the technology consulting lifestyle in the late 1990s. Granted, that picture has been repainted in recent times to reflect a massive technology recession, but the long-term fundamentals are strong. In fact, it's been said on CBSMarketwatch (see Figure 5-4 below), Motley Fool, and other financial Web sites that technology led us into this recession and it's what will lead us out of it! Keep the faith.

Figure 5-4:
The markets have been bullish on the ability of technology to lead the US out of the early 21st century recession.

Shifting supply curves

Part of the reason you should care about macro economics as a technology professional is the effect technology can have on the supply function. You've seen it play out this way. A new software release makes the setup of SBS much more efficient. So instead of being a "network installer" who could depend on $10,000 US to simply install SBS, you've seen this part of your job be reduced to a couple thousand dollars and be "commoditized." This is a fundamental shift in the supply curve caused by a change in technology (a new release of SBS). This results in a new set of prices of a range of quantities (service levels). This is not simple movement on an existing supply curve.

> BEST PRACTICE: The example above also proves that solution selling is "in" and the business of strict bits is out of fashion. One thing you can count on in technology is that progress, which will lead to shifting supply curves, is a fact of life for an SMB consultant. Resistance is futile and Luddites are losers!
>
> For those of you who skipped world economic history to go skiing in college, Luddites were weavers who were displaced by the loom and lost their jobs. Their response to this change in technology? Destroy the looms!

There are other factors that can lead to shifting supply curves, but these may not affect you as much as changes in technology. For example, macro economic leakages and injections into the economy can shift the supply curve (this could be the trading of dollars). Another is international trade (imagine that your technology work is outsourced overseas and delivered for a fraction of what you charge).

The point to this section on shifting supply curves is practical: Are you just one software or hardware product release or innovation away from becoming obsolete in your SMB consulting niche? Pretty sobering talk, but necessary as you consider what your niche will be as an SMB consultant. And fear not, I ask this question daily as I see improvements in SBS that make performing a task much more efficient than it previously was (and I can't charge as much).

Strong dollars

No macro economic discussion is complete without honoring the almighty dollar (or the currency in your respective country). On the one hand, a strong dollar is great when you've got a lot of them (dollars in hand that is) and want to vacation in a foreign land. Your dollar will buy a lot of stuff overseas. On the other hand, a weak dollar is good when you sell a product overseas as your product will become more affordable. Given you can't have it both ways, pick you poison and forever keep your peace. Seriously, the good news is that dollars go up and down in value all the time and you basically have to play the hand you're dealt. But have you ever considered, as an American, moving overseas to practice your SMB consulting craft? Then the value of the dollar must be taken into consideration.

Making sense of monetary and fiscal policy

It's all about tax cuts (fiscal policy) and interest rates (monetary policy) in this game. When the economy is boosted (okay, perhaps just sustained) with a tax cut from your elected leaders (e.g., Congress), more dollars enter the economy. Some of these dollars end up on the owners of small businesses. These owners then proceed to use these dollars to fund a technology project such as having you implement SBS. You get the picture.

So how does the Federal Reserve Board Chairperson affect your next lucrative SMB consulting engagement? First, if the Federal Reserve Board lowers the general level of interest rates, the cost of funds to businesses go down. Perhaps the business you call a client will notice it on the next draw of their commercial line of credit. That draw is used to satisfy your SMB consulting invoice. While a quarter point decrease in interest rates isn't going to make or break your SMB consulting practice, such market maneuvers signal business owners that credit conditions are loosening, the money supply is expanding, good times are ahead, and the businesses should increase their borrowings. The funds from borrowing can be used for capital expenditures, like your SMB technology engagement. Because part of my mission is to make you as much an MBA as an MCSE-type in SMB, I show in Figure 5-5 the Web site for the Federal Reserve Bank, where you can go for more information on US macro economic trends and facts.

Figure 5-5:

The US Federal Reserve Web site at www.federalreserve.gov

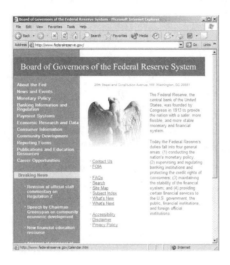

Then there's the other side of Federal Reserve life: inflation and deflation. Increasing interest rates can be a monetary response to inflation. High interest rates can dampen business borrowings and the demand for your SMB consulting services. Conversely, something to witness in more modern times (especially in Asia) is the threat of deflation. If the customer believes the technology solution you provide will be cheaper next year, they might not engage your SMB consulting services in the near-term because they have a deflationary economic expectation set. Bottom line? Either too much inflation or too much deflation can be harmful to your SMB consulting practice health. Like Goldilocks, we prefer our economy to be not too hot and not too cold, but "just right"!

Viewing the economy from a macro perspective is akin to looking at a problem child. When she is bad, she is very, very bad. When she is good, she is charming. The macro economic picture can be good and bad in a similar vein. There is not a lot you can do about it, but a heightened awareness of events that affect your livelihood as an SMB consultant will make you a better business person nonetheless.

On a positive note—the history of small business is filled with success stories about those intrepid entrepreneurs who started businesses during economic down times. Once economic times improved, these people saw many others join their ranks, providing similar services. However, history shows that, in general, those who started their small business in down times have survived and outperformed those who started a business during the good times. Because it's much easier to start a business during good times, many of those who do won't survive their first downturn. People who start businesses when economic conditions are tight really learn things, such as how to control cost and how to get by with less. They learn how to work hard and efficiently. These economic history lessons transfer to SMB consultants directly and should serve as words of encouragement for you not to let an economic downturn deter you from your goal of becoming an SMB consultant.

Statistics

Economists, while practitioners of a dismal science, love statistics. Here's some SMB numbers to chew on for a while.

- There are 22 million "businesses" as defined by the U.S. Small Business Administration (SBA at www.sba.gov). Figure 5-6 displays the SBA Web site for defining "small." Basically this is a tool for determining what businesses fall under the purview of the SBA. Typing the term "computers" resulted in the information displayed in Figure 5-7. See the "Best Practice" below for converting these numbers into meaningful values for SMB consultants.

Notes:

Figure 5-6:

The SBA's small-business-size Web page.

Figure 5-7:

Results on a small business search term.

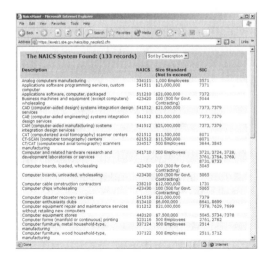

- Under the SBA's definition of "small business," there are numbers that are more on the mark for you to consider. There are 16,000 businesses with 500 employees or more. There are 100,000 business with over 100 employees. This would suggest the bulk of businesses (say 21.9 million) have fewer than 100 employees. This is a huge SMB marketplace opportunity for you.

- Small businesses contribute 39% of the US Gross Domestic Product.

- Small businesses create two out of three new jobs.

- More than half of the technological innovations come from small businesses.

- An older IDC study (late 1990s) reported that 74% of small businesses have one or more PCs. This number should be adjusted upward now.

- The same study reported that 30% of small businesses are networked. Again, this number is out of date and should be adjust upward.

BEST PRACTICE: If you refer to Figure 5-7, you'll see that the SBA's definition of "small business" is fairly generous and really converts to SMB for our purposes. If you look closely, you'll notice that a computer analog manufacturing firm (the first entry) could have up to 1,000 employees. The SBA has established a size standard for most industries in the economy. The most common size standards are as follow:

- 500 employees for most manufacturing and mining industries

- 100 employees for all wholesale trade industries

- $6 million for most retail and service industries

- $28.5 million for most general & heavy construction industries

- $12 million for all special trade contractors

- $750,000 for most agricultural industries

Note that Brian Headd from the SBS was quoted in a *USA Today* article on March 10, 2003, as saying there are 5.6 million small businesses in the USA that create the majority of jobs and typically lead the USA into economic recovery after a recession. The bottom line is that beauty is truly in the eyes of the beholder. One man's small business sector is another man's SMB sector. You get the point.

Microsoft's SBS partner page (www.microsoft.com/partner/sbs) offers the following interesting statistics for consumption.

- 4.1 million small businesses in the United States have more than one personal computer with no network installed, providing a strong market opportunity for Small Business Server as first and primary server.

- Microsoft Small Business Server sales are rapidly growing over 30 percent per year.

- Nearly 1.65 million servers are expected to ship into the worldwide small business market this year.

BEST PRACTICE: Just between you and me, you need to engage in a little expectation management here. Based on a collection of conversations around Microsoft, I believe that much of the growth in SBS is from overseas in international markets. The USA isn't driving SBS; rather it's hanging on to the tail and being dragged along. Hats off to the Aussies and others for banner years with the SBS product.

I've got more numbers to share below in the "Volatility" section.

Notes:

Sectors

Microsoft has some well-worn slides from public venues on small business customer segmentation. These are shown in Figures 5-8 and 5-9.

Figure 5-8:

Small Business Customer Segmentation

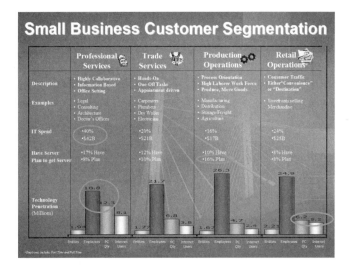

Notes:

Figure 5-9:

Small Business Segmentation by Customer Size

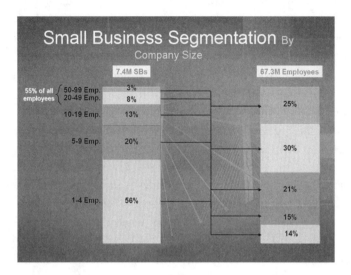

The message in Figure 5-8 is that there is some low hanging fruit out there to target your services toward:

- Professional services are a prime SMB market to target as they spend the most on computers and technology.

- Production/Operations include manufacturing and have the largest value for firms planning to implement more technology solutions.

- The trades are not considered to be an exciting opportunity for SMB consultants. You might reconsider making this your niche segment!

- Retail has an exciting statistic in that, when technology is deployed, it is aggressively deployed. This is noted by having the number of "Internet users" closely match the number of PC's deployed.

Figure 5-9 has a different view. It's the number of small businesses as acknowledged by Microsoft (7.4 million small businesses) and the number of people employed by those small businesses (67.3 million employees). Over 55 percent of the people employed in the US are employed by firms with between 20 and 49 employees. Approximately 30 percent of the employees are in firms that fall within a sweet spot for SBS: 20 to 49 employees.

Micro

Whereas all politics are local (so the old saw goes), one could say all economics apply to the firm (the singular firm being the focus of micro economics). So while hypothetically the national economy might be in the doldrums, specific firms might be having a banner year, which is a good thing for you, the SMB consultant. How can this be after the sobering macro economic discussion above? Micro economic influences (like a massive oil field being discovered just up the road from you and spurring development activity by surrounding it with industry-related firms) shouldn't be underestimated. There's nothing like being in a boomtown or inside an individual company that is booming. It's both fun and rewarding.

One place that you'll truly live micro economics is your own SMB consultant practice where "you" are the firm. You'll learn firsthand what you're willing to pay for goods and services provided to you, what your propensity for consumption of these goods and services are, and so on. You learn at times that being in business for yourself as an SMB consultant brings no financial guarantee. While I'm a big advocate of your becoming an SMB consultant and earning a large income, I want to balance that idealistic view with the stark realities of your being in business for yourself. Once you're a successful SMB consultant, having avoided the numerous pitfalls that await you, you will truly take pride in both your professional and financial accomplishments.

Volatility

It should not be lost on you from these readings or your own work experience that there is significant volatility in the SMB sector. Businesses start and fail all the time in the SMB space, many without fanfare. Here today and gone tomorrow is the rough and tumble fact of life in this arena.

This translates into opportunity for you and your services, as you can go sell the same client group several times over in a period of a few years. Each small business of any decent size needs a computer network to be competitive. This is a good thing and might help you make decisions about the type of services you'll provide.

Contrast the volatility of the SMB space with the enterprise space. With a few notable exceptions (United Airlines, US Air, Air Canada, Enron), very few enterprises fail outright and disappear (and even my examples above include some Chapter 11 bankruptcy cases as of this writing, not outright liquidations). Practically speaking, the Fortune 1000 list of enterprises remains fixed at 1,000 enterprise entities without much change.

USA Today reported encouraging words that new company failure rates aren't as high as we were all led to believe (including the old myth that 90 percent of all startups fail in the long-run). In its article titled "Study: New company failure rate not so high" published February 18, 2003, *USA Today* shares the results of an SBA study (that surveyed 12,185 companies) where, according to Brian Headd from the SBA, the 90 percent failure rate is debunked. Instead, the study found 67 percent of start-ups successful after four years in operation.

Allow me to explain. The study totals 100 percent. Of this, 33 percent of small business start-ups were outright failures within the four-year study period. That leaves 67 percent remaining, a number that needs further explaining. Subtract 17 from 67 to reflect the 17 percent of owners who closed their businesses due to retirement or via merger and you have 50 percent of all small businesses remaining in business after four years. The 17 percent value is important to understand as it's not a reflection of failure but either the sale or disposition of a successful business. Whew!

Other interesting tidbits from the SBA study include:

- The need for $50,000 US in start-up capital. The *USA Today* article tells the story of Ted Jordan, a 42-year-old Cleveland-based computer consultant who set aside $50,000 US to cover his start-up costs in 1998: salary to him, computer equipment and travel. He achieved profitability in 2001. This maps closely to my Brelsford's Dozen in this book about having 12-months cash on hand when you start your SMB consulting practice.

- Correlations between education and success. Being better educated gives the entrepreneur access to more resources and better business planning. This was a success factor.

- Home offices are cool. Not surprisingly, entrepreneurs that commence company operations at home have lower startup costs and don't have to pay rent. The commute is shorter and early-stage business owners like it. Later, when image demands it, a bona fide business office might make great sense.

BEST PRACTICE: Be sure to consult with your accountant on the deductibility of certain expenses for home offices (say part of your mortgage payment being treated as de facto rent). I'm told this is a major audit flag with the IRS in the US!

Countercyclical

This is the old zig and zag routine. When everyone else is zigging one direction, you're zagging the other way. This is especially prudent advice for the SMB consultant during bad economic times. During a downturn, many SMB consultants provide services to their tried-and-true client base. Thus, these SMB consultants likely experience a downturn in business as well. However, by being an SMB consultant who invokes a countercyclical economic strategy, and decides to provide services to entities that do well in bad times, you will likely survive and thrive. Consider the following industries to target during difficult economic times, including the following:

- **Pawn shops** — There is lots of activity to be found here as the financially challenged hock prized possessions. You might also consider casinos as part of this misery strategy too!

- **Moving companies** — Rather than fight, many people stricken with bad economic times flee to better business environments. Perhaps your local moving company needs to improve its infrastructure to handle increased business.

- **Bankruptcy courts** — More bankruptcies mean more activity at the courthouse. Target law firms that specialize in bankruptcies.

- **Educational institutions** — Historically, during economic down-turns, many people used student loans and return to school to get retrained. Ergo, smaller schools need SMB consultants to implement new technologies, such as learning labs. These schools often need adjunct technology instructors as well, so it's common for an SMB consultant to become an technology trainer when serving for an educational institution.

Areas to avoid

Old hands in business will tell you, that in the long run, you are successful just by avoiding mistakes. Same thing for SMB consultants: Just avoid the mistakes and you can't help but win. In the case of technology, that would include avoiding technology solutions that have lost the hearts and minds of the IT community. The list is long and includes IBM's OS/2 operating system, certain releases of Novell NetWare, the really old C/PM operating system (now I'm really dating myself), and so on.

Areas to focus on

Some SMB consultants niche by specific areas. You're currently seeing successful SMB consultants focus on the medical practice area because of the HIPPA compliance regulations (this is in the US). Other SMB consultants focus on law practices. I discuss niching by business area more in the Grinder section of this book.

Brelsford's Dozen: Better Business Research

For many pages, I've shared economic wisdom, studies, and statistics. But these business factoids are only as current, in many cases, as the day I wrote them. You must now march forth to the Internet and find and read a dozen updated articles on the SMB economic sector. Some Web sites to consider looking at are:

- *Entrepreneur.* Visit this Web site to learn more about SMB start up matters (www.entrepreneur.com).

- *INC.* Certainly a favorite and a source of many citations in this book: www.inc.com.

- CNN. After surfing over to www.cnn.com, click the **Business button** at **CNNMONEY** link on the left and then read the business news. Hint: Drill further into the technology and Business 2.0 links here.

- *Fortune.* As seen in Figure 5-10, *Fortune* has a dedicated small business portal (and also a magazine called *Fortune Small Business*). Visit www.fortune.com and click the **Small Business** link.

Figure 5-10:

Fortune Small Business portal

BEST PRACTICE: Consider that many SMB consultants only use the SMB space as a launching pad for enterprise engagements. IKON, the office supplies company, tried to use SBS in the SMB space to build up a list of consulting referrals so it could pursue enterprise work. Last I heard IKON was no longer in the consulting business. However, the SMB-to-enterprise strategy was sound and is often repeated. Some of you reading this book may well view your time as SMB consultants in that context. You'll be in good company down the road as many enterprise-level consultants started in the SMB space.

Packaging

In marketing, the proper packaging can make or break a product. And excellent packaging can overcome other shortcomings. Packaging yourself properly as an SMB consultant is a critical business success factor. In this section, I offer some sage advice on packaging yourself as a professional service provider.

One-to-one

You can position yourself to deliver services to individual clients (discrete business entities). This is the most common form of SMB consulting. For example, you might be a sole practitioner and have a dozen active clients. You provide services and bill on an hourly basis. As you'll learn in the Minder section of this book, this is a good life and you'll likely cap around 1,000 billable hours per year. This is one way to make six figures (say over $100,000 US) as an SMB consultant. This could be considered "bread and butter" consulting and its as straightforward as it appears. In the USA, bill rates for this type of consulting can range from $50 per hour to $150 per hour in the SMB space. Enough said for now.

One-to-C

Here is a situation where you provide quasi-management consulting services to executives (C-level, such as CEO and CFO). This discussion is applicable even for SMB, although you might have suspected it applies better to the enterprise level. The following is an example of what I call "corner office consulting."

Take SBS 2003 and one of the components: Windows Sharepoint Services (WSS). Microsoft's Sharepoint solutions, which also include Sharepoint Portal Server (SPS), are collaboration and document management tools. It's my belief that WSS in SBS will sell a ton of SPS (try saying that ten times quickly). And it's both WSS and SPS that open the door to one-to-C consulting. Why? Because the Sharepoint solutions have a real element of management consulting to them: picking best bets, information categories and subcategories, and creating document profiles. It's a consulting area that kind of combines an MBA skill set with an MCSE skill set. And it's a consulting area that allows you to charge much more per hour. Once you introduce an executive audience and management consulting deliverables, your hourly bill rate can see the other side of $200 US and maybe even approach $300 per hour! This is one way to leverage up quickly as an SMB consultant (financially speaking).

One-to-many

Something that you might not have considered is one-to-many consulting in SMB. This is where you ascend the value chain (and charge more accordingly) because you are providing more value per hour: You're dealing with an audience, not an individual. Examples of how I've employed this concept in my SMB consulting practice include:

- **Workshops**. Ever wonder why someone flies from city to city and delivers one-day technology seminars in airport hotel ballrooms? Because it pays well! Whereas a good SMB consultant might make $1,000 per day in the US, the same person could potentially earn $3,000 day or more if they successfully produce, promote, and deliver these types of workshops.

- **Train the trainer**. There is great value in a one-to-many consulting relationship when you're training someone who will then go on to train others. For example, if you trained a power user at a client site on a particular technology, and this person proceeded to train other staffers, you've added tremendous value into the equation and should charge accordingly. Read "charge more"!

- **Training staffs at competing consulting practices.** A profitable part of my consulting practice has been to train other consultants on how to be successful SMB consultants! I'm comfortable with this service, but I know other SMB consultants aren't for one simple reason: They believe they are training their competition! I don't agree with that assessment because I believe there's enough good business for all of us in SMB. The more the merrier, and I'd like to have a hand in developing competent professional SMB consultants!

And don't forget the Soft-Temps franchise discussion several pages ago, where one alternative as a franchise owner is to not even do the work. That is, you could simply be an appointment scheduler and farm out the work to other SMB consultants, taking a slice of their hourly earnings as your reward. What Soft-Temps is doing is employing a time-tested business model under these circumstances of "selling shovels to gold miners" instead of being the gold miner. It worked for the Nordstrom family over a century ago in the Alaskan Gold Rush, and guess what? The Nordstrom family survived and thrived, but I've not seen a bona fide Alaskan gold miner in years!

Dress for success

I'm guilty as charged. Early on in my technology training career in the mid-1980s, when I worked as a computer accounting instructor at a local vocational technical college, I mocked the mandatory "dress for success" course that students attended. I apologize for that and must seek to make amends. But while I'm troubled by that bad personal behavior, let me highlight a few dress code topics. And remember that dress codes vary by region, so adjust my insights for your own particular situation.

REI style

In the Pacific Northwest, there is the Eddie Bauer style of dress (also know as REI style). It's the flannel shirt and khaki pants as seen in Figure 5-11.

Figure 5-11:
Business people in the Pacific Northwest dress more casually.

So if you worked on Microsoft's Redmond campus or served SMB customers nearby, you'd be well-dressed if you sported the duds shown in the figure above. It's a casual culture thing!

Brooks Brothers style

Granted, what works in one market doesn't play well in others. Take Melbourne, Victoria, Australia for example. When I delivered an advanced SBS workshop in Melbourne in December 2002, my Pacific Northwest fashions turned heads all right, but the wrong way. Turns out Melbourne is much more conservative than I'm accustomed to. So if I wanted to be a successful SMB consultant in Melbourne, I better pay a quick visit to the fine haberdashers at Brooks Brothers as seen in Figure 5-12.

Figure 5-12:
Perhaps the finest in fine dress is Brooks Brothers.

BEST PRACTICE: When in doubt, consider it a best practice in SMB consulting to be over dressed rather than under dressed. This is of course something your mother should have taught you but you might have forgotten. Better people respect your taste in style and not remember your dress because it was inappropriate!

Pride and professionalism

Part of packaging yourself is how you portray and present your sense if professionalism. Do you take great pride in your work? People pick up on these "signals" as they're looking for the "total package" when retaining an SMB technology consultant. One avenue for sharpening your professionalism is a trade organization, the Network Professional Association (NPA) at www.npa.org. In a nutshell, the organization seeks to be the "American Bar Association" for network professionals by providing a code of conduct and professional ethics to abide by. It's a noble effort and capped by their annual professionalism awards program seen in Figure 5-13.

Figure 5-13:

Take a look at joining the NPA and perhaps you could be an award winner in the future.

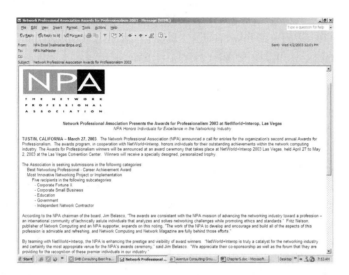

Assured Outcome

As an SMB consultant, you've got to convey a sense of an "assured outcome" for your client, that you'll do whatever it takes to make the solution meet their needs. When a client engages you, they have to know that they've hired an assured outcome. This implies a great level of trust (the proverbial trust relationship between SMB consultant and client), but it's essential you package yourself this way. Every SMB consultant wants to be the assured outcome "go to" guy or gal!

Assured outcome implies a lot of additional things in technology. I discuss the "bits" side of achieving assured outcomes in the Grinder section of this book.

> BEST PRACTICE: Be the brand! Since we're talking about packaging, take a moment to read the excellent article "Why You Are The Brand" by Steven Lang (VARBusiness, 5-12-03) at www.varbusiness.com.

Pricing

Price is the great economic rationing device. Set it too low and your overwhelmed with business and perhaps not enjoying as high of return on investment (ROI) as you might have. Set it too high and you're dance card isn't full and you might have to endure the public shame of coming down on your prices. Ouch! Few decisions you make as an SMB consultant are more important than pricing. Let's tread carefully here.

Never say no!

The great thing about traveling around and providing workshops is that you meet some great people. Often, the acquaintances provide insights you didn't previously possess. Such was the case recently in Bellevue, Washington, when a member of the audience, a long-time technology consultant, shared with me how he handles pricing. His theory and practice is to never say no to a client, but simply raise his bill rate. He reports he originally undertook this practice to ward off undesirable engagements and annoying clients. The funny thing is, says he, many prospects then stepped up to the table and paid his inflated rates. This set a new baseline for his overall billable rate schedule by allowing him to "test the market" without huge consequences. It also allowed him to earn an exceptional ROI if he indeed had to work under unpleasant conditions. His attitude for that type of work? "At least I get paid well for it!"

Brelsford's Dozen: Competitive survey

Before you get too far into this SMB consulting lifestyle and bet the family farm, please do me and yourself a favor. Undertake a survey of a dozen SMB consulting competitors in your area. This doesn't have to be as sinister as it sounds (although I'll get to that in a moment). To conduct a rate survey, simply browse (and bookmark for future reference) the Web sites of your competitors. Many post their bill rates openly. Now for the sinister part. First, you can call your competitors and ask what their bill rates are, the implicit belief being that you are a customer. To be honest, I've probably received these calls unknowingly in the past and haven't worried too much about telling all. I figure my rates are what they are and I'm confident in my role as an SMB consultant not to be threatened by competition.

Next up and farther down on the sinister bar is trade show floor walking. One of the greatest all-time tricks for surveying competitors is to attend trade shows and talk directly to your competitors in their booths. You'd be amazed at what you can learn about their business models (including bill rates).

Time and materials – an old favorite

Like the lawyer and the accountant, many SMB consultants bill the "bread and butter" method: time and materials. Nothing wrong with it and a dollar earned is a dollar earned. As you know billing for time and materials is really simple. You work an hour and you bill for the hour. Your materials charges might be product you sell to the client or an expense report you've submitted for payment. I predict that SMB consultants will continue to use time and materials as their primary billing method because it's proven to be effective and stood the test of time.

> BEST PRACTICE: In the Minder section of this book, I work through the mathematics of time and materials billing and how to earn as much as you want from SMB consulting using this approach, subject to market conditions. I also explore some of the mathematical limitations of time and materials billing and why you'll never be a millionaire if you're a strict time and materials SMB consultant without any staff to leverage.

Note that time and materials is preferred by many SMB consultants as a way to mitigate financial risk. It's far easier to manage customer expectations and have your cost overruns satisfied under a time and materials arrangement versus the next topic: fixed price contracts.

Fixed price bidding resurgence

Be careful what you ask for, the old saying goes, because you might just get it. Such is the case with the noticeable maturity of Microsoft's SMB infrastructure products. Generation after generation, Microsoft has increased network operating system stability (bye-bye Blue Screens of Death or "BSODs") and eased deployment and administration. This is in part because you, the SMB consultant, asked for it. On the one hand, some of you are grumping that Microsoft's SMB infrastructure solutions became "too easy" and now you can't make a living at it. Granted, the maturity in this technology area has forced us to reevaluate our business models to maintain and increase profitability (I do this across the pages of this book, especially the Grinder section where I emphasize solution selling).

BEST PRACTICE: You'll recall I introduced the fixed pricing concept in Chapter Four when I showed you how to create an eBay
auction entry for your SMB consulting services.

But there is another, more positive side of the Rosetta stone. It's the return of
fixed price bidding, something many SMB consultants haven't done in a long
while. First a quick history lesson in Microsoft's SMB product epochs.

In the first release of SBS in late 1997, we were actively encouraged to
engage in fixed pricing scenarios in delivering our SBS technology solution.
(This was the same epoch where Microsoft sold SBS as "just add water" to
the end user.) If you were there, you'll recall that the first release of
Microsoft's SBS product line was unstable and unreliable and resulted in
unmet customer expectations. So SMB consultants—including yours truly—
locked into to a fixed price contract with a client, ended up working tons of
hours for free (and losing money) to make the first release of SBS work.
Major ouch!

Shortly there after, we SMB consultants promised never ever to do that again
with SBS. And some of us were true to our word. We only worked the SBS
solution area on a time and materials basis. However, a funny thing started
happening on February 21, 2001. On that day, Small Business Server 2000,
the third generation of SBS, was released in Atlantic City, New Jersey, at a
Microsoft Big Day event. SMB consultants soon found this version delivered
what they'd asked for: stability, security, ease of use, etc. From that point
forward, those SMB consultants with a strong business sense (and who
weren't part of the permanently walking wounded from the first SBS release)
quickly saw the benefit of fixed price bids with SBS 2000. What follows is
the details of that insight and how it can benefit you, the SMB consultant.

Solution stability

First, a fixed price contract assume a stable product with an assured outcome.
Anything less and you'll go over your budget, cut your project ROI, and,
while doing whatever it takes to make your client happy, compromise your
profitability. So, for now, assume SBS 2000 and SBS 2003 meet our solution
stability criteria. You can go forth with confidence that, following the
structured SBS deployment process and using its built-in administrative tools,

each of your SBS customer sites will be exactly the same: stable. Each of your SBS clients will be exactly the same: satisfied.

Efficient operations

Now we get to gnaw some meat on the fixed price contact bone. If you bid SMB consulting work as a fixed price solution (say $10,000 for the SBS software, server machine, and your services), you become an SMB consultant tiger of a different stripe. All of a sudden, you're striding up staircases two steps at a time. You're concerned about time management and being efficient. If you are amazingly efficient and implement the SMB solution properly for a satisfied client, you win! That is, you implicitly make more than you would have on a time and materials basis. Is this fair to your customer? Absolutely! Both parties (you and the client) knowingly entered into the SMB technology engagement without either party being under duress. Rather, the client was able to budget a single number (say $10,000) for the SMB technology solution and they are happy with the outcome. They probably couldn't care less about the means you used to achieve this happy ending.

> BEST PRACTICE: A healthy part of this equation is that you need to use all the tools of the trade at your disposal. For example, the OEM SKU of SBS basically saves an hour of setup time in roughly a four-hour process. When the server machine that initially boots has the OEM SKU of SBS, it commences with the mini-setup phase where the client provides the registered customer name, organization name, and machine name, and agrees to the software licensing agreement. The time savings comes from the nearly complete setup of the underlying network operating system (e.g., Windows Server 2003).
>
> If you're a system builder and reseller, you already have access to the OEM SKU of SBS. You will use the OEM Pre-installation Kit (OPK) to configure the master server machine that you replicate out to the additional server machines you manufacture. I cover the OKP in Chapter 13 of this book.
>
> If you're not a system builder but a straight-up SMB consultant, consider strengthening your partner relationships with the major server hardware manufacturers in the game, such as HP/Compaq.

Financial profitability

It's all about ROI friends. Leverage up baby, as Austin Powers, the mythical movie character would say. Not to be brash or sassy, but let's go make some money honey! Fixed price bids allow the opportunity to really recast your operations from a profitability point of view. You're entirely motivated to cut out costs and engage in pure capitalism. Sure, these basic business rules apply to any SMB consulting style but with fixed price contracts, you're feedback loop is much shorter and you can see how individual projects were profitable, etc. As alluded to a few paragraphs above, you're looking for a way to leverage ahead of the time and materials crowd by winning engagements for a fixed price and then being a super human SMB consultant in successfully implementing your SMB solution for your satisfied client!

My day rate is...

Maybe I'm getting old and fussy after more than a decade (actually approaching two decades) of being an SMB consultant. I'm increasingly less excited about quarter-hour entries for telephone calls to solve an "I can't print" problem. Perhaps it's the early signs of professional burn-out. Given that might be the case, in the early part of the 21st century, I've adjusted my SMB consulting business model to take on more of a "senior statesman" role. I've not accomplished this professional paradigm shift simply by having satisfied customers ascribe large doses of credibility to me, but rather via pricing. With new clients who call to inquire about my SMB consulting services, I proudly proclaim that I bill by the day. (As of this writing, my day rate is $1,250 per eight-hour day, plus expenses).

This approach has served as a great business development filter and rationing device. Some folks can't wait to hang up fast enough, fearful that they'll be charged a full day of work for a short call to me. But others can appreciate the tack I've taken and understand that I'm a consultant, not a two-bit help desk technician. Overall, my experience has been that the quality of my new clients has improved compared to a few new clients I accepted before utilizing the day-rate method. My engagements have become more meaningful, interesting, and— shall we say—richer. And this straightforward approach has allowed me to solicit and accept engagements that are multi-day in multi-locations (including international), a strategy that lets me mitigate the negative effects of the current "dot-gone" downturn afflicting my home town of Seattle (as of this writing in Spring 2003). I'm experiencing renewed enjoyment as an SMB consultant.

> BEST PRACTICE: As you mature as an SMB consultant, experiment with a few new clients by using a "day rate."

By the way, the day rate concept is well-known in other professional services environments such as land planning, engineering, and so on. And, let me temper the above tempest with the admission that my long-time clients, dating back over five years of association with my practice, are still on a time and materials basis. Guess I'll never quite get away from those short "I can't print" missives!

Media analysis

Kiplinger's December 2002 article profiling GeekSquad and others revealed some interesting pricing information. GeekSquad charges a flat rate that is quoted in advance based on the description of the work to be performed. The lowest flat rate for any visit is $149 (this is the minimum fee). Geeks on Call franchises charge between $60 to $65 for the service call plus $15 to $20 per quarter hour for on-site work performed. Alison Stevenson, the article's author, found that sole proprietors charge $30 to $50 per hour for their technology consulting services. Granted, the *Kiplinger's* article spoke more towards break-fix technician services rather than true SMB consulting services, but the figures provide an interesting checkpoint to take under advisement.

A truly great article on TechRepublic (www.techrepublic.com) titled "Free Advice: How much is too much?" by Meredith Little (April 2002) surfaces the important discussion about the length of the SMB sales cycle and its implications on pricing. You'll recall I compared the SMB sales cycle to the enterprise sales cycle earlier in the book. But Meredith takes an interesting twist on it, suggesting SMBers might have a tendency to give away too much free advice. You might find yourself falling into this trap because you're a nice person or you're just trying to be communicative or you don't like to make pesky quarter-hour billable time entries for e-mails and telephone calls. But in all likelihood, it's because you've not developed the core competencies to close a client sooner rather than later and starting billing for your time. Consider Meredith's article to be required reading.

BEST PRACTICE: Until you consummate the consulting engagement transaction and have a signed engagement letter, you're working for free. You're likely using the sales cycle to give away valuable advice. And worst of all, you're devaluing your services and effectively lowering your price. This is not a good thing.

Closing a client sooner rather than later implicitly maintains your bill rate. This is a good thing.

Promotion

Our final P in the marketing mix is promotion. It's been said that a great consultant is a shameless, relentless self-promoter, a statement not too far from the truth. You should always be promoting yourself, and there are several ways to do exactly that.

Promoting yourself with a large marketing budget isn't hard, as you can hire an advertising agency to "buy" you market presence. However, given the world that SMB consultants live in, I've all but ruled out big-budget marketing. The real trick is to promote yourself in a dignified way with few or no budgeted dollars. That's the situation you, as a new SMB consultant, are more likely to find yourself in. In this section, I illustrate low-cost ways to get your name out in front of a lot of people.

Get the word out!

Initially, you have to get the word out somehow that you are officially an SMB consultant open for business. Simply *being* an SMB consultant doesn't generate business. You have to announce the availability of your services in some fashion.

Once established, it's in your best interest to keep your name visible so you can at least retain, if not gain, market share. Granted you'll have other, perhaps better ways of generating business (such as referrals), but as a self-employed SMB consultant you should always be spreading the word about yourself and your services.

Send press releases

One of the oldest tricks in the book is to use the sample template in Microsoft Word and write your own press release. Then e-mail, fax, or snail mail it to every paper in your area. This should include the dailies, weeklies, and monthlies.

It has been my experience that the large daily papers might not print the press release or will print just a sentence in their business announcements column. These papers get many press releases and are selective. You might have better luck with the smaller weekly business newspapers. These papers are often short on local content and may print your press release word for word. I've had good luck generating publicity with the regional weekly business papers over the years. Check out www.bizjournals.com if you live in the USA to find the business weekly in your area. This is shown in Figure 5-14.

Figure 5-14:

A huge chain of business weekly newspapers is Bizjournals.

BEST PRACTICE: Include your photo with your press release. Many papers will print your photo along with your text-based announcement. A photo has a much more powerful impact than just text. Getting your photo published with your press release is considered a major win in public relations.

You might issue a press release when you:

- Open for business

- Have an open house

- Lease new office space

- Hire a new employee(s)

- Land a new consulting contract

- Perform volunteer efforts (such as helping a school put in a network)

- Secure an appointment to a board (such as a not-for-profit board or service organization board, like Rotary).

- Win an award. Perhaps you've won an award for service. I was once named the service provider of the year for a not-for-profit. This generated both a press release and photo opportunity.

In Figure 5-15, I show a sample press release written by my good friend and fellow SMB consultant, Fredrick Johnson, announcing an office move. This e-mail sent to friends, family, clients, and media is simple and effective. You can easily do this!

Figure 5-15:
Ross-Tek Moves!

Write an article

Consider writing an article. The weekly business papers seem to be more receptive than the daily papers for this type of activity. The monthly business magazines will also accept your submission. Writing an article allows you to enjoy the good publicity of having your name and maybe a photo in print along with your words of wisdom. Perhaps you want to write an article about how Windows Server 2003 is being implemented. Articles tend to lend an air of authority, so it's a great way to build up business.

You can use the articles again and again. Attach your articles to the back of your SMB consulting proposals. Those articles can be credibility-builders with prospects in the bidding process.

Write a column

If you find you've got a knack for writing and your articles are thoughtfully received by the readership, consider leveraging your writing commitment into a regular column. This is a great way to establish yourself as an authority. More important, you enjoy the benefit of consistent publicity, appearing in print on a regular basis. This builds both recognition and a following.

> BEST PRACTICE: Manage your expectations when it comes to writing a column. You'll be on the hook for a commitment to the publisher, so first verify whether your schedule can accommodate more work. I've found writing a column to be mostly a labor of love, as it will typically bring you little or no pay. The byline, establishing you as a published authority, is your reward. And while your telephone won't ring off the hook from writing a column, you'll get a few e-mails along the way. More than anything, a column provides you some "paper" to go forward and promote yourself with. As long as you know going into the arrangement that you are making a commitment, you'll be fine.

Write a book

Writing and publishing a book on a technical topic, such as a Microsoft Servers application, allows you to ascend to the highest levels of professional status. Writing a book is a great way to generate favorable publicity and ascribed credibility if you can justify the untold hours of writing (which likely take away from your hours of billing). It's a great way to have inbound telephone calls from warm leads come your way (okay, sometime inbound e-mails, but the point is the same).

> BEST PRACTICE: If you are interested in writing a book, one of the best ways to learn more about this avenue is to visit book publishers' booths at technology trade shows. For example, *Microsoft Certified Professional Magazine*'s semiannual TechMentor trade show (www.mcpmag.com) typically has several publishers present on the show floor. These booths are staffed with acquisition editors who are on the constant hunt for the next Mark Twain.

> But another attack on this issue is to consider self-publishing. After writing eight books for traditional publishers and enjoying name recognition, I got tired of the relatively small paychecks from the royalty system. I turned to self-publishing and enjoy the benefits of being a published author, plus I've turned the books into a bona fide profit center (thanks in large part of readers like you). The vanity press that coordinates the production and printing of this book, Hara Publishing, is in the business of helping authors who would like to self-publish. Their contact information is listed on the first few pages of this book. Go ahead and give 'em a call for more information.

If you look at how the big-league consultants in both technology and business make it, you'll likely find that at some point these people have written a book. Moreover, writing a book is a time-tested promotional stunt. East Coast highbrows like James Campy, for example, built his consulting practice around his books on downsizing and reengineering during the early 1990s. The other nice thing about a writing a book is that it also helps if you want to be a technology consultant in a larger firm someday. At interview time, whipping out your latest book can be an effective way to impress your future supervisors. Firms such as Big Five accounting firms (with their respective technology practices) appreciate this approach.

Find speaking opportunities

Trade groups, social organizations, and the like are always looking for speakers for their monthly lunch meetings. In the past, I've found myself on the Rotary luncheon speaking circuit, telling SBS stories.

> BEST PRACTICE: If the cat's got your tongue, you can always join Toastmasters International, the social organization dedicated to improving public speaking and presentation skills. Visit at www.toastmasters.org.

Delivering seminars

A seminar is a tried-and-true way for an SMB consultant to engage in a little educational marketing. In many cases, it's paid marketing, where the attendees will pay for the privilege of your expertise. The key point with a seminar is that you need to know your audience and venue. If it's a sales seminar about a new service or product, you probably can't charge the audience a fee to attend. If it's a technical seminar where you offer wisdom and insight, you can typically charge a fee, say $99 US for a half day or $149 US for a day (lunch included for the participants, paid from your fee-based revenues). You need to decide if you are going to put on a sales seminar or an educational seminar or a combination of the two. If you are you trying to close business that day (the closer approach), you are clearly delivering a sales seminar. If you are doing the old soft sale, where you deliver more meaningful content, then this is the educational approach. It's up to you to decide what fits best for your personality style and the market you are trying to reach.

Established seminars

Early on in the life of Small Business Server while I was developing my reputation as a niche specialist in this area, I gave a monthly educational seminar at Microsoft's Pacific West (PacWest) sales office in Bellevue, Washington. This was part of the monthly Solution Providers program whereby you could deliver a half-day seminar using Microsoft's lecture hall. The price was right, as I had to reimburse Microsoft for only coffee and parking expenses. My topic, "Networking Basics," brought in up to 60 people each month. From that crowd, I typically enjoyed several leads and landed one engagement.

> BEST PRACTICE: Don't forget to consider joining the Microsoft Certified Solution Providers program as an SMB consultant to help build your business and interact with other technology professionals in your area. More information on the Microsoft Certified Solutions Providers program can be obtained by visiting www.microsoft.com/partner.

Note that many SMB consultants start with the lower cost Action Pack program prior to joining the full-fledged solution provider program. You can find out more about Action Pack at the above URL.

You might consider the following organizations when you're seeking out an established seminar channel through which to deliver your presentation. Be advised these environments are much more business-oriented than technical. That's not a bad thing when you're trying to earn more business.

- **Chamber of commerce** — This might be the best one. Speaking in a credible manner as an SMB consultant before a group of active business people is a great opportunity. You may need to join the Chamber of Commerce to fit into the crowd and be invited, but the $300 or so per year might be money well spent.

- **Service organizations** — These include Rotary, Masons, Moose, and Lions. Rotary leads the list as being the best selection, because, in my opinion, this organization is populated with business-oriented members, especially those who might be middle-managers who have purchasing authority. Other services organizations, such as the Masons and Moose, tend to be more fraternal and social and don't emphasize business and commerce (although many business people belong to fraternal service organizations).

- **Professional associations** — There are two types of professional associations. First, there are the paralegals, legal secretaries, and office managers who meet each month for a formal luncheon. These groups are also seeking speakers, so you're likely to have success here. Don't underestimate this avenue. Remember that office managers and the like are key influencers when it comes to retaining the services you provide as an SMB consultant. The second type of professional association includes groups who are organized for regulatory or compliance purposes. This includes accountants in the CPA Society, lawyers in the Bar Association, medical professionals, and so on. This second set of groups typical have mandatory membership (e.g. to be a CPA, you must belong to the CPA society). These groups need seminar speakers too.

- **Trade associations** — Industry-based trade associations represent a great seminar delivery avenue. Again, the monthly luncheon or the annual convention are both possibilities. Closely related are trade groups, which might not be tied to a specific entity or be as formal. I belong to one in my neighborhood called the West Sound Technology Professionals Association (www.wstpa.org) and it's been my pleasure in the past to speak before them about the benefits of SBS.

- **Clubs** — You can even successfully give a technical seminar before a club. I once gave a technical speech on how to use the Internet before the Dutch Club of Seattle. Hey, several Microsoft employees were in attendance along with many successful Dutch-American business people.

- **Regional economic development authorities** — These are typically quasi-government authorities charged with expanding the business base in a particular region. Economic development authorities facilitate introductions within the business community in the form of conferences, as well as pursue economic initiatives, such as having a certain area (say, a business park) be declared a duty-free zone for goods that are manufactured for export. Some regional economic development authorities have the power to issue bonds and debentures for financing public works projects, such as building parking garages. But the way that an SMB consultant can work with a regional economic development authority is to provide SMB technology seminars at business conferences.

- **Cause-based not-for-profit organizations** — Perhaps you support a medical research cause. The not-for-profit organization behind the cause of your choice may have a need for a seminar or speech.

- **Social organizations** — You might even get roped into giving an SMB consulting speech to a social organization, such as the Junior League.

- **Arts organizations** — Perhaps giving a speech or seminar during the dinner hour is more your style. Many arts organizations hold awards dinners and seek out speakers. The motivating factor in speaking before an arts organization is that you will find yourself before the barons and titans of industry in their off hours away from the office.

Create your own

You can also create your own seminars from scratch. The great thing about the homegrown seminar series is you control virtually everything: dates, content, promotion, and so on. One create-your-own seminar I put on with modest success was a series of executive workshops for Microsoft technologies (in this case, it was Windows 95). My feeling was that demand existed for business executives seeking to gain information on new Microsoft technologies. More important, these decision makers would be locked in a boardroom with me for a half day, a captive audience with budget authority. These seminars may not be instant money-makers, but they do pay off in the long term with new clients.

The create-your-own seminar approach has been used for years by financial planners and stockbrokers, proving they do work. The key is to target your audience.

> BEST PRACTICE: By the way, giving free educational speeches has other rewards: karma dollars. I like to think that, by giving to the business and technology community, I'll receive something in return. Perhaps it's the good feeling achieved from helping someone. Perhaps I'll be a billionaire in my next life. Whatever the payoff, it's the act of earning karma dollars and you shouldn't underestimate the power of this process.

Conferences

Another promotional avenue, used more often by established SMB consultants than those new to the profession, is speaking at conferences. Not only do you have your time in front of an audience, but also you get your name and typically a short biography printed in the conference brochure. There are three types of conferences:

- **Local** — Your efforts may be best directed to local conferences if that is where your clients are (in your local community). Since I tend to focus on small and medium-sized firms for my SMB consulting activities, local conferences make the most sense. In the Pacific Northwest, there is a local conference that travels from city to city called ITEC (recently rebranded as NEXT conferences). Perhaps your community has a similar local technology conference.

- **Regional** — These conferences tend to be larger in scope and draw people from surrounding states. The caliber of attendees may be higher as well as the quality of the selected speakers. If your SMB consulting business is regional in nature, speaking at a regional conference is a good use of time.

- **National** — Clearly, this is where the heavyweights play. The type of SMB consultant that can benefit from national exposure is someone who, quite frankly, has some thing to sell at the national level, such as a book. In the past, national conferences were focused on the enterprise level. But I'm pleased to announce that I've taken the initiative to underwrite and produce an SMB conference at the national level called "SMB Nation." Visit www.smbnation.com, and I will look forward to seeing you there sometime.

Free Marketing Opportunities

"Ah, finally!" you say, your favorite part of the chapter: free marketing stuff. I agree. Many inexperienced business people, SMB consultants included, overpay for marketing functions. There is a time and a place for top dollar and top shelf, but it's unlikely now is that time. Rather, for the SMB consultant on the way up, it's critical to keep expenses low in order to keep ROI high (more on ROI mathematics in the Minder section of this book). In this section, I spell out a few freebies you can start using tomorrow.

Brelsford's Dozen: Giveth business cards

Set a goal of giving out 12 of your business cards per quarter (every 90 days) from this point forward, which amounts to one business card per week, a modest and achievable goal. Over time, this becomes a very powerful tool, as you're name will spread exponentially in your community.

> BEST PRACTICE: The above point of "modest and achievable" shouldn't be overlooked. It's been said time and time again from the school of life to the hallowed halls of the Harvard MBA program that a successful business person doesn't do one thing great but does lots of little things well. That is, you don't need to have the wisdom of Solomon to invent new marketing models to be successful. Rather, just give away one of your business cards per week.

Consider some of the group listed in the last section (chamber of commerce, Rotary, etc.) as avenues for you to attend events, participate in meetings, AND give away that weekly business card.

> BEST PRACTICE: You can also do what Dorothy did. (No, I don't mean click your heels and say "There's no place like home!") I used to work with a seasoned professional named Dorothy a while back at a national contracting firm called 1-800-NETWORK. At the time, being full of pride, I probably didn't learn as much from Dorothy as I could have. However, reflecting back and having made amends, I think Dorothy really had a great practice when it came to giving away business cards. Dorothy's technique was to hand out two business cards at once with the phrase "...one for you and one to pass on to a friend." Needless to say, it was easy for Dorothy to meet and exceed her card giveaway quota.

> To Dorothy -> you go girl!

Brelsford's Dozen: Receiveth business cards

Not surprisingly, you now want to endeavor to obtain a dozen business cards per quarter (again, one per week). This is a fundamental SMB consulting marketing activity—and how you build your book of contacts. My premise here is simple enough. In Chapter 7, you'll learn more about being a rainmaker as I expand on the "building the book" concept.

Brelsford's Dozen: Attend a dozen marketing events per quarter

Now for one of my favorite activities: eating hotel donuts and drinking coffee at marketing functions. Seriously, your goal is to be an SMB consultant on the fast track. You need to be seen everywhere, much like a rising star in

Hollywood. You're job here isn't as difficult as the cast of NBC's top-rated show *Friends*, who necessarily need to be seen at the trendiest LA restaurants. Rather, it's to find some marketing venue to attend each week and "been seen." A couple of ideas:

- Host a table at a Microsoft Big Day/Business Solutions Seminar in the USA. I followed the Big Day circuit for over a year in the Pacific Northwest and had my table with other technology professionals in the back of the presentation room. The idea here was that local technology professionals could register to host a table for the day and speak to attendees (primarily business people) during the breaks and lunch hour. The table sign-up process is shown in Figure 5-16 and is found from the main Microsoft Business Solutions Seminar Web site (www.msbigday.com) by clicking the **Technology Providers** link on the left side.

Figure 5-16:
Microsoft's Big Day/Business Solutions Seminar is a great free marketing method for SMB consultants seeking exposure. You must register for a table to present your brochure and other marketing materials.

BEST PRACTICE: Expanding on the marketing versus sales discussion centering around Microsoft Big Day/Business Solutions Seminars, I can offer the following. When I hosted a table at these events, I found it to be true marketing. Introductions were made and it was incumbent on me to follow up on the lead I obtained. I never consummated a sales transaction at my table, thus I didn't view it as strongly as a sales event. Go ahead, host your own table, and make your own judgment. One thing is for sure—the price was right: FREE!

- Join a trade group. Earlier I spoke about the WSTPA trade group I belong to. I consider my monthly meeting to be one of my required marketing meetings. That's because the WSTPA has a real social element to it where "networking" (the human interaction form, not the multi-layer OSI model approach) is strongly encouraged. Another example shown in Figure 5-17, is the monthly chamber of commerce mixer (typically called "After Hours"). Nearly every chamber hosts such an event and, once you've paid your membership, attendance is usually free (or costs little). When you think about it, it really doesn't cost anything to stand around and talk to the membership, eh? Salute!

Figure 5-17:
As an example, here is the Bainbridge Island Chamber's announcement for the after hours event and monthly luncheon.

- Make-ups. So what if you miss a weekly marketing venue? What to do? Like the Rotary club, you need to endeavor to do a "make-up" meeting. You're not relieved of this responsibility. Like taking antibiotics for a health malady, you can double-up after missing.

Microsoft marketing machine

The Microsoft Partner's Web site provides a wealth of marketing materials at www.microsoft.com and even some special marketing opportunities. In Figure 5-18, you'll see a recent SBS promotion (the SBS 2000 channel services provider rebate program) where, after passing an SBS assessment examination, you could be listed in the worldwide partner locator tool. These deals come and go with great frequency, so please continue to monitor the Microsoft Partner Web site closely. A specific link to Microsoft marketing materials is members.microsoft.com/partner/salesmarketing/marketingtools/ default.aspx?nav=rn

Figure 5-18:

At no cost to you, by participating in the recent SBS 2000 service channel rebate program and passing the online assessment exam, you were listed for free in the partner locator tool for potential clients to find you.

Another wealth of Microsoft marketing support is the "Go To Market" (GTM) campaign I've mentioned several times in this book. A recent four-day GTM Hot Lab offered the following ISA Server resources to attendees, in the form of two discs, on the third day of the event, which was dedicated to security (Figure 5-19).

Figure 5-19:
ISA Server marketing materials (disc-based) given at the GTM campaign. You did not need to pay for these marketing materials, although there was a modest fee to attend the GTM ($50 per day US).

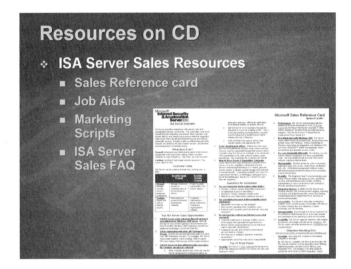

Notes:

BEST PRACTICE: If you'd like to attend GTMs and benefit from Microsoft's marketing resources, sign up via the Microsoft Partner site at www.microsoft.com/partner. One vendor that presents the GTM Hands-on Labs, Ascentus from Vancouver, BC, listed these GTM campaigns recently on its Web site at www.asentus. net (Figure 5-20).

Figure 5-20:

More and more GTMs can be expected worldwide over the next several years from Microsoft.

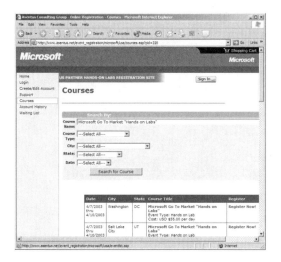

Notes:

Finally, there is the "must read" Microsoft Partner's newsletter that is shown in Figure 5-21. You can subscribe to this at the Microsoft site for partners explained earlier in this section. This newsletter is a mother lode of free or nearly free partner benefits. Get it! Read it! Use it!

Figure 5-21:

Microsoft Partner's newsletter. Notice the first item is a free support offering.

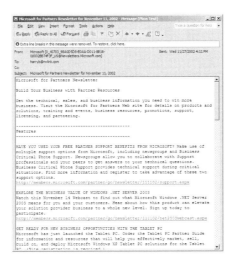

N̲otes:

Brelsford's Mailbox

Harry-

I am a consultant at a medium-sized IT firm. My company targets big projects from large corporations. I tried to sell them on the idea of a small business "practice" that would concentrate on building and supporting SBS networks. They showed no interest. Lately, I have been contemplating leaving my firm to develop an SBS consultant business. I am a good tech, but I am not a salesman. What specific steps do I take to get started?

Thanks in advance.

Sincerely,
Ladd
Dallas, Texas

# # #

Hi, Ladd!

Thanks for the e-mail and great story. I'd like to emphasize simplicity. In my writings, I speak towards something as simple as giving out your business card this week to a business person. Period. Then next week repeat the same behavior. Likewise, try to receive a business card this week from a business person and then repeat that behavior next week.

The road to SMB consulting success isn't so much knowing the nuts and bolts of SBS (which I assume you already know), but in marketing yourself. This road is paved with a thousand successfully completed simple marketing tasks, not one enormous breakthrough marketing idea. Far too many people focus on the one killer idea and don't complete very basic tasks, such as giving and receiving business cards. You get the point.

The chapter in my SMB Consulting Best Practices book, in which your e-mail appears, is loaded with tons of marketing stuff using the old five Ps of marketing lecture. Combined with the other chapters in my book, you're probably going to suffer from information overload on what your next steps are. But please! Just take one simple step at a time.

All the best to you mate....harrybbbbb

Summary

This chapter was a pragmatic and critical look at how you, the SMB consultant, will fill your marketing boots. This occurs by adhering to the five Ps of marketing:

1. Product
2. P-distribution
3. Packaging
4. Pricing
5. Promotion

It also means having a growing client list, attending marketing venues in your vicinity, and mining for clients to whom you can provide SMB consulting services. Part economics, part motivational, this monster marketing chapter has set the table for the forthcoming sales discussion in the next chapter.

Chapter 6
SMB Consulting Sales

In This Chapter

- Narrowing the definition of your SMB client

- Perfecting your sales tactics

- Developing your SMB solution selling paradigm

- Using Microsoft bCentral as a sales tool

- Understanding the role of advertising

- Discovering alternative sales models

- Sales tips you can use right now

It's time to bless the "S" in SMB. Why? Because blessing the "S" is critical to another important "S" in your SMB consulting career: sales. Even the most hardened techie can own up to the fact that sales are necessary. And in the SMB consulting community, I'm always amazed at how many people cop that "I didn't know there would be so much sales effort when I became an SMB consultant" attitude. That sentiment would be a great place to end this chapter, but there is so much more to tell you about the "S" word. Let's get started.

> BEST PRACTICE: So you could say it's time to put on your sales hat. How does that differ from your marketing hat? The last chapter on marketing was a higher level than this chapter will be. This chapter is all about putting the pedal to the metal and making it happen. A sale is a closed, consummated transaction. Sales are good.

Defining Your SMB Customer

As if you didn't have enough discussion last chapter on customer segments, I pour it on thick early in this chapter. Customer definition is a good transition from the prior chapter on marketing to this chapter on making sales.

Microsoft's take on the SMB customer

Late in the writing of this book, Microsoft started to articulate a more sharply focused SMB strategy that including recasting SMB boundaries. This is important as you look at targeting your sales efforts to specific SMB segments. This is also important if you want your sales message to be consistent with Microsoft's sales message on an SMB segment-by-segment basis. For example, you want to right-size your solution, such as SBS, for the proper segment. You get the point.

Figure 6-1:

Microsoft redefines the SMB marketplace

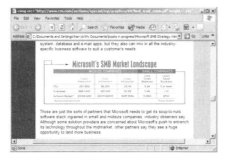

Size doesn't matter as much as you think!

No, this isn't story extracted from a men's magazine about you know what. It's more about how looks can be deceiving. Many successful SMB engagements have been completed in large firms. Take the Alaskan fishing company with 900 employees that uses SBS. It's success in using SBS stems from the fact that only 30 of the employees use computers at the home office. The other 870 employees work on factory trawlers off the west coast of Alaska in the Bering Sea. So here is a case where SBS worked in a larger company.

Other SMB customer definitions

Characteristic profiles of SMB customers observed out in the field include:

- Business advice seekers. There are certain SMB customers that retain your consulting services for business advice. This makes sense because you travel from SMB customer to customer and observe a lot of different business practices. Some practices might be better than others and some worse. You probably have the smarts to know the difference. You can benefit your SMB customers by sharing your acquired business wisdom (and billing for it, of course!).

- Reengineering. Another group of SMB customers will use technology to reengineer core business operations. The introduction of a powerful network with unimagined capabilities might act as an organizational change agent to improve the business. It could be the catalyst for the business to head off in new directions. For example, the slaughterhouse in Nebraska might decide its really in the retail butcher business and can use SQL Server in SBS to process mass quantities of customer orders.

- Keeping up with the Joneses. No doubt about it. Many successful business people have large egos. It's feeding those large egos that often motivated them to ascend to the top of the hill and be successful in their chosen craft. Ego knows no bounds and that includes SMB technology implementations. Some successful business people want to brag about their technology.

- Seeking competitive advantage. Probably most business people in the SMB space seek out technology solutions to gain a competitive advantage in the marketplace. This has been shown time and time again in SMB consulting. The consultant arrives with solution in hand, and once deployed, the business can truly point to some "wins," such as using e-mail to advertise property listings to the realtor community. Ironically, as this book was being completed, Steve Ballmer, CEO of Microsoft, sent out a company-wide memo to Microsoft employees reiterating that technology is purchased by businesses to gain competitive advantage. He was replying is his often blustery way to a recent Harvard Business Review article stating that technology had matured and new technologies offered few competitive advantages to businesses.. Ballmer refuted this point of view, saying he believes that new, exciting technology solutions will get businesses to part with their bucks to purchase new technologies that give them the competitive advantage. You, I, and the SMB consulting community focused on Microsoft solutions certainly hope this scenario plays out.

BEST PRACTICE: You might want to read the controversial Harvard Business Review article referenced above. Titled "Wringing Real Value from IT" by Nicholas G. Carr , Michael E. Porte, and Thomas H. Davenport, it can be found in the May, 2003 edition (visit http://harvardbusinessonline.hbsp.harvard.edu/b01/en/common/ item_detail.jhtml?id=3558 for reprint information). One point in the article that Ballmer wouldn't appreciate, but is well taken, is that many businesses now view the competitive advantage to be derived from technology to be duration. That is, your competitiveness is increased when you have minimized the financial outlays associated with acquiring the latest and greatest technology. Cutting costs, of course, leads to increased profits. And profits are how we keep score in business.

- Technical difficulties. A huge customer class out there includes Red Heads, Linux Losers, and Mac Attackers. Red Heads are existing NetWare sites that can benefit from an upgrade to another SMB solution such as SBS. Linux Losers are the "been there and done that" crowd. Having looked at Linux, these folks truly believe that paying for software upfront makes sense, having supposedly received it free once (and then learning it's not really free). Mac Attackers are clients that have pushed the Macintosh platform to its limits and now seek to go mainstream with a Microsoft SMB solution. Go easy on all the people from the "technical difficulties" crowd, as they're all good potential clients for you.

SMB Sales Tactics

In the MBA program, tactics are where you make it happen. Tactics are much more hands on than goals or objectives. Think of it this way: Goals and objectives are more high-level and fit the discussion contained in earlier chapters. This chapter, being on the bare-knuckled world of sales, begs for a section on tactics. Let's get started with an SMB example about how to sell SBS quickly.

How to sell SBS in under five minutes

So imagine you're working in a sales call center and you have five minutes to sell a networking solution based on SBS. How might you go about it? Consider using a sales tactics chart similar to Table 6-1. I'll provide additional context on these points following the table. Note this table refers to the SBS 2000 time frame and needs to be updated (of course) for SBS 2003 and beyond, but the all of the points below are well taken.

Notes:

Table 6-1: Sell SBS in Five Minutes

Step 1: Qualify with 3 questions

Question 1: *"What operating system will you use on this server?"*

Context/Comments:
Best chances of an SBS prospect if:
(a) Customer is buying a single server, and
(b) They plan to use Windows Server 2000.

Question 2: *"What will you be using the server for?"*

Context/Comments:
Good chance of an SBS prospect if one of the following is true; great chance if two or more fit:
(a) E-mail
(b) Database
(c) Internet access
(d) Remote access
(e) Faxing

Question 3: *"Will it be serving a standalone office with less than 50 PCs?"*

Context/Comments:
If yes, then propose SBS...SBS 2000 includes the Windows 2000 Server operating system plus:
- Email, including shared calendaring (Exchange, Outlook)
- Database for your business applications (SQL Server)
- Shared, secure Internet access (ISA Server)
- Secure remote access for mobile users, either dial-in or over the Internet

- Web server, plus graphical tool for building a Web site (IIS, FrontPage)
- Ability to share a fax, modems, printers, and files
- With integrated, graphical user management for all applications

Step 2: Explain & Close

Script: *"We can provide SBS 2000 on your server, including five client licenses, for less than the retail price of just Exchange and Windows 2000 Server. That's a great bargain!"*

Context/Comments:
- We can also provide support for SBS, so you get seamless support for hardware as well as software
- Additional client access licenses are available from volume licensing re-sellers or retail for about $50-$60 each (SBS 2000 time frame)

Question: *"May I SELL you SBS today?"*

Context/Comments:
Close the sale.

Let me explain Table 6-1 in more depth. In Step 1, you are qualifying your customer. Remember that a superior salesperson always qualifies their customer, and they do so quickly. If the customer doesn't "fit," then the salesman moves on.

BEST PRACTICE: Contrary to popular belief, a superior salesperson doesn't sell ice to Eskimos. In that case, Eskimos wouldn't need ice and would have been disqualified early in the sales cycle by the salesperson. The salesperson would have qualified a different type of customer, say beach bums in Australia! So, what is really being communicated here is that superior salespeople know how to quickly assess the customer situation and either qualify or disqualify the prospect. As rockabilly singer Dan Hicks (and his band "The Hot Licks") croons "move on." It's better for both parties early on to know if the shoe will fit, and if not, the conversation is over.

Question one in step one relates to goodness of fit for SBS with the customer. Again, you could update the question for Windows Server 2003 to make it more current. Question two in step one is "business speak" on purpose. The idea behind this question is that you'll find a business need that customer has that SBS can help meet. For example, the business person might communicate that they'd like e-mail to help their business operations. Combine that with Internet connectivity and you've met the threshold of two features meeting a business need. You're well on your way to selling an SBS solution at this point.

With business needs met in the questions above, you can further qualify the customer to determine if proceeding makes sense for all involved. Question three has much more depth to it than meets the eye. It strikes to the very essence of what SBS is. An all-in-one small business networking solution for a single office. This question asks whether the SBS solution will be used within four walls. I've seen plenty of successful SBS deployments when the SMB consultant adhered to the standalone office paradigm. I've seen plenty of unsuccessful SBS deployments when the SMB consultant attempted to make the SBS solution fit a branch office scenario (multiple offices).

> BEST PRACTICE: Please bend over backwards to keep SBS in its proper "box," an analogy that is fitting when you think of a standalone business with four walls! This is a key to your success with this product. I can tell you that many SMB consultants "make" SBS fit in branch office scenarios-and through dumb luck, reverse engineering, and a deep understanding of SBS's unique optimizations have made it work. But these multiple office SBS deployment success stories are truly the exception.

To only confuse the matter, let me mention in all fairness that Microsoft itself has sent a mixed message. Whereas the left hand speaks publicly about SBS being the first and essential server for a standalone office, the right hand released a white paper titled "Connecting a Remote Office to a Small Business Server 2000 Network" (which can be found as of this writing at http://members.microsoft.com/partner/products/servers/smallbusinessserver/ConnectingRemoteSBS2000Network.aspx). Regrettably, this confuses the SMB consulting community because you might now ask if it's cool or uncool to use SBS in branch office scenarios.

If I can spend some of the political capital I've built up with you, I'd like to recommend that you not use SBS in branch office scenarios. Please use the full Microsoft Servers product SKUs for such scenarios.

The second part of question three relates to the licensing that defines SBS. As of this writing, SBS has a 50 client computer limit. The license agreement speaks clearly to this and it relates to the number of client computers attached to LAN A (attached to the network). The licensing is per server, because all SBS applications are required to run on a single server. It is likely the licensing limitations will change in future releases of SBS, so you are encouraged to research this matter at www.microsoft.com/sbs for the most current licensing terms and conditions. There's some lawyer talk for ya!

The end of step one has the sales talk shifting to a more technical realm. Given that you've qualified your prospect this far (determined SBS will meet business needs, single office, small-size business, wants to purchase an operating system that is Windows Server-based, etc.), you can now drop to a more detailed level. Thus, the discussion shifts to actually mention specific application names. It's important to note that applications haven't been mentioned by name up to this point. Why? Because there is no need to start defining Exchange Server until you know you've got a fish on the line!

Moving on to step two, it's important to appreciate that a superior salesperson is a "closer." If you can't close the deal, you're not going to make it in SMB consulting or last long as a salesperson. BE THE CLOSER! It's in the closing arguments in step two that we play out our trump card: the value equation. SBS is priced such that it is cheaper than any two individual components combined, just as the statement about Exchange and the network operation system suggest. Fact of the matter is that SBS is the same price, as of this writing, as the standalone ISA Server standard edition SKU! Such a deal! Typically, if you can get your prospect to this point where you can present the SBS value equation, you've made the sale!

It's "shark in the water smelling blood" time! The final script item is to ask for the prospect's business. You be amazed how many inferior sales people will complete all of the steps in Table 6-1 and then FORGET to ask the prospect for his business! This is akin to completing a lengthy job interview process and then forgetting to ask the potential employer for the job itself. My assertions in this area about "not asking for the business" are well supported in many sales books (see the end of this chapter for a short list of sales books I'd encourage you to read). So, be the closer-come out of the bullpen (a baseball analogy) and end the game with a victory!

I'll say the obvious. A superior salesperson is a superior closer.

> BEST PRACTICE: Microsoft often places sales tools on its Partner site. An example was a "flash sales demo" titled Small Business Server 2000 Benefits Demo that was placed on the Partner site in the SBS area. This demo is shown in Figure 6-2 below. Continue to monitor the Partner site for such tools in the future, but as of this writing, the demo was found at: http://members.microsoft.com/partner/products/servers/smallbusinessserver/SBS2000FL.aspx.

> Be sure to review the readme.txt file that ships with this flash demo to learn how to customize the flash demo with you company name, logo, etc. Consider using this flash demo as a crowd warm-up when you give SBS speeches. Oh, and you'll like the snazzy jazz music in the background of this flash demo.

Figure 6-2:

Flash demo from Microsoft to sell SBS.

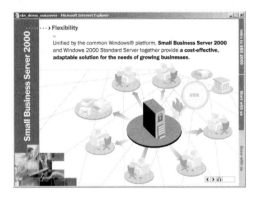

Notes:

Overcoming objections

It's been said many times, including books dedicated specifically to sales, that a superior salesperson knows how to overcome objections. This would, of course, be one of the most important points you could take from this book. You, too, must find a way to overcome objections to make the sale happen!

I'll provide a wide range of SBS sales objections followed by how to overcome them below. These objections are specific to the SBS 2000 era, but could easily be updated for SBS 2003 and beyond (in most cases, just change the number 2000 to 2003 in the scenarios below).

Question: Do I need to purchase Windows 2000 Server in addition to Small Business Server 2000?

Answer: NO. Small Business Server 2000 contains Windows 2000 Server.

Optimizations to Windows 2000 Server:

- No trust relationships between domains in SBS

- Must be root of Active Directory Forest

- Per server licensing

Context: I encountered this situation while competing to win an SBS engagement at a small Seattle biotech business. My competitor's bid had both SBS and the underlying Windows 2000 Server operation system. His bid was "redundant," because SBS contains Windows 2000 Server. Once I demonstrated this to the client, I was awarded the engagement. Cool!

Q: Can I add Small Business Server 2000 to my existing Windows 2000-based network?

A: YES!

Subject to a few considerations:

- Small Business Server 2000 must be installed as the root of the Active Directory (AD) forest. This means that SBS much be the first server installed on a LAN. Additional servers can be installed next.

- Suppose you have an existing Windows 2000 Server acting as the root of the AD forest. You will need to demote this existing Windows 2000 Server DC back to WORKGROUP mode and then join the Small Business Server 2000 domain. You will use the DCPROMO tool to accomplish this.

Context: This situation was created by the one-year gap between the release of Windows 2000 Server (February 2000) and SBS 2000 (February 2001). Many great small businesses, unable to wait a year for SBS 2000 and desperate to get off of Windows NT Server, jumped ship and deployed the standard version of Windows 2000 Server. Later, when SBS 2000 was released, many of these same firms asked whether they could upgrade their existing Windows 2000 Server machine to SBS 2000. Ergo-the answer that overcomes this sales objection.

One additional thought in this area concerns the two-server scenario. You could take the existing Windows 2000 Server machine and demote it/promote it back into the SBS 2000 domain as a second server (either member server or domain controller). This is a great way to solve a problem where a firm is currently running Windows 2000 Server and they'd much rather be running SBS 2000.

Q: I want to run ISA Server 2000 on a second Windows 2000 Server, separate from Small Business Server 2000.

A: NOT SUPPORTED out of the box.

This is not supported out of the box because of the following reasons:

- Per server licensing won't allow this from Small Business Server 2000 media set

- Purchasing second Windows 2000 Server, second ISA Server 2000 negates economic benefits of Small Business Server 2000.

Context: As of this writing, the cost of SBS 2000 is the exact same price as ISA Server 2000, thus ISA Server 2000 is essentially free and should be utilized. If for some reason, someone had political or religious objections to ISA Server 2000 (such as one and the same machine as IIS, running on a DC, acting as a software-based firewall, etc.), you might encounter a situation whereby said client would want to move ISA Server 2000 to a standalone perimeter server. This isn't groovy because SBS licensing in the SBS 2000 time frame is per server, so you can't use "our bits" to do this. Furthermore, the purchase of an additional Windows 2000 Server and ISA Server 2000 SKUs, plus to dedicate another server machine, would exceed $4,000 USD! I've got only one word for that: OUCH.

> BEST PRACTICE: Let's quickly resolve the ISA Server on SBS debate. People coming down from the enterprise level to the SMB world are typically really uncomfortable with this. However, the fact of the matter is that ISA Server 2000 is working VERY EFFECTIVELY as a multi-layer firewall (packet, session, application) for my clients and my clients are happy! I've done right by these folks and am kicking ass as an SMB consultant. Use ISA Server 2000 on SBS 2000 at a minimum (see the next sales objection about dual firewalls, etc.).

Q: Can I use my hardware-based firewall instead of ISA Server 2000?

A: YES!

Perhaps you've lost the battle but not the war. The client asks the above question and the answer is yes as per the following points.

- The Internet Connection Wizard (ICW) inside Small Business Server 2000 supports the existence of a hardware-based firewall.

- You may still use ISA Server 2000 for DMZ, caching performance gains in a dual-firewall scenario.

Context: Okay-repeat the sales mantra: A good salesperson will always overcome objections! This includes objections from the folks who simply don't like ISA Server 2000. Here the situation is that you can turn lemons into lemonade. First, you can effectively disable the firewall capability of ISA Server 2000 and have a hardware-based firewall do the heavy lifting. The ICW supports this natively. Second, you can satisfy everyone by using both ISA Server 2000 and a hardware-based firewall solution set to create a dual-firewall DMZ! Cool!!

Q: Isn't the server machine running Small Business Server 2000 "too busy" to run efficiently? Should Exchange 2000 Server run on a separate server?

A: NO.

- Small Business Server 2000 is optimized to run effectively on a single server machine.

Context: Enterprise-level technology professionals who often dabble with SBS as a hobby or weekend project (say to install it at their church) will conclude erroneously that no single server machine can run that many programs (Exchange 2000 Server, ISA Server 2000, SQL Server 2000, faxing, etc.). WRONG! SBS works very well on a capable server machine (late model, 256 MB RAM minimum, but 512 MB RAM preferred, 8GB + hard disk free space, etc.). This single server fear is misguided and easily addressed with a site tour to an existing SBS network. Simply walk up to an SBS server machine in production at a client site, right-click the Taskbar, select Task Manager and click the Performance tab. You'll see processor utilization rates and memory consumption well within acceptable limits.

Q: In prior releases of Small Business Server, I purchased a third-party faxing application to achieve the stability and capabilities I needed. Do I still need to do that?

A: NO. The Shared Fax Service in Small Business Server was completely rebuilt on the Windows 2000 Server code base.

Context: Microsoft Israel recoded the Share Fax Service in the SBS 2000 time frame to improve its performance and reliability. That resulted in such a good faxing solution that it was "borrowed" by the Windows Server 2003 team and is now a standard component in that network operating system! Be sure to honor the faxing process to attain the highest performance levels from the Shared Fax Service. This would be accomplished by using a superior fax modem, such as the external V.Everything model from 3Com/US Robitics. At a minimum, use an external fax modem, such as the USR Sportster. Do not use a cheap internal PCI modem.

Q: Do I need to master Active Directory?

A: NO!

- Active Directory is configured and managed in the background.

- Add User Wizard adds users and computer to Active Directory.

- Setup creates default organizational units (OUs), such as MyBusiness.

Context: A common fear expressed by clients is that they'll need to master Active Directory to successfully deploy an SMB solution such as SBS. This is not the case, but I have seen the client's kids seek to master Active Directory for ulterior motives: to earn the Microsoft Certified Professional designation. Fair enough. The native Active Directory tools, such as Active Directory Users and Computers, are exposed (but some functionality, such as trusts, are disabled).

Q: Can my remote workers run Terminal Services (TS) sessions on the Small Business Server 2000 server machine?

A: NO! NO! NO!

- TS is placed in Remote Administration Mode.

- Add second member server running TS in Application Sharing Mode.

- Possible Licensing Issues! (SBS CALs aren't TS CALs, Win9x legacy OSes need TS CALs, etc.)

Context: It's been accepted by SMB consultants that you would never seek to have mere mortal users log on via a TS session on an SBS server. That is because the TS session is a locally logged-on session; the user is logging on directly to the server console, which is risky! And to have more than two users log on via TS to the SBS server, you would need to place it in Application Sharing Mode. The problem with placing SBS in TS Application Sharing Mode is that the TS sessions receive foreground resource priority. That means you're remote TS users will get their slice of the pie at the expense of the LAN users who will suffer greatly!

On the other hand, Microsoft gives mixed guidance on this matter. Placing TS in Application Sharing Mode to accommodate remote workers is discouraged. But because so many SMB consultants and SBS clients were doing it, Microsoft released a white paper that provided prescriptive guidance on how to actually place TS in Application Sharing Mode. I'm inclined to not reveal where this white paper is located...but I'll tell you anyway: www.microsoft.com/partner/sbs. Please don't read it!

Q: Do I need to purchase another copy of Microsoft SQL Server 2000 to run my Line of Business (LOB) application?

A: NOT NECESSARILY!

SBS 2000:

- Contains Standard Edition

- Has no database size limitations

- Has no restrictions on number of databases

Context: SBS 2000 is a great infrastructure platform to deploy business solutions. But some people remember the early releases of SBS where the SQL Server database had restrictions. Such is not the case anymore and SBS will gladly support numerous LOBs. Read the next objections for further SQL Server discussion.

Q: My accounting consultant said I need to have SQL Server 2000 running on a separate Windows 2000 Server server machine. Can I do this?

A: YES!

- Common to have second Windows 2000 Server running additional SQL Server 2000 application for LOB

- Recommended by many ISV consultants

Context: This is the story of Vernon, the Great Plains consultant, who has his own deployment methodology. Vernon insists on his own server machine running just the operating system and his beloved Great Plains application. He has said he wants the ability to isolate the problems he might encounter with supporting Great Plains and not have to fiddle with Exchange, ISA, and so on. Fair enough. And more evidence to support Vernon's need for a second server is the fact that his Great Plains Dynamics deployments are often in the neighborhood of $50,000 and a second server running SQL Server is a small part of the overall cost.

One additional consideration on the second SQL Server discussion. An acceptable compromise in many dual-consultant situations that involve infrastructure and LOB (read Harry and Vernon) might be the following. Perhaps Vernon gets his second server but uses the SQL Server application contained in SBS. This could be accomplished by a program such as Great Plains Dynamics mapping a uniform naming convention (UNC) path to the database in SQL Server. A win-win and cost-saver for the client as well.

Q: How can I setup a Windows XP Professional client computer on a Small Business Server 2000 network when the client setup disk does not natively support Windows XP setup?

A: Refer to the following KBase article: Q316418: "How to Set Up a Windows XP Professional Client in an SBS 2000 Network."

Context: The issue here is about a software suite released at a certain point in time being able to support future desktop operating systems. This is a challenge. Whereas the "magic disk" in SBS 2000 natively supported the operating systems in existence when the SBS suite was created, its support for Windows XP and beyond was lacking. The above KBase article addresses the obvious issues about how to connect a client computer running Windows XP Pro to the network. However, it doesn't address the oddities that exist in introducing a more current client computer operating system on a "legacy" SBS 2000 network, such as the client-side Shared Fax Console not functioning.

Q: I'd like to automatically deploy my business applications on client computers. The Define Client Applications link isn't robust enough for me. Help!

A: Use the software deployment capabilities of Group Policy Objects (GPO) in the underlying Windows 2000 Server operating system.

Context: The Define Client Application in the SBS 2000 time frame didn't interact with MSI files and other sophisticated application installation approaches. You had to use Group Policy in the era to really install client-side applications from the server. Moving forward, you can anticipate this will be an area of improvement in the SBS 2003 release.

Q: Can I host my Web site on my Small Business Server 2000 server machine?

A: Yes and no!

• Technically-yes you can. Recognizing this, Microsoft has a Web cast on this topic.

• However-it is a best practice to host your Web site at your ISP for performance reasons (fat Internet pipes, backup power generators, etc.).

• Unless you are the ISP!

Context: This topic frequently comes up in client discussions with the SMB consultant. A client, seeking to extend SBS to the maximum and beyond, asks if the firm's Web site can be hosted on their SBS server machine. However, SBS really isn't the best way to handle this (even though it technically is able to). You are advised to introduce the client to Microsoft bCentral as the small business Web hosting solution that's a better fit.

Q: Does Small Business Server 2000 have an anti-virus application built-in?

A: No, it does not. Many popular server-based anti-virus products exist on the market specific to Small Business Server 2000. Check with your favorite anti-virus ISV.

Context: This is a critical sales discussion item. Clients can typically handle the truth that they'll need to spend extra to purchase and deploy a capable anti-virus program. The challenge is to explain why such a capable anti-virus program can cost nearly half the purchase price of SBS! Your response is that it's necessary to have such protection today. And you, the SMB consultant, might view this as a business development tool. If a client balks on purchasing a capable anti-virus application, then you should probably walk away from the engagement. This client is demonstrating serious warning signs and, worse yet, will probably blame you for viruses on the Internet (true story!).

> BEST PRACTICE: Late in the writing of the book, Microsoft announced it was acquiring the Romania-based anti-virus vendor GeCAD Software. This is a developing story, so bring yourself current on the matter by following the account at CRN (www.crn.com).
>
> The initial story on this purchase can be found at: http://www.crn.com/sections/BreakingNews/breakingnews.asp?ArticleID=42590 (published at CRN on June 11, 2003).

Q: Does Small Business Server 2000 have a tape backup program built in?

A: Yes, it does, and it's certainly better than no backup at all. However, strong consideration should be given to a more capable third-party backup solution.

Context: The native NTBACKUP program is good for making general backups of data and e-mail at the information store level. But there are limitations. One such limitation is the ability to quickly restore e-mails without restoring the entire information store (which you would have to do on a second server with the exact same naming convention because you can't realistically restore an information store on a production server).

Q: Must I purchase two network adapter cards to operate Small Business Server 2000.

A: Not necessarily. If you are not connected to the Internet-or you are connected to the Internet via a firewall-based router-a single network adapter card is typically sufficient. However, ISA Server functions fully with two network adapters.

Context: There are a couple of different viewpoints on this. First, there is the cheapo client that wants to pay as little as possible for anything and balks at the prospect of purchasing a second network adapter card to place in his server. Second, there is the great client who wants to use a hardware-based firewall and not have two network adapter cards in the server machine. Fact of the matter is that we can accommodate either client type and overcome this objection. But, remember the best solution of all would be to have a dual firewall on your SBS network (which would include two network adapter cards in your server machine).

Q: I have concerns about being able to establish a Terminal Services session directly over the Internet. Any better way of launching a Terminal Services session?

A: Force the remote user to establish a VPN connection first. This would be accomplished by disabling direct Terminal Services connections via the ICW and allowing VPN sessions via the VPN Connection Wizard.

Context: Remember that Terminal Services natively provides 50-bit encryption (and the new version in Windows Server 2003 provides stronger 128-bit encryption). But some clients have this feeling that it's not really secure. Rather than duke it out over this minor point, you're money ahead to follow the advice above and simply force a VPN connection prior to launching the TS session.

Q: Just to clarify-my company has 900 employees in the fishing industry. But I only have 30 client computers for the professional staff. Will Small Business Server 2000 work for me?

A: Yes, very well. The key to understanding Small Business Server 2000 limitations is that it applies to client computer count, not employee head count.

Context: SMB consultants constantly undersell SBS! Companies far larger than the licensing restrictions in SBS can benefit from the product. I've seen a landscaping company with 125 employees use SBS just fine. Ditto construction companies, manufacturing companies, timber companies, and numerous other companies with a small professional staff (using computers) and many blue collar workers (without computers).

Q: Can I use my Small Business Server machine as an FTP server to transfer large files to my clients (e.g., CAD drawings for an architect)?

A: Yes. It is permissible and the FTP port can be opened via the ICW. You will need to install the FTP service manually. This would be acceptable for low-volume usage-say, with clients-but not the general public.

Context: The context here is that SBS has some capabilities that many clients don't use and but can benefit from to solve a business problem. In this case, the printing company was trying to send and receive AutoCAD files from customers. E-mail wouldn't work because the file size (often approaching 60MB) would realistically be too large as an attachment. One consideration with the FTP service: You might have the users establish a VPN connection before using their FTP client so that the logon authentication isn't passed as clear text.

Q: I'm a photographer/printer. I need to interact with my Macintosh computers while on the Small Business Server 2000 network. Is this possible?

A: Yes. Manually install Services for Macintosh.

Context: This is one of the great underserved markets in SBSland! Macintoshes can connect to an SBS-based network for file and printer sharing, e-mail, Internet connectivity, and so on. There are limitations, as the Macintosh doesn't fully participate in the domain, but that's a topic best left for another white paper.

Q: I'm the IT manager for a not-for-profit organization. We need to keep our UNIX server to run the FundWare development program. Possible?

A: Yes. Small Business Server 2000 supports services for UNIX, NFS clients, and, as often seen, client computers running terminal emulation software such as Ice Ten to connect to UNIX servers.

Context: This objection can be easily satisfied when the client already has an existing UNIX network and would consider introducing SBS. I've seen this scenario in retail (point of sale) as well. Also, remember that SBS can modify its default local area network subnet to accommodate an existing UNIX network (that is, the 192.168.16.2 IP address can be changed during setup compared to prior SBS releases).

N̲otes:

Q**:** I'm now hearing that Small Business Server 2000 can't be customized to meet my needs-that's its methodology is too strict. True?

A**:** Not True. You can customize the consoles, create custom templates to add users, etc.

Context: Early users of the first two releases of Small Business Server found it to be too rigid. Starting with SBS 2000, the native tools were exposed and customization is not only possible, but even encouraged in some areas (such as the SharePoint Technologies in SBS 2003).

Q**:** Isn't Small Business Server 2000 hard to install?

A**:** NO.

- The baseline SBS installation is often a "click Next" experience and, with adequate server and network hardware, is an assured outcome.

- The OEM preinstallation option insures a successful outcome. This is also a "rapid deployment" method that is appealing to both customers and technology consultants (on a fixed bid installation contract).

Context: Those SMB consultants who worked with early SBS releases were frustrated by points of failure in the product (such as an incorrectly detected modem resulting in setup failure during the Shared Fax Service installation, etc.). SBS setups are much more refined, and if you use the OEM SKU, where much of SBS is installed at the factory, the setup is even more positive. I discuss the OEM SKU for SBS in the final chapter of this book.

N otes:

The following objections were taken from a different slide deck and relate to Microsoft Windows Server 2003. The context of the first objection is the popular mantra to upgrade Windows NT Server environments to Windows Server 2003. That is followed by a slide on upgrading from Windows 2000 Server to Windows Server 2003. The objections end with a security slide and an Exchange 2000 slide.

Q: Why should I upgrade? My NT 4.0 Servers are quite stable.

A: There is much to be gained by migrating to Windows Server 2003:

- Many-to-one management with group policy

- Increased end-user productivity with the obvious dependability improvements in Windows Server 2003

- Improved Terminal Services functionality, because it's built into the core operating system and not a separate SKU

- Easy PKI and Kerberos security via the new security domain model based on Active Directory in Windows Server 2003

- World-class application and Web servers, given the two-generational increase in operating system technology.

Context: Remember that Microsoft's Windows Server 2003 mantra is to upgrade existing Windows NT Server sites first. This is truly the low hanging fruit of the technology industry in the 2003/2004 time frame for SMB consultants to go after.

Q: Why should I upgrade? Is WS 2003 really much different than Windows 2000 Server?

A: Selling points for customers with Windows 2000:

- Active Directory improvements

- Group Policy Management Console

- Volume Shadow Copy Restore

- IIS 6.0

- Integrated .NET Framework

Context: This is a tougher sales area. Folks running Windows 2000 Server aren't entirely unhappy with their lot in life or their LAN! The first two selling points about Active Directory and Group Policy are improvements that relate best to the enterprise space. Volume Shadow Copy Restore is a cool tool that can be used by organizations of all sizes. Improvement to IIS 6.0 will appeal most to medium-sized and enterprise organizations that host Web sites. It's the .NET Framework that's perhaps most interesting and will yield the greatest long-term benefits in SMB. Think back to the mid-1990s when any line of business applications were being ported from being NLM-based applications in the NetWare environment to Windows NT. The thrust was to convert from Novell's network operation system to the new one from Microsoft. There was good work in SMB at that time taking folks from NetWare 3.x to SBS 4.0 (which had just been released).

Fast forward to late 2004 (which might be when you're actually reading this) and the .NET Framework has been improved upon and embraced by ISVs that are creating new LOBs based on the .NET Framework. It's likely your clients will receive a letter from their ISV advising them that Windows 2000 Server is no longer supported and they must upgrade to Windows Server 2003. This is a built-in consulting opportunity for SMB consultants to upgrade SMB client network infrastructures! I show a recent letter received by an actual client regarding Timberline discontinuing support for older operating systems in Figure 12-16 of Chapter 12. It's likely this same client will receive a similar letter from Timberline soon that communicates its latest release needs to use the .NET Framework and they must upgrade to Windows Server 2003.

Q: I'm concerned about all the security issues with Microsoft products.

A: Suggested talking points:

- Trustworthy Computing initiative that started in early 2002
- Products shipped secure by default
- Necessary components must be installed and enabled-eliminates risk
- Example: IIS 6.0 is not installed by default in Windows Server 2003
- Security and Critical Update program

Context: I have a strong response to this type of objection being raised by an SMB client: What better company than Microsoft to address the security issues in technology? Microsoft has the financial resources and the staff to jump right on security matters! The weekly security bulletins that ship to security professionals are not only welcome missives on how to fix shortcomings, but they have a soothing and comforting effect on clients, giving the impression that Microsoft is "all over" the security thing. Hey-at least clients don't feel they have to wait for a young man in Finland to return from cross-country skiing to create a bug fix when they deal with Microsoft!

BEST PRACTICE: Be sure to subscribe to Microsoft's security bulletins at www.microsoft.com/security to receive announcements.

Q: What about running Exchange 2000 on Windows Server 2003?

A: Suggested response:

- Changes made in WS2003 as part of Microsoft's Trustworthy Computing initiative prevent Exchange Server 2000 from being installed on a server computer running WS2003.

- Some of the changes required to support Exchange on WS2003 are architectural work beyond what is normally expected or welcomed by our customers in a service pack release.

- As a result, the Exchange team has decided to build that work into Exchange "Titanium," scheduled for release in mid-2003.

- "Titanium" will be fully supported on both Windows Server 2003 and Windows 2000 Server.

Context: This is a bona fide issue you might confront in SMB consulting. In-place upgrades from the 2000 to 2003 server platform on machines running Exchange 2000 have a big problem. Exchange 2000 will not run natively on Windows Server 2003. Thus, you are often looking at a dual upgrade, including the network operating system and messaging application. This is exactly where you don't want to be during an upgrade process. Ouch!

> BEST PRACTICE: You can read more about this specific issue in the April 22, 2003, article titled "Exchange 2000 Won't Run on Windows Server 2003, Partners Gripe" by Paula Rooney at CRN (www.crn.com).

No Money? No Problem!

A classic overcoming-the-sales-objection scenario is that of the client without money. So the joke goes like this: The client communicates that he'd love to retain the SMB consultant, but has no money to do so. The SMB consultant replies, "No problem," and proceeds to ask about the client's new Hummer H2 SUV automobile in the parking lot. The punch line comes with the SMB consultant magnanimously offering to do a trade out of his services for the Hummer H2-instead of working for cash.

Seriously, there is a method to my madness in presenting this section: trade outs. Off the top of my head, I can think of two times I've done this (although I've probably done it more than that). Both experiences were satisfactory, and you should consider trade outs to grow your SMB consulting practice.

Take my paint, please!

During the depths of the early 21st century recession, I entertained different ways to make sales and attract more business. This included accepting a promising retail client who was tight on cash because of a recent business move and expansion. The client wanted my SBS consulting services, and I wanted to raid his home supply store in return for badly needed gardening supplies, wood stains, and paints. This relationship worked very well and resulted in a-you've already guessed it-"win-win" for everyone. His SBS network hums and my house looks great!

Life's a beach!

This client, a resort lodge on the ocean, was part of the hospitality business (which I learned is not wealthy and typically undercapitalized). While good souls, these people typically paid their bills about 60 days late and often questioned minor legitimate expenditures to whittle down the amount owed. But overall the business relationship was fine, and there were reasons I wanted to continue doing business with this client.

One fall, the lodge was planning to close for 20 months to renovate. Faced with a $3,000 USD accounts receivable and a soon-to-be shut-down, slow-pay client, I did what any reasonable SMB consultant would do: I partied hard! That's right. I took friends and family down for a long Labor Day holiday weekend and treated everyone to an all-expenses-paid PARTY. I was able to blow through the entire invoice in four days. Moving forward from the weekend, the client and I started with a clean financial slate. It was a great time fostered by a great SMB consulting business decision.

> BEST PRACTICE: Be creative as an SMB consultant when making sales. There is a lot of great work out there, some of which might not fit the 30-day, cash billing cycle. Speaking of cycles, perhaps you're partial to Harley Davidson motorcycles. It's a poorly kept secret that many self-made, wealthy business owners own Harleys. Perhaps you could trade your SMB consulting services for a new LOUD ride!

One-Hour SMB Sales Effort

You must seek to limit your SMB sales efforts to a modest amount of time. Why? Because SMB consultants don't have the engagement margin that enterprise consultants do to absorb and amortize an extended sales cycle. Let me make the point by focusing on a potential small business engagement. Let's assume you're looking at installing SBS at a client site for about $5,000 in billable time (you will bill 50 hours over 60 days at $100 per hour). If all goes well, you're looking at $500 in profit after everyone (including you, the landlord, and the utility company) are paid! If your sales cycle exceeds one hour (a reasonable time allocation), then you are really starting to eat into that modest $500 profit.

> BEST PRACTICE: Use this one-hour rule as a way to gauge the fitness of the potential client. If the client can be closed in an hour and there is a mutual feeling of trust, you've had a good day of sales as an SMB consultant! A client that takes tens of hours to close for such a small engagement is likely taking advantage of you and isn't a suitable match for your talents.

So you'll need to find yourself signing that engagement letter sooner rather than later in the SMB consulting space. I've already highlighted that this preserves your profit margin and pride, but it also mitigates a gray area of paid planning. In SMB consulting, it's often difficult to know when you've crossed the line from sales effort to technology planning. Some prospective clients are very crafty and will trick you into giving away hours of planning advice, all in the name of "sales calls."

The goal is to get paid for your planning. You are a skilled professional as an SMB consultant. You need to be treated with respect and not be taken advantage of. It's a reasonable request. A client who can't pay you for adding value via the technology planning process, probably shouldn't be a client of mine or yours. Case closed.

Be sure to see more discussion on client selection, and the tools used to select clients wisely, in Chapter 7.

Goofy Sales Tactics

Close your eyes and think for a moment about the different sales approaches you've seen in your lifetime. It's safe to say that you probably think you've seen it all. To some extent we all feel that way and our assumptions are likely correct: We have seen it all. Perhaps you've seen the hucksters hacking sharp kitchen knives at the county fair. That's about as low as you can go, and I'll not have you go there. And, oh yeah, "goofy" in this case isn't in reference to a snowboarding style, but rather refers to the strange, the unheard-of, and perhaps the effective.

Condo King

Talk about branding! This real estate salesperson gives out a business card that shows him wearing a crown. He calls himself the "Condo King." It's goofy but I'm sure it's effective in his line of work.

Rainbow Lady

Talk about someone who must have enjoyed the 1960s as a hippie! The Rainbow Lady is an entertainer for kids' birthday parties, etc. She drives a rainbow-colored car and has even been known to attend funerals and hand out her business card in the receiving line. It's true and admittedly a bit over the top in the sales category.

SMB Solution Selling Paradigm

Long-time observers in the SMB space know all too well the problems associated with selling into SMB. Everyone from Microsoft to IBM to Novell to Oracle to Gateway (and I'm forgetting several others) have tried to find the silver bullet for selling into SMB. For the top tier players, it can be a daunting proposition, because the 30-second TV commercial you run during an episode of Friends on NBC requires you to push a heck of a lot of SMB product to just pay for the advertisement! At the middle tier, which would be large consulting firms trying to sell into the SMB space, you have a potential cultural and business sector mismatch. In this case, you likely have 100 percent commission salespeople who are accustomed to landing IT consulting gigs that start at $500,000 USD. The problem is these same commission sales people aren't nearly as excited as pursuing a $5,000 gig with its corresponding lower payout. Even if you teach them the one-hour rule of SMB sales, it's still not exciting for these folks. So read on for SMB solution selling paradigms that work.

Map to your constituency

It's a well-known fact in Seattle that Boeing (the huge aerospace manufacturer) uses Perkins Coie as its law firm because "big" firms like "big" law firms. Perkins Coie is one of the largest law firms in the country and maps well to Boeing's sheer size of 250,000 employees. Likewise, if you serve small business, it's best if you're a small business yourself. You'll have a deeper cultural understanding of what these folks are going through on a day-to-day basis.

More important, as a small business serving small businesses, you have a cost structure that is similar to that of your clients. You can make a profit on a $5,000 SMB consulting engagement, whereas larger firms can't. It unlikely you have a larger corner office and fancy company car to support for your executives (that's you!).

Suffice it to say, we like doing business with ourselves, as the old saying goes. Ergo, your small business clients will enjoy working with an SMB consultant who runs a small business himself. You'll laugh at the same jokes, eat the same foods, and drink the same drinks. You get the picture. Live small business if you plan to serve small businesses.

Stay current!

So theories on selling into the SMB space come and go. Business models are continuously tweaked to find ways to sell profitability into a largely diverse, widely disparate heterogeneous SMB marketplace. These are scary words to MBA marketers, because they suggest your selling costs will quickly outpace your revenues. So what's a poor SMB consultant to do, faced with such structural barriers? One of the best things you can do is to educate yourself and stay current on topics relating to SMB consulting. A site I highly recommend is CRN's SMB portal at http://www.channelweb.com/sections/newscenters/default.asp?newscenterid=32, where many articles relating to channel sales in SMB can be found. Knowledge is power, so make this a power tool!

Hidden jewels

Possibly you like to engage in the same relaxing behavior I enjoy when you're all burned out after a long day of SMB consulting: surfing around for SMB sale materials on the Internet. This mindless clicking can sometimes lead to some real finds out there including a sample I want to share in this section on the Microsoft Solution Selling (MSS) model. I was digging for gold on the Internet one day and found an incredibly valuable PowerPoint slide deck on the MSS at a Microsoft vendor site (Sales Performance International) at www.solutionselling.com/mspartners/fusion.html. Admittedly, this slide deck is being using to sell a three-day intensive sales course, but the "teaser" you will view at the above Web site is excellent. This sales approach is more enterprise-oriented than SMB, but I share with you a few hidden jewels from the presentation (which is copyrighted by Sales Performance International, so I can't reproduce too much here).

- Customers want technology advisors, not just vendors.

- Managing Difficulties: We lose to "no decision" more than to any single competitor.

- Be the Eagle. Eagles are the top 20 percent of the sales force.

- Buyers expect the following from Eagles: situational knowledge, capability knowledge, people skills, and selling skills.

- Only 10 percent of potential buyers are really "looking" for a solution.

- MSS is used internally at Microsoft.

Figure 6-3 displays the MSS process in graphic forms with pointers about which worksheet to use at what stage.

Figure 6-3:
Even though MSS is enterprise-focused, you can appreciate how this basic structure would help you boost SMB consulting sales.

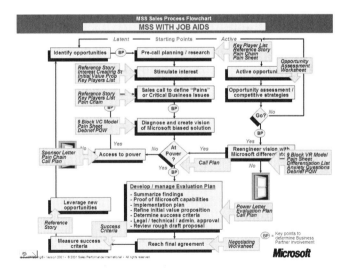

From Figure 6-3, cherry-pick the points that work for you. I think you can intuitively walk through these steps in the lean and mean SMB sales environment and improve yourself (and your bottom line) as an SMB consultant.

bCentral Time, Baby

This section on promoting bCentral is presented to you as a "look and see" overview. You can follow up at www.bcentral.com, and you are encouraged to incorporate this SMB portal as part of your SMB consulting sales tool kit! Let's get the tour started!

Sales and marketing

The sales and marketing area of bCentral provide these features and capabilities to help the SMB consultant increase business activity:

- Sales Leads. The bCentral Sales Leads gives you access to comprehensive and up-to-date databases of more than 14 million businesses and more than 250 million consumers. With Sales Leads you can (1) pull mailing addresses, phone numbers, and other data for new, qualified customers for your direct-mail marketing efforts, (2) select customers based on your own demographic criteria, (3) choose the types of customer data most useful to your marketing needs.

- Search Engine Submissions with Submit It! You will optimize your Web site for submission to top Web search engines. This is followed by the actual submission process followed by weekly ranking reports. You also are allowed to use the Web analyzer tool called FastCounter Pro to monitor, analyze, and further optimize your Web site. I have personally used this service to drive clicks to my Web site if someone searches on Small Business Server and other SMB-related terms.

- E-Mail Marketing With List Builder. This is a service that I use to distribute my monthly SBS newsletter to over 5,000 readers. I'd encourage you to use this capability to create your own newsletter to generate demand for your SMB consulting services.

- Business Listings. This will help new customers find your business with a premium listing in one of America's largest online business directories. Powered by Verizon Superpages.com, a bCentral online business listing will (1) give you exposure to over 9 million unique monthly users who are ready to buy, (2) cost you a fraction of what you might pay for a traditional business listing (3) list your business in up to five search categories that you select.

- Banner Network Ads. Use this tool to display your service as a banner ad on numerous Web pages.

The bCentral Sales and Marketing page is shown in Figure 6-4.

Figure 6-4:
Take a moment to learn how bCentral might serve as an SMB consulting sales tool even though its primary focus is consumer-oriented businesses.

BEST PRACTICE: There are frequent promotions on bCentral that bundle many of the above services together for a lower overall than the individual services purchased alone. You are encouraged to visit the bCentral site for the latest promotional opportunity.

Web sites and commerce

This next set of services from bCentral was clearly intended for the consumer market, but I encourage you to consider using these services for your SMB consulting practice. All of us can benefit from having our Web pages hosted by a robust Web hosting service with fat Internet pipes, stability, and big backup batteries! I use bCentral to host my SMB Nation Web site, and I can report it meets my needs. Other Web sites that I've hosted at my office on my own servers have been subject to windstorm-induced power outages, failed hubs, etc.

The e-commerce function at bCentral has been beneficial in providing a payment mechanism for my SMB Nation conference series. An SMB consultant might use the e-commerce function to sell services and products at a fixed price (remember the fixed price SMB consulting package on eBay in Chapter 4 of this book?). So put on your creative thinking cap and determine who you might sell yourself via an online e-commerce function.

The bCentral Web Sites and Commerce page is shown in Figure 6-5.

Figure 6-5:
With a little bit of thinking, you'll be able to think of ways to exploit the Web and commerce functions at bCentral to benefit your SMB consulting practice.

BEST PRACTCE: Don't forget that what you learn about bCentral by using it might well develop into a service you can deliver to clients. I discuss bCentral consulting opportunities in Chapter 12.

AOL for small business

bCentral finally has a competitor! America Online (AOL) has a small business portal similar to bCentral. I've not used the service and can't speak to its capabilities. At first blush, it didn't appear to have as many features and functions as bCentral. More information can be found at aolsvc.aol.com/small_biz.

Advertising

One of the great debates of our time amongst SMB consultants, vendors, software manufacturers, and the like is the value of advertising. Here's the problem. In the SMB space, the cost/benefit ratio typically doesn't work. That is, you can spend a ton of funds on advertising, but will you recapture it in increased sales and profits? For example, if Microsoft decided to spend $50 million on promoting SBS 2003, it might have to sell $200 million in additional product just to pay back the cost of the advertising. That might be a good deal none the less, but the highly fragmented SMB marketplace makes it expensive for the right eyeballs to see the right advertisement. You might end up paying for a lot of visual impressions from folks who have no interest in SMB technology.

> BEST PRACTICE: Indeed I do sound like I'm trying to discourage you from advertising. In SMB consulting, I've always seen advertising as a warning sign that you're not making it on referrals. That is, you're not growing by word of mouth, and you're relying on expensive advertising. Expensive advertising will not hide fundamental flaws in your SMB consulting practice!

Okay, since you asked for it, now some thoughts on advertising. In this section I'll present image, display, and channel versus consumer advertising. That's followed by a "Brelsford's Dozen" on great advertising mistakes.

Image

This is often reserved for large companies that are effectively engaging in public relations or that want to paint a broad brush stroke to deliver a message. I cite two examples from the Pacific Northwest. Boeing will occasionally run advertisements on television that show a plane flying or a spacecraft entering orbit. While it's unlikely Boeing would ever sell a commercial aircraft or spaceship based on a TV ad, it is committed to fostering strong positive relationships in the communities it serves. Thus the image advertisement on television.

Microsoft also has been engaging in image advertising lately. As these pages are written, there is a general Microsoft television advertisement oriented toward small business where the viewer is told Microsoft software solutions inspire creativity and success. The advertisement ends with a small bistro restaurant growing into a thriving eatery with long lines to get in (perhaps you saw this advertisement that made extensive use of white color crayon outlining and drawing). In this image advertisement, Microsoft never mentions a single product, such as Office or SBS.

> BEST PRACTICE: Of all forms of advertising, this is the least likely to have high ROI for the SMB consultant. It's great to put yourself out there in a positive way, but practically speaking, is that really what will make the telephone ring with lucrative new business?

Display

Display advertising is much more specific and typically includes purchasing information, such as price and location. Think thick Sunday paper overflowing with ads and you've got display advertising! I've seen many SMB consultants engage in display advertising. For some, it's worked well if product (such as white box clones) are sold in addition to services. Others have had success if positioned as break-fix (e.g., Harry's Repair Shop). True SMB consultants who sell billable hours alone have run ads where they offer a package deal — e.g., "Install your network for $1,999 between now and June 30th."

A display ad can take many forms, including television, radio, print (newspaper, magazine), and-what the heck-throw in billboards and postcards! Often, a display ad makes the person running the ad feel great to see their business baby in shining lights! But again, cast a wary eye to the cost of business advertising versus the incremental revenue you will generate from such efforts. It's gotta be such that the benefits outweigh the costs when making the display advertising decision.

BEST PRACTICE: Now to reverse myself. I'm a huge fan of display advertising when it involves Other People's Money (OPM). If the question is whether Microsoft should advertise its SBS product to specifically generate more product awareness and demand, then I'm all for it. I've sat in many meetings with other SMB consultants where we've preached and beseeched Microsoft to engage in display advertising to pump up SBS. To its credit, Microsoft has engaged in some display advertising for SBS, although primarily in the channel. But this display advertising hasn't been focused on the customer.

So if someone else is willing to pay for your display advertising, who is complaining, eh? Surprisingly, there are some OPM avenues readily available to you. One is called "Market Development Funds," or MDF, which are allocated for spending by software manufacturers, hardware manufacturers, and distributors, to name a few. Here's an example of how this might work. A computer/software reseller (and SMB consultant too) opens a shop in a town. This shop participates in different vendor reseller programs. The vendors have funds earmarked to spend on advertising for the shop to sell its products. A real world example of this was how Egghead Discount Software ran full-page Sunday ads listing many different software packages for sale (and did so with very little of its own money!).

When you go forth with your plans to run display ads, for God's sake, do it right. While I've preached you should be a finder, minder, and grinder (as well as butcher, baker, and candlestick maker) across this text, I didn't include camera-ready graphic artist. Consider farming out your actual advertising production to a specialist. This could be an advertising agency for those SMB consulting practices who are especially well-heeled. It might be a graphics arts student at a local college for the rest of us SMB consultants.

BEST PRACTICE: Consider a trade-out as you dip your toes into the world of display advertising. In my case, I traded out a SMB Nation conference booth and sponsorship to CRN magazine for four display advertisements to promote my event. Because CRN's readership exceeds 100,000 technology resellers and consultants,

I thought this would be a great way to reach my target. I'm pleased with the results, as it raised awareness of my SMB Nation conference and made it "legitimate" in the eyes of many.

The type of trade-out for display advertising you might engage in with a publication could very well be different from mine. Perhaps you could provide SMB consulting services to a local business newspaper in exchange for advertising space!

Channel vs. consumer

It's a debate as old as mankind itself. Should advertising be directed to the channel (that's you, the SMB consultant) or the consumer? The debate continues, and you see both sides of it daily. If you scan a recent issue of CRN (www.crn.com), you'll see technology ads directed to the SMB channel for products, services, etc. But if you read INC magazine (www.inc.com), you'll see (albeit fewer) technology ads directed to the consumer.

Microsoft

Historically, in the SMB area, Microsoft has made channel plays. This is particularly true with SBS 2000 (and earlier releases), where ads directed specifically to SMB consultants appeared in numerous trade magazines. What advertising was allocated to the consumer channel was either image advertising (as discussed above in this section) or advertising by partners. Partner advertising included Dell running its consumer ads for workstations, laptops, and servers in newspapers and magazine where SBS was listed as an "add-on." Another form of partner advertising was the localized advertising conducted by individual SMB consulting firms to sell products such as SBS. One example of this was a firm in my area, Autonomix (www.autonomix.com), which advertised SBS in the regional business monthly Kitsap Business Journal.

The advertising example set by Autonomix (and other SMB consultants) raises a question that is being debated in the Microsoft SMB community. Should Microsoft's partners such as Autonomix be implicitly responsible for advertising Microsoft's SBS product to the consumer? There are two sides to this debate. On the one hand, many SMB consultants feel it's not necessarily their job to go out and sell Microsoft's product for them ("them" being Microsoft itself). This viewpoint is akin to owning a franchise whereby the franchisee (the SMB consultant) looks to the franchisor (Microsoft) to conduct advertising to drive business to the franchisee. This is how a sandwich shop franchise, such as Subway Sandwiches, operates.

But on the other hand, if Microsoft isn't stepping up to the table with sufficient levels of consumer advertising, then you could argue that someone has to do it! And if the benefits outweigh the costs in advertising a product such as SBS, then the SMB consultant should just do it! That is the framework of the Microsoft consumer advertising debate in SMB, and you'll need to decide which side of the fence you sit on.

Oracle, Novell, IBM, Others

With its Small Business Suite providing a range of business accounting capabilities and less of an infrastructure focus, Oracle has used consumer advertising as its mainstay. Ads have appeared in numerous business magazines including INC. Novell has, on occasion, advertised its SBS networking bundle to consumers. Other SMB-related advertisements include Intuit's small business accounting software. It's interesting to note that one segment of the market with the great affinity for SMB consumer advertising has been the hardware manufacturers, including Gateway, Dell, HP, and IBM. For example, in Spring 2002, IBM sent out over 1 million postcards to North American small businesses promoting SBS 2000! More on the IBM mailing later on in this chapter.

Brelsford's Dozen: Great expectations

A key element to success as an SMB consultant is to avoid making mistakes along the way. The world of advertising is littered with great mistakes, and by acknowledging and appreciating these mistakes, you can avoid repeating them. So as an SMB consulting/Brelsford's Dozen exercise, let's compile a list of advertising approaches you might want to avoid. Consider this the "Brelsford's Dozen of Great Advertising, Sales, and Marketing Mistakes to be Avoided." I'll provide the first two and then send you on your way to research another ten to complete the list as part of this SMB consulting assignment.

1.   Coke Classic. Every business student studies this faux pas, where Coke broke something that was fixed when it changed the positioning

of its mainstay cola beverage by introducing a "new and improved" version. Ouch!

2. Nike's Olympic Chain Saw Massacre. In the 2000 Summer Olympics (Australia), Phil Knight, CEO of Nike, Inc., came up with the idea of recreating a scene from a popular horror movie: A killer wielding a chain saw chases Olympian Suzy Favor in a television advertisement. Suzy makes a clean getaway, supposedly making the point that Nike shoes allow you to outrun killers, etc. However, the ad was taken the wrong way by the public and reflected an abusive and violent tone towards women.

3.

4.

5.

6.

7.

8.

9.

10.

11.

12.

Microsoft SMB Sales Resources

Many think of Microsoft as a marketing machine. In this section, I expose some Microsoft SMB sales resources for you to take advantage of. And while I discuss some of these resources in other book sections, the context here is sales!

Microsoft TS2 events

Not enough US SMB consultants know that a technical sales training seminar called TS2 is hosted over 800 times per year. This translates into quarterly TS2 events in the host cities, which makes sense because the TS2 content is updated every 12 weeks. A TS2 half-day event emphasizes Microsoft SMB solutions and how to "sell" such solutions to clients. It's a mixture of technical content delivery combined with sales best practices.

Figure 6-6:

Microsoft TS2 seminars (held in the US) are the best way to sharpen your sales saw for free!

BEST PRACTICE: By the way, many SMB consultants who seek closer ties to Microsoft not only attend TS2 events, they also buddy up with the TS2 instructors, go out and have lunch, etc. It's worth your effort, as you'll have quality time with quality technical sales professionals who are presenting the TS2 content. It also helps the TS2 instructor, as they have a "face time" requirement to be in front of SMB consultants, hearing their concerns, etc. It's a win-win for both parties.

Microsoft Go To Market

This will hardly be the last time I discuss Go To Market (GTM) in the book. GTM is made up of four methodology elements (I discuss the GTM methodology much more in Chapter 11):

- Learn It!

- Sell It!

- Deploy It!

- Build On It!

Here I focus on one of the GTM elements: Sell It! Typically at the Microsoft Partner site (www.microsoft.com/partner), you will find competitive analysis documents, sale tools, etc., under the Sell It! GTM category. In Figure 6-7, a recent Sell It! view from the SBS partner page is displayed.

Figure 6-7:
Note the product competitive analysis papers on the SBS Sell It! page. A good salesperson knows the competition and how to reposition to it.

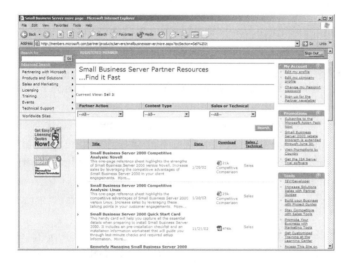

> BEST PRACTICE: Note that Microsoft uses different language across its public and partner Web sites to describe the four-stage GTM methodology. For example, whereas in this discussion I refer to the first element as "Learn It," in other sections of the book you'll see it called "Learn About It." This merely reflects how Microsoft handles the four GTM elements across the company.

Microsoft partner materials

So here's my sales pitch for you to consider becoming a Microsoft partner. Do it not so much because of the free not-for-resale software you will receive, but because of the sales support you can take advantage of, such as partner and project guides.

> BEST PRACTICE: In parts of this book, I suggest you start with the Action Pack program instead of becoming a bona fide Microsoft

Partner. I stand by those words, because the context is to start with Action Pack and grow into becoming a Microsoft Partner. Once you become a Microsoft Partner, the best practice I want to impart to you is "You get what you put into it." If you simply wait for the monthly partner mailer, that's all you'll get out of it. If you build upon the partner relationship with your district office, you'll reap more rewards than not.

Moving on now.

There are basically three levels to partner with Microsoft that might interest the SMB consultant. The first, simply being a registered member, allows you to access certain content on the Microsoft Partners site. The second level, Microsoft Certified Partner, requires two Microsoft Certified Professionals (MCPs) on staff. The highest level, Microsoft Gold Partner, requires a significantly higher number of certified professionals on staff. Note the Gold Partner has many different designations (security, learning, global, managed) that are beyond the scope of this SMB consulting text. More information on the Microsoft Partners program can be found at http:// members.microsoft.com/partner/partnering/programs/default.aspx?nav=ln.

> BEST PRACTICE: One benefit that might compel an SMB consult-
> ant to become a gold partner would be the golden opportunity to
> develop Microsoft district office relationships. Gold Partners have
> better access to district office employees. Plain and simple, that's
> how the game is played and won-through strong Microsoft rela-
> tionships.

One additional program that might be of interest is the System Builder designation. I've found many SMB consultant who are also system builders belong to this program and speak highly of the support they get. I've only met one SMB consulting practice (Paladin Data Systems in Poulsbo, Washington, at wwwpaladindata.com) that is also a Certified Technical Education Center (CTEC). A CTEC delivers Microsoft Official Curriculum courses.

Another way to acquire partner materials is by surfing the Microsoft Partners Web site and clicking down into the content of the partner and project guides.

These guides are the focus of Chapter 11 (presented in the context of methodologies), so I'll not bother to repeat the details here.

Last and certainly not least is the Microsoft Momentum conference, formerly branded FUSION. This is the annual partners conference held over a weekend that is 50 percent party, 30 percent business, and 20 percent technical, in that order! I've learned more about sales by socializing with successful partners at this conference than any other conference I've attended. I consider attendance mandatory-once you develop your SMB consulting practice, can afford to go, and want to take your practice to the proverbial "next level." Figure 6-8 presents information for the current Momentum conference in New Orleans (did I mention party?).

Figure 6-8:
Make a date to attend a Microsoft Momentum conference once your SMB consulting practice can afford it!

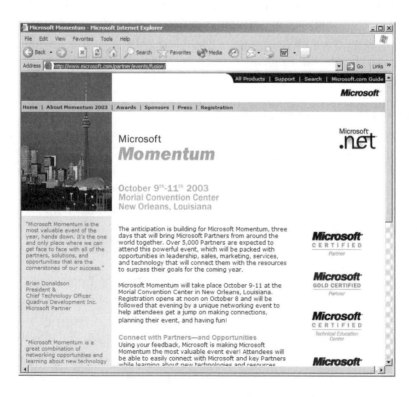

BEST PRACTICE: As of this writing, there is a cheap and effective way to attend the Microsoft Momentum conference and rub elbows with the other half. I've encouraged SMB consultants on a low budget to simply purchase the evening party tickets and partake in the partying. Historically these tickets have been $100 USD for the weekend compared to $1,500 USD for the entire conference. But the SMB consultants have been able to meet folks from numerous Microsoft marketing teams and get their fill of merriment. You can use other conferences for technical knowledge transfer!

Note that to purchase the party tickets, you typically need to have a bona fide conference attendee purchase them for you. Details. Details.

SMB Sales Alternatives

Time to think outside the box. We're all different and what works for Peter might not work for Paul. More importantly, as you will learn in Chapter 8, our professional personality types differ. Sales may come naturally for some and prove elusive for others. So this section looks at some sales alternatives that you might consider as an SMB consultant including telemarketing, mass mailings, SPAM and faxing.

Outsourced telemarketing

Perhaps you don't have what's called a telephone personality or you suffer from "phone fright" when faced with the prospect of making tons of cold calls. Perhaps your stockbroker buddy scared the wits out of you when he spoke of making 300 cold calls per day! Maybe you don't even use a telephone, restricting your communications to e-mail and instant messaging. Then the prospect of farming out the telemarketing function will hold high appeal.

When I worked for a Boston-based technology contracting firm called "1-800-NETWORK," the use of telemarketing was one of our marketing mainstays. But recognizing that technology types tend to be introverted, many offices farmed out this function to telemarketing firms. In the Seattle office, we retained "Janet" to work our call lists, which we purchased from some list brokers. Janet's mission was to generate warm leads we could follow up. I'd give the effort a passing grade on the whole, but recognize that these warm leads were consistently of lower quality than other methods suggested in this book, such as relationship selling.

Another firm that provides outsourced telemarketing services for SMB consultants is AllySMB (www.allysmb.com). I've met Scott Dow, its president, only once, so I can't speak to the effectiveness of its approach.

Of course, you don't need to outsource the telemarketing function at all. You can certainly do it yourself. It's simple. Pick up the telephone and start calling small and medium-sized businesses to offer your technology consulting services.

Mass mailings

Who would have thought I'd be writing that IBM is an SMB player? It's true. As mentioned earlier in the chapter, in the spring of 2002, IBM mailed over one million color postcards promoting SBS to North American customers. The card promoted IBM servers running the OEM SKU of SBS. A potential customer, upon receiving the card, would ring an 800 telephone number and be connected with an IBM server sales representative.

Back at the aforementioned 1-800-NETWORK, mass mailings were another sales and marketing mainstay. Experience showed that, while response rates were always in the single digits, a postcard had a longer life than you might imagine. For example, when a humorous postcard was mailed out, it often found itself being posted on the cork board in the employee kitchen. Many months hence, an inbound call generated by the postcard would occur. It was like manna falling from the heavens! The author is shown in a 1-800-NETWORK postcard (under its "Enterprise" trade name") in Figure 6-9 .

Notes:

Figure 6-9:
Tricky postcards probably will result in a greater number of customer impressions than "bland" cards.

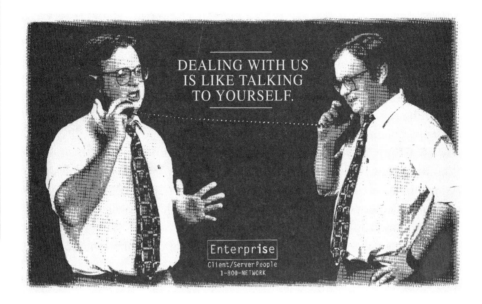

So go ahead and add the mass mailings arrow to your sales quiver. The point is to generate inbound customer calls. These inbound calls are somehow less threatening to many SMB consultants with some introverted traits. For the rest of us, it's a sales vehicle that, when it works, allows use to sit back and let the money roll in!

> BEST PRACTICE: In summer 2003, I ordered 5,000 four-color postcards to promote my September 2003 SMB Nation conference in Indianapolis, Indiana, USA. I did this after consulting with conference producers, who suggested a mass mailing to my target audience who lived within a day's drive of the conference site would be a good use of my marketing dollars. I was able to reuse the TIF art file that had been created for my CRN magazine advertisement (mentioned above in the display advertising section of this chapter) for the front of the postcard. For the back of the postcard, I wrote text about Leadership, Knowledge Transfer, and Celebration as

reasons to attend the SMB Nation event. What was surprising to me was how cheap the postcards were to order and have printed then shipped to me. The entire bill for the postcard product and shipping was $500! I used PrintForLess.com (www.printforless.com) and found the work to be of high quality and ready to go about a week AHEAD of schedule!!! Highly recommended if you need postcards.

Who knows? Maybe you should order up a bunch of postcards and use them secondarily as a brochure.

Spam

It makes the headlines daily and is proving to be one of the roadblocks to further success in implementing technology. I'm, of course, speaking of SPAM! As of this writing, Microsoft has filed law suits against 15 bulk e-mailers and the US Congress is entertaining legislation to make spam illegal. It's trench warfare and the battle lines are shifting daily.

The practical effect of spam is negative on the SMB consultant. Not only will it consume your own time managing your Inbox, but it overwhelms your clients as well. Selling your SMB consulting services via e-mail advertisements is likely to fail because such spam approaches generally backfire. Put yourself in your recipient's shoes. Would you want to receive a spam e-mail for SMB consulting services? What does that say about the SMB consultant?

The spam problem extends beyond advertising to other e-mail communications, such as electronic newsletters. I can speak from firsthand experience in publishing my free SMB newsletter (www.nethealthmon.com/newsletter.htm for more information) that the negative response to spam is hurting the effectiveness of my newsletter. In some cases, my newsletter is being blocked from readers by spam blockers. While I understand why that happens, it does prevent me from communicating with my readership in these cases. Take this experience into consideration if you launch a newsletter to communicate with clients and drive business to your SMB consulting practice.

> BEST PRACTICE: Spam is a strange beast and continually morphs itself to stay one step ahead of the good guys. Pop-up ads are a variation of spam being used to attract attention and sell low interest mortgages, etc. I hardly need to say that pop-up ads probably wouldn't benefit your SMB consulting sales efforts!

Fax blasting

This is something of an old-school approach, but back in the days when knights were bold and "spam" was a form of canned meat, business people relied on faxes. So did salespeople. One of the all-time great SMB consulting practices, the Center for Computer Resources (CCR) in Detroit, made its name and built its practice by sending out fax notices for a free "Network 101" seminar. This fax sales approach-announcing and then giving seminars-reeled in clients like fish, quickly exceeding 300 SBS installations!

Ironically, there is something of a budding neo-fax movement building in response to spam. Perhaps you've discovered that if you really want to reach someone, sending them a fax instead of an e-mail let's you rise above the spam "noise" in their Inbox.

> BEST PRACTICE: Be sure to inquire with the telephone company about fax sales campaigns. Some jurisdictions do not allow unsolicited faxes to be sent to recipients. That's because, believe it or not, there was a period of faxing abuse similar to spam today.

More Sales Tips

With the end of the chapter near, what follows is a bundle of little sales snippets that you can implement today to improve your success as an SMB consultant. Remember that a truly great salesperson does many small things well and not one big thing better than everyone else. That is, just repeat a series of small successful sales behaviors daily and don't look for the "big kill," and you'll be on your way to success.

Document footers

As an SMB consultant, you'll pick up sales tips and tricks along the road of life. Such is the case in this example, where I witnessed a fellow consultant I mention several times in this book (Vernon) adding his name, company name, and telephone number to his technology proposals as a document footer. This accomplished several things for Vernon. It, in effect, implied something of a copyright on his works, so if a proposal was circulated for "bid shopping" by unscrupulous prospects, the other firms being asked to bid against Vernon's proposal would smell a rat. But, on a more positive note, as Vernon's awesome proposal was circulated around the prospect's office, Vernon was imprinting his name in the minds of decision makers! And having his telephone number on each page certainly enhanced his accessibility. A tip of the hat to Vernon.

E-mail signatures

Run and check your Sent Mail folder in Outlook (then immediately return to this page!). Perhaps you have thousands of items in it, reflecting e-mails you've sent to other parties over time. Let's assume you're a prolific e-mailer and you've sent out 15,000 e-mails over the past year. Did you know, that in many cases, those e-mails offer a subliminal sales opportunity via your e-mail signature? Your e-mail signature, which should include your name, title, company name, contact information, and perhaps a business tag line ("We do SBS right!") is really an advertisement making an impression on the recipient! Take advantage of this sales "quick hitter" to improve your success as an SMB consultant.

Instant messaging

Sometimes you've got to use the tools available to you. As of this writing, instant messaging (IM) is still something of a business novelty in the SMB space. Ergo, it's an attention-getter and might make sense to use as a sales tool for prospects. I could see a situation where you'd "IM" (yes, it's both a noun and verb) a prospect, asking if she had read your SMB consulting proposal and had any questions. Don't overdue the IM thing and annoy potential clients, though.

Trade shows

There is always great debate over the value of trade shows. Renting booth space, preparing your booth, and traveling to the show can be very expensive. Large manufacturers and vendors see value in this because they can amortize some of these costs over many shows in several geographic regions. The SMB consultant typically doesn't have such advantages, because his business is much more localized. But what the heck-as your SMB consulting practice grows, go ahead and give it a try. Man a booth at a trade show and see what the response is. To be honest, it probably won't become a large part of your SMB consulting sales effort. Figure 6-9 displays the ITEC show series (www.goitec.com), which has an SMB focus.

Figure 6-10:
The regional ITEC trade show might be your avenue for testing a sales booth at a trade show.

BEST PRACTICE: I participated in the ITEC shows as a Microsoft vendor in the Gateway booth. Gateway invited some of its partners (known as Network Solution Providers) to stand in the booth as well. You might consider approaching a large vendor to see if possibly you can test the trade show waters by standing in their booth!

BEST PRACTICE: Please continue to monitor the SMB Nation Web site at www.smbnation.com. It's my intent, as the show's founder, to build a trade show element into the conference. Who knows? You might want to have a booth there someday.

Seminars and workshops

And again, what the heck, why not host a seminar or a workshop for business decision makers in the SMB space to drive business to you? Pick a compelling business technology topic, create a presentation, rent some space, run an ad in the local business paper to promote your event, and GO FOR IT!

In the past I've held such workshops directed at business decision makers and even charged for event attendance. One program, titled the "Executive MCSE," attracted business people who wanted to learn more Microsoft technologies. This event was patterned after the ever-popular local college course titled "Financial Analysis for Non-Financial Business People." So, not only was the workshop successful, but the $99 USD entry fee paid for my advertisement in the local paper. That's called "paid sales" and that's a good thing!

Telephone book advertising

Lots of discussion to be had here on the effectiveness of telephone book advertising. On the plus side, it can work very well when you resell and support a product such as Inuit's QuickBooks. On other hand, it can be very expensive and is ineffective if you sell a service that doesn't "translate" well into a small display advertisement. I frown upon telephone book advertising, because the clients it attracts tend to be bottom feeders. Hopefully, I present enough alternative sales and marketing approaches in the Finder section of this book that are cheaper and more effective in driving business to your SMB consulting practice!

Killer presentations

On occasion, you'll have the opportunity to make a sales presentation in front of a client. It's been said that in sales you get only one chance to make a great first impression. So your presentation needs to be effective. You should beg, borrow, and (yikes) steal existing PowerPoint presentations so you can cherry-pick the best and brightest slides when you create a slide deck. Truth be told, you don't even need to beg, borrow, or steal at all. Microsoft generously posts slide decks on its sites. In Figure 6-10, you can see the TS2 presentations that are available via the Downloads link at the TS2 site (www.msts2.com).

Figure 6-11:

The TS2 presentation decks are an excellent source of sales slides for your SMB consulting efforts.

Notes:

Another resource is a presentations newsletter I've read for several years. It offers lots of different news for presenters, including new equipment, presentation software, and tips and tricks. This newsletter, shown in Figure 6-11, can be subscribed to by visiting www.presentations.com.

Figure 6-12:
Industry Presentations allows you to track trends in delivering effective presentations.

Sales books

Time to hit the books (sales books that is). To supplement the sales and marketing wisdom I've imparted in the Finder section of this book, you should follow up by reading the following two texts.

- How to Master the Art of SELLING (Tom Hopkins, Warner Books, ISBN: 0-446-38636-7)

- Strategic Selling-The Unique Sales System Proven Successful by America's Best Companies (Robert Miller, Stephen Heiman, Warner Books, ISBN: 0-446-38627-8)

The book by Tom Hopkins is especially well done and he brings honor to the sales profession!

Brelsford's Mailbox

Hi,

I aspire to be a computer consultant. I read your book titled MCSE
Consulting Bible. The book is excellent in providing structured guidance to a
novice consultant. Although the author has elaborated several marketing
methods to launch the business, he hasn't mentioned anything about direct
marketing strategies, e.g,. cold calls or solicitation letters.

I'm wondering how direct marketing methods stand against indirect methods.
Also which one is more effective-cold calls or solicitation letters ?

I'd really appreciate your professional opinion on this matter. Thank you!

Regards,

Dan

Hi, Dan!

*Thanks for the e-mail and kind words. I've taken your advice to heart in
writing the SMB Consulting Best Practices book. This chapter addresses
many of your questions. Personally, I'm more comfortable with the written
word (the solicitation letter) versus the spoken word (cold calls). I think
receiving a heartfelt letter is less intrusive than an annoying telephone sales
call. Of course, you need to weigh my preferences against budget. Telephone
calls are essentially free and mailing letters costs money. But I'd recommend
you start with a solicitation letter and then follow up with a telephone call
(write that into your letter that you'll be calling in a week, etc.).*

Best of luck to you, mate!

Cheers...harrybbbbb

Summary

If you think this chapter took a while to read, just imagine how long it took to write. I've laid it all out on the line for you here in the sales department! I assume one of the main reasons you purchased a book such as this one was for meaningful and applicable sales advice. Hopefully, no sales stone was left unturned. The sales stones I turned over in this chapter include:

- Building on the definition of an SMB customer that started in the prior marketing chapter

- Honing in on effective sales tactics, such as selling SBS in five minutes

- The all-important sales method of overcoming objections

- Fortifying your SMB sales efforts with sales tools, including sales information from leading periodicals such as CRN

- Using the Microsoft Solution Selling approach to develop your own SMB selling paradigm

- Looking at bCentral's sales and marketing tools as a way for you to develop SMB consulting business activity

- Traditional sales approaches, such as advertising, mass mailings, telemarketing and fax blasting

- Looking to the countless free Microsoft sales resources

- The many end-of-the-chapter "one-minute" sales tips and tricks you can start implementing immediately, such as adding headers and footers to your documents with your name and telephone number

Chapter 7
Be the SMB Rainmaker

In This Chapter

- Creating and using good business development habits

- Building your book of business

- Being a discerning rainmaker is a good business development practice

- How to write a technology proposal, including effective scoping and defining work boundaries

- Making every client referable and referenceable

- Building skills to create client trust relationships

- Negotiating fairly with clients in order to consummate transactions

This chapter is all about being an esteemed rainmaker. A rainmaker is a vital cultural role that is present in every successful business, including SMB consulting firms. Granted, there might not be an official job title of "Rainmaker" in a company, but this critical role exists or else the company doesn't! Let's get started.

Good Business Development Habits

I've mentioned it once or twice along the way so far, and I'll mention it again. Being a great "finder" of business (aka "rainmaker") isn't about having one breakthrough marketing idea. It's about repeating relatively small sales and marketing "tasks" over and over again in a competent and consistent manner. That's it! End of chapter. Well, not quite, but you get the point.

Win-win

Back when knights were bold and Microsoft owned all the gold, there was a popular management theory espoused in the hallowed halls of MBA programs called "win-win." The phrase grew and grew to become part of our everyday nomenclature and that apple lost a tad of its polish along the way. But the underlying tenant of win-win is still applicable today as it will be tomorrow: an effective negotiation results in a business transaction that works for all parties involved. It's gotta be a win for the seller. It's gotta be a win for the buyer. It's gotta be a win for all of the stakeholders. In the absence of a win-win basis for your business transaction, the deal is likely to unravel. Later in this chapter, I'll go into more detail on this concept.

The win-win notion is also a long-term view of business development. The reason you are motivated to consummate transaction in which everyone wins is that you're in the SMB consulting game for the long haul. You're not the furniture salesman today who will be a hi-fi stereo salesman tomorrow. Long-term success can only be achieved from a win-win business development philosophy.

Fair zone

Another good business development habit is to operate within the fair zone. As seen in Figure 7-1, the fair zone is where business people and SMB technology consultants have a meeting of the minds. This is "agreement" and the hallmark of sound business development.

Notes:

Figure 7-1:

Finding the fair zone is something good rainmakers are conscious of in their business development approach.

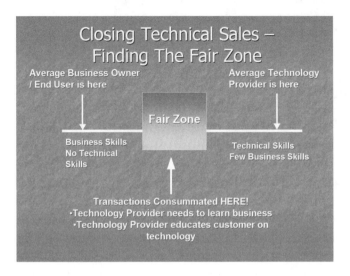

The point being made in this figure is that, in this day and age, you need to reach out as a technical professional and understand the business of your clients. I've heard this time and time again when I've traveled and presented my "MBA" talk to SMB consultants. Job one is to be more businesslike in both dealing with customers and in the management of your own firm (I discuss practice management matters in the Minder section of this book). Likewise, it's time for you to assert yourself as a confident SMB consultant and deliver a dose of tough love to your beloved client. Get them to stretch intellectually and tune in to the technology that you're implementing for them. To enter the "fair zone," you must have "business buy in" for the SMB solution you're selling

Pain charts

A great rainmaker will focus on the client's pain points. I share with you the Pain Chain methodology from the Microsoft "Go To Market" campaign in Spring 2003 in Figure 7-2.

Figure 7-2:
Microsoft's Organizational Pain Chain for Windows Server 2003.

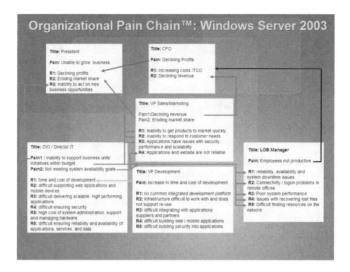

So what's really occurring here is that Microsoft has outlined a chart that relates business pain to technology solution. Here you are shown pain points confronted by business executives and managers. Your role as a superior rainmaker is to propose (often while thinking on your feet) how a technology-based solution can alleviate pain. For example, perhaps the firm in question here had focused on the line of business (LOB) manager's concern at employee productivity. Assume this firm is using Windows NT Server 4.0 and never upgraded to Windows 2000 Server. Today, your technology solution based on Windows Server 2003 could easily address this by providing much more stability than the old NT infrastructure days.

In another Microsoft slide-deck view of pain (Figure 7-3), I show you how folks think at different levels of the organization and what their worries are. I find the chart is accurate based on my experience in consulting to all levels of SMB organizations. However, I'd clarify the first entry: the role of the CEO and president. It's been my experience that the CEO in most companies is the chief salesman and visionary. The entries about investor's expectations, shareholder value, and the ability to exploit new business opportunities clearly relate to the CEO role. But the company president is typically more focused on day-to-day management issues in the same vein as the Chief

Operating Officer (COO). If I were in charge, I'd separate out the CEO and president roles, as they are truly different positions.

Figure 7-3:
This Key Player list from the Microsoft Go To Market campaign shows more pain points.

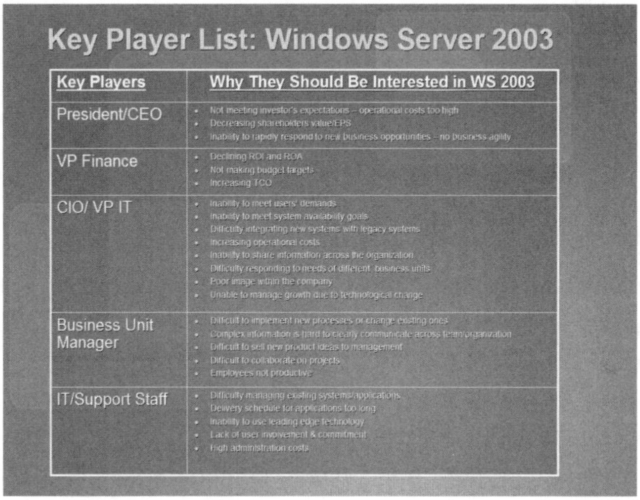

Key Player List: Windows Server 2003

Key Players	Why They Should Be Interested in WS 2003
President/CEO	• Not meeting investor's expectations – operational costs too high • Decreasing shareholders value/EPS • Inability to rapidly respond to new business opportunities – no business agility
VP Finance	• Declining ROI and ROA • Not making budget targets • Increasing TCO
CIO/ VP IT	• Inability to meet users' demands • Inability to meet system availability goals • Difficulty integrating new systems with legacy systems • Increasing operational costs • Inability to share information across the organization • Difficulty responding to needs of different business units • Poor image within the company • Unable to manage growth due to technological change
Business Unit Manager	• Difficult to implement new processes or change existing ones • Complex information is hard to clearly communicate across team/organization • Difficult to sell new product ideas to management • Difficult to collaborate on projects • Employees not productive
IT/Support Staff	• Difficulty managing existing systems/applications • Delivery schedule for applications too long • Inability to use leading edge technology • Lack of user involvement & commitment • High administration costs

BEST PRACTICE: There is a method to my madness in showing you the information above. It's my hope that you'll operate as part super-computer in your rainmaker efforts. You'll want to commit these charts to your memory. In the case of Figure 7-2, you'll be able to rapidly generate an organizational pain chart when you walk into a new client opportunity and scan the horizon. I'm also asking you to be part super-feeler and have an intuitive feel of who holds power in a company, who doesn't, and what the power holder's pain points are. It's been said great rainmakers can quickly determine who the key decision makers are in a company.

Make your client look good

A superior rainmaker will make those around him, especially clients, look good. This can come in the form of a well-timed compliment in a social situation. Or, more likely in SMB consulting, a technology infrastructure that the client's peer group finds impressive. When you engage in this process of making your client look good, you're "managing up," as the trendy business phrase says. While delivering a Microsoft Go To Market workshop in April 2003 in Omaha, I bumped into an article titled "The art of making others look good" that was actually a reprint from the *Philadelphia Inquirer*. This article summarized the Mercer Human Resource Consulting's 2002 survey of 2,600 working adults. Granted, this survey was about employees and their relationships with bosses, but a few key points listed here are applicable to consultant and clients.

- Communicating goals and objectives. When goals and objectives are clearly communicated, only 18 percent of employees were seeking to leave the situation. I suspect the same could be said for the relationship between consultant and client.

- Head, heart, hands. Management consultant Elizabeth Gibson is quoted about her "head, heart, and hands" managing up theory. It applies to consultant/client relations where the client is the boss. Her point is that different things are important to different people. Gibson says some are motivated by status, others by recognition, and yet others by the opportunity to be creative. A key point from Gibson is "…when we propose something to the boss, we are up against the way they thought about the situation before."

• Head—Looking and listening to the world through the boss's (client's) eyes. Understand his terrain, responsibilities, pressures.

• Heart. Answer the emotional question asked by the client of "what's in it for me" You need to appeal to a very basic Maslow's Hierarchy need here about what the client gets, both tangible and intangible, from having a consulting relationship with you.

• Hands.This reflects the actual behaviors of the client. The consultant must manage the behavioral outcomes of the client. An example might be to have the client not log on to the SBS server machine and perform tasks that the consultant ultimately has to clean up (and embarrasses the client in front of staff).

New work — Following the last consultant

A favorite business development best practice for the rainmaker is to come in second, not first, in the SMB consulting race. Second means you are following the first SMB consultant who has been shown the door unexpectedly. My favorite scenario is when — via word of mouth — I'm invited to an SMB client site following another consultant who was unsuccessful. After assessing that I can be more successful than the last consultant, which is always a legitimate concern, I arrive at the site and engage in problem discovery and start to perform my work.

In general, these follow-up situations are marked by technical-related clean-up activities that enable the client site to return to a functional state. More important, they allow you to be a customer service hero!

Building Your Book

If you ever have the chance to overhear old professional service providers, since put out to pasture, talk about their younger days, they'll inevitably speak about the trials and tribulations of building up their book of business. Doesn't matter if you're an insurance agent, attorney, or undertaker, the steps are the same. The book of business must be built from the ground up—or purchased from someone who built it from the ground up. I'm assuming you're not planning to purchase an existing SMB consulting practice with an established book of business (although that is a great way to grow quickly).

Try this hypothetical on for size. If you want to be a superior alpine ski racer, how might you go about it? Would you (a) ski on the modest slopes and be the king of the hill in front of a crowd or (b) try to hang with the advanced racers who are far better than you? Hopefully you would select option (b) above. Now, extend that thinking to becoming an SMB consulting rainmaker. Find someone who is successfully rainmaking and become their next best friend. Pull a trick right out of their business book and have them over for a Texas-style BBQ! Make them your mentor.

Contacts

Consider reading the article on Keith Ferrazzi, widely known as the man who needs two PalmPilots to keep track of all of his contacts. Keith was featured in the article "The 10 Secrets of a Master Networker" by Tahl Raz in the

January 2003 edition of *INC* magazine. As of this writing, you can find the article at: www.inc.com/magazine/20030101/25049.html and is shown in Figure 7-4.

Figure 7-4

This article on Keith Ferrazzi is must reading for the up-and-coming SMB consultant.

Notes:

Keith shared his ten rules for success as a master rainmaker in the article, as listed here in Table 7-1:

Table 7-1
Master Networking Rules

Rule	Description
Rule One: Don't network just to network.	Know what you want from networking. If you want to be a power broker, you don't get there by knowing a lot of mid-level managers.
Rule Two: Take names.	Keith constantly harvests names from articles and magazines, such as the Top 40 under 40 lists that business newspapers run in major metropolitan markets.
Rule Three: Build it before you need it.	Build your network before you need it. Keith tells the story of a "soft landing" as he left one company and sought other opportunities.
Rule Four: Never eat alone.	Enough said. Let's do lunch!
Rule Five: Be interesting.	Have stories to tell, secrets to share, and make yourself interesting to others.
Rule Six: Manage the gatekeeper. Artfully.	Learn to work effectively with the office manager.
Rule Seven: Always ask.	If you don't ask for it, you won't get it. Keith shares a story of his childhood break through because his father asked his boss if Keith could perform some work. Audacity is often the only thing that separates two men from their job titles.

Rule Eight: Don't keep score.	Not only get what you want but make sure the people important to you get what they want as well.
Rule Nine: Ping constantly.	My personal favorite. Keith quotes a Woody Allen phrase that 80 percent of success is just showing up.
Rule Ten: Find anchor tenants. Feed them.	Throw parties such as Texas BBQs and build your anchor tenants who attend these parties and attract others.

BEST PRACTICE: The article has a side bar you might find interesting on where to meet people. This includes political fund raisers, not-for-profit boards, and conferences. I discussed your potential to interact with political campaigns and not-for-profit organizations in Chapter 4 of this book. I discuss conferences in Chapter 9.

Business card scanning

You know the drill all to well. You go to a meeting, conference, or workshop and gather a bushel of business cards. You then promptly do nothing with the business cards you gather. Worse yet, months later you find this and other stacks of business cards and you can't remember *who* these people were much less *where* you got their business cards.

Enter my esteemed, blue-chip client Robert Wallace. Bob, one of my long-term SMB consulting clients in the Seattle area, is a real estate broker and syndicator from a long-time Seattle family. He is socially and political active in a lot of causes and organizations (too many to list here but including all the local major chamber of commerce organizations, etc.). His business card collection and his book of business is the envy of everyone in the Seattle real estate community. So how does he manage his newfound business friends and their business cards?

Bob uses the CardScan (www.cardscan.com) software application and the accompanying mini-scanning device. He sits there and feeds the new business cards through the scanner, verifies the optical character recognition (OCR) integrity of the card scan (this mean you occasionally correct the spelling of a name that didn't OCR correctly) and then save the contact records in Outlook. His real estate business has thrived in part because of his big business book of contacts. Your SMB consulting practice can do the same.

> BEST PRACTICE: Suppose you're too busy to diligently scan your business cards in CardScan and categorize them shortly after each business opportunity or gathering. Join the club. What I've done in the past is perform batch scans of cards at a fixed point in time (say once a month on a slow night). While the business card batch job waits to be processed, I simply keep the cards separated in letter-sized envelopes. In my case, the envelopes are labeled by city name: Dallas, San Jose, Denver, Omaha, etc. On the back of the business card, I write a comment about the card holder (e.g., "knows the Circuit City procurement process") to help me categorize my cards later on and allow for "data mining" of my rich contact list at a future date. Note I discuss data mining in the Grinder section of this book.

Notes:

The setup and use of CardScan is very easy. After scanning a business card, you will see results similar to Figure 7-5.

Figure 7-5
A contact record and business card displayed in CardScan.

Updating your Outlook Contact records with Plaxo

Another group of folks who have much motivation to manage their business cards and contacts well are news reporters, such as writers for the technology weekly rags and monthly magazines. One such individual, a very senior editor with Ziff-Davis (publishers of *PC Magazine*), recently e-mailed me and asked that I click on the link to update his Outlook Contact records via an application service provider (ASP) process on the Web called Plaxo.com. In the figures below, you can see how Plaxo.com is a tremendous business building tool. The idea is that you could periodically ping your contact list, have them complete a simple set of steps at Plaxo.com and you're Outlook Contact records will automatically be updated. Yee-haw! The only thing better than a ton of contacts is current contacts!

Notes:

Figure 7-6

Start with the Plaxo.com site to update your Outlook Contacts.

Figure 7-7

A notice will be received by your contact list members. They will complete the simple update process.

BEST PRACTICE: Yes, the Plaxo process does require your clients or customer contacts to take a moment and participate in updating their records. But it's been my practice not to encounter resistance in asking for this form of cooperation. Why? Customers and clients not only have an appreciation for your moxie, but it's in their interest to have their contact records current in your Outlook Contact list so everyone can get together and do good business.

Be a Discerning Rainmaker

There's a whole darker, sinister side of business development that I now need to introduce. It's called the legal department approach to becoming a rainmaker. I know that on the surface this sounds like an oxymoron along the lines of "military intelligence" and other well-worn one-liners. But hear me out on this one as I have firsthand experience with this approach and can appreciate what the cast of characters accomplished.

Enter my brother Jim stage right. An intellectual property lawyer with significant experience, Jim made the jump to a well-known Silicon Valley "dot-com" firm in the late 1990s after seeing his clients getting rich on stock options while he made a law partner's pittance (relatively speaking). In addition to his change of employers, he also changed careers from law to business development. And while Jim is an extrovert and well-spoken, being a salesman wasn't the first career change opportunity that came to my mind when I heard this.

But brother Jim explained it this way. While he had significant experience in the rainmaker role of "hunting and gathering" clients for his old law firm, he had even more experience at being a "deal killer" (which is how some people in business refer to attorneys). To Jim, being good at business development is finding all the reasons you shouldn't enter into a sales contract or a new client relationship. It's about being a discerning rainmaker who says "no" more often than "yes." It's about turning down more client leads than you accept as new clients. Others in the professional service realm have recast this argument as "the best engagement I ever had was the one I turned down." That's because a bad client will bring you down emotionally and deplete your energy. And a bad client is not only a distraction, but unprofitable. Be selective and earn Jim's respect!

Call it firing your client (see Chapter 4) revisited. There's the former CEO of Egghead Software who once spoke at an introductory management information system course I taught as an adjunct instructor at Central Washington University in the Seattle area. This CEO shocked the business students when he proclaimed he'd never fired an employee or client too soon. Rather, it was his weakness and that of his organization to keep bad fits too long. I tabled this "art of war" thinking for a few years until I was at a TechMentor conference in 2000 and met with a leading SMB consultant who had niched on SBS. He recast the Egghead CEO's philosophy that you should, once a year, drop a "class C" client or two from your consulting roster to clean house, allowing you to take on new clients. I consider this portfolio management function to fall under the purview of the rainmakers responsibilities. All's fair in love, war and SMB consulting.

Environmental Scanning

As SMB consultants age and mature, they start to become more strategic in their thinking. Terms like "the 50,000-foot level" and "in the long run" start to enter their business vocabulary. These people may be reading some of the higher-level business magazines I've mentioned on the pages of this book like *INC* and *Business Week*. Hell, a few of you Yankees might even read the high flouting *Harvard Business Review* (*HBR*). If you did read the *HBR* with any great regularity, you'd likely have encountered a business Zen term called "environmental scanning." This is an activity where you put on your big-thinker hat and "monitor" business news events that might impact your business and livelihood. I have three examples of environmental scanning for you to consider adding as arrows in your business development quiver.

> BEST PRACTICE: You know more than you think you do and you should fluff out your tail feathers. Those braineacks at Harvard don't know everything. Here's what I'm getting at with these in-flammatory statements. I had the great pleasure of having a one-hour meeting with an editor of the Harvard Business School Press in her Madison Avenue office in Manhattan a couple of years ago. I was introduced by a friend of a friend to secure this prime time appointment. In that meeting, I pitched her on the book you are reading as a combo MBA/MCSE type book oriented towards the SMB space. She graciously declined my proposal, citing the lack

of demand for such a combination text. Fast forward to the current time frame and, as you know, SMB is the hottest strategy within Microsoft today! It only proves that you might harbor an idea that has merits beyond the criticism that the so-called experts will level upon you. Always believe in yourself.

Who's who

An outstanding rainmaker knows that successful people like to do business with successful people. Thus if follows you should target your business development efforts towards the power elite of your community and ignore the laggards and losers. One way to identify the best and brightest achievers in your area is to conduct interlocking analysis. Follow these simple six steps.

1. Gather a list of the boards of directors and officers for public corporations, not-for-profit organizations (e.g., American Lung Association), service organizations (Rotary, chamber) for your area. You might limit yourself to just your local community or you might expand it out to include your entire state or region of nearby states. Note that your local library can be very helpful in providing these lists.
2. Create a simple data base in Microsoft Access or SQL Server. Create at least the following fields: Last name, First name, Organization, Title.
3. Enter each individual from each list you collected in Step #1 above.
4. Sort on last name.
5. Observe how many times certain names keep reappearing. In Seattle, the name I used in the chapter of Bob Wallace would appear several times as business owner, board member, community leader, etc., as evidenced by this analysis.
6. Find a way to meet these movers and shakers of your community. These power brokers should be one of your marketing targets for your SMB consulting practice.

Web page cycling

Something to consider each morning, as well as at the top of each business hour, is to cycle through a short list of Web pages as part of your environmental scanning efforts. I like to click through and quickly view the following Web pages to keep a pulse on the world:

- CRN (www.crn.com) for breaking news on SMB technology matters.

- MarketWatch (www.marketwatch.com) for breaking news in the world's financial markets.

- CNN (www.cnn.com) for breaking world news.

- *Seattle Times* (www.seattletimes.com) for breaking news in my local community. Substitute your local TV or newspaper Web site here.

I've even seen this form of environmental scanning extended to include a mounted TV in a business office with financial TV networks, such as CNBC or Bloomberg, playing continuously. These are the channels where the stock ticker trading information scrolls on the bottom of the screen, etc.

Directions on Microsoft

A final pillar in your environmental scanning efforts should be a subscription to the *Directions on Microsoft* newsletter (found at www.directionsonmicrosoft.com). Why? Because this newsletter complements your SMB consulting environmental scanning efforts in three ways.

Microsoft's SMB strategy

There is really no better way to track Microsoft's strategic SMB thinking than to peruse copies of *Directions on Microsoft*. The writing staff of this journal, many of them former Microsoft employees, has insights into internal Redmond thinking that other publications don't. More important, as you make big decisions about "going small" in the SMB sense, you need to hear all sides of the Microsoft story. Imagine if you missed some critical Microsoft communication, such as an emphasis being placed on a new SMB product. Such an omission could be costly.

Organizational chart

Perhaps even cooler than the newsletter is the organizational chart. This organization chart shows who's in and who's out at Microsoft. And given Microsoft is known for musical chairs in its management ranks, the organizational chart is invaluable if you want to monitor who the key stakeholders in SMB are.

How to do business with Microsoft

Some of the most popular topics for mail that I receive are "I've got this great idea I want to tell Microsoft about" or "How do I do business with Microsoft?" I always tell these kind folks to visit the Web site for *Directions on Microsoft* and educate themselves on the vendor advisory services. Not only does *Directions on Microsoft* offer exclusive content on how to do business with Microsoft, but the staff conducts a multi-day workshop on the same. It's my opinion that investing in the Direction on Microsoft package (newsletter, organizational chart, vendor advisory services) will dramatically shorten the line between point (a) you and point (b) Microsoft.

The *Directions on Microsoft* Web site is shown in Figure 7-8.

Figure 7-8:
A must read is this important newsletter and organization chart detailing on Microsoft itself at the Directions on Microsoft Web site.

BEST PRACTICE: If you're ever at Microsoft in Redmond and waiting in the lobby of a building to gain admission for a meeting or conference session, look on the top of the waiting room tables for an extra copy of *Directions on Microsoft*. Take a moment to thumb through it and see if it makes sense for you to subscribe. I bet you an SBS t-shirt that you'll do so! Each building on Microsoft's Redmond campus has a "lobby copy" of *Directions on Microsoft.* Just please don't steal it!

Another interesting newsletter to look for in a Microsoft building lobby is the internal *Microsoft News* daily journal. Microsoft has been liberal about posting these in public places and, if you have a chance to glance through an issue, you glean internal Microsoft SMB strategy. Apparently, they print all the news that's fit for public consumption or you wouldn't see this newsletter left in public places.

Writing Great Technology Proposals That WIN!

Consider the following. Were you the high school student that aced Honors English and professionally wrote papers for other students? And did you go on to pursue the MCSE certification program? And, finally, did you decide you wanted to be a consultant? If you answered three out of three in the affirmative, then this chapter is for you. This chapter will show you how to merge your technology prowess and writing skills to become a successful SMB consultant.

But even if you answered "yes" to none of these three questions, please read on. Why? Because if you don't feel that writing is your strong suit, then this chapter can provide you with the style elements you'll need for creating a winning proposal. In short, over the next several pages, I'll address what might be one of your weakest links as an SMB consultant: writing proposals. By the time you've reached the end of this chapter, and factored in a dose of real world experience, I'll just bet you can add "writing winning technology proposals" to the other skills you've already mastered in technology (e.g., like knowing how to write stored procedures in SQL Server).

Writing 101

People often ask authors what it's like to write a book. Some authors have been known to respond by handing the person a dictionary. "Here, take this," he'll intone seriously. "All the words in my book are in there. You just have to put them in the right order." Then the author punctuates this clever piece of wisdom with a doltish grin. Of course, writing a technology proposal is much more than just putting the words in order, which is a small part of the writing process. Many preparatory steps occur before you start tickling the ivories and that is the focus of this section. A little sage advice is a great place to start.

- **Just do it** — You basically have to launch Microsoft Word and start with Document1 (an untitled blank page). Hopefully, if you're properly prepared, the writing is easy.

BEST PRACTICE: Be sure to build your own collection of proposals stored as Word documents for use in generating future proposals. That way, after you create your first successful proposal, you don't have to look at the Document1 blank page described in the point above. See the next point on using preconfigured documents provided by Microsoft. I also share additional points on how to build a collection of other's proposals.

- **Just do it smarter** — You can visit Microsoft's document Template Gallery (http://officeupdate.microsoft.com/TemplateGallery/) for Office document templates to get started (Figure 7-9). Such document templates help guide you, help fight off that writer's block you feel, and make you more efficient. I list several applicable templates later in the section as "proposal starters."

Notes:

Figure 7-9:

You will find a rich collection of business forms at the Microsoft Template Gallery. This includes Microsoft project templates and other non-Office file types.

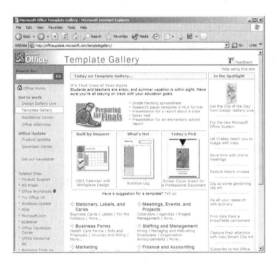

- **If you can't beat them, join them** — If you are soundly beaten time and time again at the SMB consulting proposal phase, a critical look in the mirror of self-assessment may be necessary. If the factors contributing to your failures are not your skill set or the fees you are charging, then perhaps your writing skills need some help. In this case, don't hesitate to ask a lost client what they liked about the winning proposal.

- **Best of breed** — Similar to the preceding point, start and maintain a file of competitors' proposals. You can then use these proposals as examples, selecting a format here, a well-worded paragraph there, and so on. Of course, I'm not suggesting that you break into you competitors' offices and photocopy their proposals, but rather that you ask for proposal copies from friendly competitors, mentors, and clients. This practice is used in many professional services environments, so you're not really breaking new ground here. You're just invoking the IBM mantra of "think" that really means "work smart."

- **Hire the best** — Manage your writing weakness and hire the best writer you can find. Many times, companies that provide typing services (typically located around college campuses) also provide excellent writing services.

- **Surf the net** — Search the Internet. You can also surf on your own using your favorite search engines such as Google, Yahoo!, Northern Light, Dogpile, and AltaVista to find technology proposals that have been advertently and inadvertently posted to the Web. Using Web-based search engines, you'll want to search on terms such as *proposal* and *technology*. The more focused your Web search query, the better chance you have of eliminating millions of worthless sites that contain the word *proposal*.

When searching the Web for technology proposal samples, I have some of the best resources to be government sites. Government entities are often subject to full disclosure laws, such as the Freedom of Information Act in the United States. Government sites, therefore, publish mass quantities of information, including request for proposals (RFPs) and winning technology proposals from incumbent private sector technology consulting firms that have been awarded government work.

SMB consulting framework

The SMB consulting proposal framework is shown in Figure 7-10 and outlines the start-to-finish process for generating a winning SMB consulting proposal. This is a conceptual framework that is your map and global positioning system to lead you to SMB consulting work.

Notes:

Figure 7-10:

Use the SMB consulting proposal framework to generate winning bids.

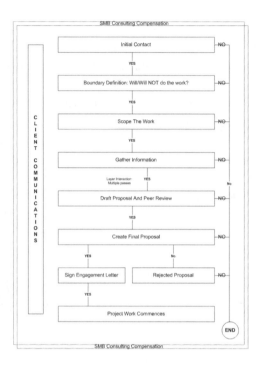

The first block is the initial client contact that results in an RFP from the client. Next you decide if the work outlined in the RFP is work you will perform. If yes, then continue to the third box down where you scope the work. The scoping activity is connected with the information-gathering stage (you will gather information to write the scope and use the scope to determine what additional information you need to gather). This results in the draft proposal that you review. Hopefully you have a chance to send this draft out for peer review among your fellow partners, co-workers, or friends to make sure the proposal is sound. The feedback you receive on the draft proposal will allow you to create the final proposal.

Finally, either the proposal is accepted by the client or not. If the proposal is accepted, you start the work. Note that the SMB consulting proposal framework displays lines to the "No" vertical line on the side. At any step, it's possible the proposal generation process might end. Perhaps you have decided that, quite frankly, the engagement you're pursuing just isn't for you. Salute!

> BEST PRACTICE: By now you're starting to get the message that communication is important in SMB consulting. This point has been and will be made in each chapter of this book. So it's no surprise that the other vertical box in the SMB consulting proposal framework is COMMUNICATION. An SMB consultant acting in an extroverted communicative mode will proactively schedule appointments with the potential client to see if he or she is on the right track. This valuable client feedback can be used to add value at each stage of the model and create a winning proposal. And that's the secret to success: client communication during the proposal stage. This level of communication is critical consulting behavior that will allow you to separate yourself from your competition.

> What I suggest really isn't that strange. Think about how a commercial real estate leasing agent consummates a lease transaction. The leasing agent will typically call the client every day to stay in touch, clarify a small point, etc.

Paid proposals

Another component of the SMB consulting proposal framework is to be compensated by the client for your proposal generation efforts. Granted, this is a tough argument for me to make in the SMB space. Compensation for creating proposals is an ambiguous area encountered by consultants of all types. However, public accounting firms typically view such proposals as part of a bill-for-everything perspective (and that perspective is one of the key ways you will make money as an SMB consultant).

> BEST PRACTICE: Getting paid for proposal generation will really work best at the medium-sized level or higher. It's unlikely that you'll truly be paid by the smallest of businesses to write technology consulting proposals. Say ye so spoken.

The idea behind that CPA perspective is that an hour worked that produces bona fide value-added results for a client should be compensated. Putting together a technology proposal that is well-scoped is often akin to writing a technology planning document (complete with needs analysis) that is of great value to the client. In the best-case scenario, such a technology proposal allows you to show how good you are at what you do and results in a winning proposal.

> BEST PRACTICE: Let's assume you draw a line in the sand and decide getting paid for proposal creation is critical to you. Then you may use the compensation issue for proposal writing to assess whether or not a client is a good fit for you. Chances are a medium-sized or larger client will understand the value of a well-scoped proposal and is gladly willing to pay for your services is a good client to have.

> And there might be variations on the "pay for proposal" thinking. Perhaps if you win, the hours spent writing the proposal are paid for by the client (and if you lose, the hours aren't paid for). Or conversely, you'll charge for the proposal writing work but forgive the amount if you're selected for the overall job.

Bid shopping is bad

Flip this discussion 180 degrees and look at the worst-case scenario: unscrupulous clients might take your technology bids and go bid shopping. It has happened to me, and quite frankly, you can't do much about it beyond picking your prospective clients better next time. One legal step you can take is to insert language in the cover letter accompanying your technology proposal indicating that "this proposal is submitted in confidence." You might also have document footer notices on each page of the proposal that says "Confidential" and lists your name and date. That way the client will think twice about photocopying it for distribution. You should never submit an electronic version of your technology proposal to the client, as this form would more easily allow the client to copy and paste your work into a RFP that could be bid shopped all around town. An exception to this might be a text document that was saved as an Adobe Acrobat Reader PDF file.

In a bid-shopping scenario where other technology consultants bid against your technology proposal, it's entirely likely you would lose the job because the other bidders, using your proposal information, could minimize the time spent bidding on the project, and allowing them to undercut your price. The other bidders may also point to the tasks you have listed and claim, "We can do that for a lot less" and "You don't need to do that step." Many clients are receptive to this message. Maybe it's in your best interests to let these clients go.

Bid shopping as a revenue opportunity

On a more positive note, you can institutionalize the bid-shopping process and get paid at the same time. If the client recognizes the value of receiving a well-written technology proposal from you, the SMB consultant, then such a proposal can become a for-hire work element. You scope the work and prepare a technology RPF/proposal for the client, for which you are a paid a reasonable amount of money, with by the hour or for a flat fee such as $500 (a fee I've pulled out of thin air for an example, but you get the point). This document then serves, of course, as the RFP on which you and other consultants submit bids. You've read correctly, it's possible that you may bid for work where you have created the RFP. I've seen it done several times and it is common in government bidding scenarios (local governments, school districts, etc.) where there is a "favorite consultant" who has the inside track and it's their job to lose.

Moving on, if you're bidding on your own RFP, you'll have several distinct advantages over the competition at this point:

- **Relationship foundation and continuation** — You have completely assessed the client's situation while preparing the technology proposal, and you can decide if you want to continue the consulting relationship. This is akin to job hunting as a temporary employee where you try before you buy. You go in, look around, prepare a technology proposal for which you are compensated, and then decide if you want to go any further with this client. The answer might end up being a resounding "no," because you've seen behind the curtain and discovered there's some serious dysfunction going on.

  BEST PRACTICE: Who would have thought I'd be writing a BEST PRACTICE that tells you how to lose a bid. One way to get out of a dysfunctional relationship such as the one described above is to bid the actual work at a high rate so you effectively lose by choice.

This allows everyone to save face in a situation that just isn't working out right.

- **Strong working relationship** — Working side by side with the client while preparing the work-for-hire technology proposal or RFP, you develop a working relationship that shouldn't be undervalued. In these scenarios where you divide the project up and are paid to develop the technology proposal, the client tends to develop a very trusting relationship with you. (I discuss trust relationships later in the chapter in more detail.) More often than not you'll be asked to evaluate the competing proposals because the client trusts you to work at arm's length and to represent her best interests by picking the best technology proposal for her business. Hopefully the best technology proposal for the client is also the best technology proposal for you (that is, your proposal is justified and selected).

Why would the client let you (the fox) guard the hen house? He does so not only because he trusts you for having developed the initial technology proposal used for RFP bidding purposes, but because you have the technical expertise to assess the fitness of the competing proposals. Typically the client hasn't the time, interest, or expertise to read the technology proposals that are returned.

Part of your being paid to write the initial technology proposal that was turned into an RFP is to purchase your independence in helping the client select the consultant who will perform the work. The planning work that generated the RFP may turn out to be the end of your engagement. The work from that point on may be awarded to another consultant. The good news is that under this business model, you won't be doing the planning work for free.

Further, when you're paid for writing a proposal and find yourself helping the client solicit other bids, you are a better SMB consultant for it. You can't help but become a better SMB consultant by seeing how your competitors are soliciting work, what their costs are, how they format a proposal, and so on. As long as you are party to this information in the capacity of serving the client, no one can fault you for becoming a better SMB consultant by what you hear and see.

- **Favorable perception of qualifications** — If you write the technology proposal that is used for the RFP, the client may have the perception that you know the project best. I liken this to an adjunct instructor's getting a tenure-track teaching job at a public university. This gives that instructor the inside track, meaning the tenure-track teaching position is his lose. The university must still run ads announcing the opening for a tenured professorship for equal employment purposes, but a favorite candidate for the job already exists, one who has been working with the school and the department offering the job. Your role in preparing the technology proposal used for the RFP gives you the inside track for being selected as the incumbent technology consultant. The job is yours to lose.

BEST PRACTICE: Call it winning by losing. Assuming you're awarded the work and acknowledged as the most qualified, don't overlook that the competing technology proposals can help you to deliver a better technology solution. Your competitors may well expose some weaknesses in your approach that can be corrected.

Building a paramount reputation

Your reputation in the technology community is important when you are paid by the client to write the technology proposal used as an RFP. If other consultants and vendors sense an insincere or less-than-competitive bidding situation, they won't bid because it isn't worth their time. This process must be aboveboard or you'll only attract bids from SMB consultants who are true bottom-dwellers. More important, your professional reputation in the SMB consulting community will suffer.

BEST PRACTICE: Walk in your competitors' shoes for a moment and consider the reverse situation. You are asked to bid on a technology project not only for which another technology consultant has prepared the RFP but also on which that same consultant is bidding. At a minimum, when you are bidding on technology engagements, ask the client who else is bidding and whether or not an existing technology consultant is bidding for the work. This might help you avoid committing a lot of bidding time to an engagement you are unlikely to win.

So the bottom line for this section is this: If you can develop client relationships where you get paid for your proposal generation efforts, consider yourself ahead of the game.

Defining boundaries

Part of the SMB consulting proposal framework is to know what work to pursue and accept and what work to avoid and from which to run. As an SMB consultant seeking to build your business, you will need to be part salesperson and part lawyer when it comes to the boundary definition area of business development. Boundary definition is about deciding what work you will perform (profitably) and what work you will reject. So what about being part salesperson and part lawyer in the business development realm? Here is what I mean. Lawyers look at business deals (such as technology consulting engagements) differently than commission salespeople often do. Many commission salespeople will sell into any deal that walks through the door. As presented earlier in my business development discussion, attorneys tend to scrutinize deals more closely and don't hesitate to recommend against those business arrangements that seem less than beneficial. You need to adopt both personas to be an effective SMB consultant in the boundary-definition area.

One way to face the challenge of deciding which technology engagements are acceptable is to know what and who you are and what and who you are not. That's called "boundary definition." It strikes at the core of how you present yourself as an SMB consultant— whether you're a specialist or a generalist and so on.

My point about boundary definition is simple. Don't be afraid to put on your lawyer-turned-business development professional hat introduced earlier to reject work that doesn't feel right. On the other hand, don't reject so much work that you starve.

Understand that defining boundaries is a dynamic process, not a static line in the sand. Your skill set changes, allowing you to consider more difficult, more challenging, and perhaps more rewarding technology assignments you previously might not have considered. Perhaps you've grown into a bona fide SMB consulting practice and added some fresh talent to your staff that allows you to bid for work you previously turned away from. Conversely, with your fingertips burned by stretching too far on the last SMB consulting engagement, you might retreat. These are all acceptable outcomes as you understand the shifting nature of defined boundaries.

Scoping the work

Scoping is the job of a pre-sales engineer. Pre-sales engineers typically put together the scope of work that allows a technology proposal to be generated. But to be honest, as an SMB consultant, you wear so many hats that adding the responsibility of pre-sales engineer shouldn't surprise you at all. Just part of another day's work as an SMB consultant.

In construction, scoping is performed by estimators. For example, in construction project management, scoping might be called "developing the work breakdown structure" (WBS). The WBS is used to create the project schedule. Specifications follow and are used to create construction blueprints.

Scoping is busywork performed by someone with sufficient technical knowledge to call around to get part numbers and pricing from hardware resellers and so on, to collect cost estimates from other services providers (Internet service providers, etc.), and to estimate the hours necessary to successfully complete each work area. Scoping is hard to teach someone and it's a baptism by fire learning experience.

Brelsford's Dozen: Scope a 12 percent fudge factor

All of your proposals should include at least 12 percent padding or inflated cost estimates to account for unknowns and mistakes. In actuality, this 12 percent value is pretty lean, because it doesn't take much of a mistake to cut through 12 percent padding. In your niche area of SMB consulting, you can probably get away with 12 percent padding. However, if you are bidding outside of your niche, consider 30 percent padding to cushion your lack of experience and to account for the unknowns and the unpredictable.

Gathering information

While the scoping discussed in the last section tends to have a quantitative bent to it, the information-gathering stage is typically more qualitative. This is more akin to high-level needs analysis, an art that has enjoyed resurgence in popularity due in large part to Microsoft's emphasis on Go To Market business-technology planning. Questions like "Tell me what your organization does" are being asked by the SMB consultant.

Experienced technology consultants will concur that the best way to gather information in an organization is to interview management, staff, and possibly suppliers and vendors, depending on the size of the technology project for which you're preparing a proposal. Adjust accordingly for SMB engagements where the planning dollars may be restricted by the client.

> BEST PRACTICE: When constructing a list of interview questions, work smart. Go to college libraries and thumb through books on systems analysis to gather interview questions to add to your list. A few hours of research can save many hours.

Creating the proposal

There are a number of ways to create the SMB consulting proposals you provide to clients in hopes of being awarded business. You can create a unique and custom proposal for each bidding situation. Or you can create a "form letter" style proposal in a word processing program like Microsoft Word. Here you would open the proposal document file and insert the date, client's name and address, and some limited customized information, such as pricing, and print it out. However, both of these approaches have some drawbacks. First, a customization approach for each bidding situation might clearly take too much of your administration time to effectively implement. The second approach with a form letter might be too robotic and make the customer feel that you haven't paid attention to her needs. However, I have found tools that strike the balance between customization, time savings, and a form letter. These are listed here:

Microsoft Template Gallery

The Microsoft Template Gallery was introduced earlier in Figure 7-9. If you select the Bids and Proposals from the Business Forms category, you will find 12 bid and proposal templates to help your proposal efforts, including:

- A cover letter for the cost quotation for a project.

- A memo outlining a proposed project.

- A reminder that the prices in this quotation are good for a limited time only.

- Final reminder: The terms and pricing on this quotation are guaranteed for only a few remaining days.

- I have outlined a different option on the following pages.

- Please let me know if you are still considering our quotation.

- Shown below are my recommendations and my brief proposal.

- The enclosed proposal outlines what we'll do and how successful we've been.

- This correspondence outlines the work you requested, including objectives, procedures, identification of responsibilities, and estimated fees.

- We propose to furnish the following goods for this project.

Microsoft Great Plains

As mentioned before, Great Plains is Microsoft's business accounting software solution (www.microsoft.com/greatplains). This group at Microsoft has its own partners who can take advantage of PartnerSource, a program that provides ready-made tools to generate proposals, increase sales, etc.

TechRepublic

This technology portal offers a disc-based "IT Consultant's Tool Kit" that provides 20+ templates for contracts, project planning, collection letters, and more. Details at www.techrepublic.com.

Google search

Search on key words such as "consulting proposal software" at Google and you'll see numerous hits for ISV proposal-building applications. One firm that appeared during my search, Advantage Consulting Inc. (www.acibiz.com), offered Proposal Development and Management Software.

Draft Version

So far this leads up to the first draft of the SMB consulting technology proposal. The major sections should be completed, and the draft should have an appearance similar to a filled-in proposal. But the first draft is not intended to be a final version of your technology proposal. Not only may your proposal contain grammatical errors (reflecting poorly on you), but mathematical errors may bedevil the cost estimates. Making math errors in an SMB consulting technology proposal can cost you real money.

Feedback

Nothing improves a technology proposal like getting feedback in time to revise the draft. Accordingly and as mentioned in passing earlier in this chapter, you will want to meet with your prospective client to review the draft proposal and solicit feedback. This is typically a session that allows you to express what you thought you heard from the prospective client and find out if your proposal reflects that understanding. Often you'll find small errors that need correction, and, hopefully, you'll have a satisfied prospective client who will be impressed with your work style.

Peer review

I've hinted at this earlier in the chapter, but allow me to expand on peer review. If you have this option available, you should consider submitting your draft technology proposal to peer and superior review. Peer review is having a fellow employee look over the draft of your technology consulting proposal to make suggestions and corrections. Even a lone ranger SMB consultant should have some type of peer review process, though this process could be as simple as e-mailing your draft proposal to a buddy.

If you are in a larger consulting organization, consider having a superior review your SMB consulting draft proposal. This review process is typically seen in two types of consulting practices — (a) consulting practices that have learned the hard way and made a mistake somewhere along the way (which is the basis for most rules and procedures in business) and (b) consulting firms that work on enterprise-level projects in an environment that requires such review. An example in the medium space might make more sense. If your firm is bidding on government contracts or military work, senior review of proposals is just a necessary step in the process. Sometimes the legal department or outside counsel even gets involved and lends another set of eyeballs to the proposal review process to make sure the firm isn't making commitments it can't even hope to honor.

Know your audience

As the SMB technology proposal writer, you bear the responsibility of knowing the audience for whom you are writing. It's considered rule one in writing. If you're working with dairy farmers in Wisconsin, your approach may be different than one you would employ for a big-city, fat-cat entrepreneur. You'll be the best judge in this qualitative area, but all proposals should be well-thought-out and professional with the end reader in mind.

Final Version

The technology proposal draft and subsequent corrections lead to a final copy, which you submit to the prospective client. A final technology proposal should be devoid of mistakes and professional in appearance. It should represent you in a competitive and competent way as you try to win the business of the client. Take a bow—getting a proposal the door can feel like moving a mountain.

> BEST PRACTICE: In many cases, the technology proposal is the first meaningful extended communication you will have with the prospective client. I've won many wonderful and lucrative consulting engagements not necessarily because I had a cheaper or better solution than my competitors had, but because the client responded more warmly to my well-written technology proposal and my verbal communication at each step of the process.

Bad proposals

Just as your proposal file should contain great proposals to model, it should also contain examples bad proposals to show you what to avoid. It's amazing what you see floating around the SMB consulting community. There are some real stinker proposals being written. My all-time favorite bad proposal was the Microsoft Small Business Server (SBS) 4.x proposal that scoped out the additional purchase of Windows NT Server 4.0 and Microsoft Proxy Server, apparently ignorant to the fact that SBS includes these two items as part of the bundled package, making the purchases of the additional software components unnecessary. I prevailed in that bidding situation simply because my proposal was factually correct.

You won't have to look far for similar bad proposal examples in your SMB consulting career. Let's face it. There are more bad proposals in the world than good. Hopefully, your days of committing such gaffes are behind you.

References and Referrals

If you're going to make it in the long run as an SMB consultant, you need to strive to make every customer a bona fide reference. If for some reason you're "hiding" clients because the client wouldn't give you a satisfactory reference, then that speaks volumes about the state of your client relationship: poor. Granted, there is a little academic theory behind this lofty goal, as your circumstances and situation will dictate whether all of your clients can truly be references. Rare are the times in my own SMB consulting practice where I would truly list all clients on a reference sheet. There's always a top-of-mind "I can't print" situation at one client or another that wouldn't make them the best reference of the day (ironically I typically return the client's good graces the next day when the printers work again). I continue the discussion on references near the end of this section, but now it's time to talk about the good stuff: referrals.

Time for some tough love. You can't afford to buy enough display ad space, yellow pages ads, or even skywriting airplane services to be a successful SMB consultant. Sure, you can certainly purchase these high-priced advertising avenues, but the cost will far exceed what you could reasonably expect to earn as an SMB consultant. I've seen it done countless times by my misguided competitors.

Your success as an SMB consultant will depend on the referrals you receive. A referral from a client is a vote of confidence and an "Atta boy" slack on the back. It's the best form of feedback you can hope to receive. Most SMB consultants in their formative years don't get as many referrals as they would like, so any referral shouldn't be taken lightly. It has been my experience that referrals are earned later rather than sooner in your SMB consulting career. Manage your expectation about the time it takes to get the referral food chain going and understand that success here demands commitment to being an SMB consultant for many years.

Brelsford's Dozen: Nine out of 12 new clients must be referrals

In the long run, nine out of 12 new clients (three-quarters) must be referrals or else you are facing an uphill battle to be truly profitable as an SMB consultant. "The long run" means different things to different people. Stock market day-traders view the long run as holding a stock overnight. Real estate investors view the long run as 30 years until a property is free and clear. For an SMB consultant, the definition of "the long run" lies somewhere between these two extremes. I've been an SMB consultant in the same market for over a decade and it's just in the past couple of years that I've actually had referrals coming in on e-mail, by voicemail, and through face-to-face conversations over lattés. You, too, will build your ability to gain referrals in your own time.

So just what tree do you shake to get all these inbound referrals to drop in your lap? Being a competent technical professional with great customer service skills is the first step. Look around right now and see if there's just one tiny thing you could do better. Have you answered that client's e-mail sitting in your Inbox? No? Then right here, right now, put this book down, double-click on the client's e-mail, and hit "Reply." I'm betting in less than ten minutes you can complete a customer service task that'll make your client feel good. Still sitting here? Go do it. The SMB consulting book will be here when you return.

> BEST PRACTICE: If you really want to impress your clients, call them up and ask how things are going since your last visit. Tell your client you just wanted to check in and make sure the fix you implemented is working as planned. Few people in the SMB consulting industry do this and you'll stand out in a very positive way.

A great way to boost the number of referrals you get is to look closely at the industries you are serving. Some industries and sectors of the economy lend themselves to being better referral sources than others. For example, excellent referrals are freely given in the not-for-profit sector, where the organizations keep in close contact with each other and are known to gossip! You might be serving the wrong type of business if you're seeking to grow by referrals and the businesses in that industry don't talk to each other via lunches, trade associations, etc. A friend of mine in the not-for-profit niche as a Chicago-based SMB consultant pointed out that many small businesses are so busy working 18-hour days that they literally don't talk to each other. His level of referrals and his success as an SMB consultant increased when he focused on the not-for-profit sector.

> BEST PRACTICE: Remember that these same referral sources in your various channels can turn against you if you disappoint any of them. Do a poor job at one not-for-profit organization and you can be blackballed from all the rest.

Don't forget I discussed a similar topic, the client rejection ratio that specifies how many leads you should reject as a healthy business best practice, in the early part of Chapter 4 of this book.

Small Business Server Partner Locator Tool

Another way to get referrals is via vendor reseller programs. For example, from time to time Microsoft implements bona fide referral programs, where referrals are actively pushed to solution providers and other Microsoft friends and partners. Microsoft provides a technology provider look-up page for its Certified Solution Providers. There is still a look-up tool for students seeking to take a course at a Certified Technical Education Center (CTEC). I once wrote a business book in the late 1990s where I commented that Microsoft hadn't really developed a credible locator tool for its SMB partners to receive referred business. But all changed on August 1, 2002, when Microsoft announced its Small Business Server 2000 Channel Services Rebate program, whereby technology providers (e.g., SMB consultants) could receive up to a $500 rebate for providing SBS services to new clients who had just purchased the underlying SBS product. The program had a few conditions, including a stipulation that the technology provider needed to attend a one-day SBS Hands-On Training Lab (HOT Lab) or pass a basic competency exam. If you passed the exam, you were included in the Small Business Server Partner Locator Tool, shown in Figure 7-11.

Notes:

Figure 7-11:

As of this writing, the SBS referral tool had over 6,000 SMB consultants worldwide.

Other Microsoft referrals

So how do you get other referrals from Microsoft? It's been my experience that you have to cultivate and develop personal relationships at your regional Microsoft sales office. Business at Microsoft is still done, at some level, with the people they know. Having contributed my expertise to the SBS team in the form of beta testing and joint development products to implement the SBS solution at real client sites, I've been rewarded with referrals directly from guys and gals in Redmond, Washington. By developing a rich relationship with your nearest Microsoft sales office and contributing specific expertise to the Microsoft cause, it's possible you'll benefit in a similar manner.

One Microsoft referral tool that is very SMB-specific is the bCentral Technology Consulting Directory that allows customers to search for an SMB consultant by location and product type. Shown in Figure 7-12, you can click over to it at http://directory.bcentral.com/ITConsultant/.

Figure 7-12:

Microsoft' bCentral technology consultant Web site is targeted right at the type of customers an SMB consultant would seek.

There still exists the "traditional" Microsoft Resource Directory (http://directory.microsoft.com/resourcedirectory/solutions.aspx) that allows a customer to search by language, region, solution, software, training, and hardware. The results will only return certified partners (compared to the SBS referral tool discussed above that will present non-certified partners to the customer).

As mentioned earlier in this chapter, the *Directions on Microsoft* (www.directionsonmicrosoft.com) newsletter is a great way to learn who's who at Microsoft and then proceed to develop business relationships.

Finally, a source of Microsoft referrals is their Great Plains partner group. Great Plains is the accounting package software vendor acquired by Microsoft a few years ago. If you are a Great Plains reseller in good standing, you will receive bona fide customer opportunities to follow up. You can tap into this good mojo by clicking over to www.microsoft.com/greatplains. I've seen this program in action and was always just a little jealous that the Great Plains consultants got warm leads referred to them. Great Plains has a quality control program where clients complete a post-project survey. Scoring poorly on this customer satisfaction survey results in a low or no lead flow of future referrals. It's a good program and surfaces a valid issue for SMB consultants to consider: whether or not you should take on an application-level line of business software product as part of your offering. If you do, I think it's a wise addition to your SMB consulting practice in this era of maturing infrastructures and so on.

> BEST PRACTICE: One important point should not be lost on you and thus will allow you to sleep better at night. Microsoft doesn't directly compete against its partners. This is a long-standing truism that isn't adhered to by major software vendors, including one in Islandia, New York, and a large database vendor in Redwood City, California. Let's give credit where credit is due. Microsoft supports its partners in a straightforward manner. This adds tremendous value to the Microsoft partner relationship.

Vendor referrals

Other vendors have referral programs that might complement your Microsoft-centric SMB consulting practice. For example, perhaps you want to look at Trend Micro and Veritas for their reseller/partner programs. Other third-party application vendors work this way (too many to list), so it's likely the product you're interested in has some form of consulting support program. I've even seen ISPs with partner programs where referrals are dished out for customers who sign up for Internet accounts.

Making every client referenceable and referable

So, how do you get the reference and referral food chain going? Start asking your existing clients for a reference letter. This might get them thinking about how you're doing; but more important, it'll get them thinking about helping you get business. In many cases, if you don't gently nudge your clients into a referral mindset early, they'll forget about you and your business-development needs. You can't blame them, as they've got their own business challenges to confront.

Another way to get the referral ball going in your SMB consulting practice is to give a referral. It's the old "you've got to give a referral to get a referral" theory. On occasion, I've been known to give referrals for "Bob," who works for the real estate services firm that I serve. Heck, one real estate leasing referral that I recently gave Bob was for one of my SMB consulting clients (a manufacturers representative) who was looking to move into larger and better office space. It's not lost on Bob that I've been buttering his bread, so he occasionally remembers to butter mine.

> BEST PRACTICE: Remember that you would never recommend someone you didn't feel was qualified, no matter what the reward.

Losing a reference and referral is costly

There is an old adage in business that an unhappy customer will tell ten of his friends about the negative experience. That was likely true in the days of Abraham Lincoln as well as today. There is nothing worse than a "reverse proxy" in rainmaking: someone who actively campaigns against your SMB consulting practice. Avoid it!

Building Trust Relationships

There are two trust relationships an SMB consultant needs to be concerned about. There is the Active Directory trust relationship better left to more advanced texts. And then there is the client trust relationship, which is central to the business development mission of the SMB rainmaker.

Sell trust, not bits

As for me, I'm in the business of selling trust, not bits. Hear me out on this. It's my belief that I want my clients to continue to use my SMB consulting services because they trust me and I'm their "go to guy." They trust me implicitly in the field of technology, regardless of the product release version. I don't sell the fact I know it all with products like SBS, but rather that they can count on me to go forth and get the right answer to solve a problem. Hopefully, they'd sell their first born son before getting rid of me. But seriously, I don't want to be tied to or branded by a specific product release cycle. I want my SMB client relationships to last longer than any one release cycle of a product or a brand. For example, I wouldn't have been thrilled about being called "BackOffice Brelsford" now that the BackOffice branding has gone away. You get the point.

> BEST PRACTICE: You'll know you've gained the trust of your clients when you enter the power circle, where you're bosom bud-

dies with the accountant and the attorney. These are the long-time trusted advisors of any small business owner. Welcome to the club!

I discuss accountants in the next section.

Exit barriers

An esteemed instructor that I've worked with on Microsoft's Go To Market campaign in early 2003 has a well-constructed and lengthy lecture about building up exit barriers so a client company isn't inclined to get rid of you. I'm not speaking about unscrupulous underhanded consulting behavior like withholding a password, but about providing invaluable services to the client. For example, by continually introducing bona fide solutions to your client, such as the Excel Data Analyzer tool for "business intelligence" analysis as a way to extend the SQL Server component in SBS and Excel in Microsoft Office, you're building exit barriers.

Additional work

Another customer service barometer that reflects on your trust relationship with your client is the area of additional work. If you're doing a great job as an SMB consultant, you may find yourself overwhelmed with opportunities to do additional work for existing clients. Clients give you additional work when they trust you. That is the bottom line. Receiving additional work is very advantageous (and profitable) to you, the SMB consultant, because it lets you:

- **Sell yourself to existing clients** — This is a case of familiarity breeding comfort. It's always easier to sell yourself to existing clients. Not only that, but it's easier for you to be successful, given you already know the client site, the computer system, and so on.

- **Market yourself in the most effective way possible** — Hour for hour, obtaining additional work from your existing clients is the most effective marketing program you'll ever launch. Think about that the next time you're stuffing direct mail envelopes to promote your practice.

- **Market yourself in the cheapest way possible** — Having an existing client walk up and say, "Harry, could you spend a few hours looking at this?" is much cheaper than purchasing display advertising or otherwise marketing to attract new clients.

Partnering

Another way to obtain referrals to grow your practice is to partner with other closely aligned professional services firms. In other words, it may be advantageous for you to partner with like-minded professionals where organizational synergy exists.

Partnering with accountants

CPA firms long interested in technology for their clients (especially technology that runs accounting systems) have sometimes aligned themselves with SMB consultants. It's a popular marriage, enabling accounting firms to provide a breadth of services to clients without having to build full-fledged technology consulting practices. More important, it's a practical marriage. The CPA firm protects its clients from other, larger CPA firms that have a full-fledged technology practice, and the MCSE consultant picks up client referrals. In fact, Microsoft touts the value-added provider (VAP)/accounting firm relationship as one of the smarter business decisions a VAP can make (the term "VAP" is interchangeable with the term "SMB consultant" for our purposes). A few years ago, when Microsoft had its Direct Access site in the Value-Added Forum, there was a story of a VAP who aligned with a CPA firm, doubled its revenue, and cut its marketing expense 35 percent in one year. Rumor had it this VAP, working alone, had billings in excess of $500,000 per year.

> BEST PRACTICE: I've found, after working in the technology consulting division of a CPA firm and now partnering with CPA firms, that the purse strings prevail when it's time to sign an engagement letter. Accountants and clients tend to have really long-term relationships, often exceeding ten years in length and even passing from one generation to another. The accountant becomes a trusted business advisor (when it comes to money, a fair amount of trust is necessary).
>
> The accountant also interacts with the top decision-makers at the client site: the owners and the chief financial officer (CFO). Not only does the buck stop here, but the accountant knows how many bucks are being stopped. To put it briefly, there are few business relationships stronger than the one between an accountant and a business owner. Understand that, and you'll do fine in the accountant/SMB consultant partnership.

Brelsford's Dozen: Partnerships!

If you thought Enron, with its financial wizardry and web of complex partnerships, was too much, consider this piece of advice: I suggest your rainmaking efforts might heavily focus on entering into and managing partnerships to drive your SMB consulting business. Could you imagine, over time, building up a dozen marketing relationship where you partner with different accounting firms? It's not beyond the realm of possibility and might just be the right fit for your marketing efforts.

Marketing to accountants

You need to become a trusted party to the accountant as part of your rainmaking practices involving accounting firms. An accountant is less impressed by stories of bleeding-edge beta releases than by the fact that you strive to make every client referenceable and referable. A promise that you'll call and provide the accountant with an update after each client visit (that is, those clients which he has referred to you) is solid marketing talk when you're dealing with an accountant.

As with any sound marketing effort, you should know your customer. Similarly, you should be familiar with the different designations within the accountant continuum.

The Certified Public Accountant (CPA) designation is analogous to the certification earned by an MCSE designation in technology consulting, with one minor difference. The CPA designation is required by law for public accountants, whereas the MCSE title is not required by law to be a technology consultant. There are accountants without the CPA designation working in-house in firms and government agencies, but not serving the public. These individuals have no public accounting responsibilities. There are other accounting designations, such as Certified Management Accountant (CMA), which won't be discussed here. Basically, technology professionals have their designations and accountants have theirs, and since professionals like working with professionals, technology professionals and CPAs can coexist just fine.

The services offered by accountants fall into a few distinct areas:

- **Accounting** — This includes financial statement preparation, setting up the chart of accounts in an accounting system all the way down to bookkeeping. Professionals who work in a true accounting function learn a great deal about the businesses they serve and may be your best resource for landing technology engagements as an SMB consultant.

- **Auditing** — This is a true public accounting function and involves testing the validity of a firm's financial reports, transactions, and systems. Every CPA must spend a certain amount of time in auditing, but most accounting professionals move on to other accounting areas.

- **Taxes** — It has been said that from January through April, every accountant in a public accounting firm is involved in the tax area. To some extent this is true. But tax season aside, there are specialized tax accountants who help wealthy individuals year round with tax advice and so on.

- **Specialized niches** — Many accountants specialize after gaining general experience. Specialized niches I've witnessed include estate planning, pre-IPO accounting services, divorce and litigation-related accounting, and so on.

- **Business advisory services** — Seasoned accountants with years of experience under their belts sometimes gravitate away from accounting and become general business advisors. These individuals provide business planning services and lead strategic planning seminars.

Another consideration when marketing to accountants is the size of the accounting firm you're partnering with. I've heard it said that large clients like large accounting firms and small clients like small accounting firms (and the lower bill rates). Because my primary SMB consulting niche is Small Business Server (SBS), I have partnered with smaller accounting firms (with small business clients) who can benefit from what I have to offer, and vice versa.

One additional consideration when marketing the "partnership" idea to accountants is the calendar. In the USA, there are at least two times per year you won't receive much attention from the accounting firm you've partnered with: the regular tax season and the mini-tax season in October, when firms file mid-year returns. If the accounting firm you've partnered with has a not-for-profit clientele, the month of June is busy when tax and accounting information is prepared for this area.

Doing business with accountants

So you're sold! You are going to partner with accounting firms to fill your SMB consulting book with referrals! Early on, you'll have to confront certain mechanical issues. For example, will you carry your business card — or theirs — to their clients?

Fee splitting

There is the question about charges to the client. Will the client receive multiple bills, including your bill for SMB consulting services? Most clients would probably agree that the fewer bills they have, the better. If the arrangement is to have the accounting firm you're partnered with handle the billing, you'll realistically need to do some fee splitting to compensate the accounting firm for its administration and collection activities.

This arrangement can be viewed from this perspective. As an SMB consultant, you really have two bill rates. You have your retail rate, which we'll say is $100/hour for our example. When you bill this rate, you've gone out and marketed, won over the client, performed the work, and handled the administration and collections. You also have your wholesale rate. Your wholesale charged to your accounting partner might be $70/hour. The account firm then bills you out for $125/hour. The difference is the amount contributed to the accounting firm's overhead and profit. I actually like the wholesale rate arrangement, as it allows me to let someone else handle the marketing, administration, and collections. When you step back and lucidly look at the difference between your retail and wholesale rate (and what the difference means practically), the bottom line is about the same, give or take a dollar or two per hour. Don't overlook the opportunity, under the right conditions, to bill at the wholesale rate.

Under any financial arrangement, bend over backwards to honor the fact that the accountant owns the client if the client was delivered via your accounting firm partnership. Watch the accountant's backside at the client site (i.e., pass on gossip you might hear about the accountant in a professional way). Be technologically conservative. Few accountants who partner with you will appreciate an aggressive, bleeding-edge SMB consulting attitude. Note in this context, "bleeding-edge" is a well-accepted phrase in the technology community (including SMB consultants) that refers to the propensity to implement newly released technologies that aren't debugged or stable. Many business people shy away from the latest technology releases, opting for more mature technology solutions.

Regulations

Be advised that you, as an SMB consultant, cannot and should not provide accounting advice. Likewise, you might ask your CPA buddies not to provide infrastructure advice. Since the fall of Arthur Anderson, a huge international accounting firm that had problems resulting from its client called Enron, the accounting industry has become more regulated. I don't claim to know the rules and regulations in this area, but there are restrictions on the type and amount of outside consulting that accounting firms providing auditing services can provide.

The bottom line

Accountants are bottom-line professionals with a focus on profits, a fact that is not only well-known and appreciated, but common to many business people and SMB consultants as well. And because of the regulatory nature of the accountant's job (such as auditing and taxation), accountants must be more conservative than other types of business professionals. More important, accountants, more so than other professionals I've observed, have very high standards of professionalism. So if you can partner and get referrals from an accountant, you're doing a great job with customer service!

> BEST PRACTICE: To better understand accountants and technology, as well as improve your stature in this unique role (bits and debits), consider learning more about an organization dedicated to technology in the accounting profession. This organization, Pencor LLC, previously hosted the "SuperConference," which brought together accounting firms that had their own technology

consulting practice or partnered with other technology consulting providers. I was fortunate enough to speak at the 2001 SuperConference in Chicago and truly enjoyed the experience. If SuperConference returns, please join in the fun. Visit www.pencorllc.com for more information.

Paying a Finder's Fee

The finder's fee issue has been a hot topic on the SMB consulting newsgroup at Yahoo! (join SmallBizIT "Small Business IT Consultants" at http://groups.yahoo.com/group/smallbizIT/?yguid=26422569). Some SMB consultants pay finder's fees for bona fide work opportunities presented herein; some do not. It's a simple as that, and the reasons are as varied the imagination. Some feel it's unbecoming and uncouth to pay such blood money. Others take the Al Davis approach to SMB consulting practice management and say "Just win, baby!" For those of you not familiar with Al Davis, he is the owner of the Oakland Raiders in the National Football League in the USA. He's got a lot of moxie and is known for doing what ever it takes to win. If Al Davis were an SMB consultant, I can assure you he'd pay finder's fees to get the business!

The Yahoo! SmallBizIT group is shown in Figure 7-13.

N otes:

Figure 7-13:

This is a forum for you to trade business practices with other SMB consultants.

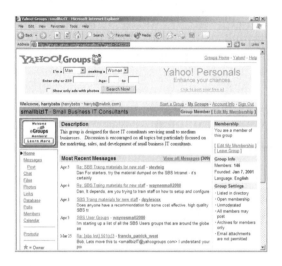

Brelsford's Dozen: Finder's Fee

When you consider the explicit and implicit cost to secure a client, it's surprisingly expensive (especially if you consider the time you devote to the sales process). So go ahead, try putting out the word that you'll pay a finder's fee for bona fide customers that are delivered "as advertised" and secured under an engagement letter. Tell the "finder" that you'll pay a 12 percent finder fee on the first 12 months of business. This should be fair, as the "finder" earns a commission that should be a source of motivation. And often, in SMB consulting, some of your best client billing opportunities occur within the first year of the relationship when the workload is highest.

Guerrillas and Cheese

There are many great business books that will be your logical next step after you complete this book. Two stand out as worthy of mention and are profiled in this section.

Guerrilla sales and marketing

There is a business book series based on guerrilla tactics (not gorilla tactics). The basic idea in the business guerrilla books is that sometimes you have to get wild and crazy to make things happen. Beyond the guerrilla books, there is a guerrilla conference series that further promotes the "guerrilla" approach. I attended a guerilla sales seminar where I found a combination of crowd exercises to warm up the audience, solid sales tactics, and marketing discussion delivered to eager students by a darn good instructor. Information on the guerrilla approach to business can be found at: www.guerrillabusiness.com and is shown in Figure 7-14.

Figure 7-14:
Consider guerrilla tactics in SMB consulting to get ahead.

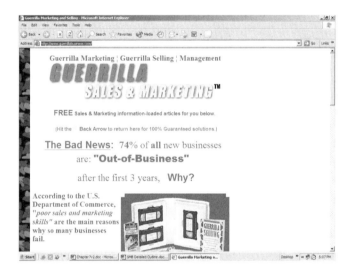

One guerrilla book in particular stood out for me: *Guerrilla Selling*, which *INC* magazine called one of the top ten business books of the 1990s. I agree. As proof, I cite a passage from the start of Chapter 7: The Need Stage, where the authors, Bill Gallagher and Orvel Ray Wilson, state:

"The objective of the Needs Stage is to verify, up-front, that your product or service matches, or is very close to matching, your prospect's wants or needs. If there isn't a match, the guerrilla asks for referrals and exits, saving everyone's time."

I couldn't have communicated this business best practice any better.

Who Moved My Cheese? thinking

Granted, the "cheese" thing, which is a national business phenomena based on the best-selling book *Who Moved My Cheese*, by Spencer Johnson, MD, deals more with organizational change than business development. But then I attended a Microsoft TS2 event where one of the themes was "Who moved my margin?" in SMB consulting! The point is that change and your ability to deal with it, whether the change is new technology or shifting margins, will affect your success as a rainmaker. Learn more about the "cheese" way at www.whomovedmycheese.com and add another arrow to your quiver. Figure 7-15 is your entry point into the cheese movement.

Figure 7-15:
This site features cheese updates and even information on cheese (not cheesy) seminars.

Brelsford's Dozen: Scanning contemporary texts

The next time you're traveling and you check in and clear security at the airport, spend some time (at least 12 minutes or more) and scan the business book section at the airport bookstore. I'd like you to discover at least a dozen contemporary business book titles that might help you develop your SMB consulting practice. No need to purchase all these books; you'll just get a handle on what current business best practices are being communicated, such as Guerrillas and Cheese!

Bottom Line:

Negotiating and Consummating Transactions

The exhilaration you feel when being awarded an SMB consulting technology engagement is wonderful, albeit quickly tempered when you need to sit down with the client and sign an engagement letter. An engagement letter is typically the contract between SMB consultant and client. You will find that it is one thing to win a bidding war with a superior technology consulting proposal, but it's an entirely different thing to get a signed engagement letter. The chasm can be wide.

In the leasing of commercial real estate and other business transaction environments, there is a phenomenon called signature fright. By all appearances, the client may have awarded you the SMB technology engagement, but the deal isn't done until the engagement letter is signed, sealed, and delivered. Clients sometimes back out of technology engagements when it comes time to sign the engagement letter for a number of reasons. Perhaps they had a traumatic childhood and their basic MO (shorthand for the Latin "modus operandi," which means "manner of working") is to avoid commitments. Maybe they have a newly developed case of buyer's remorse. Other clients who might balk at signing are the "conditioners." These clients—also known as "moving the yardsticks"—often change the terms of the consulting engagement right at the end and are hard to do business with.

Other points to consider while negotiating include the following (I realize these points are covered in more detail in other parts of the book, but the shoe fits to quickly repeat here):

- **Win-win situations** — Management texts abound espousing the need for win-win negotiations. In plain English, that means don't thump your clients so hard in the negotiation stages that they'll never do business with you again. Pursue long-term relationships, which require give and take.

- **No money, no problem** — Sometimes a potentially good client doesn't have the money. I've found that these clients are occasionally diamonds in the rough, so I work the deal to make it fit for everyone. For example, perhaps the client can pay for the majority of the work on the back end, so the engagement can be staged over a longer period to account for this.

- **Equity** — In today's dot-com business world, professional services providers, such as accountants for example, are taking equity in the form of stock instead of cash payments. Perhaps this strategy works for you, too.

- **Trades** — I'll occasionally provide services such as articles and book excerpts to publications in order to receive free ads to promote my consulting practice. The publication saves money, and I take advantage of another marketing avenue.

Being a Karass negotiator

So you're sitting on an airplane reading the in-flight magazine and you see a glossy two-page ad for a negotiating seminar series, the Karass System. This multi-day negotiating workshop is about getting what you want by negotiating, not because you deserve it. So 14 points to consider, from the Karass System, are:

1. You Pick the Best Place and Time to Negotiate.
2. What Is Our Next Choice If This Negotiation Breaks Down?
3. Be Stingy With Your Concessions and Leave Room to Negotiate.
4. If You Are a Buyer, Don't Give the Seller a Quick Counteroffer to the Asking Price.
5. Don't Say "Yes" Too Quickly.
6. Buyers Should Always Try to Get Cost Breakdowns. Sellers Should Not Give Them.
7. Don't Make the First Major Concession.
8. Watch Your Concessions as the Deadline Approaches—Big Mistakes Are Often Made Here.
9. Shut Up!
10. Be Skeptical. Things Are Not What They Appear to Be.
11. Stop Hoping for the Best: How Winners Become Losers.
12. Watch Out for Funny Money.
13. Do's and Don'ts If You Have to Compromise
14. Be a Super Winner: You Can Always Find the Better Deal for Both Parties.

Signing the engagement letter

It's the end of the process and it's time for the rainmaker to sign an engagement letter! You will recall that I highlighted the engagement letter in the prior chapter on sales in the section on the one-hour SMB sales effort. This time, the context is that all successful negotiations should result in a signed engagement letter allowing you to commence your SMB consulting work. That's the bottom line.

Brelsford's Mailbox

Hello Harry,

I have been reading one of your past consulting books, and it has been "awesome" so far. The only problem is that the proposal builder has been moved or removed. The Direct Access is now MS Partner. Were to go from there?

I currently work for a consulting firm, and I am responsible for the networking side of the house. Your book has been very enlightening for me, but, like other people, I have the "BLANK PAGE STARE." I need help with a proposal, or how to start one.

Can you point me in the right direction for starts? Thanks!

Bart
SBS Consultant

Hi, Bart!

Thanks for the e-mail and kind words. You are correct, sir! The Direct Access program changed and its proposal builder tool disappeared. Darn it! I hate it when things like that happen. Fortunately, in my SMB Consulting Best Practices book, I suggest several other tools to help build your technology proposals. In a nutshell, these include:

Microsoft Template Gallery at http://officeupdate.microsoft.com/ TemplateGallery.

Microsoft Great Plains (www.microsoft.com/greatplains)

TechRepublic at www.techrepublic.com has an IT Consulting Kit with proposal templates.

Search on Google and other search engines with keywords such as "technology proposal" and see what the cat brings home!

Cheers...harrybbbbb

Summary

This was an important chapter in your journey as an SMB consultant. Being a rainmaker is your long-term path to success as an SMB consultant. A large part of successful rainmaking comes from writing winning proposals, a skill just as important as your technical, sales, and management capabilities. If you can't hook the business at the technology proposal stage, and close it with an engagement letter in the negotiating stage, not much else matters as an SMB consultant. This chapter presented:

- Creating and using good business development habits

- Building your book of business

- Being a discerning rainmaker is a good business development practice

- How to write a technology proposal, including effective scoping and defining work boundaries

- Making every client referable and referenceable

- Building skills to create client trust relationships

- Negotiating fairly with clients in order to consummate transactions

Part Three
MINDER

Chapter Eight
CRM: Client Relationship Management

Chapter Nine
SMB Practice Management

Chapter Ten
Financial Management

Chapter 8
CRM: Client Relationship Management

In This Chapter

- Sharpening your human communication skills

- Engaging in effective project management

- Improving the management of ongoing engagements

- Managing your consulting practice effectively to better serve client

- Recognizing the importance of solid on-going client communications, including status meetings

And you thought this would be a chapter on the "bits" of CRM software, didn't you? Really, it's another "b"— the "business" of living and breathing strong and effective client relationship management in your SMB consulting practice. It all starts with basic communications, as the next section demonstrates.

Human Communications 101

Perhaps you skipped class the day your communications instructor in college gave the proverbial sender/receiver (S/R) model discussion. The basic premise with the S/R model is that a sender "sends" a message that is "received" by the receiver. The model becomes more complex when the receiver hears something different than the sender intended.

When you think about it, both human communications and modern computer networking are based on this basic S/R model. With human communications, typically one person speaks (sends a message) while the other person hears (receives a message). Now extend the S/R model to a computer network. A sending host sends a message (in the form of a packet) to a receiving host. The receiving host accepts the packet and typically replies with an acknowledgement packet. After processing the packet, it's common for the second host (the original receiving host) to send a packet of information back to the first host (which likely requested some information be returned as part of the communication sequence). In Figure 8-1, Network Monitor, a network sniffer tool introduced in Windows NT Server and included in Windows Server 2003 shows the S/R communication handshake.

Figure 8-1:
Packets 31 to 33 in the packet capture show the follow of communications from the initial send (S) packet to the final acknowledgement (A) packet.

This computer network procedure for communicating is very similar to how humans communicate between each other, taking turns to talk. Don't believe me? Let me use token ring networking as an example. Turn the clock back in time and look at how Native Americans managed communications with a talking stick. When you held the talking stick, you could talk and the others would listen. This is analogous to how hosts on a token ring network communicate. The host holding the token is allowed to communicate on the network.

BEST PRACTICE: Like human communications, the computer network can have incomplete communications, including packets dropped (the communication not being received by the receiver), or there might be excessive network noise. Computers deal with this malady by retrying communications until there is an acknowledgement that the communication was successfully received or the session is ultimately terminated via timeout. So what is the human translation? You should practice acknowledgements to confirm that you've correctly received a message. This is commonly done in two places of human communications: sailboat racing and marriage counseling. In sailboat racing, the crew acknowledges the skipper's command, such as "raising spinnaker." In marriage counseling, a distraught couple will, under the guidance of a trained counseling professional, engaged in dialog where the receiving party recites what they've just heard. And since a long-term solid client relationship is much like a marriage, maybe you can take something like this from the home front to the office.

I've emphasized communication skills as much as technical skills for defining the prototypical successful SMB consultant. I stand by that base argument now as before, because communication is the answer to my basic question as to why widely divergent salary ranges may exist for two comparable SMB consultants stuck side by side in traffic.

The first SMB consultant is making in excess of $100K US per year. The second SMB consultant is making $40K per year as a glorified break-fix technician. Both are experienced in the field and considered technically competent. But the first SMB consultant is driving a nice "ride," such as a late model luxury car, while the second, less successful SMB consultant is stuck in a clunker. It's about attaining different stations in life, a disparity often determined in part by a person's communication skills. In the example above, the first SMB consultant more than likely is superior in this area.

The first SMB consultant doesn't necessarily have a huge Harvard vocabulary or use more technical terminology. Rather, the first SMB consultant communicates clearly and consistently. This SMB consultant conveys both good and bad news to the client immediately, and the client can handle truths such as "You need a new server" or "I'll be an hour late to your site." Because this form of communicating is direct, the client receives the same message the consultant intended to send. That's the definition of effective communication and is your ticket to purchasing a great new car with your profits as an SMB consultant.

The second SMB consultant in my example is the one we've all seen or heard about. He walks in, performs the technical work, and leaves without telling anyone at the client site what work was accomplished, what the next steps in the process are, and so on. This client feels disenfranchised and disconnected. But, ultimately, it's this SMB consultant who is disconnected by the client and will feel economically disenfranchised as his peers move ahead financially in life.

Myers Briggs

An unusually effective personality test used in business is the Myers-Briggs Type Indicator. It's known as a tool to allow people to take a personality inventory to determine how they fit-or don't fit-in organizations. The belief is that leadership, change, and empowerment affect individual and interpersonal effectiveness, personal and professional development of intellectual capital, and bottom-line satisfaction. As of this writing, it's safe to say that millions of people have experienced some level of the Myers-Briggs Type Indicator® (MBTI®) globally. This intellectual capital tool, developed by Isabel Myers and Katherine Briggs, is based on the writings and insights of C.G. Jung, the Swiss psychiatrist and spiritualist, who studied people's behaviors and invited them to honor each other's differences. A key point about Myers-Briggs follows. Like any tool, its usefulness and accuracy depend greatly on the craftsman's creativity and innovation and his/her practical and common sense application both personally and professionally. It's not a form a medication that can be self-administered.

The MBTI® describes personality preference styles with four bi-polar scales that occur in daily interpersonal and intrapersonal interactions, both proactively and reactively.

- **Extrovert** and **Introvert** focus on our personal *Energy* level.

- **Sensate** and **Intuitive** are perceptions of *Information*.

- **Thinking** and **Feeling/Valuing** differentiate *Decision Making styles*.

- **Judging/Organized** and **Perceiving** manage daily *Life Style*.

One's personal preferences may vary as to strength and application. When you take the exam, you'll see that you can be strong in one area and weak in another. That's the real world and should sound familiar to the SMB consultant. Preferring one behavior listed below in Table 8-1 more than the other is similar to people preferring to be either right-handed or left-handed. Most people have both hands. People use both hands, but one is more effective, the other less. One is natural and habitual; the other takes more time and effort to accomplish similar tasks. The strong hand is the leader and the weak hand is the supporter.

Notes:

Table 8-1:
Eight Personality Preferences

Extroverts (E)	Introverts (I)
Talk Things Out	Think Things Internally
Actions and Stories	Ideas and Values
Energy = Outside Focus	Energy = Inside Focus
Speak to Think and Feel	Think and Feel to Speak
When Speaking-*not necessarily decided*	When Thinking-*not necessarily shared*
[Exaggerate & Repeat}	[Withhold & Contain]
Sensing (S)	**Intuition (N)**
Five Senses, Experience	"Sixth Sense," Options
Past and Present	Future and Present
Facts and Details	Big Picture and Patterns
Practicality	Innovation
Live Life and Let Live Now	Change and Rearrange Life in the Future
[Misses Big Picture]	[Misses Details]
Thinking (T)	**Feeling (F)**
Objective-Fair	Subjective-Supportive
Impersonal and Brief	Personal and Friendly
Analytical Truth, Principles, Competency	Human Values, Needs, Spirituality
Intellectual Criticism	Loyalty and Caring
Costs and Benefits	Value-Added
[Can Be Insensitive]	[Avoids Conflict]
Judging (J)	**Perceiving (P)**
Focus on Decisions	Focus on Information
Thinking-Feeling	Sensing-Intuition
Closure with Planning and Systems	Possibilities with Brainstorming
Finish Tasks-Closers	Begin Tasks-Starters
[Decide too soon]	[Inform too much]
[Right/Wrong]	[Procrastination]

MBTI® can be a great tool for the SMB consultant in several ways. You can use it to:

- Have yourself assessed to determine if you'd make a great SMB consultant

- Understand where your clients are coming from (strengths, weaknesses)

- Assist in the hiring of complementary coworkers who can effectively contribute to your SMB consulting practice

Generically, speaking, the MBTI® has practical applications for leadership and management within corporations, education, personal and career development, cultural understanding, research and spirituality. Further professional information about the MBTI® may be attained by contacting the Association for Psychological Type (APT) at www.aptcentral.org. or calling (847) 375-4717.

BEST PRACTICE: Perhaps some of the best hours I ever devoted to the "minder" management function of the SMB consultant were spent taking the MBTI®. I've done so on two occasions. First, I took the MBTI® several years ago when I was considering ways to improve my station in life as an SMB consultant working under the employ of a great regional accounting firm. The MBTI® told me that I was a better sole proprietor consultant than an employee and my effectiveness would be greater on my own. I promptly resigned, started my own SMB consulting practice, and moved to an island outside of Seattle. The next time I took it under similar circumstances when I wanted to take my growing SMB consulting practice to the next level. MBTI® confirmed that I needed to scan the horizon and create value with new ideas, such as the SMB Nation technology conference I've created.

You should run, not walk, and find a competent professional who can administer the MBTI® for you. It's one of the best investments you can make in your SMB consulting practice (beyond the price of this book of course!).

The body politic

Of course many of us become SMB consultants in order to escape the politics of the enterprise. But when more than two humans gather, politics are bound to occur. It's truly human nature. So you'll need to develop a political skill set to be successful as an SMB consultant in client situations. Perhaps your form of playing politics is to exchange morning pleasantries where you might not have done so in the past. It doesn't mean you need to be smooth as silk or as effusive as an elected official. You'll recall I discussed politics in the consulting game in the "not for profit" discussion in Chapter 4.

The Wall Street Journal, not especially known as a political journal, published an insightful article in March 2003 about thinking like clients do. This was in the context of management consulting. Not bad advice if you'd like to increase your profitability as an SMB consultant.

Brelsford's Dozen: Communications

Communicate with your clients frequently on a clear and consistent basis. For clients with whom you have an ongoing relationship, communicate every dozen business days. I selected this number as it fits with my style of checking in with my portfolio a couple of times per month. I've found that not adhering to this rule of communications results in the following outcomes:

- **Crises-based negative communications** — If you don't proactively communicate a couple of times per month with your active clients, the communication channel can take on a consistently negative tone. That is, the only time you communicate with your client is when there is a problem. Perhaps you've had those clients who call only when something is broken! This is not the firm foundation of communication you're seeking as an SMB consultant. I, for one, got tired of the "911" emergency mentality that can bedevil less experienced and less knowing consultants.

- **Manufactured information** — I've also found that if I don't proactively initiate communications a couple of times per month with my clients that, with the passage of time, clients will start to manufacture information, resulting in an unintentional fabrication. In order words, a lack of clear and consistent communications from you will create a void in the client communication model that will be filled by your clients. That sounds risky to me! I'll never forget a time when I was breaking my own rule and not being communicative with my client. Having not heard from me and having misinterpreted my parting comment one visit about performing surgery on a server, the business owner called one day to find out if I was out of the hospital yet. He had confused my surgery comments in his own mind and, when he didn't hear from me again, assumed I'd gone into the hospital. We enjoyed a good chuckle when we found out that information had been manufactured, but it sure illustrated the power of imaginary information. You should strive to prevent this with constant communication-because the outcome might not always be so humorous. In other words, if they don't hear anything from you about what you're doing and how their system is running, the client will interpret for himself how you and the system are performing. This is an EXTREMELY DANGEROUS WAY to operate, as most manufactured information is NEGATIVE (e.g., "That •@?#!$+% darn computer system isn't working again!")

By saying that you should communicate with clients a couple of times per month, I don't mean to suggest you need to sit at a telephone and "power call" for several hours straight. Mix it up. Some weeks call a few clients. Other weeks e-mail a note to different clients. The communications can often just be a quick: "How is it going?" I've found clients appreciate the gesture, and such behavior has resulted in additional work for me.

I discuss telephone calls and e-mails to clients near the end of this chapter.

Notes:

Project Management

A critical part of managing the SMB consulting engagement is project management. All SMB consulting engagements, whether ongoing or truly project-based, benefit from project management. This section defines project management by looking at specifications, which drive the creation of the work breakdown structure, which drives the project schedule. Got it? I'll spell it out in more detail.

Secrets of great project management

Being a good SMB project manager is more than writing reports and creating charts. There are a few secrets to successful project management that I'll share with you here.

Balancing time, budget, and quality

A good project manager tries to achieve high marks in three categories: time (staying on schedule), budget (coming in at the proposed cost), and quality (delivering what the client expects). The trick is to balance these three dimensions. And you guessed it. These three dimensions are often at odds with each other. In Figure 8-2, I show the project management triangle that depicts the legs of time, budget, and quality.

Figure 8-2:
Time, budget, and quality legs form a triangle in SMB consulting project management.

Crashing

The focus of project management is to get the work done successfully. Often you have to crash a project to achieve this goal. In the technology arena, in particular, crashing a project to reach completion is not uncommon. Crashing a project is done in several different ways:

- **Budget busters** — Assuming the critical element is a time deadline, a project management ploy is to throw money at a maligned project. This could involve hiring more laborers on a construction project or hiring more contractors (developers and so on) on a technology project. I've seen cases where the project manager doubled the size of the staff to get a project done on time.

- **Missed deadlines** — Another way to crash a project is to let the date slip, but stay on budget and at the same level of quality. This option is much less common in the world of project management, as the emphasis often is placed on meeting deadlines more than on meeting the requirements of any other category.

- **Cut feature sets** — A common project crashing approach in software development is not only to freeze the feature set, but also to cut features not critical to get the software shipped. You've unknowingly or unwittingly seen this in Microsoft solutions you've purchased. Cut features typically appear as a new feature in the next software release. How does this relate to general product management in the SMB consulting field? Often in the professional services area, the scope of the work is scaled back in order to crash the project. That is, the project is effectively made smaller by reducing the tasks that must be completed and the deliverables that are expected.

BEST PRACTICE: The law of crashing is this: You can trade off any leg of the project management triangle (time, budget, or quality) to crash the remaining two legs.

Backward pass

My favorite trick in project management is the backward pass. All too often when people sit down to create a project schedule, they work from left to right. That is, they start at time period zero and work toward the project deadline. This approach tends to create schedule creep as people add more time to tasks, extending the project to the right. This is a true luxury in project management and one that isn't a best practice for the SMB consultant.

A backward pass is project scheduling going from right (the end) to left (the start). You commence the project scheduling process with the final deadline and work your way left, determining what day you should start the project. But be advised that the backward pass tends to have an outcome that can be mildly upsetting to the SMB consultant: You should have started your project yesterday and you are already behind!

Showstoppers

The following is a short list of roadblocks that can result in the failure of your SMB consulting engagement. Be aware of showstoppers and be prepared to take corrective action as necessary.

- **Opinions from everyone.** Also known as the too many cooks in the kitchen. Leadership is necessary to prevent a project or engagement from being bogged down in a quagmire of unfocused work efforts.

- **Baseline project schedule rules.** Being too focused on a static project schedule that doesn't allow for the ebbs and flows of real-world timing adjustments can bog down an engagement. Stay flexible, as the last project schedule you print will look far different from the first project schedule (baseline) you create. It's natural for a project schedule to change during the course of a project, so go with the flow.

- **Delays caused by vendor and service providers.** You've done everything right on your end, but the telecommunications company is late getting the DSL service to your client site. Dependency on third-party services providers is an uncontrollable area of project management that can truly be a showstopper.

- **Can you just help me with....** This is the "Oh by the way..." method of a client adding work on to an engagement. Not only does the added work delay the project but it can result in billing disputes if your perform work outside the scope of your contractual engagement without client approval to do so.

- **Phase-skipping to save time and money.** You eliminate a critical phase to save either time or money (or both) on an engagement. But have you really accomplished anything if you haven't truly completed the project as intended. Nope!

• **Incompatibilities.** Since SMB consultants work primarily with technology, the likelihood that you'll discover incompatible hardware and software is entirely plausible. You must exercise great care in not letting software and hardware incompatibilities be an engagement showstopper.

• **Pirated software.** It's not in your best interest to perform work on an SMB consulting engagement with unlicensed software present at the client site. Why bother with the mess when there are plenty of honest consulting opportunities for you? And don't ever loan your software to a client with the understanding that the client will "order their own copies." They won't. Seen it too many times.

Specifications

Specifications are what define the work at a granular level. In construction, specifications are the quantities ordered, the length of wood cut, and so on. With technology, the specifications are the scope of work. Scoping was discussed Chapter 7 in the section on writing great proposals. A specification might contain the following Statement of Work (SOW):

"Develop a relational database system to drive business processes in the firm. Adequately train staff."

Notes:

Work breakdown structure

The work breakdown structure (WBS) is based on the information provided by the specifications. The WBS organizes work into manageable groups of tasks. The WBS is the way in which tasks are listed in a Gantt chart. A WBS looks like Table 8-2.

Table 8-2
Work Breakdown Structure

Task	Subtask	Description
1.0		**Start Small Business Server Implementation Project**
	1.10	Client engagement letter
	1.20	Determine client needs; purchase
	1.30	Assess current situation
	1.4	Inventory
	1.4.1	Inventory existing solutions
	1.4.2	Inventory existing hardware
	1.4.3	Inventory existing software
	1.5	Order necessary hardware and software (order SBS)
2.0		**Install SBS**
	2.1	Complete installation checklist with user names, etc.
	2.2	Configure server hardware
	2.3	Install SBS operating system and applications.
	2.4	Configure SBS via To Do List, Console, etc.
3.0		**Testing**
	3.1	Develop test plan
	3.2	Create model office and test SBS
4.0		**Deploy SBS to staff**

Project schedule

The outcome most identifiable with the practice of project management is the project schedule. The two types of project schedules are Gantt charts and critical path method (CPM) charts. In this section, both the Gantt and CPM charts are shown for the database development example started in the previous specification section and detailed in the WBS in Table 8-2. As mentioned once before, the WBS drives the project schedule, which is exactly what I'm doing with the SMB consulting example in this discussion. The list of tasks in the WBS must be assigned durations and resources. Set this information on a chart, and you have a project schedule.

Gantt

Gantt charts are basically horizontal bar charts that show activity against the y-axis of time. For example, a two-day task would be a horizontal bar that occupies two days of time. A Gantt chart is the easiest form of project schedule to interpret. However, a Gantt chart doesn't display the finer points, such as interdependencies between tasks, which might be something like a predecessor and successor relationship.

Critical path method

The project management diagram chart of connected boxes uses the critical path method (CPM). Task boxes are connected to each other by lines. The longest path through the project, measured by time, is the critical path. Tasks on the critical path have no slack time or room for slipping the schedule without affecting the entire project. While considered a more sophisticated form of project schedule than the Gantt, it's more difficult to read at a glance and requires some study. A CPM chart might also be considered overkill for SMB consulting engagements, which are typically simpler than enterprise engagements. And something that bewilders folks who view a CPM chart is that the length of the line doesn't correlate to the duration of a task. That is, the line used to connect tasks isn't speaking to how long something will take to complete. A short line doesn't imply a short task.

In the next section, you will develop a Gantt chart for a sample SMB consulting engagement.

Using Microsoft Project

SMB consultants will want to purchase the Microsoft Action Pack (details at www.microsoft.com/partner) so that you have a bona fide copy of Microsoft Project. You'll want to have basic familiarity with this application, but not necessarily mastery of Microsoft Project as it can be overkill for many SMB consulting engagements. Note that later in the book, I profile Microsoft Project again in it's client/server format as a possible consulting niche in SMB land (you could become a Microsoft Project consultant to engineering and architectural firms for example).

Defining Microsoft Project

As a program, Microsoft Project is relatively mature, exceeding ten years in age and evolving through numerous upgrades during that time. Microsoft Project was originally released as version 1.0 in 1990. At its heart, Microsoft Project is a resource-based project management system running on Microsoft desktop operating systems, such as Windows XP Pro (although the latest release has a variation on this as there is a server component available in the Microsoft Project family). It has the following features:

- **Calendar** — You may view task information set against a traditional 30-day calendar.

- **Gantt Chart** — This is the default view in Microsoft Project and shows tasks set against time.

- **Network Diagram** — This shows the critical path method project schedule view. Task boxes are connected by lines.

- **Task Usage** — This is a spread view of tasks. Tasks are listed in a table format similar to a WBS.

- **Tracking Gantt** — This is a modified view of the Gantt Chart to show percentage of completion on the list of tasks.

- **Resource Graph** — This view shows resource allocations in a histogram view. This is the chart where you learn you've assigned someone to work 80 hours per week for the next three months.

- **Resource Sheet** — This is a table view of the resources you have available. Resources are listed by type, such as people (by different labor classifications), machines, conference rooms/facilities, and so on.

- **Resource Usage** — This is a table view of how you've committed your resources.

- **Custom views, reports** — Microsoft Project is very strong in the customization area, especially with views and reporting.

BEST PRACTICE: Microsoft Project was designed to be used in the following fashion. First, you enter your resources, such as labor units (people) or machinery. You then enter tasks with durations and assign resources to the tasks. You proceed to manage the resources as much as the tasks themselves throughout the project so that no one resource becomes overburdened and the project can finish on time.

Installing Microsoft Project

You install Microsoft Project just like any other Microsoft application (insert the disc and let the autorun.inf file display the product setup screen). The Setup Wizard behaves similarly to that of other Microsoft products, where you click Next and accept the typical installation defaults. Because installing applications, especially Microsoft applications, is top of mind with folks, I've elected to forgo the step-by-step in this section.

BEST PRACTICE: Earlier I hinted that you can acquire Microsoft Project from the Microsoft Action Pack subscription. While that is true, you can also download a sample, time-bombed, full version of Microsoft Project 2000 from Microsoft's Project Web site at www.microsoft.com/project or install the sample version from the TechNet monthly subscription. This is a great way to try before you buy or, better yet, manage a one-time project that is 60 days or less in duration. If you don't yet own Microsoft Project and would like to complete the example below, then simply download and install the trial version prior to continuing.

Step-by-step Microsoft Project use

In this section, you will open a sample project template from Microsoft, open it and modify the tasks. The intent is to teach you good behavior on several fronts. I want you to go out to the Microsoft Web site and download a contemporary project schedule template. You then save time by modifying the template to meet your needs rather than creating a project schedule from scratch.

The intent of this step-by-step exercise was to show you how easy it is to manage your SMB consulting engagements with Microsoft Project. This is a very powerful project management tool that finds its greatest relevancy within medium-sized projects. Later I discuss other, more elementary project management tools that might make more sense for small-sized engagements.

1. At your workstation that is connected to the Internet, launch Internet Explorer and surf over to the following address: http://officeupdate.microsoft.com/templategallery/.

2. Select the **Project Management** link under the **Meetings, Events and Projects** category in the center of the screen (be advised this may change over time, so you might need to find the Project Management link).

3. Observe the numerous project templates listed on the Project Management page (see Figure 8-3). Select **Infrastructure deployment project plan**.

Figure 8-3:
Several project management templates are available for your use in the Microsoft Office template gallery.

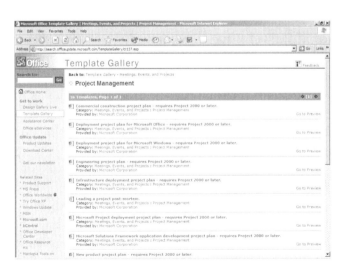

4. Observe the project schedule preview and click the **Edit in Microsoft Project** button.

5. Microsoft Project launches and displays the infrastructure template. You will now save the template to the file name **SMB Consulting Network Plan.mpp** from **File, Save**.

6. Modify the following tasks. You can delete a task by highlighting it and then selecting **Edit, Delete Task**. You can modify task duration by right-clicking a task and then selecting **Task Information**, followed by your adjustment to the **Duration** field on the **Resources** tab.

   • Delete Task #4: Secure project sponsorship

   • Delete Task #15: Review geographic factors

   • Delete Task #24: Identify mitigation of geographic factors

   • Change all task durations for tasks #3 to #32 to one hour each to reflect a realistic SMB environment.

BEST PRACTICE: To save time, you can delete multiple tasks at once by using the CTRL key to make multiple task selections. You can also do the same with the tasks when you change the duration to one hour.

7. Change the resources assigned on tasks #3 to #31 to SMB Consultant. This is accomplished by using the **CTRL** key to select all of the tasks and then select **Assign Resources** from the **Tools** menu. When the Assign Resource dialog box appears, type **SMB Consultant** in the **Resource Name** field. Then click **Assign**. If any other resources have a checkmark on the left, highlight the resource and click **Remove**. You have now assigned the SMB Consultant as the resource on these tasks. Click **Close**.

8. Change the timescale of the project schedule to have it reflect hours instead of days. Double-click on the project time scale (located to the right of the tasks) and the Timescale dialog box will appear. On the Top Tier tab, select **One tier (Middle)** in the **Show** field under **Timescale options**. In the Middle Tier tab, select **Hours** in the **Units** field under **Middle tier formatting**. Click **OK.**

9. Your completed SMB Consulting Network Plan should look similar
    to Figure 8-4.

Figure 8-4:

The result of completing this exercise and using Microsoft Project to manage your SMB consulting engagement.

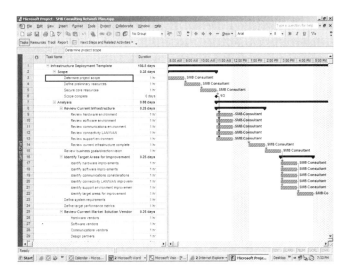

Sample templates

Above and beyond my step-by-step example above utilizing Microsoft Project, you have to give the Microsoft Project program managers credit. They have included sample templates on the Disc as timesavers for the SMB consultant. These templates are wonderful and should be on your short list of client management tools. However, these templates are dated as of the Microsoft Project product release date and aren't updated like the templates available from the Microsoft Web site (you should visit the Microsoft Project Web site for new and exciting templates). The existing project templates that shipped with the software are found from File, New, and General Templates.

> BEST PRACTICE: So you don't have time to go earn an MBA in project management, eh? And heck, you're so busy running your budding SMB consulting practice you can't even earn the project management certificates offered by different project management

associations. Fair enough. There is a shortcut. To learn more about project management, see the excellent online help system in Microsoft Project. It's a project management textbook.

Other Project Management Tools

To be honest, Microsoft Project can be overkill and too large for a typical SMB engagement. Therefore, you need to know about some other project management tools that might be of value to you. These include Microsoft Outlook, Visio, Windows Sharepoint Services, and the online service eProject.com.

Microsoft Outlook

In the keep-it-simple-stupid (KISS) school of project management, consider using Microsoft Outlook as your project scheduler until you out grow it for that function. Just enter tasks and appointments, as seen in Figure 8-5.

Figure 8-5:

An Outlook calendar, teamed with the tasks, can be an effective way to manage your SMB consulting engagement.

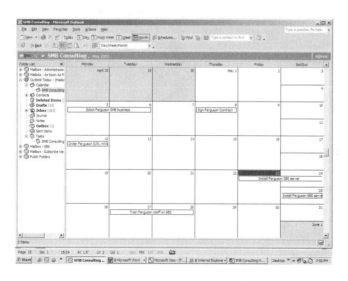

Visio

Another Microsoft product, Visio, has a project management template that is reasonably useful and receives high marks for presentation. I rate this product as slightly more sophisticated than Outlook and less sophisticated than Microsoft Project. In Figure 8-6, I display the project management templates available in Visio. Visio is also a great client relationship management tool for presenting information graphically. Remember that flow charts are very often used as a project management tool to communicate direction, progress, and accomplishments. In that sense, Visio is kinda an "MBA in a box" and deserves your full consideration. In the Grinder section of the book, I discuss using Visio as a tool to build your SMB consulting niche by delivering services such as IT as-built drawings.

Figure 8-6:
Use Visio as a project management tool and a communication tool to foster better SMB consulting client relations.

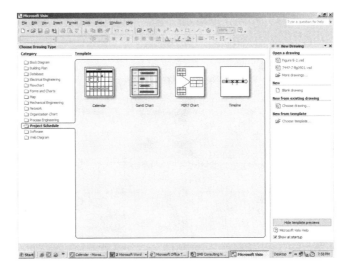

Notes:

Windows SharePoint Services

Some of you have probably asked "What ever happened to Outlook Team Folders?" And indeed Outlook Team Folders disappeared from the Microsoft Web site. But fear not, as the same concept and functionality has been reborn as Windows SharePoint Services. The idea here is that project groups can create a workspace to share documents, collaborate, and maintain a project-related Intranet site for communicating with team members. So the content of Windows SharePoint Services in this chapter is one of "eating your own dog food" or that you, the SMB consultant, should use this tool to better manage your own practice and projects.

Windows SharePoint Services ships natively with SBS 2003. It represents a great consulting platform for the delivery of customer solutions. This concept is further explored in the Grinder section of this book, where SharePoint technologies are highlighted. You can gain more information on Windows SharePoint Services at www.microsoft.com/sharepoint.

eProject

This is something of a dot-com survivor success story. eProject is a project management portal that has survived the crushing dot-gone downturn of the early 21st century. It's worth a look at www.eproject.com.

Notes:

CompTIA IT Project+

Late in the writing of this book, Certification Magazine reported that the Computer Technology Association (CompTIA), the vendor-neutral trade association that provides technology certifications (visit www.comptia.com), was upgrading its project management certification (see the article at www.certmag.com/articles/templates/cmag_nl_extra_content. asp?articleid =318&zoneid=37). Basically, outside of executive development programs at colleges or project management institutes (which often teach project management in a non-technical environment), CompTIA provides the only technology project management course of study and certification. It's a great way to learn about project management and then validate what you know via a certification exam. The exam reportedly has the following breakdown:

- IT project initiation and scope definition: 20 percent
- IT project planning: 30 percent
- IT project execution, control, and coordination: 43 percent
- IT project closure, acceptance, and support: 7 percent

To find out more about IT Project+ certification and the certification exam, go to www.comptia.org/certification/itproject.

> BEST PRACTICE: If you really want to go overboard in the project management area, consider a degree in project management. Yours truly got his MBA in "construction management," which was really "project management" by any other name, from the University of Denver more than a fortnight ago. In the Grinder section of the book, I again discuss project management in the context of this being a niche consulting area you might consider.

Managing Ongoing Engagements

"Son, you'll never make it in this business if you can't manage the work." So said a former managing partner at an accounting firm where I learned some of my early SMB consulting best practices. At the time, I figured this father figure was simply taking his son to the woodshed. But many years hence, his wisdom is much more appreciated. Consider the following Brelsford's Dozen.

Brelsford's Dozen: Analyze this!

Pop therapy meets SMB consulting reality. Consider that out of a dozen failed engagements (God forbid you never have so many failed engagements), you'll find the vast majority of engagements didn't fail for technical reasons, but rather because there was a communication breakdown with the client. If you're shown the door because of a "blue screen" on a misbehaved server, you were probably in trouble for months over poor communications. So, stand up and look at yourself in the mirror. Are you doing the best job you can to communicate with your clients currently? Can you improve your communication skills? Probably so. Read the next section on analyzing personality types and understanding where people are coming from.

Stated another way, may I propose for your consideration that an engagement is 12 times more likely to fail as a result of poor client communications rather than technical failure — a sobering thought when you think about it.

And analyze that!

Another take on the engagement management topic comes with assessing your own shortcomings, trips to the therapist's office included. Back when I worked for the consulting division of the accounting practice (mid- to late 1990s), the managing partner's advice about long-term success as a professional service provider (including SMB consultants) requiring great management skills was well-taken. I discovered that when it came to management tasks and roles, resistance is futile, and you'll either accept the management role with open arms or be dragged into it kicking and screaming. But if you want to last more than a fortnight as an SMB consultant, you've got to demonstrate at least basic engagement management skills.

On a more hopeful note, it's been said that of the three main areas of professional service delivery (and the broad outline of this book) — finder, minder, and grinder — that you can only master two out of three. Take your pick! Some people focus on management and technical services, leaving the marketing to others. Other folks like to get the work (finder) and then perform the tasks with little interest in management functions. It's okay to have strengths in two out of three key consulting areas, but you can't completely ignore any of the finder, minder, grinder functions as an SMB consultant.

Status Meetings

Some of us became SMB consultants in part to rebel against the enterprise organization. This might be our reaction to a bad case of meetingitis whereby we've sat in one too many mid-level management meetings. It's fine to have an aversion to meetings, but don't let that be an impediment in any way to solid client communications. This section outlines some communication best practices for you to employ.

Formal meetings

Engaging in formal meetings with clients is a fact of life in SMB consulting. You benefit from the face time and the dialog by facing your client from across the table. Typically the formal meetings allow you to review IT strategy, such as an upgrade or a Web site deployment project. I've also a found formal meeting to be a great trust-building exercise. You show up on time, groomed and dressed to the nines, to communicate with your client. Formal meetings are also a great way to introduce new players in the game. For example, I referred in my friend David, a Web master, to a client and the formal meeting served as the setting for the introduction.

Telephone calls

People often ask "How do you a grow from a one-man SMB consulting practice to a profitable, large consulting practice employing tens of technology consultants?" The answer is... telephone calls. And I'm not talking about playing the cold calling numbers game where you dial for dollars. Rather, I'm talking about a form of overcommunicating with your clients, which is a good thing. Imagine the following script, with you in the role of Saint Peter, the ultimate SMB consulting manager.

St. Peter Scenario

Saint Peter runs one of the most successful SMB consulting practices in all of Seattle. He's built his empire using two successful approaches. First, he is no longer "technical" and, ergo, doesn't work with computers on a day-to-day basis. Second, he spends his entire day receiving field reports from his employees and then making follow-up calls to his clients. Imagine the following scenario. Saint Peter SMB Consulting is engaged by a client to perform troubleshooting on an errant server machine. No one can easily identify what the exact malady is. Saint Peter's crew of SMB consultants undertakes the assignment and performs the typical troubleshooting steps, including modifying one variable at a time and testing the outcome. Saint Peter receives regular updates. Let's listen in on his client call on the third day in the next section to the client.

St. Peter Script

Saint Peter calls in as promised at exactly 11:00am with a client update. The client, Todd, is in a meeting and Saint Peter's call goes into voicemail:

"Hi,Todd, Saint Peter here, calling at 11am as promised. Listen, my guys are still working on the server problem and I really don't have much to report since my call to you yesterday morning. The latest hardware drivers didn't make a difference yesterday and neither did the reboot. Today the guys are going to try adding some additional software patches that might make a difference. They'll need to reboot as part of that process, so you might advise your staff there will be another reboot overnight. I'll call you again tomorrow, at 11 am with another update. Bye-bye."

St. Peter Postscript

So what really transpired in the above scenario? On the one hand, you could say that Saint Peter called, left a message saying his company billed a lot of time and nothing was accomplished. On the other hand, you could say Saint Peter engaged in superior client communication and the client, appreciating the technical efforts and being kept informed, will gladly pay Saint Peter's bill with no questions asked. Why? Because Saint Peter didn't let questions go unanswered with his daily client communications. And thus client concerns weren't allowed to fester. Clients dig this communication stuff. Saint Peter receives more than his fair share of blue chip referrals for new work and he has no trouble recruiting top talent. He is truly blessed.

Site status reports and invoices

Right here, right now, you can make an immediate positive adjustment to your your SMB consulting practice. Perform the following tasks: After completing work at a client site, take a spare moment while still on the clock to write a quick e-mail to your client. This is your site status report that informs the client of the work performed during your visit and encourages them to ask any questions while the assignment is still top of mind to both parties. What you want to avoid is having the client question your work a month hence when the invoice arrives and neither party can completely remember the assignment and the outcome. Better to take your lumps and write your billing report upfront rather then a month later at invoice time (when you've forgotten the work details).

Here is sample site status report from Burl Carr, an SMB consultant who works in my consulting practice:

Jeanette,

On Sunday evening I cleared the Exchange server queues of some 80+ rogue Non-Delivery Report (NDR) messages. On Monday evening I again cleared out a significant number of newly created NDRs. Today, with the assistance of Microsoft Product Support Services, I was able to identify the root causes of the problem and made some configuration changes to your Exchange server that should help in significantly reducing the amount of NDRs and dramatically increase the performance of the server, your network, and Internet access. I have sent Pat a message detailing the problems identified and the resolutions taken. I will be closely monitoring the server and the Exchange queues for the next few days.

For this work I am billing 3.75 hours at $100 per hour for a total of $375.

Thanks for your good business!

Burl Carr

> BEST PRACTICE: A key point to this section is that clients will gladly pay for your communication. That's why I suggested you take a few moments to write your client a note while still on the clock. I, and other peers in the SMB consulting industry, feel it's only fair that a minute worked is a minute billed. It's the key to success-and being a PROFITABLE SMB consultant-to get your clients to understand that they'll implicitly be paying for some of your management time, such as the communication function. You could always offer them the alternative to save money: not communicate with them!

SBS Server status reports

In "C" programming, this would be called a pointer. I want to point you to the Grinder section of this book where I discuss the SBS Server Status Reports and Health Monitoring as a consulting opportunity to provide real, on-going value to your clients. Briefly note here (and I repeat this info in Chapter 13), the idea is that you have your clients under some form of ongoing maintenance agreement where you provide daily server status monitoring with the SBS Server Status Reports. Not only do you glance at these reports each morning to eyeball the fitness of your client's system, but, more important, you hit "Reply" and communicate back to your client that all is well. The value here is the communication with the client on a daily basis, typically in a positive vein (maybe with a tad of humor like the phrase "TGIF!" in the return e-mail to humanize the communication). People who have heeded this advice and made the SBS Server Status Report part of their daily best practices have seen improved client relations, dramatically cut client portfolio turnover, and significantly increased referrals from existing clients. All good stuff.

Client Service

Technical types often cringe at the term "customer service." Such verbiage is usually followed by a load of marketing hype, which only takes you and me away from the server bench, right? Fair enough, as I've been there and tend to agree with you. My second point is that technical types aren't especially good at customer service in the Nordstrom school of customer service sense. We might prefer to arrive late to scheduled events as a form of technical rebellion, not return calls in a timely manner, let inbound e-mails fall into the void of the unanswered, etc. You get the point. Tech heads are technical and humanoids simply get in the way of a raging SBS blowout! For that reason I'll call this discussion area "client service" and see if we can't get off to a better start.

Perhaps poor client service has its place. Such thinking isn't necessary wrong if:

- You're a tenured faculty member in the technology area at a college.

- You're effectively tenured at your day job as an in-house, on-staff, irreplaceable technical guru.

- You are wealthy and play with your own server farm all day in your home lab at your waterfront estate. (That's when you're known as having "the hell with ya' money" in your life.)

- You're an introverted hot-shot programmer or database developer and people not only accept that in you, but gladly slip slices of pizza under your locked office door.

But for the rest of us, especially those of us who are, or are aspiring to become, SMB consultants, we must march to the beat of the client service drummer. That's because SMB consultants depend on clients for their livelihood. No doubt about it.

Client service isn't about being the corporate cheerleader. You know the type of annoying character I speak of. These are the chronically cheerful people, usually mid-level managers without technical skills sets, who overpopulate the hallways of large enterprises. It's corporate cheerleaders that drove many of us into SMB consulting in the first place. Rather, client service is about managing your clients expectations, not BS-ing them and generally being nonoffensive. (Okay be cheerful if you must!).

Here is a short list of client service attributes you should strive to live your SMB consulting life by. Please add on to it as you see fit.

- Managing the client's expectations about Microsoft technologies, such as Small Business Server.

- Meeting client needs in a timely manner. Clients like to know you're dependable and will come through.

- Clients trust what you say. Good client service is gaining the trust of your clients. They believe what you say.

- Performing as expected or better. You arrive at the client site, do your work, communicate what you did, and leave.

- Model of consistency. Clients like consistent behavior. From that view, it's actually okay to be ten minutes late (did I really say that?) if you're consistently ten minutes late. I speak from experience. More important, are your billings consistent with the billable time you said you would bill?

What you really want to avoid is the following and final definition of customer service, so kindly provided to me by a Microsoft Solution Provider consulting firm in deep decline. Tongue-in-check, one staff member shared with me that his firm no longer had any problems with their client service, but his competition did. His point was that his firm was losing customers in droves to its competition. Not only did they not have any "customer service" problems, ultimately their SMB consulting firm had no customers. That's not exactly the type of customer service I want to teach you.

The ultimate feedback loop

Whether you like it or not, you will get client feedback. So your goal as an SMB consultant is to make sure the client feedback is both honest and as positive as possible. False platitudes of "atta boy" are easily unmasked as just cheer and glee.

The feedback you receive is largely based on the level and quality of client service you provide. It's the ultimate feedback loop about whether you're making it as an SMB consultant. Superior client service is what will lead to referrals, a key point of this chapter. If you're delivering great service to your clients, the referrals will take care of themselves. Case closed.

> BEST PRACTICE: Here's one way to force client feedback that won't cost you any money. Simply walk into your client's office and ask "How am I doing?" Such proactivity is actually pretty darn impressive. And caught slightly off-balance, it can defuse consultant/client tension with the client. Often the client exhales a sigh of relief, and then proceeds to give you an earful (both good and bad).

Client surveys

Another no-cost way to not only garner client feedback, but engage in good old-fashioned customer service is to periodically survey your clients. If you work for yourself, you might simply send out an informal e-mail asking questions, not tipping your clients off to the fact that your conducting an official and scientific poll.

Consider sending a five- or ten-question survey form to the client contact at predetermined points of the engagement, say the 33 percent, 66 percent, and 100 percent milestones. Surveying the client at mid-point affords you the opportunity to make course corrections while you can still make a difference. Surveying the client at the end of the project allows you to see how you did and determine if this client will be either a referral source or at least a reference for you in the future.

It's critical the client survey process not be a shame. Let me share a quick case study with you to make my point. At a consulting firm I was with, a fellow consultant I'll call "Linda" was a chronic underbiller, in part because of her abruptness with clients. Instead of improving professionally, Linda elected to harass the overachievers and big billers in the practice, as if dragging them down would validate her own shortcomings as a consultant. Part of the ongoing ploy was to administer the survey process. Well, after a few surveys, a few of us on staff got a firsthand lesson in push-polling that politicians both commend and complain about. I noticed two survey delivery problems that invalidated the results. First, the way in which the questions were worded pushed the client into selecting a negative response. Second, the only clients surveyed were problem clients. Other staff members had similar or worse survey-related experiences, resulting in a de facto rejection of a very valuable process. It was very sad to witness. Promise me now you'll strive to avoid politicizing the polling process.

Improving Quality

So why the soapbox speech on client surveys? The bottom line is to improve quality. The cheapest route to financial success as an SMB consultant is to have a high-quality practice that is not only on autopilot, but has referrals fed to it.

Part of improving quality is having thick skin. Your first reaction to unsettling feedback is often fight or flight. But hang in there, as the feedback is, more often than not, sincere and on target. The good news is that you get used to client feedback over time. One reason is that some of the comments become familiar to you. ("Harry accommodates our business work schedule by coming in after hours.") Another reason is that you, knowingly or unknowingly, develop a large data set of responses to inherently compare any new responses to. It's your own form of filtering that allows you to determine whether a particular piece of feedback is in or out of bounds, given the feedback you've received over the years. Having such a reference point is refreshing on those particularly stormy days of SMB consulting.

Brelsford's Dozen: Client treatment

This proverb is simple to state. Treat your clients a dozen times better than you treat yourself, because an unhappy client will tell a dozen people about his unhappiness with you. Thus, it's in your interest to bend over backwards to have happy clients.

In the long run

On the whole, you'll be judged as an SMB consultant not for what you know but for the business relationships you build. Talk to management consultants who aren't necessarily practicing a technical craft, and you'll consistently hear the emphasis that's placed on strong consultant/client relationships.

The outcome of building successful relationships with your clients is trust. Trust worked for Abraham Lincoln over 150 years ago, and it still works today. Trust between a consultant and client will survive operating system releases, application versions, and anything else in the fast-changing world of technology.

Notes:

Brelsford's Mailbox

With a chapter focused on customer care and feeding, I couldn't resist reprinting Steve Ballmer's infamous "Connecting With Customers" e-mail which was sent out to countless Microsoft partners, consultants, et. al., on October 2, 2002. Here it is.

Connecting With Customers

Oct. 2, 2002

Steve Ballmer: I spend a lot of my time thinking about how Microsoft can do a better job of serving its customers. I'm convinced that we need to do more to establish and maintain broad connections with the millions of people who use our products and services around the world. We need to more thoroughly understand their needs, how they use technology, what they like about it, and what they don't. I'd like to share with you some of what we've recently begun to do and are planning for in the future to better connect with our customers.

First I should give you some context on why I am sending you this email. This is one in an occasional series of mails that Bill Gates and I, and periodically other Microsoft executives, will be sending to people who are interested in hearing from us about technology and public-policy issues that we believe are important to computer users, our industry, and everyone who cares about the future of high technology. This is part of our commitment to ensuring that Microsoft is more open about communicating who we are, what we believe in, and what we are trying to achieve.

If you would like to hear from us in the future, please click here (http://register.microsoft.com/subscription/subscribeMe.asp?lcid=1033&id=155). If you don't want to hear from us again, you needn't do anything. We will not send you another of these emails unless you choose to subscribe at the link above.

Software and Snack Food

In my career, I've worked at only one other place besides Microsoft. I marketed brownie mix and blueberry muffin mix for one of the largest consumer products companies. I'm glad I decided to join Microsoft 22 years ago, when it was a little software startup, but I have great admiration for successful consumer businesses, and I believe Microsoft can learn from them.

Behind the leading brands are companies that really know their customers. These firms devote a great deal of time and energy to gaining an intimate understanding of consumers, their reactions to every aspect of products, and how those products fit into their lives. Even so, not every new grocery or drug-store item succeeds. But by using the huge volume of data that feeds back from the daily purchase decisions of millions of consumers, marketers manage over time to figure out what consumers want in cake mix, soft drinks, shampoo, and so on. And these same products often go on satisfying consumers for decades.

Satisfying customers is what it's all about with technology products, too. And customers expect the same high quality and reliability in computing devices and software as they do in consumer products. But meeting their expectations is much harder, and not just because information technology is more complex and interdependent. The challenge has more to do with the flexibility of technology and its continual, rapid advance. To take advantage of this and expand what people can do with hardware and software, computer products must constantly evolve. As a result, products are seldom around long enough in one form to be fully time-tested, let alone perfected. And customers continually come up with new uses for their technology, new combinations and configurations that further complicate technology companies' efforts to ensure a satisfying experience, free of hiccups and glitches.

If technology products are to approach the satisfying consistency of consumer staples—and clearly they should-then we in the industry need a more detailed knowledge of customers' experiences with our products. We must do a better job of connecting with customers. For a company such as Microsoft, with many millions of customers around the world, the connections must be very broad. While we are working to deepen our relationships with enterprise and other business customers, we also need to make innumerable, daily connections with the very wide array of people who use our products-consumers, information workers, software developers and information technology professionals.

In the past year, we specifically identified some near-term objectives on the road to further product improvements and greater customer satisfaction. Among them:

- *Obtain much more feedback from our customers about their experience;*

- *Offer customers easier, more consistent ways to update their products;*

- *Provide customers with more effective, readily available support and service.*

We have a long way to go, but we're excited about the results so far from some of our recent efforts. I'd like to share just one great example, and then I'll tell you how you can learn more about what we're doing along these lines.

A New Pipeline for Customer Feedback

Let's acknowledge a sad truth about software: any code of significant scope and power will have bugs in it. Even a relatively simple software product today has millions of lines of code that provide many places for bugs to hide. That's why our customers still encounter bugs despite the rigorous and extensive stress testing and beta testing we do. With Windows 2000 and Windows XP, we dramatically improved the stability and reliability of our platform, and we eliminated many flaws, but we did not find all the bugs in these or other products. Nor did we find all the software conflicts that can cause applications to freeze up or otherwise fail to perform as expected.

The process of finding and fixing software problems has been hindered by a lack of reliable data on the precise nature of the problems customers encounter in the real world. Freeze-ups and crashes can be incredibly irritating, but rarely do customers contact technical support about them; instead, they close the program. Even when customers do call support and we resolve a problem, we often do not glean enough detail to trace its cause or prevent it from recurring.

To give us better feedback, a small team in our Office group built a system that helps us gather real-world data about the causes of customers' problems—in particular, about crashes. This system is now built into Office, Windows, and most of our other major products, including our forthcoming Windows .NET Servers. It enables customers to send us an error report, if they choose, whenever anything goes wrong.

There are risks in offering this option to have software "phone home" like E.T. One risk is that error reporting could compound a customer's irritation over the error itself. We therefore worked hard to make reporting simple and quick. We developed a special format, called a "minidump," to minimize the size of the report so that it can be transferred in a few seconds with a single mouse click.

Also, customers may wonder what we do with their reports and whether their privacy is protected. We use advanced security technologies to help protect these error reports, which are gathered on a cluster of dedicated Microsoft servers and are used for no other purpose than to find and fix bugs. Engineers look at stack details, some system information, a list of loaded modules, the type of exception, and global and local variables.

We've been amazed by the patterns revealed in the error reports that customers are sending us. The reports identify bugs not only in our own software, but in Windows-based applications from independent hardware and software vendors as well. One really exciting thing we learned is how, among all the software bugs involved in reports, a relatively small proportion causes most of the errors. About 20 percent of the bugs cause 80 percent of all errors, and-this is stunning to me-one percent of bugs cause half of all errors.

With this immensely valuable feedback from our customers, we're now able to prioritize debugging work on our products to achieve the biggest improvement in customers' experience. And as the work proceeds based on this new source of systematic data, the improvement will be dramatic. Already, in Windows XP Service Pack 1, error reporting enabled us to address 29 percent of errors involving the operating system and applications running on it, including a large number of third-party applications. Error reporting helped us to eliminate more than half of all Office XP errors with Office XP Service Pack 2.

Work continues to find and fix remaining bugs in these and other existing products, but error reporting is now also helping us to resolve more problems before new products are released. Visual Studio .NET, released last February, was one of our first products to benefit from the use of error-reporting data throughout its beta testing. Error reporting enabled us to log and fix 74 percent of all crashes reported in the first beta version. Many other problems were caught and eliminated in subsequent testing rounds.

And we're not keeping this great tool to ourselves. We're working with independent hardware and software vendors to help them use our error-reporting data to improve their products, too. Some 450 companies have accessed our database of error reports related to their drivers, utilities and applications. Marked decreases in some types of errors have followed. Those involving third-party firewall software, for example, have dropped 67 percent since the first of the year. Also, we've created software that enables corporations to redirect error reports to their own servers, so that administrators can find and resolve the problems that are having the most impact on their systems.

This Is Just the Beginning

We're working to make error reporting a much more supple tool that provides helpful information to customers while enabling us to improve their experience in new ways. As we understand more errors, we're adding an option for customers to go to a Web site where they can learn more about and even fix the errors they report. In the future we want to enable customers to look up the history of their error reports and our efforts to resolve them. And we're trying to create easy ways for customers to send us more nuanced feedback about their experience with our products-not only about crashes, but also about features that don't work the way or as easily as people would like.

Microsoft Error Reporting is just one of the ways in which we're trying to create broader customer connections. Another is through our software update and management services, which make it easy for customers to keep their software current. We're also making significant changes in our product service and support to enhance their value, and to speed the resolution of customer problems. Soon we will commit to a new policy that will give customers greater clarity and confidence about our support for products through their lifecycles.

There's much more I would like to share with you about these and other initiatives on behalf of customers, but I wanted to be (relatively) brief. If you would like to know more, you'll find information and links to help you drill down even further here.

Ultimately, we're trying to change how software developers do their jobs on a daily basis. We're working to establish more of a direct, interactive connection between developers and customers, leading to better software and happier customers. To get there, we intend to listen even more closely to our customers, consult with them regularly, and be more responsive. This is the message I am sending to all of Microsoft's employees, and it is my commitment to you.

Thanks for taking the time to read this.

Steve Ballmer

For information about Microsoft's privacy policies, please go to: http://www.microsoft.com/info/privacy.htm.

Summary

In this, perhaps one of the most important chapters in this book, you and I have discussed the importance of great client relationship management in the world of SMB consulting. This chapter started with a discussion of the sender/receiver communication model and ended with a school lesson on client service. Specifically, you read about:

- Communication fundamentals

- The role Myers Briggs tests play in assessing personalities

- What the key elements of project management are

- Using project management tools such as Microsoft Project, Outlook, and Visio

- How to effectively manage ongoing engagements

- Improving client relations via status meetings

- How to consistently deliver great client service

Chapter 9
SMB Practice Management

In This Chapter

- The "M" word explained: MANAGEMENT!

- Tips for managing organization workflow

- Best practices for managing staff

- Improving your organizational skill set(s) with training

- Human resource management tips

So perhaps you were the one, growing up, who thought business people were boring. You mocked the bald-headed businessman in your neighborhood, who was similar to the "organizational man" as portrayed in William H. Whyte, Jr.'s *The Organization Man* (published in the 1950s), who drove a sedan and wore a grey suit to his desk job every day. Well wake up. By the time you finish this chapter, you'll be a biznesssssman yourself, as members of the Russian Mafia like to say. You might be surprised at how much "organizational man" management techniques, albeit boring to perform, you must engage in.

Fact of the matter is, you might be surprised how much time the act of practice management will consume in your day as an SMB consultant. You've already learned that finding the work (in the Finder section) of this book consumes much more time than you probably anticipated. You're about to learn the same about management, and you're probably asking if there is any time left to actually perform that work (the Grinder section that concludes this book). Good for you if you're having these natural thoughts that afflict all of us SMB consultants! Being an SMB consultant can be both enormously time-consuming and extremely rewarding.

So let's get started on learning about effective SMB practice management.

Managing Workflow

Birds do it. Bees do it. Even your own SMB clients do it. And you'll do it: manage workflow. If you must conjure up images of cubicle characters pushing paper à la the popular *Dilbert* business comic strip, so be it. But effective management of the flow of SMB consulting operations is essential to your profitability.

Land, labor, and capital

In the classic economic viewpoint, as an SMB consulting practice owner, you'll be a baron of commerce and manage land, labor, and capital! Okay, maybe the land will be the leased office space from which you run your practice, you might be the only labor component, and the capital might initially come from your hard-earned savings. But darn it, you're in charge and running the show! You've got all the economic pieces in place. And I like the "land, labor, and capital" analogy to emphasize how many hats you'll wear as an SMB consultant!

Growth strategies and organizational structure

This section highlights a few ways to grow your practice and how the organizational structure might impact that.

One-man band

In keeping with that rousing "master of your own destiny" speech in the last section, most SMB consultants are one-man bands and are truly self-employed without staff. I base this professional opinion upon my interactions with many SMB consultants who aren't large consulting practices and have no desire to become large consulting practices! All too often, these SMB consultants are sole proprietors without the corporate shield to protect their assets.

The good news is that being a one-man band can be very profitable for the SMB consultant. Your operations are scaled to serve your clients without excessive overhead and the only payroll to meet is your own. It works very well.

Hiring staff to leverage up

But there is another side to the story. Many folks who truly become wealthy from running professional services firms, such as law firms and accounting firms, did it by hiring staff and "leveraging up." This is a proven business model that typically involves keystone pricing (a doubling of price over cost). For example, you hire the young attorney for the law firm at $50,000 per year and you bill him out at $100,000 per year. For some, scaling up to an SMB consulting practice with staff is desirable and profitable. Simply stated, it allows them to earn more with the productive labor of their staff.

This leveraging formula works well while you're able to deliver the business to keep the staff busy. But it also entails certain risks, including getting hit with "bench time." Bench time, a popular consulting industry euphemism, describes the coffer-draining practice of paying to have a staff on hand even though they have no work to perform. Another consideration is that you'll need to devote significant time to staff management. This is something you should expect to do, as most people need to be managed. Many people aren't especially good at management; personally, I've found it's not exactly my calling. Some people aren't willing to do this, seeing it as a big headache.

As you know, I've seeded this book with sections called "Brelsford's Dozen," which are little tidbits for success submitted for your consideration. But here's a "reverse Brelsford's Dozen" that an SMB consultant in Pittsburgh shared with me in the Spring of 2003. He said that he'd been there and done that with respect to running a large SMB consulting practice. He'd never been so miserable in his professional life. When he downsized his SMB consulting practice from 12 employees to one (himself), both his profitability and his attitude improved dramatically.

Organizational structure

Time for a primer on legal structures. This section will discuss sole proprietorships, partnerships, and corporations. Note I'll assume you conform to all legalities for your area, such as obtaining a business license, etc., as you read about these organizational forms.

Sole proprietorship

This is simple. Start with yourself, mix in a business license, add a few business cards, and voila! You're a sole proprietor SMB consultant. It's possible you're doing business under your own name, so clients write checks directly to you. Perhaps you use your own personal checking account. In fact, your checkbook may well be your accounting system. This is how most SMB consultants begin operations. This system may meet your needs only for a short while, or it may meet your needs over the long-run.

Partnership

Now envision two or more SMB consultants, a partnership agreement, a business license, and business cards, and bingo! You have a partnership! While many different types of partnerships exist, most are forged by SMB consultants who have grown beyond the sole proprietorship stage. It is common to see SMB consultants form a partnership together after they've been working side-by-side on common projects and the clients are tired of receiving two separate bills from two, separate, sole proprietor SMB consultants.

Notes:

BEST PRACTICE: If you elect to conduct your business as a sole proprietorship or a partnership, remember you don't have some economic and legal protections that a corporation have (explained below). And even if you're incorporated, the following tip will still apply to you. RUN OUT AND PURCHASE PROFESSIONAL LIABILITY INSURANCE RIGHT NOW! You can't afford to function without it, as you're placing your net worth at risk. One site where you can learn more about professional liability insurance is www.techinsurance.com. This is shown below in Figure 9-1.

Figure 9-1:

Start your research on professional liability insurance on the Web to find the best policy for you.

Corporation

Another viable business organization, which comes in different shapes and sizes, is the corporation. Here you have SMB consultants working together but seeking the corporate shield of limited liability to protect their assets. Running a corporation is more complex than other organizational forms. There are reporting requirements, especially if you are a public corporation (you will then need to file numerous reports with securities regulators). There are more administrative tasks, such as the issuance of corporate stock certificates and the procurement of a corporate seal. There are increased communication requirements for corporations, as certain forms of information must be shared with shareholders and the public (if it is a public corporation). Complete all that and you've got a multi-headed beast called a corporation.

> BEST PRACTICE: Understand that all of my discussion about organizational structures needs to be followed up with a visit to the business attorney of your choice. A business attorney is best qualified to advise you on what organizational structure will suit your situation.

Management tips

In this world, there is no shortage of business people willing to give you free advice. Typically such advice is worth exactly what you paid for it: nothing. Part of your maturation process as an SMB consulting practice manager will be your ability to separate the good advice from the bad advice. Better yet, you'll want to develop your own management "dos and don'ts" based on your own experiences. It's something that managers do and haughty MBA texts call "developing your own management philosophy."

Having said that, here's one piece of free advice that could save you some headaches: Don't grow too rapidly. This is an easy trap to fall into, given an SMB consultant's natural enthusiasm to do more, take on more work, and so on. In your SMB practice, assuming you are competent and do good work that is appreciated by your clients, you're more likely to set yourself up to fail from growing too quickly rather than from not growing fast enough.

Perhaps you've seen this with other consulting practices in your area. A couple of technology practitioners get hot in the marketplace soon after launching their practice. Late nights and a flurry of activity follow, with maybe even a few hurried hires along the way. This upward slope of activity continues unimpeded for a while. Then an implosion occurs. The consultants miss deadlines because they took on too much work. Client dissatisfaction grows. New business dries up and existing contracts mature, strangling cash flow. And as that famous American radio pioneer Paul Harvey says, "…you now know the rest of the story."

BEST PRACTICE: There is a financial side to the rapid growth equation. That relates to the old MBA in finance maximum of going broke while making money (I discuss financial matters in more detail in Chapter 10). Essentially your growing so fast that your accounts receivables get out in front of your cash flow. That is, your payroll comes faster than your payments from your clients. More later.

Brelsford's Dozen: Daily limits

Taking a page right from the airlines and railroads labor agreements, I want you to consider imposing a daily limit on your business activities. That limit is a maximum of 12 hours per day. Let me explain.

Airline pilots and railroad engineers have daily work limits in order to insure the safety of passengers. A fatigued pilot is a dangerous pilot. The same can be said for SMB consultants who overwork themselves and "get stupid" out on a client site. I've done it and perhaps you've done it as well! Granted, it's one thing to have an especially long day on a "911" emergency call and work the hours of a gifted surgeon. That's not my primary concern. It's about working too many long days in a row where the cumulative fatigue not only causes you to think unclearly but to burn out on being an SMB consultant. Too many back-to-back days, weeks, months, years of outrageously long work days will drive you from this line of work, which would be unfortunate.

Now exactly how do you measure 12 hours? Clearly I'm not talking about 12 billable hours. That's because, as you'll learn in the next chapter, a solid SMB consultant has a 50 percent utilization rate and 12 billable hours would translate into a 24 hour work day. Ouch! Rather, I'm talking about a maximum of 12 hours per day away from other activities, such as family and fun (although, of course, SMB consulting is fun). Translation: Count your drive time, telephone time, think time, and so on and you'll quickly hit 12 hours in a busy work day. Then I'm asking you to back off and not even do this too often. Ideally you're billing four to five hours per day and working, in aggregate, eight to 10 hours.

Time management

A few workflow mistakes I've seen committed time and time again (including by yours truly), concerns time management. The most grievous sin is the failure to record quarter hour increments, such as telephone calls with clients. Over the course of a year, this clearly adds up to a lot of billable time. When I looked at my time entries in detail once, it added up to over 100 hours per year, which is a full 10 percent of my annual goal of 1,000 billable hours!

> BEST PRACTICE: Bill to the quarter hour as a general rule in running your practice. This allows you to accurately capture the time and effort consumed by short client calls. It also has the effect of training your clients to think twice before calling you with a simple question (such as printing an envelope in Word). As an SMB consultant, you're striving for exciting and value-added work and typically want to deemphasize application-level help desk duties. A quarter hour minimum billing time slice will help filter out unwanted telephone calls.

One of the great pleasures in writing a third-party book is that I can suggest third-party solutions to make your SMB consulting practice more effective and efficient. The area of time management is one such area. In this section on time management, I'm pushing Timeslips For Windows, an application from Best Software (visit www.timeslips.com). I feel very strongly that it's the best standalone timekeeping software on the market, and managing your billable time is paramount to your success as an SMB consultant. Hey, in many cases, billable time is all that the SMB consultant sells.

> BEST PRACTICE: As of this writing, Timeslips has a "sole practitioner" version that allows time and billing for up to two employees. It starts at $199.99 USD. This might be the best fit for the majority of SMB consultants.

Timeslips has been around for a number of years and is popular in professional service environments, such as the legal community. Not only does Timeslips provide the functionality you need to keep track of your billable time and bill clients, but it also interfaces with popular accounting programs such as QuickBooks. Another appreciated feature is the Timeslips personal digital assistant (PDA) interface. You can load Timeslips on your Windows Pocket PC-based PDA and keep your time while at the client site. Once you return to the office and synchronize your PDA with your personal computer, the billing information is uploaded to your full version of Timeslips.

Timeslips is also available in application service provider (ASP) mode. Sage has introduced Timeslips eCenter where you can log on over the Internet to enter your time and billing information. This is shown in Figure 9-2.

Figure 9-2:
Consider using Timeslips over the Internet.

BEST PRACTICE: Ideally, you and the other SMB consultants you work with would enter your time and billing information from a Web browser at a client site while the information is still fresh in your minds. That's a critical step because making your time entries at the moment you perform the work is the easiest way to remember billing details. Clients appreciate detailed billing entries so they understand the work you have performed.

Working smarter

Management time needs to be devoted to simple office tasks such as maintaining a useful filing system to manage your documents. Here are a few suggestions.

Client file system

You need to have an updated client file system to manage each engagement. This file system can be a simple notebook for each client or a manila folder in a filing cabinet. Not only should the client file contain client engagement documentation, including the engagement letter, contracts, change orders, field notes, receipts, bills, and so on, it should also contain the network notebook and programming comments, along with related documentation, which I discuss next. Finally, be sure the client file also contains logon passwords, contact names, and so on. You would be amazed at how many SMB consultants try to keep all that information in their heads. Without a file system in place, if something should happen to the SMB consultant, there is no way someone else can easily step in and pick up the pieces, a clear example of bad engagement management.

SharePoint technologies

I call it a case of eating your own dog food (a popular Microsoft phrase for using the software that they create). As this book is being completed, Microsoft is making great strides on its next generation of SharePoint applications including SharePoint Portal Server (SPS) and Windows SharePoint Services (WSS). WSS has many of the document management features that were previously found in SPS, and WSS ships with Small Business Server 2003, so it's readily available to the SMB consultant. Figure 9-3 displays Microsoft's SharePoint site.

Figure 9-3:
SharePoint is a hot application area in the Microsoft product family and can be used at your client sites and as well as for your own internal operations.

Here's my point. You should use the document management features of WSS to manage your SMB consulting practice workflow. You'll go through the same steps for yourself that you would undertake for your clients, as seen in Table 9-1.

Table 9-1: SharePoint Steps to Manage Documents

Current Assessment	Look at how you manage documents today. You likely have some documents stored on your local C: drive under My Documents, some stored under the Users share and some stored under the Company share.
Plan of Attack!	Decide how you would store your documents on a server. What would the SharePoint categories be? Perhaps client, technology, location, etc. What additional fields would you add to a profile beyond the standard author, title, date and keywords field? Perhaps you'd add client, operating system, bill rate, etc. Finally, you'll need to decide what names you'll give to the enhanced folders that store the documents (e.g., Consulting). Last, you'll need to come up with a file-naming convention, as SharePoint doesn't have auto-naming capabilities like other high-end document management programs.
Just Do It!	Now the hard part. You've got to manually move your documents into the new system, complete the profile for each system, etc. This will take some time (time you probably don't have), but it's essential for bringing order to your operations.
Keep Doing It!	I've found that an ongoing "working smarter" challenge is to keep using the document management system after you've set it up! It's easy to get burned out on the process of check-in/check-out but those

	extra few seconds yield great benefits in terms of robust document management.
Go Forth and Multiply!	By "eating your own dog food" and getting your own act together internally with SharePoint-based document management, you're also increasing your SMB consulting skill set. By that I mean you can learn on your own time with your own data, and then turn right around, go out, and sell your newfound SharePoint expertise!

STOP THE PRESSES! Late breaking news. There is an SBS-specific document management solution from Portland, OR-based ColumbiaSoft Corporation (www.documentlocator.com) called Document Locator. This provides much more robust document management capabilities on SBS than the Microsoft Sharepoint-based applications. It's affordable with pricing starting at $1,500 USD.

Documentation

Put yourself in the client's shoes. Part of the value they receive from the SMB consulting relationship is the documentation of the work you do. If anyone follows in your footsteps, they will easily start work where you left off.

Network notebook

At my sites, I maintain a network notebook with anything and everything related to infrastructure operations. This includes an as-built drawing created in Microsoft Visio, site visit reports, user account information, vendor application information, and so on. I discuss the network notebook concept further in the final chapter of the book (Chapter 13) in the context of SMB consulting services you'll provide related to SBS.

Programming comments

One SMB consulting engagement I remember in particular is the time I was hired by a lumberyard owner to verify the work of his database administrator. While I wasn't qualified to verify the development work in a database program called Clipper, I was qualified to look at how well the database was documented. What I found was a pleasant surprise. The database administrator had commented out his work, had printed out the comments, and had saved them both in a fireproof file cabinet and as comment files to the server (which meant a bona fide tape backup system with off-site storage was protecting the comments). The lumber owner slept much better at night knowing this.

Forms

Something mentioned several times in this book is the use of existing templates and forms to ease the burden of creating business documents from scratch. I direct your attention to the Microsoft Template Gallery at search.officeupdate.microsoft.com/TemplateGallery/ct102.asp. Investigate which forms can assist you in more effectively running your SMB consulting practice.

Administrative functions

You can run but you can't hide from basic administrative functions. It's a fact of life — you'll have to perform some administration in order to successfully practice your SMB consulting craft. This includes some accounting, some human resources, some filing, and even running errands. One SMB consultant commented that he spent all day performing administrative work and didn't do the "real work" of SMB consulting (e.g., working with computers) until night!

Outsourcing

Part of the trick to running a successful SMB consulting firm is to do what you do best and outsource the rest. I jest, of course, to make a point. You typically can't truly do it all and perhaps outsourcing certain management functions will allow you to capitalize on your strengths and shore up your weaknesses with a little help. Consider availing yourself of outsourcing firms in the following areas:

- Accounting and bookkeeping

- Payroll

- Human resources

- Marketing

- Public relations

- Legal

BEST PRACTICE: Another management consultant I speak with occasionally told me about a CEO he was advising. This CEO had retained this consultant as a success coach. A success coach is someone who, for a fee, makes executives more successful. In this case, the success coach worked with the CEO to let go of his weaknesses and outsource those weak areas to service providers that could perform the work in question much better than the CEO could. This CEO was especially strong in selling, but weak in administration, so he let go of the business administration functions. This is an application of the old "You're only as strong as your weakest link" theory of running a company. That is a way of saying that by propping up your weaknesses, which in this CEO example was the act of seeking help in the administrative area, your greater overall work effort is stronger and more effective.

ConnectWise

A long-time respected SMB consultant who is especially keen with SBS, Arnie Bellini, has taken his years of SMB practice management and packaged it as a deliverable service and product for other SMB consultants to use. That is, Arnie is selling shovels to gold miners as part of his SMB strategy. As you can see in Figure 9-4, Arnie's ConnectWisePSA product assists SMB consultants and other service providers with business development, project management, service and support (including time and billing), and financial management.

Notes:

Figure 9-4:

ConnectWisePSA is one of the first administrative support software packages built from the ground up for the SMB service provider space.

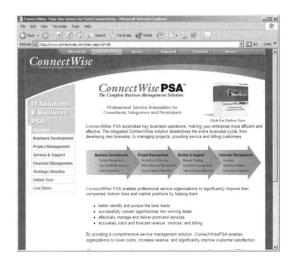

I recommend you complete the live demo of the ConnectWisePSA at www.connectwise.com before you get to the next chapter where I'll feature the financial features of this SMB solution.

Managing Staff

Once you've made the decision to scale your practice beyond your capabilities, you have to hire the staff. In this era of IT downsizing and excess capacity, many skilled professionals from both business and technology have found themselves being consultants — and not by choice. This, of course, is a play of words on an old joke. The joke has an embarrassed unemployed professional at a cocktail party telling others that he is a consultant — the punch line being an unemployed professional is really a consultant looking for a permanent job. And if you've heard that one already, get used to it, as you'll hear it again in the real world.

Because of the current state of the economy as of this writing in mid-2003, there are many candidates seeking work and many of these have inadequate technical skills. Nearly all are seeking the compensation promised land of yesteryear and have some hard facts of life ahead of them when it comes to current IT-related pay scales. You'll have to plow through all this malarkey and more as you review the stack of résumés and conduct a handful of interviews. When you look up and catch your breath, you will have invested significant time in the recruiting process. And that's before you've extended an offer to the incumbent and trained and indoctrinated them in your SMB consulting ways!

> BEST PRACTICE: Hell hath no fury like a bad hire. Much like saying the best client you ever had was the client you rejected, the same could be said for hiring. The best employee you'll hire would be the job candidate you rejected! Not only can a bad hire be demoralizing and technically incompetent, but different cities, states, and countries have different employment laws regarding terminations. I've been told by one of my SMB clients — but not actually verified the statement — that it's difficult to terminate someone in Canada who is under your employ. So take your time up front and hire wisely.

Beer and buddy system — NOT!

A time-tested lesson in business is to avoid hiring your friends. I present that point by taking a moment to discuss what SMB consulting is *not* about in the recruiting area. It isn't an exercise in getting the fraternity brothers together and hanging a shingle outside announcing yourself as an SMB consulting firm. The way you used beer and buddies to move from your apartment to your first house doesn't work here. In fact, SMB consulting is such a high-caliber occupational endeavor, I've not seen much success where good friends are recruited to help out. Is that another way of saying you shouldn't do business with friend? You'll have to decide for yourself as you take the SMB consulting journey.

Attracting top talent

You have to sell yourself to potential employees. Top talent in the SMB consulting field — hopefully yourself included — will typically receive multiple offers when job hunting. Or more realistically in today's world, they will not be looking for new opportunities. If you're the employer, how on earth do you attract the best employees?

First you have to create an attractive work environment to procure top talent. Second, you need to commit yourself to hiring standards, such as hiring only the top 10 percent of a peer group. Such a high bar means that you'll be sitting through tons of interviews just to hire one person.

> BEST PRACTICE: It's widely believed in the Silicon Forest of the Pacific Northwest that Microsoft's success is as much attributable to Bill Gate's early recruiting strengths as it is to anything else. Apparently, Bill Gates is mesmerizing in telling the Microsoft story and painting his picture of occupational opportunity. The tradition continues today.

I'm sad to say there's no snake oil solution you can buy for successful recruiting. The process is clearly trial and error. But the next section on hiring strategies will give you a head start.

Hiring strategies

Just do the best you can do when it comes to hiring SMB consultants to work for you. This section presents some proven hiring strategies that should be very helpful.

Homegrown talent

A break-fix repair business in North Seattle that I have the utmost respect for is well known for being an SMB consulting training ground. They believe in growing your own when it comes to recruiting. You are initially hired as a break-fix technician, often starting at the bottom cleaning printers. Slowly the person is given more challenging assignments and ultimately allowed to assist in the management of the client relationship.

This approach often means you train many people and lose a few good ones along the way. Sometimes you even train your competition, as the people you train may open up shop using many of the same consulting techniques you use. But that's life in the wacky world of SMB consulting. More important, in the case of the respected break-fix shop, the SMB consultants who came up through the ranks and stayed on were real gems.

Outsourcing

You can outsource the human resources function in three ways. First, you can subcontract out a lot of your work to other firms. In that case, your role as an SMB consultant is more that of project manager or prime contractor.

You can outsource the human resources function by using headhunters to do your recruiting. A headhunter will work on a fee basis to find, screen, interview, and otherwise qualify (check references and work history) candidates for you. Headhunters typically charge a percentage of a candidate's first year's salary (sometimes as high as 30 percent), payable after a 90-day warranty period. This warranty period, which starts on the date of hire, ensures the candidate fits in your organization before the headhunter is paid. Many headhunting firms can also provide you with temporary employees and contracts.

Finally, there are organizations in the business of serving as your human resources department on an outsourced basis. These firms assist not only in the hiring process, but also in developing, maintaining, and enforcing employee policies. Other services provided by outsourced human resources departments include conducting salary surveys, helping to set compensation levels, and performing terminations.

> BEST PRACTICE: Monitor trends in outsourcing to see if this approach makes sense as part of your SMB consulting business model. Sometimes outsourcing is favored in the technology community; other times it is not. A recent article by Bonnie Markowitz, titled "Alternative Supplies of IT Talent" (VARBusiness, May 6, 2003), put a positive spin on outsourcing trends. That article can be read at: vb.channelsupersearch.com/news/var/41676.asp.

Using temps and contractors

Past newspaper articles in the Seattle area, where Microsoft is located, have estimated Microsoft's workforce as consisting of up to 30 percent temporary employees and contractors. When you interact with Microsoft, that percentage seems a lot larger, let me tell ya. Just about everyone seems to be a temp or contractor on the Microsoft Redmond campus. Microsoft and other companies pursue this workforce strategy for a number of reasons, including the following:

- **Lower benefit costs** — Temporary employees and contractors typically don't receive benefits, and if they do, the benefits don't closely compare to those received by full-time employees. This translates into lower benefits costs.

- **Flexible staffing levels** — On a macro level, executives like the flexible staffing option as a human resource policy in order to be able to shift the focus of the company quickly. Imagine this: You're a large SMB consulting firm (which kinda sounds like an oxymoron). You decide to pursue consulting opportunities that are in alignment with Microsoft's dot-NET (.NET) direction. One day down the road, Microsoft abandons the .NET initiative. If you have a staff augmented for .NET, you could be faced with the extremely unpleasant task of large-scale terminations. With a flexible staffing solution in place, you can call the temporary agency or contracting house and have them adjust your staff to eliminate the unneeded workers. A few days later, that same temporary agency or contracting house can send over a workforce that meets the needs of your new direction.

- **At-will terminations** — On a more individual basis, substantial legal maneuvering is avoided when you want to terminate an incompetent individual. I discuss termination of full-time employees at the end of this chapter, but suffice it to say, the standard that must be met to terminate a temporary employee or contractor is much lower. And the temporary agency or contract house can conveniently perform the termination for you.

- **Try before you buy** — Many firms use the temporary employee and contractor approach to test-drive employees before hire. There's nothing like seeing someone in action for several months before you extend a full-time offer. Many temporary agencies and contract houses have turned this "try before you buy" option into a service offering by including a break on the headhunter placement fee you ultimately pay.

One of the odd jobs I had on the way up in the technology community was as an account manager for a national temporary agency. It provided an interesting look inside the placement field. One thing I learned that has been invaluable to me is that temporary agencies and contract houses enjoy significant markups on the rate you are paid as the temp. A markup is the difference between the price paid by the customer and the cost paid for something. In the retail field, 100 percent keystone pricing markups are common on merchandise. But back to the temporary agency story, where for your purposes, a markup is the difference between your labor rate per hour and the charge to the customer per hour. The high-volume national temporary agencies can afford to have lower markups, because of the vast number of placements they make. The markups here can be in the 20 percent range. The middle-tier placement agencies that tend to be more specialized operate with markups in the 50 percent range. Very specialized placement agencies enjoy markups in excess of 100 percent.

> BEST PRACTICE: If you work with temporary agencies and con-
> tract houses, understand that the placement field if full of unsa-
> vory characters. Ask what the person being placed at your site is
> making. Be sure to receive assurances that the person being placed
> knows what you are paying the temporary agency or contract house.
> If the agency or contract house isn't willing to participate in the
> full disclosure of this information, then you are advised to shop for
> another placement firm.

Full-time employees

You might just want to hire a full-time employee (FTE) as your next SMB consultant and be done with it. It's what most of us do. It's what our parents and our grandparents did. Adding FTEs to your SMB consulting practice is a sure sign of maturity. You've become a real business with real employees at that point.

Compensation Guidelines

There are many ways to pay your staff. I discuss a few approaches here, including the popular salary and per-hour wage options.

Salary

There are numerous salary surveys in the technology area. Two surveys that warrant further review and continuing coverage are *CRN*'s Salary Survey and *Microsoft Certified Professional (MCP) Magazine*'s annual salary survey. To be honest, *CRN*'s salary survey is more closely aligned with the life and times of an SMB consultant and is listed here first. *MCP Magazine*'s salary survey is a good reality check and is listed here for reference.

CRN

In its 2003 salary survey, *CRN* declares that an aggregate 2.1 percent increase was half the increase seen the prior year for technology service providers (VAPs, VARs, consultants, resellers). The article, found at www.crn.com/sections/special/ssurvey/ssurvey03.asp?ArticleID=42733, lists salary ranges from roughly $110,000 for an executive manager to $69,000 for a technical staffer with no certifications. The average compensation was approximately $82,000. Interestingly, the salary survey was divided into management, sales, and technical roles, which maps very closely to the finder (sales), minder (management), and grinder (technical) outline for this book and the three functional areas of being an SMB consultant. By classification, management paid the best (note this was skewed towards executive management). Next on the pay scale was sales, followed by the technicians. In all likelihood, in most technology service provider environments, sales-related compensation is typically higher than most management roles, except executive management. What's very interesting is that the "lowest" paid were the technical staff. Don't take this the wrong way, but that thinking "maps" to my philosophy of SMB consulting where management and sales are typically more important to SMB consulting than the actual technical work. It's all in the numbers of this salary survey! And more proof of the pudding is that the jobs in greatest demand in the survey where general sales. Technical roles related to infrastructure were way down on the list, due to the glut of talent. Demand for management roles, including project management, were in the middle of the list.

> BEST PRACTICE: Take a quick gander or look at the *CRN* salary calculator at www.crn.com/sections/special/Salarysearch2003/SalaryCalculate.asp and compare different job roles based on region and experience levels. This might help you understand what you'll need to pay for top-flight talent and also what you should be earning as an SMB consultant.

So what's my point in emphasizing *CRN*'s findings about management and sales compensation over the technical work? If you can find a multi-tasking finder, minder, grinder individual as your next SMB consultant, or if you're such a person, this is obviously an INCREDIBLY VALUABLE SKILL SET! My interpretation of the *CRN* salary survey also suggests that, in the view of society, management and sales are "harder" tasks to perform than the technical work (ergo the higher compensation levels). But the final word is this: Technicians who become SMB consultants remark many times over that they didn't realize how much sales effort was required in SMB consulting. They're probably surprised at how much management time they will need to commit to their craft as well.

> BEST PRACTICE: Set your sights high! The only thing holding you back from the six-figure compensation earned only in management in the *CRN* survey is yourself. Just because you read somewhere that very few people make six figures doesn't mean it can't be you. More pragmatically speaking, consultants are typically compensated as well as business managers and sales people (that's why many hot-shot MBAs become management consultants). In Chapter 10, I show you specific steps to earn six figures as an SMB consultant, assuming you've got the finder, minder, grinder skill sets working for you.

Microsoft Certified Professional Magazine

It's fun each year when the *Microsoft Certified Professional (MCP) Magazine* Salary Survey hits the streets. MCSEs across the WAN (and the land) become deeply concerned about how much money they are making. In some cases, they're deeply concerned about how much money they're not making. Now, granted the *MCP Magazine* salary survey isn't a perfect fit for the SMB consultant seeking compensation guidance, but it's interesting nonetheless. Visit www.mcpmag.com.

> BEST PRACTICE: The *MCP Magazine* salary survey and many other salary surveys (say *ComputerWorld*), typically exclude consulting income and self-employment income because it doesn't fit the "employee" mindset of such salary surveys. So use these salary surveys as a reference only.

Per-hour wages

It may make more sense for you to pay helpers by the hour, especially if you're at the low end of the SMB consulting market where you still perform break-fix work. Certain work environments are traditional wage environments, and it's not the intent of this book to address that issue.

Assuming you work in a per-hour environment (where you pay employees per hour instead of salary), think through your financial business model. If the SMB consultant under your employment earns $30 per hour and that includes many hours of shop time (since not every hour is billable), then you've got to bill out this person at two times or more than that hourly wage. A good SMB consultant has a 50 percent utilization rate, an observation I've made several times in this book. If you pay someone $30 per hour for full-time employment (about 2,000 hours per year) and he or she bills only 1,000 hours per year, their effective wage rate matched against the billable hour is $60 per hour. In that scenario, you should bill out at $120 per hour. Viewed a different way, the MCSE consultant employee might think he or she is earning only $30 per hour and being billed out at $120 per hour (and may feel he or she is being taken advantage of). You'll want to be sensitive to this issue and work through the math with your employees.

Eat what you kill

Another type of compensation method, one that I personally like, is the "eat what you kill" method. Basically this involves an agreement or understanding with a consulting firm where you will earn a percentage of what you make for the firm. To make my point, I cite an example of an SMB consulting firm in the Pacific Northwest. The owner — I'll call him "Wayne" — recruited SMB consultants. His compensation system was easy. He paid you half of what you earned. So if you billed out at $120 per hour, you earned $60 per hour. More important, and here's the part I like, you were part of an organization with infrastructure and support that theoretically allowed you to earn more money more easily than if you were on your own. Wayne's support structure was particularly effective in generating workflow. Free to market and manage, Wayne brought the business in and kept his consultants' plates full. Also, this form of compensation is a lot like a commission environment: You can earn whatever you want. So if you want to work enough to earn $60,000, Wayne's "eat what you kill" approach works (and Wayne enjoys gross billings of $120,000). If you want to earn $80,000 per year, Wayne's world likely works for you too (and, here again, Wayne's gross billings would be $160,000 per year).

BEST PRACTICE: You've now been exposed to keystone pricing several times in this chapter by definition and examples. So the rule here is that you've got to keystone price pay rates to essentially break even and not lose money.

Partnerships

You might consider partnership distributions as a form of compensation. Given the right situation, you might take on a partner in your SMB consulting practice. The only caveat in this scenario is never to forget that owners are always the last to get paid. If you have ever run a business, you may recall that only after your suppliers, vendors, and employees are paid do you finally get paid.

Profit sharing

You can consider offering profit sharing to employees to sweeten the compensation pot. In this day of dot-coms gone, compensation forms like profit sharing bring a twinkle to the eyes of prospective SMB consultants you're recruiting. But be advised that twinkle might be tears from someone who got duped in the late 1990s with promises of riches and now has nothing to show for it. Nonetheless, if you are organized as a corporation and have hopes of going public, you might grant stock options to your employees to give them a sense of ownership.

Equity

Equity is the foundation of riches, not a bi-weekly paycheck. You'll learn that at any "rags to riches" motivational seminar. Equity is a great motivator when you recruit staff. This is different than the partnership discussion above which was really about having a bona fide partner. Here the discussion is about giving some ownership equity to an employee and how you might go out and perform work for equity in another company.

Financial equity

This is the old carrot-and-stick compensation approach where you motivate employees with equity nibbles. Someone who hasn't had ownership in their lives can be very motivated by this equity kicker approach. This might be a stock grant (not options).

Sweat equity

This next example applies more to the sole proprietor SMB consultant. My favorite equity compensation form is a deal that, unfortunately, never happened. I was looking at the manufacturing molds of the San Juan Sailboat Company, a business that needed a new network, but didn't have any money to pay for it. In fact, the company was in an early form of bankruptcy. No problem, I thought. I'll just take a San Juan sailboat in return for my services. I thought perhaps I could turn the job into a multiyear engagement and get a really big sailboat in return. As fate would have it, however, the sailboat company went deeper into bankruptcy, and I never got my sailboat. However, I'd sure entertain the same deal today, and I'd encourage you to do the same. Certain industries use this form of barter, including construction and construction materials. Think about that the next time you want to get a free hot tub installed on your patio deck in exchange for installing a Windows 2003 network.

Benefits

Another part of the managing staff puzzle is the benefits area. This is a complex area. Some benefit consultants make a good living advising small business owners, such as you and I running SMB consulting firms, on what benefit packages to provide. The good news is that, in addition to retaining a benefits consultant (who might be compensated on commission for the benefits they suggest to you), shopping among insurance companies is a great way to get free information.

Health and life insurance

Without tackling the complexities of the health and life insurance policies, I can share the following observations. Health insurance is increasingly not offered to SMB consultants who are self-employed or working for small consulting firms. If it's offered, it is typically a co-pay situation.

Life insurance is another one of the disappearing employee benefits. In general, employees and independent contractors are on their own when it comes to having any meaningful life insurance coverage. The Pacific Northwest regional consulting firm that I worked for as an MCSE consultant for a spell had a basic $10,000 life insurance policy for each employee. That policy would have about covered the funeral expenses. Having gone out and purchased my own life insurance, I can tell you that some ratios exist. At a minimum, you want three times your annual salary, roughly enough to pay off the house and provide several months cash for your family.

> BEST PRACTICE: Bite the bullet and sit through a couple of insurance sales presentations. However, make sure you've fortified your constitution so that you don't get sucked into purchasing policies before you step back from the process and consider them as a rational buyer. You can also compare insurance benefits at a host of online insurance clearing houses, such as www.insurance.com.

Additional benefits to offer

Additional benefits are an area in which you can shine as an SMB consulting firm trying to hire SMB consultants without an enterprise-level benefits package. People appreciate creativity in the benefits department. Here are a few things I've seen offered to recruits that fall under the creative benefits category:

- Work from home arrangements
- Elder care subsidies
- Childcare arrangements
- Tickets to sports team events
- Occasional use of the owner's ski condo!

> BEST PRACTICE: Many wonderful human resources sites are on the Web to guide you. For example, you can find sites that provide information on compensation. There is a small business Web portal with a bevy of human resources links and information. Go to BizBuilders.com (www.bizbuilders.com) and select the human resources link in the Small Business category.

Training Yourself and Staff

So now that you've got your sights set on being a big-time SMB consulting firm with staff, have you thought through how you'll develop the staff's talents? Typically when you hire a technology professional, they're as current as the current release of their niche product area. Fast forward a year or so and you'll find yourself with a staff that needs additional technical training to "stay current," as the saying goes. It'll shake you to the bone when faced with some of the expense training options in the marketplace. You'll question whether you're really the "learning organization" you professed to be when you were interviewing the incumbents. And don't forget about your own skill set. You have to stay current as well (especially if you're a sole proprietor without staff!).

> BEST PRACTICE: I've found the whole training area to be a great "filter" when recruiting staff in the SMB consulting area. I like to steer the job interview into the old "We're a learning organization here" discussion and see how the candidate responds. I'm looking for them to shine here and speak towards being a "life learner" and attending night courses at a college to keep their minds active, etc. A great response would be that they'd indicate they need to make sure they've completed their duties by 4:30pm on Tuesday and Thursday so they can get to their marketing class on time at the university. This would likely be a candidate with a track record for a commitment to continuing education and one that would have my consideration for hire, all other things being equal. That is, given the chance, I'll hire a true learner over a non-learner any day!

So how much to spend per year on yourself or an employee for technical training? There are several considerations here. First, training has to have a bona fide return on investment (ROI, which is discussed more in my next "Best Practice") and, as such, you might consider it an expense akin to the way corporations view research and development (R&D). Most corporations will say they spend 5 percent of revenues on R&D. Perhaps you can pick a similar figure for training. For a modest-sized SMB consulting firm with gross revenues of $200,000 USD, that would amount to $10,000 USD per year for training (company-wide, not per person!). I've seen other SMB consulting practices say that an employee receives $1,500 per year for training (which could be used for any of the methods below, including conferences).

Then there is the CPA firm view of training. A managing partner of a CPA firm told me that he committed $5,000 per year to his CPAs so they could meet statutory continuing education requirements in their profession. But he found he had to pay that and often more — up to perhaps $10,000 per year — for his MCSE consultants on staff to maintain their certifications. His frustration was that his accountants required less training then the MCSEs, who seemed to need to always go back and learn the latest products from Microsoft. Yet the CPA and the MCSE, put side by side, brought in about the same amount of billable hour revenue to the firm. Just food for thought!

> BEST PRACTICE: The ROI of training dollars is very similar to the dynamics expressed in an article I once wrote for *MCP Magazine* on the ROI of certification dollars. The article highlighted two points: lower study costs will boost ROI and any certification must result in greater consulting revenues (e.g., getting certified in SQL Server might allow you to garner new work). The same thoughts apply to training dollars: Do it for as cheap as is reasonable and make sure it benefits your billable hours.

Fear not. In this section, I list some training options that are available to you and your staff ranging from no cost to high cost. Let's get started.

Go To Market and HOT Labs

By now you've likely memorized the Go To Market (GTM) message of learn about it, sell it, deploy it, and build upon it. Here I focus on the "learn about it" message. GTM learning opportunities take various forms, many of which are listed in this section (such as HOT Labs). But a key point of the learn about it message is that SMB consulting firms could send one person from the office to attend a GTM learning session and then have that person return and train the remaining staff. This is the old "train the trainer" trick, but it helps reduce costs.

Laugh if you must about train the trainer, but I really saw that process play out in San Diego in mid-2003 near the end of a four day GTM HOT Lab tour. A student, Ed, from Coronado Island (a suburb of San Diego) runs a small SMB consulting practice with five SMB consultants. As the owner, he sets his own schedule and he elected to attend the four-day workshop. His intent was to learn the materials, gather the hand-outs and then return to the office and train his staff. Little did Ed know, but he was exactly what the Microsoft GTM team had been hoping for. One day of the four really stood out in terms of GTM train the trainer. It was the ISA Server day, where students left with a disc containing the VMWare HOT Lab sessions. In this case, Ed could return to his Coronado Island office and install VMWare workstation to run the complete ISA Server HOT Labs for all staff members. Brilliant!

Online

Whereas Ed in the example above had the freedom and flexibility to leave the office to attend training, some folks don't. It might be they're too busy to get out of the office. Or it might be that in-person training opportunities don't exist where able and willing SMB consultants live and work. That's where the promise of online learning pays off! This section reviews different types of online learning: e-learning, Webcasts, and online Hands On Training HOT Labs.

E-learning

Microsoft has posted a large number of e-learning courses, including, as of this writing, an eight-hour e-learning course on Small Business Server 2000 created in conjunction with SmartForce, an e-learning developer. The course experience itself is similar to working with Apple's HyperCard environment. HyperCard was a "flash card" learning paradigm, similar to the three-by-five-inch cards that many students used to memorize topics in grammar school. Throw in hyperlinks, animation, and other tricks, and you've got a Microsoft e-learning course. It is anticipated that other SMB e-learning courses will be posted as well at www.microsoft.com/partner.

Webcasts

Another online learning avenue is Webcasts. This allows staff to actively learn from their own desks using several senses such as visual, audio, tactual, etc. I've found that rural SMB consultants appreciate the live Webcast interaction the most because, unlike their urban counterparts, they can't just drop by a conference or workshop. Two sites to monitor for Microsoft-related Webcasts are: www.microsoft.com/usa/webcasts/ondemand/default.asp and support.microsoft.com/ default.aspx?scid=fh;RID;webcst&style=type2&sd=gn. Note *CRN* and other magazines are also big on Webcasts (visit www.crn.com for more details on its Webcast offerings).

Online HOT Labs

Microsoft is pushing HOT labs as a low-cost and effective way to learn its solutions. These HOT labs have limits with respect to the technical depth encountered, but given that they're free, the format is typically well-received. In my research for this book, as of mid-2003, I found four online portals providing online HOT labs that related to the SMB consulting space. These are listed as:

- Microsoft SBS 2003 Release Candidate HOT lab at: microsoft.com/windowsserver2003/sbs/lab.mspx#XSLTsection123121120120

- Handsonlab.com (name and address the same)

- Granite Pillar at microsoft.granitepillar.com/partners/

- Entirenet at www.entirenet.net/registration/

Microsoft official curriculum courses and certifications

Delving deep into the certification community to write this book, I spoke with a Senior Editor at Microsoft Certified Professional (MCP) Magazine (visit at www.mcpmag.com). He indicated that, as of mid-2003, he is witnessing some interesting certification trends. First, Microsoft is looking way beyond its traditional certification strongholds of enterprise, developers and database administrators. It's looking at more desktop certifications, certifications based on job function and SMB-related certifications. It's that last point that is most exciting to us SMB consultants.

Course

The SMB-related course is known as MOC 2395A Designing, Deploying, and Managing a Network Solution for the Small and Medium-Sized Business. This course helps students determine the appropriate Microsoft products to use to facilitate networking in their small to medium-sized business environment. It covers networking opportunities ranging from peer-to-peer solutions, including Microsoft Windows XP Professional, to deploying and managing solutions using Windows Small Business Server 2003 and Microsoft Windows Server 2003. The course will be available in September 2003.

Certification exam

The SMB exam is known as MCP Exam 70-282 Planning, Deploying and Managing a Network Solution for the Small and Medium-Sized Business. This exam will support the release of Windows Server 2003 and Windows Small Business Server 2003 by accurately identifying consultants who can successfully design, implement, and manage a technology solution for small and medium-sized environments. The exam will be available in November 2003.

Conferences

I can truly add value here. Simply stated, there aren't many SMB conferences, which is why I started the SMB conference series (www.smbnation.com, Figure 9-5). This conference is all about supporting SMB consultants with special attention given to SBS. It has two tracks: technical and business.

> BEST PRACTICE: It's my intent to continue to build a list of SMB-related conferences. Make sure you've subscribed to my SBS newsletter (sign up at www.nethealthmon.com/newsletter.htm) to monitor my findings.

Figure 9-5:
SMB Nation is anticipated to occur twice a year in the USA. International delivery is also planned.

> BEST PRACTICE: You and your staff should be attending one or more conferences per year. Chalk it up to "professional development," if you must, but know that this is just what you do when you're a leader in your chosen field.

Another conference (really a trade show) to consider is the Microsoft Partners conference called Microsoft Momentum (formerly known as Fusion). This conference, while more enterprise-oriented, has an overwhelmingly business orientation, which is refreshing. Technically speaking, it's not really a technical conference (okay, that was a bad pun). The evening events (read "PARTIES") are worth the admission alone. You can find more information on Microsoft Momentum at www.microsoft.com/partner/events/fusion.

> BEST PRACTICE: If you or your staff attend Microsoft Momentum, make sure you are taking advantage of the partner meet and greet tables. It's here that you'll want to sign up to meet like-minded partners who have completed a survey where they indicated an interest in SMB and SBS. You get to look at the survey results to find such people and when you meet with them, its worthwhile to sit and talk about business models, etc.

Finally, a USA traveling conference series with an SMB focus is the ITEC conference. Details can be found at www.goitec.com. Admission is typically free, and it's more sales-oriented than educational, but touring the floor and sitting in on a few of the one-hour speeches can be educational. I had the pleasure of working the ITEC conference series in the fall of 2001 and can attest that it draws in the hard-core SMB crowd (heck, there were event booths leasing photocopiers to small business owners).

Training centers

SMB consultants shouldn't overlook traditional classroom training environments such as Microsoft Certified Technical Education Centers (CTECs) and other similar venues (e.g., Gateway stores have classrooms). You can find CTECs in your area by visiting www.microsoft.com/traincert. You will note that some training organizations focus on the SMB space more than others, so you'll want to shop around. For example, in the Seattle area CTEC community, Paladin Data (www.paladindata.com) has a strong SMB focus while other CTECs are content to focus on large enterprise training accounts, such as Boeing. Paladin Data is shown in Figure 9-6.

> BEST PRACTICE: Don't forget courses at training centers offer another opportunity: being a trainer yourself! It's widely accepted that if you want to really learn a subject area, then go out and teach it. Enough said!

Figure 9-6:
Paladin's training center is located in a rural part of the greater Seattle area, thus its focus tends to be more SMB-oriented.

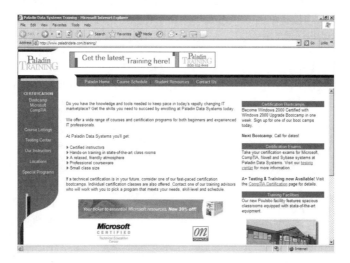

> BEST PRACTICE: It's important not to get so focused on training as a means to acquire certification that you forget about knowledge transfer and learning. For many years, everyone wanted a CNE from Novell followed by an MCSE from Microsoft. That's tamed down a tad in recent times, but there are many great courses out there that might focus on second-tier certifications, such the CompTIA courses on hardware, security, and project management.

Additional educational opportunities

So far, a fairly straightforward, traditional view of training opportunities has been presented in this section. But you and I as SMB consultants are always learning. It may not be in a classroom, a ballroom with a HOT lab, or an online course. Rather, it may reveal itself in other unique ways. Here are a few possible additional training opportunities:

- **User Groups.** In early and mid-2003, numerous SBS user groups were formed in response to a "call for action" by leading SBSers to build "community" from the ground up. My SBS newsletter, referenced below, frequently lists user group meetings. Wayne Small, a leading Australian SBSer, maintains a worldwide list of SBS user groups. Roger Otterson (aka Mr USA SBS User Group), has a primer on how to start an SBS user group, if you're so inclined, at http://www.sdsbsug.org/star.htm (shown in Figure 9-7). Of course, you can find a local user group in your area that best meets your social and professional interaction needs by asking at local computer shops!

Figure 9-7:
The San Diego SBS user group is reaching out to help start other SBS user groups.

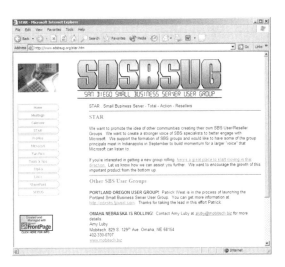

- **Trade Associations.** Consider joining the Network Professional Association to engage in the "bird of a feather" thing as a consulting professional. This group focuses more on medium-sized and enterprise folks, but it'd be good for you to get out and circulate with them nonetheless. Details at www.npa.org as shown in Figure 9-8.

Figure 9-8:

The NPA has recently warmed up to the SMB community and has been supportive of SBS!

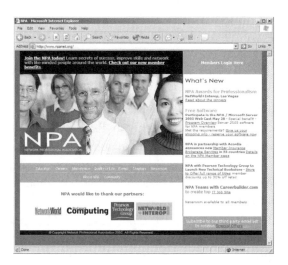

- **Microsoft Events and Stuff.** Across the pages of this book, I'll mention numerous Microsoft learning resources (if you already haven't figured that out!). For SMB-related matters, key in on the Microsoft TS2 series (details at www.msts2.com) as your primary portal followed by close monitoring of the broader partner site (www.microsoft.com/partner).

- **College Courses.** One of the most accessible and reasonably priced training opportunities can often be found at your local college. Go ahead, take a break right here and drive over to your local college and peruse the catalog for both applicable business and technology courses.

- **Professional Development Courses and Workshops.** These range from local colleges with one-day management summits to the traveling seminars that hold one and two events at airport hotels. You know them when you see them. A popular topic for the professional development circuit has been project management courses. One great organization that delivered many technical workshops has disappeared (Data Tech Institute). No other details at press time, but it must have been the victim of the technology downturn.

BEST PRACTICE: It's the intent of SMB Nation to also deliver one-day seminars in the USA, Canada, and other English-speaking countries (UK, Australia) starting in late 2003. Continue to view www.smbnation.com for updates on this.

- **Newsletters.** A shameless plug, followed by legitimate content. I'm honor-bound to ask you to subscribe to my *Small Business Best Practices* so that I can continue to feed you important SMB content well after you've purchased — and read — this book. Visit www.nethealthmon.com/newsletter.htm to sign up — why not, it's free! A recent issue is shown in Figure 9-9. Consider a few other informative newsletters as well. Sign up for the *IT Consultant Republic NetNote* at www.techrepublic.com to receive advice on business development and technology trends. Another is Ramon Ray's *Small Business Technology Report* newsletter at www.smallbiztechnology.com. Long-time small business technology writer Josh Fienberg writes a newsletter that you can sign up for at www.smallbiztechtalk.com (be advised that Josh's bark is worse than his bite, as he comes across as ANTI-SMB consultant!). And don't forget Stu Sjouwerman's infamous weekly newsletter (over 500,000 readers) at w2knews.com. Lastly, make sure you receive the *Microsoft Partners* newsletter (Sign up at: members.microsoft.com/partner/help/newsletteroverview.aspx)

Notes:

Figure 9-9:

Small Business Best Practices is my free SMB/SBS newsletter that extends many of the topics discussed in this book.

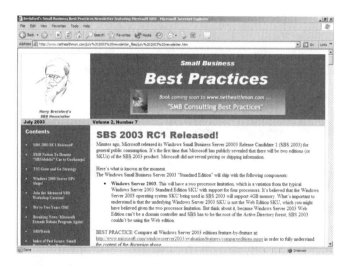

- **Free seminars.** So why buy the cow when you can get the milk for free? Keep an eye cast on the calendar of events in the business section of your local paper. Typically major hardware and software vendors will put on free public seminars (okay — these are disguised sales efforts). Oracle, Computer Associates, HP, and others have long used the free seminar trick. There are some educational gold nuggets at these events and it only costs your time! You should attend at least a few of these a year under the guise of "training."

BEST PRACTICE: Just an FYI for USA readers. I make it a practice when traveling around on day-time business to different cities to give a free Advanced SBS workshop in one evening. This was implemented in spring of 2003 when I traveled to 20 USA cities on unrelated Microsoft business. In most cases, my free Advanced SBS seminars, held offsite on Wednesday nights, outdrew the day-time official audience! My newsletter shown above will post my free workshop schedule. Hope to see you at one of these events in the future.

Oh, and to answer the obvious question — Why would I take time to give a free seminar? Simply stated: I like to earn KARMA DOLLARS, so good fortune will rain down upon me. Perhaps you'll do as I say and do and give some free seminars in your community as well.

So what's the bottom line on training? Focusing on the technical realm of SMB consulting for just a moment, you're only as current as your last product release. If you stop learning, you stop earning!

Retention and Termination

This chapter closes with some future human resource issues that will bedevil you: retaining your great staff and terminating the not-so-great staff!

Retention strategies

As you mature as a consulting manager and as your SMB consulting practice matures, you'll place emphasis on retention. Seasoned human resources managers know that it's far cheaper to put a few dollars into retention rather than lose their talent. Staff turnover involves a very real cost. Here is a short list of retention considerations:

- **Paying for certifications**. You might pay for certifications, such as the Microsoft MCP related to SMB or the CompTIA A+ certification. As an SMB consulting manager, recognize it's in your best interest to sign a loan agreement with your employees whereby they pay you back for all or part of the certification courses if they leave within 12 or 18 months. This is common practice when a company pays for a graduate degree for an employee too.

- **Paying for cost of courses**. As the previous point suggested, paying for an employee's course work is a valid retention strategy.

- **Paying for time away from the office**. You might grant paid hours away from the office both to attend class and to study for SMB-related certification exams. Employees appreciate it when their time isn't docked.

- **Increasing compensation for designations and certifications earned**. A popular retention strategy is to pay your SMB consultants more money as they earn more certifications. Perhaps you'll offer a $1,000 salary bump for these employees for each certification title. In consulting, this retention strategy makes sense. An employee with more certifications should have a higher bill rate, and the whole arrangement should be both cost-effective and revenue-generating.

Mentoring your hires

Part of being an SMB consulting manager is to be a coach and mentor to your staff. You'll likely mentor a few great SMB consultants right out of your organization who will go on to do bigger and better things with their lives, but what goes around comes around (read "KARMA DOLLARS"). Sometimes those mentored SMB consultants refer new candidates for hire to you.

Brelsford's Dozen: Annual departures

No matter how wonderful you are, your firm is, and the salary is, you will lose some SMB consultants in your practice. It has been my experience that four out of 12 employees will leave per year in high technology consulting. That's the complex paradox of managing human beings. Some are unhappy with their career choices. Others are unhappy with you, but not their career choices. I've observed the following reasons for departures:

- Better offers
- Family matters (divorce and so on)
- Relocation
- Job not being a good fit

Terminations

Terminations happen. While I haven't been involved in many terminations, I cite the advice of a one-time speaker before my college class, the CEO of Egghead Software. He commented, and I believe correctly so, that most terminations occur too late. For the benefit of both employee and employer, issues surrounding termination of employment should be addressed earlier, not later. "No one ever got fired too early" were his exact words.

> BEST PRACTICE: Retain and seek the counsel of a labor lawyer in all matters involving employee terminations.

Brelsford's Mailbox

Wow! Harry...I've read your books, attended your talks @ Techmentor, etc.....I'M A BIG FAN!!!

Seriously, your *MCSE Consultant's Bible* book played a large role in providing the structure (and the confidence) for me that I could go out on my own and be a Small Biz technical consultant — and for that, I thank you! I also greatly appreciate your generosity to the Small Biz tech consulting community, such as putting many of your consulting docs online and your SBS tips. Not many gurus are as generous as you are!

Thanks again! We're looking forward to the SMB Nation conference, and I can't wait to see the new book!

Britt

Britt—

What can a say (after I stop blushing). I wanted to share your e-mail in the book you can't wait to see (this book, which you're obviously now in!) because you mention conference attendance. MCP Magazine's TechMentor conference continues with a heavy technical emphasis at the enterprise level. I look forward to catching up with you at SMB Nation!

And once you get to the big time, be sure to give back just a little more to the SMB community than you take. It's a strategy that's personally paid off for me and it's in part why I post content on my Web site for download.

Forward!

cheers...harrybbbb

Summary

This was perhaps the most management-oriented chapter you and I will have the pleasure of spending time with in this book. It's easy to get caught up in the hysteria of sales and marketing and the fun times of being a techie, so much so that management is forgotten. But face it, you'll learn management one way or another. You can study it, plan for it. and be prepared. Or you can ignore it and only learn management when you must. I'd prefer this chapter be your management primer for being an organized planner-type, but none of us can completely escape the school of hard knocks where we emerge "streetwise managers." So forward!

This chapter covered:

- The "M" word explained: MANAGEMENT!

- Tips for managing organization workflow

- Best practices for managing staff

- Improving your organizational skill set(s) with training

- Human resource management tips

Chapter 10
Financial Management

In This Chapter

- Understanding the difference between financial and management accounting

- Learning what popular accounting software packages might improve your SMB consulting money management

- Looking at financial traps, such as going broke while making money

- Appreciating ways to boost SMB consulting return on investment, including lowering costs and increasing revenues

- Follow-up steps in the money management area for you to take, including reading additional accounting and finance texts, watching financial news programs on TV, and attending money management seminars.

Call it accounting for non-accounting majors, but this chapter is important because it deals with money management. Not only is money necessary to sustain you and your SMB consulting practice, it's also one measure of your success. It's how we keep score. Let's get started with discussion on financial accounting and then move to management accounting

Financial Accounting Matters

Financial accounting is the form of accounting most often thought of when you look at a bookkeeper or an accountant hard at work. It's the debits and credits that record economic activity. Financial accounting typically reports information as a flow of activity over time (an income statement) and a snapshot at a point in time (a balance sheet). You'll need tools to record your economic activity, such as ConnectWisePSA, Timeslips, Microsoft bCentral's Small Business Manager or QuickBooks (all four are highlighted in this section).

Accounting systems

There are numerous accounting systems on the market. I've had the chance to interact with them on multiple levels: user, consultant, trainer. What I've found is that, for the most part, accounting systems are a very nichy (or specialized) area, with a few notable exceptions. Many accounting systems specialize in one form of accounting, such as hotel and restaurant management. Other accounting systems specialize in performing just one part of the accounting function and then integrate with bigger, more comprehensive packages. And others try to be broad enough to support multiple industries, such as Intuit's QuickBooks and Microsoft Small Business Manager. So here is a starting point for your journey into selecting and implementing a "best fit" accounting system for your SMB consulting practice.

ConnectWise PSA

In the prior chapter, you were introduced to ConnectWise for its management tools. But in case you forgot, ConnectWise PSA is the outcome of a seasoned SMB consulting firm with onboard CPA and MBA talent creating a comprehensive practice management solution for SMB consultants. The idea behind ConnectWise PSA is to offer solution sets for the following practice areas: time and billing, service and support, CRM, sales, marketing, and projects. These solution areas are then implemented with the following features:

- block time tracking

- proactive service requests

- scheduling & escalation of technicians in real time

- custom hourly rates for every client and project

- continuously current time sheets

- radar screens for time, service, sales, and projects

- access to all data anytime, anywhere over the Internet

The time and expense data you input into ConnectWise can be integrated with QuickBooks and other more robust financial account systems to generate profit and loss statements, etc. ConnectWise PSA's Service Board, which is a primary interface to using the solution, is displayed in Figure 10-1.

Figure 10-1:

The ConnectWise PSA's Service Board.

> BEST PRACTICE: While I don't have extensive experience with ConnectWise PSA, I do believe it's worth your further investigation. The president, Arnie Bellini is a well-respected SMB consultant a CPA and an MBA. Visit www.ConnectWise.com for more information or email Arnie@ConnectWise.com

TimeSlips

This program is addicting once your start to use it as a professional service provider. For me, it solved a long-time problem of time management. Timeslips is best known for its positioning in the legal arena, but it'll work just fine for SMB consultants as well. I actually use Timeslips as part of my own fledgling SMB consulting practice and can give you a firsthand recommendation for this product. Timeslips comes in different forms including a version for larger professional services offices, two-person offices (again, this might be the perfect fit for the new SMB consulting practice), and an online version (previously mentioned in Chapter 9). More information on Timeslips can be obtained at www.timeslips.com.

Small Business Manager

Call it "Great Plains Lite." Small Business Manager is Microsoft's "QuickBooks killer" entry in the small business accounting area. Perhaps the best news is that, as of this writing, it is now second generation and incorporates feedback from the business user community. The basic features including the following modules:

- Sales

- Purchasing

- Inventory

- Banking

- Payroll

- Financials

- Reports

For more information on Small Business Manager (shown in Figure 10-2), visit www.bcentral.com/products/sbm/default.asp.

Figure 10-2:
Notice that Microsoft has brought Small Business Manager into the market-place for just under $1,000 US to compete directly with QuickBooks.

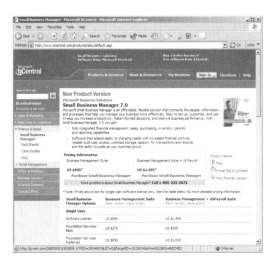

QuickBooks

This is the holy grail of small business accounting systems, the one application that has taken on Microsoft and won to date! It's sufficient for meeting most of your business accounting needs, as it's built to serve a broad market. But I've found one of the great strengths of QuickBooks is its ability to integrate with a wide range of narrower accounting solutions via its import and export functions. For example, Timeslips data (which is essentially only time and billing entries) can be seamlessly imported into the main QuickBooks accounting module. You are encouraged to visit www.quickbooks.com for more information on QuickBooks. And if you decide not to use it yourself, you may well be introduced to QuickBooks at one of your SMB client sites. Count on it!

> BEST PRACTICE: With the exception of Timeslips from the above discussion, the financial accounting packages presented in this section are "true" double-entry accounting packages. That's important to know because, if you're going to go to all the time and effort to implement an accounting system, you should do it correctly. A double-entry accounting system makes you, in many ways, a true business and "bankable." That last term, "bankable," relates to how you can create financial statements that are acceptable to a bank for borrowing purposes.
>
> Contrast the above double-entry discussion with single entry accounting packages like Quicken. While fine for home use to manage the check book, Quicken isn't really "compliant" with what are called "Generally Accepted Accounting Principles" or GAAP in the US. When you're a business, it's better to be GAAP compliant rather than not (again, especially if you want to borrow funds from a bank). Visit the American Institute of Certified Public Accountants at www.aicpa.org/index.htm for more information on accounting principles.

Financial accounting potpourri

Just two miscellaneous points to wrap up the financial accounting section before moving to management accounting.

- **Going broke while making money.** This is a classic eye-opening business school lecture about how companies go under while on top.

It works like this. A firm grows so quickly that is gets into a cash crunch. Perhaps it lands a US Navy contract that pays out near the end of the contract, but the cash demands on the firm are more frequent. For example, imagine landing a $1 million contract that will pay you in 18 months, but you've got biweekly payroll and other expenses to meet in the interim. This short story could have an unhappy ending, as your great account receivables are lagging behind your accounts payables and creating a cash crunch. Don't think this can happen in the consulting world? Think again. Better yet just ask EDS of Dallas, Texas, how it encountered this exact problem in the 2003 time frame with some large enterprise outsourcing work.

BEST PRACTICE: If you think that you might encounter such cash flow management problems in your SMB consulting practice, you'll want to apply for a commercial line of credit with your lender that you can draw down upon during lean times and replenish (pay back) during fat times.

- **Taxation.** Talk about a book unto itself. The world of taxation is not only complex, but depends on your unique situation, your location, etc. But there are a few things to watch out for (amongst many "gotchas") on which I feel comfortable advising you (for my US readers, that is). First, beware of the home office deduction. The Internal Revenue Service (IRS) has been known to cast a wary eye on home office deductions and this is considered an audit flag. Second, research current tax trends in the SMB area. For example, the *INC* magazine article titled "IRS Targets Small Biz" at: www.inc.com/magazine/20030401/25303.html speaks to renewed IRS auditing vigor in the SMB space (which could potentially affect both you and your customers).

Management Accounting Matters

Let's leave the debits and credits of financial accounting behind us. This section addresses management accounting matters that relate more to business planning, execution, reporting, and real-world results. Time's-a-wastin', so let's get started.

How much do you want to make this year?

So now you and I finally get to one of the important reasons we're really here as SMB consultants: making money. You don't need to apologize for such less-than-pure motives. Speaking only for myself, I've got kids to get through school, house and car payments to make, and a retirement to fund. So making money is not only okay, but it's kind of cool.

The next step after deciding you want to make money is to determine how much money you want to make. You should assess your basic needs, what your other wants and desires are, and what foolish luxuries you would like. Somewhere between basic needs and foolish luxuries is the amount of money you need to make as an SMB consultant. This amount will vary by individual.

> BEST PRACTICE: Notice I underlined the term "need" above. The amount of money you want to make will likely be greater, as wants often exceed needs. Wanting to make more than your needs is entirely acceptable and is encouraged between the covers of this SMB consulting guide.

Speaking more pragmatically, determining what you want to make is a function of many variables beyond your control. One of those input variables is what the marketplace will pay for your talents. The place to start this investigation is with salary surveys you'll find hither and beyond this book, as well as by heeding the words I share with you. Consider the following salary survey sources such as *CRN* (www.crn.com), *Microsoft Certified Professional (MCP) Magazine* (www.mcpmag.com), *Robert Half International* (www.rhii.com), and *ComputerWorld* (www.computerworld.com). You'll recall I presented the *CRN* and *MCP Magazine* salary surveys in Chapter 9 of this book in the context of what to pay employees and yourself. I won't repeat that lengthy discussion here.

The next step is to realistically quantify your financial compensation expectations. Read on.

50 percent utilization rate

I encourage you to consult with other SMB consultants to confirm the observations that I present in this section. In plain English, you bill only half of your hours in a given year. Ergo—the section header called "50 percent utilization rate." I'll explain why this is.

A utilization rate is the ratio of billable hours to available hours, the standard measure used in professional services, such as consulting, law, and accounting. In fact, the regional consulting practice I worked with in the mid- to late 1990s had a weekly charge hour report that displayed a column with the calculated utilization rate.

With SMB consulting, your utilization rate is typically 50 percent. This is a truism, observed year in and year out, due to non-redundant tasks, incalls/outcalls, and recurring charge hours.

Non-redundant tasks

Accounting has certain roles that are rote by nature, allowing efficiencies to be gained because of their predictability. For example, auditing and tax preparation tend to have more of a step-by-step workflow than many tasks performed by SMB consultants. SMB consultants often perform one task (for example, implementing a service pack) and then move on to another client site and perform a completely different task (a data restoration, for instance). Different task sets eat into billable hours because the SMB consultant has to shift his or her mindset continually and can't leverage up from repetition.

Incalls/outcalls

No, this isn't about call girls and the like. Strictly business here. Accountants tend to work at their desks in their offices. The nature of the workflow is inbound from clients. That is, clients typically deliver paperwork to the accountant's office, a process often combined with a meeting in the conference room.

With SMB consultants, the process tends to be exactly opposite. The work is performed at the client site instead of at the SMB consultant's office. Performing outcalls instead of receiving incalls contributes to a lower utilization rate.

Recurring charge hours

Let's take a moment to look at how accounting firms bill for hours of work, then I'll transition to the SMB consulting environment. It is a fact that the regulatory environment in which businesses operate dictates that certain accounting-related jobs, such as tax preparation and auditing, be performed once per year. Accountants are also retained to assist in the annual budgeting process and, perhaps, to update the business plan. To say that accountants are offered recurring billable hour opportunities in the context of their client relationships is an understatement. Basically, if you're an accountant, once you land a client account, you can count on certain types of work year after year from that account without additional marketing. And in many cases, state and federal law, tax rulings, and good old-fashioned government regulation mandate the work be completed.

SMB consultants in general perform more project-oriented work than other professional services—like my oft-cited accounting field—perform. SMB consultants start many client relationships with a project, such as implementing an SBS network. Many times the greatest number of hours occurs early in the SMB consulting relationship. In fact, it's not uncommon for SMB consultants to make off-color comments around the espresso machine that their better hours on a mature account are behind them. Long-term client relationships in the world of SMB consulting are more than desirable, but you will rarely exceed the billable hours that you'll enjoy at the beginning of a project.

> BEST PRACTICE: Some SMB consultants, having wised up to the peaks and valleys of project-based consulting, sell maintenance contracts to their clients to increase recurring charge hour revenues and stabilize cash flow.

For these reasons and more, SMB consulting is different from many other professional services. Without naming the guilty party, I can't help but smile at the long-time career CPA who boldly stated he wanted to run a technology consulting practice just like his accounting practice. That is, he expected the same utilization rate from his technology consulting accounts as he did from his loyal accounting accounts. Given his lofty expectations, I regret to say his career could have ended only in disappointment. The point is this: SMB consulting is different from other types of professional services-based consulting.

Use of remaining hours

If you've accepted the premise that an SMB consultant bills only half of the available hours in the long run, you may be curious as to what happens to all of those remaining hours. For some consulting managers, it's one of the greatest mysteries of running a consulting practice. Some skeptical businesspeople think consultants, under this scenario of a 50 percent utilization rate, are working only part–time—and that the out-of-sight consultants in the field are really sneaking in Bondi beach time in Sydney, NSW Australia!

Marketing

Certainly near the top of the time-robbers list is the marketing function. Something you already know from reading prior chapters is that SMB consultants are constantly marketing themselves, placing numerous follow-up telephone calls to track down hot leads, attending a chamber of commerce after-hours mixer, writing and delivering a proposal, and so on. SMB consulting is as much a finder exercise as it is a minder and grinder exercise.

One interesting point about marketing and the SMB consultant is this: Because much of the new work awarded to an SMB is project-based, it's not uncommon for an SMB consultant to put in the same marketing effort to land a one-time SMB consultant engagement that an accountant expends to land an account with recurring annual work and a very long life. In other words, the lunches, letters, and telephone calls requisite to consummating a professional services transaction (such as landing the client engagement) are often nearly the same when comparing accountants and SMB consultants (although in the Finder section of this book I stress the importance of trying to limit your sale time per account to boost profitability). The difference is that the SMB consultant may well be expending nearly the same marketing effort for a one-time event that an accountant puts forth for a ten-year relationship and constant workflow. This drives the marketing time commitment and associated marketing expenses higher for SMB consultants than for those in other professional services capacities. It has the net effect of reducing your utilization rate down to the 50 percent range.

Administration

Assuming that you're a sole proprietor SMB consultant or you run a small SMB consulting firm, you clearly perform much of your own administration (perhaps with the assistance of your long-suffering spouse or soul mate). It's shocking how much time the administrative function takes in the day-to-day world of SMB consulting. Faxing a document or mailing a letter at the local post office can take a significant amount of time. It's these administrative tasks that often result in your looking up at the clock at midday and not only feeling like you haven't accomplished a thing, but also pondering where all the time went. E-mail may be the biggest culprit. It's surprising how many e-mails you read and answer in a day.

One administrative task of critical importance is the accounting function. The hours spent billing your time and recording your financial activity are well spent and necessary.

In larger consultant organizations, the administrative function is ever present as well. While you may have administrative minions to send your faxes and mail your letters, you have to contend with a whole different layer of paperwork, such as time and expense (T&E) reports. I've personally found big company paperwork and reporting requirements to be more frustrating than the mindless tasks of mailing my own letters as a lone ranger SMB consultant.

Full cost principle

Accounting recognizes an idea known as "full cost principle" that basically says you must realize and recognize the full costs associated with your revenues. In SMB consulting, if you want a way of truly appreciating the hours you put in (both billable and non-billable), you have to realize and recognize your learning hours. It's the only fair way of truly assessing how hard you're working for those SMB consulting revenue dollars. Under this full cost model, you'll probably find you're working more than you thought.

Learning activities

Do you recognize any of the following learning behaviors?

- You've followed many of the sage tips presented in this book, and you subscribe to the local business newspaper (typically a weekly business journal in your region), which you read for one hour per week.

- You read the business section of the local paper each day, looking for interesting stories that might spur some creative SMB marketing ideas. You are also on the lookout for articles about troubled businesses so that you don't perform services for such entities and unwittingly become an unpaid creditor.

- You purchase third-party computer books on products, such as Windows Server 2003. You then proceed to spend hours reading the book at night and tinkering with step-by-step exercises in your home computer lab.

- You delve into the resource kit of a Microsoft application, such as Exchange Server, in the middle of the night to resolve a bedeviling conflict that has turned into a recurring nightmare (such as an impossible-to-solve open relay condition).

Assuming you've displayed any of these symptoms before, you are suffering a lower utilization rate as an SMB consultant than you likely know. If you spend 15 hours per week reading, these hours need to be thrown into the mix of total hours worked. This has the practical effect of lowering your utilization rate as an SMB consultant. Why? Because time dedicated to the SMB consulting professional is time taken away from other endeavors. This time must be added to the utilization rate equation. It is added to the denominator value, which is the whole of the hours you've committed professionally to being an SMB consultant—say, on an annual basis). A larger denominator with the same size numerator (the actual hours you bill) in a fraction equation results in a smaller decimal value. In this case, the decimal value (say 0.50) is the utilization rate of the SMB consultant. Go ahead and try the math yourself. Such an equation might be expressed as: 1000 hours/2000 hours worked = 50 percent utilization rate.

Rest and relaxation

So has it occurred to you that a few hours here and there will be consumed by simple, old-fashioned rest and relaxation (R&R)? Give yourself permission to sneak in a nap (yes, you read correctly). Burn-out would be far more devastating to your SMB consulting career than a short snooze one afternoon. R&R is even built into some union contracts, such as shift workers who built the trans-Alaska pipeline a generation ago.

Strategies on How to Make Money

So time for a bevy of Brelsford's Dozen offerings that will serve as strategies for making money.

Brelsford's Dozen: Bill 1,200 hours per year!

Armed with the understanding that a great SMB consultant has a 50 percent utilization rate, I challenge you to attempt to bill 1,200 hours per year, which would be at the extreme upper range of billable hour possibilities as an SMB consultant. This challenge assumes you are working 2,400 hours per year. Did you know that translates into 50 hours per week (each and every week)? That, my friend, is a busy week.

Fortunately—or unfortunately, depending on your viewpoint—you may occasionally work 80-hour weeks; however, few do this for extended periods of time. It's these 80-hour work weeks that can skew (not screw!) your average up. But remember that, in the long run, for every 80-hour work week in SMB consulting, there is a shortened week of 10 work hours lurking out there. The law of consulting that states "For every peak, there is a valley" holds true for SMB consultants. The key point is that the hours tend to balance out to a 50 percent utilization rate. You should keep short-term long hour aberrations in proper perspective.

Brelsford's Dozen: 12 percent profit margin

For the sake of argument, use a simple 12 percent profit margin rate in the world of SMB consulting. This number is actually close to true, once you do the math for a large sample size of professional services firms. Consider that large accounting firms, after everyone is paid, are darn lucky to have a 12 percent profit margin (something they'd freely admit to you). And this profit margin calculation accounts for the compensation paid to the employees and partners of the law firm. It also accounts for the depreciation expense over three years to recover the costs of the state-of-the-art network that the hardworking SMB consultant implemented (that's you!). So if accountants will accept a 12 percent profit margin, then you should happily accept it too!

For SMB consultants, understanding that profits are truly the bottom line is critical. After you have paid yourself a salary and have paid all of your taxes and expenses, you need to have about 12 percent of the gross revenue left (this is your 12 percent profit). Profit is the reward above and beyond just making a living as a consultant, the reward for taking a risk to start your own firm. It's also the money used to pay for capital additions and acquisitions.

> BEST PRACTICE: If you're not making a 12 percent profit margin in the long run, consider packing up your SMB consulting shingle and becoming someone else's employee. Why bother with the headache and frustration of running your own consulting practice when for nearly the same compensation you could work as an employee? This is a strict financial argument that doesn't account for the freedom you have as an SMB consultant, but you get the point. And perhaps you are really happy as an SMB consultant and don't want to assign a financial measurement to everything. But my point here should at least be taken under advisement.

Brelsford's Dozen: Calculating true costs

If you assume a 12 percent profit margin, you now need to understand how expensive your marginal costs are. That personal digital assistant (PDA) you've been eyeing to keep track of your tasks, address book, and calendar is more expensive in reality than it first appears to be. Getting certified, such as earning the MCSE or the Certified Cisco Internetwork Expert (CCIE), can be surprisingly expensive.

Something like a PDA is useful to the SMB consultant (I have one myself). A good PDA, for the sake of argument, costs $500. Assuming a 12 percent profit margin in SMB consulting, it takes just under $4,200 in revenue to earn a $500 profit. That PDA you want to purchase for $500 will suck the profit out of $4,200 of billable time. If you didn't buy the PDA, your profit would be $500 higher. Addressing the $4,200 in billable time, if your bill rate is $100 per hour, you would need to bill at least 42 hours to generate the profit needed to pay for the PDA (actually slightly more hours when you account for write-offs, which are discussed next).

> BEST PRACTICE: Perhaps you're a certification addict. Many SMB consultants are. You're satisfied with your life as an SMB consultant and now you want something more. You want to validate your professional technical qualifications with an MCSE. Your hard costs for an advanced certification, such as the MCSE, may exceed $10,000. This is a staggering number when you consider that $10K

just ate all of the profit out of $83,000 in SMB consulting rev-
enue—very possibly all of your profit for one year's worth of work.
Don't forget your SMB consulting utilization rate is going to take a
hit for the hundreds of preparation hours you'll incur to pass the
intensive MCSE exams. You really have to ask yourself whether or
not such an expensive technical certification designation will truly
pay off for you as an SMB consultant.

Brelsford's Dozen: Assume a 12 percent write-off rate

Another Brelsford's Dozen in the world of SMB consulting concerns write-
off rates. All SMB consultants should and do take write-offs. Believe it or
not, it's good SMB consulting practice management.

Dissatisfied clients

Some time or another, you will have one or more dissatisfied clients. You
may not know it from their communication with you, which might be very
pleasant when held face-to-face. Rather, you'll know it by observing your
accounts receivable balance. When a client's account ages 30, 60, or 90 days,
they are typically showing with their pocketbooks how dissatisfied they are
with your services.

Client dissatisfaction results for many reasons, such as technical
incompetence and poor communications, which are explored in various parts
of this book. The specific reason for the client dissatisfaction is not the point
here; rather, be aware that unhappy clients will shrink your consulting
revenues as an SMB consultant.

Learning curve analysis

You have picked a niche, have mastered client relations, and are making
money. Do you really need to recognize this 12 percent write-off rate? Yes.
For example, suppose you are an SMB consultant in the networking niche
who started in the Windows NT 4.0 days. Over the years, you mastered
Windows NT 4.0 and enjoyed client respect. Then Windows 2000 was
released, and you ran head-on into Active Directory. Billing adjustments are
made to account for time you spend learning Active Directory at the client
site. This is time you can't reasonably expect the client to pay. So, you've got
a legitimate write-off on your hands. Such write-offs are an acceptable part of

being an SMB consultant. You need to factor in learning curve analysis for product upgrades and new releases. It's all part of your budgeting model.

Trying new niches

Professional services firms are often looking for new opportunities. One reason is that niches, while well-defined and lucrative, can also mature and dry up. For example, suppose you're a SBS nicher in the SMB consulting game and Microsoft decides to release no future SBS upgrades. Over a couple of years, your SBS niche can be expected to dry up.

Be thinking about and developing new niches. Such professional development is just good SMB consulting management. The drawback is that, in developing new niches, you often have to take significant write-offs (which some SMB consultants call "write-downs") as you refine your consultant methodology and technical expertise. Many times such development comes through an implicit understanding with clients that you'll work for half-price on their job in order to break into that niche.

> BEST PRACTICE: A good consulting manager knows to expect reasonable write-offs. In fact, if such write-offs are absent, the consultant manager knows that either the SMB consultants on staff are hiding mistakes, loafing on the job, or not expanding their professional and technical boundaries. A small number of mistakes go with the SMB consulting territory. And if you are developing a new consulting niche, your propensity for making mistakes is higher while you are learning and mastering a new area.

Bartering

Another interesting way to make money is to effectively disregard money as a medium of exchange. Perhaps you really want a water skiing boat and you're engaged by a boat reseller. There exists an opportunity to get what you want, financially speaking (a new boat in exchange for services), and thus make money, even though money never changed hands. Just something to think about. Searching on Google (www.google.com) under terms such as "barter" will allow you to find business bartering networks.

Budgeting

Time to convert the preceding billable hours and profitability guidance into a practical outcome: an SMB consulting practice budget. So far you've thought about what you want to make (for example, $100,000 per year gross revenue) and you've learned how the 50 percent utilization rate applies to you.

Your supported bill rate

Part of the budgeting process is gathering information. You clearly need to know what markets you plan to operate within when it comes to bill rates. In general, urban markets tend to pay more than rural markets, reflecting increased cost of living. An SMB consultant who bills $125 per hour in San Diego, California, may only bill $60 per hour in Louisville, Kentucky, and $6 per hour in Tijuana, Mexico. This example isn't completely far-fetched (except for my point about Tijuana). Big cities offer a wonderful top line (the revenue picture), but sometimes the rural market offers the same bottom line with its lower cost of living. Two very different markets might offer the same relative financial compensation when all factors are taken into consideration. Read on.

Establishing your bill rate is critical because other key budget variables, such as number of hours billed per year, profit margin, and the write-off rate, have been established. In my simple examples in the next sections, I'll assume a bill rate of $100 per hour.

> BEST PRACTICE: Consider standing out from the crowd when it comes to bill rates. When I traveled across the US in the spring of 2003, delivering my free Wednesday night Advanced SBS workshops, I found a most interesting SMB consultant in Denver, Colorado. He approached me after my three-hour presentation, and we retreated to the hotel lounge. There he told a true tale of how he effectively flat-fees each client. His logic is simple and his method is surprisingly effective. This fella tells a prospective SMB client (typically closer to medium size) that it would cost $45,000 per year to have a competent computer support professional on staff. And this staffer wouldn't have the exposure to numerous other sites (including the latest workarounds, tips, and tricks). Every task would be performed for the benefit of only this site. You get the picture.

Now the financial part. This Denver SMB consultant goes on to say that he'll support the client site, lock, stock, and barrel (that is, completely) for $30,000 per year. A qualified SMB consultant will be only a simple telephone call away and on site within two hours. For this Denver SMB consultant, this business model is working very well. It should. Could you imagine pulling in $30,000 per SMB client site each year? Cool!

So the bottom line is that this SMB consultant is using the perma-temp in lieu of full-time IT professional argument. Try it out some-time.

Creating a budget

Microsoft Excel is the SMB consultant's tool of choice when it comes to using a spreadsheet application to create a budget. Figure 10-3 shows the typical layout of a budget. The top section typically reflects revenues, both total gross revenues and the gross margin (which is net of write-downs). The middle section reflects expenses. The lower section speaks to profitability.

Figure 10-3:

An SMB consulting budget

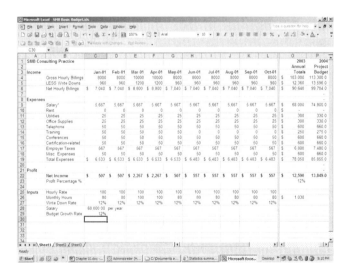

Notice across the side of the budget, going from left to right, are dates. These are typically displayed by month with an annual total after 12 months. The consultant referenced in Figure 10-3 earns $68,000 annually (this is his salary).

Extrapolation

A popular way to budget is to simply add a growth factor to the prior year's budget. An example would be to add 12 percent to last year's budget to account for higher costs, new consulting activity, and so on. Figure 10-4 displays this practice where an additional annual column for the year 2004 has been added to reflect 12 percent growth in everything across the board.

Figure 10-4:

Extrapolated budget growth of 12 percent

This form of budget is a massive oversimplification of how the real world works. Nonetheless, it's a favorite among entrepreneurs and SMB consultants alike who just want to get the general picture about how things look now and in the future.

> BEST PRACTICE: The 12 percent growth in revenues can be accomplished one of two ways. The first method is to work 12 percent additional hours. This increases your total working hours for

the year when you factor in the 50 percent utilization rate. The second method for increasing revenues is to increase your bill rate. It is common for professional services firms to announce rate increases to reflect inflation, increased efficiency, more value-added services, and so on.

Zero-based budgeting

My favorite budgeting method is zero-based budgeting. This method, from the land of MBAs, is detail-oriented, and surprisingly accurate. With zero-based budgeting, you typically use linked spreadsheets that allow you to enter the details of a particular budgeting category, such as the telephone expenses seen in Figure 10-5, on a child spreadsheet. The detailed information is then summarized as a category in the parent budget spreadsheet (which was shown previously in Figure 10-3).

Figure 10-5:

Details for the telephone expenses in a linked spreadsheet

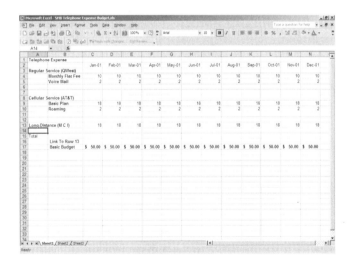

In a true zero-based budgeting scenario, you create a child spreadsheet for each budget category. These child spreadsheets are then linked to the parent budget spreadsheet. You then call around to get costs (for example, estimated utility expenses) or look at actual bills (say, from the telephone company). For the client billings, your spreadsheet may look similar to Figure 10-6, where the clients are listed by name and the monthly billings are inserted into the appropriate spreadsheet cells. To arrive at these billings, you would be advised to sit down with your clients and discuss their expected needs over the next year (monthly maintenance, upgrades, and so on).

Figure 10-6:
The framework for estimating your client billing on a monthly basis

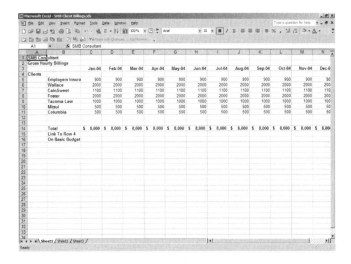

Break-even analysis

Budgeting has a very important role in the SMB consultant's life. But a budget requires you to make assumptions. In budgeting, especially the extrapolation method, the inherent assumption is that you have an operating history on which to base your budget numbers.

So what's an SMB consultant to do if they have no operating history and just want to know if they'll make it or not? To answer that, I use the break-even analysis method in Microsoft Excel. I've changed the SMB consulting scenario slightly so you can see the outcome in detailed numbers. As seen in Figure 10-7, the SMB consultant wants to gross $125,000 per year, billing at $105 per hour. The answer, via break-even analysis, is to bill 1,190 hours, which is a considerable amount of work but close to the aforementioned 1,200 hours per year (see the Brelsford's Dozen above).

Figure 10-7:
Break-even analysis using Microsoft Excel

In break-even analysis, you interpret the results by asking yourself if you believe you can bill that many hours at that rate in your marketplace. If you feel confident about it, you have your answer. Break-even analysis, in spreadsheet form, is wonderful for playing "what if" or what is more formally known as "sensitivity analysis." In this form of analysis you change your variables to create different financial scenarios. For example, perhaps you think billing the nearly 1,200 hours mentioned in the previous example is too aggressive. What if you raised your bill rate to $125 per hour as part of testing a different scenario? As seen in Figure 10-8, in this new scenario you have to bill only 1,000 hours.

Figure 10-8:
Engaging in sensitivity analysis using different break-even scenarios (such as changing your bill rate to $125 per hour)

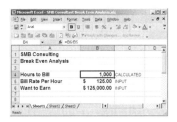

Boosting Your SMB Consulting ROI

Once you've looked at making money from an SMB consulting point of view and considered how to account for this money, it is important to visit the mathematics of return on investment (ROI). That is, how has the decision to become an SMB consultant panned out? Has it truly made money for you and how can you boost your ROI?

ROI mathematics

An ROI equation has three variables:

- **Costs** — These are your SMB consulting practice startup costs, which include marketing expenses, printing expenses, office rent, and so on. In this example, I'll assume $10,000 in costs to get started as an SMB consultant (I realize this might be too low, but it keeps the example simple).

- **Inflows** — Inflows are the extra cash you will make because you are an SMB consultant. For this example, assume that you will enjoy an extra $5,000 per year once you become an SMB consultant compared to your salaried day job.

- **Duration** — How long is the ROI relationship valid? Does your skill set as an SMB consultant have a useful life associated with it? You bet it does. Assume the useful life for the MCSE is about four years, because within four years it's likely you'll need to pursue yet another round of technical training to stay on the cutting edge of your field as an SMB consultant.

The ROI formula is as follows: ((Inflows x Duration) – Costs) / Costs. In English, you invest $10,000 to become an SMB consultant and receive an extra $5,000 a year for four years because of your wise investment. Here the ROI is 100 percent, which means becoming an SMB consultant was a good investment in this case.

Lowering your costs

There are several ways to boost your SMB consulting ROI. An often overlooked way is simply to lower your costs. Instead of renting great office space and running up that $10,000 startup bill, perhaps you could get your SMB consulting practice off the ground for as little as $1,000. If you were able to do lower your SMB consulting startup costs from $10,000 to just $1,000, your ROI (based on the same assumptions from the previous example) increases dramatically to 1,900 percent. That clearly demonstrates the power of controlling your costs.

Raise your bill rates

I've saved the best advice for last. Clearly one of the most obvious ways to boost your ROI, based on the mathematical equation, is to raise your effective bill rate. There are several ways to effectively raise your bill rate:

Inflation

The old saying that "all politics is local" could be changed to "all inflation is local" when SMB consultants look at reasons to raise their bill rates. Here is what I mean. You could track the broad inflationary measures, such as the Consumer Price Index (CPI), and impute how that relates to you, but you're far better off looking at how costs around you are rising. I recently raised my bill rates $5 per hour to account for my health insurance costs going up. In the past, for my family, I was paying $400 per month for full health insurance coverage. When it came time to renew, the costs for the same policy had increased to $650 per month. It was necessary for me to increase my SMB consulting bill rate slightly to pay for this inflationary effect of increasing costs for my health insurance.

> BEST PRACTICE: Be sensitive to the deflation argument that is occurring in the world today. Instead of inflation, many folks are afraid of deflation and simply trying to maintain their prices (e.g., SMB consulting bill rates). In this situation, it's not a good idea to propose a increase in your bill rate.

Skill set improvements

Suppose you've added another certification from Microsoft. This effort to gain another certification represents an increase in your basic skill set. Perhaps a bill rate increase of $10 or more per hour can now be justified. Again, use your best judgment.

Billable hour minimum

Another way to raise your ROI via your effective bill rate is to impose a two-hour minimum per client call (instead of a one-hour or zero minimum).

Think about it. If you tell your clients that you have a two-hour billable minimum, the clients will think twice about calling you out for small tasks they can solve on their own. And these are typically tasks that you have little interest in solving. This is also a legitimate way to bill up. If you make five client visits in an eight-hour day with a two-hour minimum (assuming all parties are in agreement with this provision), you will have mathematically billed for ten hours while only putting in eight. This has raised your effective bill rate by approximately 20 percent.

Travel time

Another overlooked billing category that will contribute to your profitability is billing for travel time. Think for a moment about what you sell in any workday: time. At some level, you are indifferent as to whether that time is billed sitting in a car commuting to an engagement or working at a client site. When I was with a large consulting firm, we billed for travel time. This act had a way of contributing positively to the bottom line of the financial statements.

Just because

There are numerous other reasons to raise your bill rate to improve your lot in life as an SMB consultant. I throw these into the "just because" bucket.

I recently mentored a new SMB consultant along the path to profitability. When I met James, he was billing at a rate nearly 40 percent below market. He was booked solid on his consulting schedule, to the point that he was fatigued and not giving his best effort to any one client. So in the final analysis, both James and his clients suffered from less-than-stellar outcomes. Later, when James raised his rate to market, he lost a couple of cheapo clients, but ended up making more money because of the higher bill rate. His schedule wasn't booked solid, he had time for technical training to increase his skill set, and he enjoyed a few afternoons of long-deserved rest. He thanked me for teaching him how to work smarter and more profitably.

Another situation was the "Bray School of Business" approach. Here a banker named Mr. Bray told me I wasn't being taken seriously enough because my bill rate was too low (this is in the mid-1980s, and my bill rate was an astounding $20 per hour). He told me to raise my bill rate to market immediately and start earning what I was worth. Mr. Bray must have been right as I went from apartment renter to home owner along the way and sometimes now make more in three months than I made in a year when I was young!

Intellectual capital investments

It's not breaking news to you if you've been reading this book from start to finish that Microsoft has certain opportunities available to you to boost your SMB consulting ROI. Two Microsoft opportunities worth mentioning are the Action Pack subscription and occasional "spiffs," such as the channel services provider rebate program for Small Business Server. Information for these types of opportunities is typically found at the Microsoft Partner site (www.microsoft.com/partner). The Action Pack subscription boosts your ROI by lowering your software purchasing costs. (Action Pack is a great deal for acquiring much of the Microsoft infrastructure software library.) Rebate programs and the like are cash directly to you, the SMB consultant, and as such immediately boost your RO!

Another consideration is to boost your ROI by letting someone else manage it. I use a firm called CFO2Go in the north Seattle area (a neighborhood called Bothell) that allows me to focus on SMB consulting and not financial accounting. Because I've sought out and actively used this type of help, I've been able to improve my financial performance by, ironically, worrying less about financial matters. Kinda strange but true, nonetheless.

> BEST PRACTICE: This section on ROI ends with a true gold nugget mined from the hills of California. Microsoft SBS "most valuable professional" (MVP) Susan Bradley posted a slide deck titled "Profitability and Financial Metrics in Consulting" from an accounting conference she recently attended (Tech2003) on the Yahoo! small business technology consulting forum at http:// groups.yahoo.com/group/smallbizIT/files/ and select the consulting.pdf file. Take a 15-minute break right now to go do this, print out and review the file.

> (15-minutes pass here)

> Now take another 15-minutes to go review Forbes well-done SBS ROI study that was written in 2002. It can be found at: www.forbes.com/whitepapers/microsoft/index.shtml.

Welcome back! Betcha were impressed with the financial analysis in that presentation eh? You should also look into some of the other great consulting files posted at the above address for more consulting practice management documents.

Resources

So, not to leave you hanging, here are a few additional financial resources to go forth with in your SMB consulting career. You'll want to add to this list by finding additional accounting texts, financial television and radio shows, and money management seminars that interest you.

- Suze Orman on CNBC. Suze is unusually entertaining in the dry world of money management. CNBC is a cable channel which is widely available in the US and Canada. Suze is shown in Figure 10-9 below.

- Bruce Williams. This radio announcer provides a wealth of money management advice for business people in an especially insightful way. Learn more about Bruce at www.brucewilliams.com.

- *Money Magazine*. There are so many money magazines out there, but *Money Magazine* is the grand daddy of them all. Learn more about this at http://money.cnn.com.

- Millionaire Mind seminar series. T.Harv Eker delivers a series of workshops that allows you to recast your financial blueprint so you can increase your earnings and overall wealth. I attended the free three-hour evening seminar recently and was very pleased with his motivational message. I did not attend the three-day seminar, but I'd like to do so in the future. Details at www.peakpotentials.com/homepageframes/homepage.html.

- TechRepublic. This site, at www.techrepublic.com, has much financial advice for technology consultants.

Figure 10-9:

Tune in to Suze Orman as you educate yourself more on financial and money management matters.

Notes:

Brelsford's Mailbox

Here's an interesting e-mail that was posted to the Yahoo! SmallBizIT list for small business IT consultants (more information at groups.yahoo.com/group/smallbizIT/?yguid=26422569. Because I'm on that list and know both of the authors (and have their permission), I reprint it here for your enjoyment. The topic is collections, an accounting matter if there ever was one. More specifically, it's a proven fact your ROI will be higher if you collect all of the monies you bill for! Here's the dialogue between Wayne Small and Eli Blank:

——Original Message——

From: EBlank1 <eblank1@yahoo.com> [mailto:eblank1@yahoo.com]
Sent: Tuesday, 10 December 2002 6:57 AM
To: smallbizIT@yahoogroups.com
Subject: [smallbizIT] Collections

I would like some advice about how to go about collecting from a client that seems not willing to pay outstanding invoices. We have tried to be in contact via phone and email with no luck. Our calls are not returned. The problem is that we are in Los Angeles and this particular client happens to be in Virginia. The total owed to us is approximately $2200. Thanks in advance for any help.

Eli

——Reply——

Eli,

The conditions may differ in the US from Australia, but here we have a few courses of action available to us.

> *1. Write them a letter via registered post (they have to sign to pick up the letter from the post office, therefore giving you proof they received it)*
> *2. Have your solicitor write them a letter called a "Final letter of demand"—this normally gives them 7 days to pay up else face legal action.*

3. In Australia, if they owe you more than $2000, then you can go to the courts to issue a wind-up order which gives them 21 days to pay or challenge your invoices before the government can start to wind up and close down their company. This is not the thing to do if you want to have any form of ongoing relationship with them, but will get you your money. I had a friend recently issue a wind-up order for an outstanding amount of $5000 to a company that had a turnover of $60M. They paid on day 20 the full amount, including legal costs.

The credit circle is becoming tighter down here and we're watching our credit control more closely than ever before. In total in the last 7 years, we have only written off $10,000 in bad debts — 75% of this has been in the last 6 months! Not a happy story.

Regards,

Wayne Small [SBS-MVP]
MCSE+I MCSE 2000
Technical Director – Correct Solutions Pty Ltd
For more information on us - check out www.correct.com.au

Notes:

Summary

What can be said about the importance of managing money in your SMB consulting practice? I've used 30 pages or so here to impress upon you the need for an accurate and robust financial accounting system, the importance of managing your financial affairs from a management accounting point of view, including planning, and strategies for boosting your ROI.

Specifically, this chapter covered:

- Understanding the difference between financial and management accounting

- Learning what popular accounting software packages might improve your SMB consulting money management

- Looking at financial traps, such as going broke while making money

- Appreciating ways to boost SMB consulting return on investment, including lowering costs and increasing revenues

- Follow-up steps in the money management area for you to take including reading additional accounting and finance texts, watching financial news programs on TV, and attending money management seminars

Part Four
GRINDER

Chapter Eleven
SMB Consulting Methodologies

Chapter Twelve
SMB Consulting Niches

Chapter Thrirteen
Microsoft Small Business Server

Chapter 11
SMB Consulting Methodologies

In This Chapter

- Adhering to the one-hour rule

- Using the "Go To Market" methodology of learn about it, build on it, sell it and deploy it to your advantage.

- Availing yourself of countless Microsoft methodology resources, including partner and project guides, Microsoft Operation Framework and Microsoft Solution for Internet Businesses.

- SMB methodology tips and tricks such as franchising, evergreens, and exit barriers.

Resistance is futile. Try as you might, even if you run as fast as you can, you can't get away from one fact of life in profitable SMB consulting: You need to have consulting methodologies that you adhere to. Oh sure, you can say you're an "artist" and need creative space. To that I say "Right on, baby" followed by "Be prepared to be broke most of the time," much like starving artists often are. The key point is that it's essential you embrace consulting methodologies in the flight to SMB consulting profitability. "Why?" you ask? Please read this chapter and ask the same question again at the end. I suspect you'll be able to answer it yourself.

Don't Reinvent the Wheel

A methodology is a set of consulting practices that provides the command and control you need to achieve profitability as an SMB consultant. You want this set of steps and procedures to sanely guide your practice and avoid mistakes and box canyons and the like.

Maturing as an SMB consultant

Don't put too much pressure on yourself in this chapter if you're just starting out. Methodology development is a function of experience, the kind of experience you'll gain over time as you mature as an SMB consultant. And it may be true that methodologies are appreciated more by the older crowd—also known as the "no hair" or "grey hair" crowd—than youngsters. Younger SMBers seem to enjoy the "process" of discovery and don't seem as interested in performing the same set of tasks over and over again in the name of efficiency and effectiveness.

Characteristics of a mature SMB consultant are:

- **Awareness.** To even utter the term "methodologies" proves your professional maturity an SMB consultant. Go ahead and say it now—yes, out loud. LOUDER! If you're not even aware of consulting methodologies or can't say "methodologies," it's highly unlikely you're actually using one.

- **Reflection.** Here I'm speaking towards an SMB consultant who is living, breathing, and performing at a higher level on the food chain than a break-fix technician who basically takes orders for a living. This is a reflective soul who is contemplative and has the ability to reason and think.

BEST PRACTICE: Remember back to Chapter 2 of this book, that focused on business planning? In that chapter I encouraged you to develop a business mission statement that worked for you. You might be interested to know that a motto from IBM, which could be woven into your business mission statements, is THINK! You have to admit that single word is short, sweet, and effective.

- **Seasoning.** In all fairness, we don't arrive at the start of our SMB consulting journeys thinking and breathing consulting methodologies. Part of what introduces the methodology mindset into an SMB consultant's behavior is experience. Over time you learn what consulting approaches work and don't work. This seasoning alone allows you to develop a casual, living SMB consulting methodology, something akin to a living theology in religious quarters.

- **Professionalism.** When you work with executive-level clients, being able to articulate your SMB consulting services in the context of a methodology gains the client's confidence. Having a consulting methodology puts the word "professional" back into professional services.

- **Structure.** Perhaps the real point I'm trying to make in this chapter is that formal methodologies bring necessary structure to your consulting practice. As you mature as an SMB consultant, ad-hoc approaches will serve you less and less effectively. You are encouraged to both embrace and celebrate the introduction of formal consulting methodologies as a sign that you're making it as an SMB consultant. Congratulations!

Snatching victory from the jaws of defeat

Working smarter, such as using methodologies in your SMB consulting practice, will have profound effects on your success or "win" rate. I liken it to snatching victory from the jaws of defeat. It's about having good sense and judgment in the heat of SMB consultant battles on what surgical procedure makes the most sense. It's about having an innate ability to maintain order and procedures in a SMB server deployment so you don't chase your tail and repeat steps.

My take on consulting methodologies is pragmatic: avoid defeats. There's enough good work out there and you can be plenty successful by simply not making mistakes. This is another way of saying that, if you consistently deliver what you promised, making money and enjoying your engagements won't be problems. Consulting methodologies bring the consistency element and effectively allow you to avoid defeats.

Depending on your consulting philosophy, you may be playing to win or you might be playing not to lose. The playing to win approach includes such things as introducing bleeding-edge solutions. You're trying to hit the home run. Many times you do, but other times you strike out. The playing not to lose approach is more akin to the public accounting approach to consulting: conservative. Here an emphasis is placed on risk adversity, management of the engagement, and avoiding surprises. Both approaches can be profitable, but the playing not to lose approach is clearly a more consistent delivery mechanism and in alignment with consulting methodology thinking.

Value of repetition

Not reinventing the wheel inherently recognizes the value of repetition. SMB consultants develop a deeper skill set in their niche when they perform the same process over and over again. Hardly anything surprises them. Clients like specialists who have performed a certain procedure many times in the past. The value that repetition brings can be measured in an assured outcome. Clients love assured outcomes.

So this view of SMB consulting methodologies is to appreciate the value of repetition. Repetition breeds familiarity and allows you to debug your process. And in plain East Texas talk, it's a heck of a lot easier to bid work when you've done it several times before. In fact, there is an entire school of consulting that believes sound consulting practice management involves performing the same work over and over again. I've seen this first hand with accounting application installers who install the same package week after week at different client sites. It's a good living for these people, so who's complaining.

> BEST PRACTICE: Granted, too much repetition can be boring with a capital "B." I'm clearly not talking about a lot of personal enjoyment and fulfillment here. So my advice is deal with it and find satisfaction where you can. I'm teaching you how to make money as an SMB consultant! Business isn't always barrel of monkeys.

Another take on the value of repetition proposition is that an SMB consulting manager can avoid having a key man on staff. The "key man" concept, taken from the insurance industry where key man insurance is actually underwritten and sold, refers to an individual who is so critical to the business entity that if that key man leaves, the business could be devastated. Some people believe Bill Gates is a key man at Microsoft.

Here's how the key man concept plays out in SMB consulting. You grow your SMB consulting practice to the point that you start to hire additional staff. Some of these people act as "mini-me's" or junior SMB consultants. Try as you might to impress the value of the built-in deployment methodology in Small Business Server (something I cover in Chapter 13), you have one or two loose cannons (this is a legal term believe it or not). One of your loose cannons, Joe, likes each client site to be different. This includes different naming conventions, different subnet structures, etc. Because of his style, Joe evolves into somewhat of a key man. Then, suddenly, Joe meets a key woman and flees to the Florida Keys. You must step in to manage his clients and you discover Joe was very creative. You proceed to engage in significant unbillable rework to make every client site Joe maintained adhere to your remaining client sites in terms of layout structure, style, etc.

Finally, a war story from years gone by of demonstrating the value of repetition as a baseline SMB consulting methodology. I lent a hand to Gateway, the computer maker, with its retail store network, functioning in a few different capacities. One role was to provide my own opinion on the intrinsic value of its individual stores being SMB consulting practices. The idea was that Gateway, with its technology focus on SMB solutions (selling the software, hardware, and services combined), could in effect become a national SMB consulting firm a là IBM Global Services at the enterprise level. There would be sufficient training for the Business Solutions Advisors (BSAs) in the store and the Network Solution Provider (NSP) technicians who were contracted by Gateway to perform the actual deployment and maintenance work. Gateway was discussed at length in Chapter 2.

The grand plan with Gateway, based on my memory, was that Gateway stores could niche on specific SMB products, like SBS. Each store would have a reasonable sales goal such as ten SBS solutions per month. Given there were over 300 Gateway stores at the time, that's 3,600 SBS solutions sold and deployed per month or over 36,000 such solutions annually. This would have single-handedly made Gateway the largest SBS reseller and provide much appreciated work to fleets of aspiring SMB consultants acting as NSPs. Central to the success of this strategy was adhering to a strict SBS solution deployment methodology, where every customer site had to be exactly the same. Because Gateway sold the original equipment manufacturer (OEM) stock-keeping unit (SKU) of SBS, it was responsible for the initial free follow-up technical support (two incidents) for the consultant and the client.

So here's the bottom line to the story. If each site varied in its deployment, the potential for the server support call center in, say, North Sioux City, South Dakota, to get "slammed" was enormous—not to mention that a scenario of no strict SBS deployment methodology would likely leave many unhappy customers in its wake. And Gateway, which has an internal cost assigned to each support call received, could quickly eat up the profit from the sale of a complete SBS solution via its stores. Ouch. I think you can now see the tremendous value of having an SMB methodology.

> BEST PRACTICE: So why all this talk about efficient studies (the time and motion stuff)? If an SMB consultant is working in a time-plus-materials world where the more hours you work, the more money you make AND YOUR CLIENTS WILL PAY IT, then my arguments in this section fall flat. But two obstacles conspire to work against unlimited time and materials billings. First, clients have billing limits and won't continue to pay for your learning time over the long run. Second, fixed bid scenarios and maintenance contracts have reemerged as a favorite practice again. That's because in a leaner economic era, customers have more say in how much will be spent on information technology (IT) (read "spend less") and your hungry competitors will undercut you with their own fixed bids.

> Fixed bids shift the financial risk from the customer to the SMB consultant. Also note that fixed bids and maintenance contracts are in vogue again because the Microsoft SMB infrastructure solutions have become much more stable in the Windows Server 2003 time frame (a trend that started in earnest in the Windows 2000 Server time frame). SMB consultants can eek out profits under fixed bid pricing, whereas a decade ago that might not have been possible.

One-Hour Rule

This section addresses something so obvious, its one of the great mysteries as to why SMB consultants don't do it: seek help when they can't solve a problem. It's easy enough to commit yourself to better business practices and promise to work more efficiently and effectively. However, a combination of human nature and Murphy's Law can highjack our best behaviors, and we find ourselves engaging in what is known in the recovery movement as "insanity." We repeat the same behaviors over and over again expecting a different outcome. We simply don't admit our powerlessness on occasion and ask for help.

Been there and done that. But I did learn the value of the one-hour rule—where you call for help after one hour of troubleshooting—after I hired employees and took on consulting manager responsibilities. Here I witnessed firsthand, as sometimes only a person removed from the problem on the outside looking in can do, the phenomenon called "heads down." I've seen an individual put in nearly twenty billable hours on a dot matrix printing problem (of course the client could have purchased several dot matrix printers for the equivalent cost). I've seen a person accrue ten billable hours on an "I can't log on" workstation problem (again, you could have purchased a new workstation for that amount). This concept leads us into the following Brelsford's Dozen.

Brelsford's Dozen: 12-to-1 Odds

I propose the following SMB consulting theorem for your approval. If you don't adhere to the one-hour rule, you run significant risk of going heads down and putting in a dozen hours before you look up again and, enlightened by your defeat, finally ask for help. Prove me wrong on this but I believe, based on my own observations, that I'm on target here.

Specifics

Here are the seven steps for successfully implementing the one-hour rule.

1. **Keep time.** You must glance at your time piece when you start a specific task, such as trying to resolve an "I can't print," so you know when an hour would have passed. It's easy to forget that you've even committed an hour to the problem if you don't know what time you started.

2. **Wear the extrovert hat.** Don't sink into introverted mode, as it'll be especially difficult to look up after an hour and make an outbound plea for help.

3. **One hour.** At the one-hour mark, call your consulting manager or a peer in the industry. Granted, if you work for yourself as an SMB consultant, you are the consulting manager, so you'll need to call a peer to describe the situation and brainstorm some ideas to solve the problem.

BEST PRACTICE: So you don't have any friends in the industry, eh? Then be sure to either join or start an SMB-related user group in your area. Information on starting a user group was presented in Chapter 9 in the "Managing Yourself" section.

4. **Newsgroup postings.** Minutes later, if after speaking to someone in step #3 above and the problem is still unresolved, immediately post your troubleshooting scenario to a couple of newsgroups. This can include the Microsoft newsgroups accessed from the support link on any Microsoft product page or the Yahoo! third-party newsgroups. Be the extrovert and post to newsgroups after one hour. These links are found in Appendix A.

5. **Walk away.** Go take an early lunch to clear your head out. Walk away from the problem and take a fresh look at it when you come back. It works wonders to see the sunshine and then return to the server room refreshed.

6. **White board**. If the problem escapes a solution, do as I say and as I try to do: Use a white board in a conference room to "map it all out." I once was bedeviled by a complex server upgrade from NetWare to NT for a 500+ user site. Long story short—problems were encountered using the NT based NetWare emulation feature as part of the migration process. The situation became so confusing—not to mention stressful—it took a few hours in the conference room to draw out where we'd been, what we'd done, and where we were headed to get it all straight! Use the white board as a tool in your methodical approach to SMB consulting.

7. **Call Microsoft Product Support Service (PSS).** When all else fails, call for bona fide Microsoft support earlier rather than later. There are at least four ways to engage PSS:

   •Small Business Server free support incidents. Specific to the world of SMB consulting and the SBS product, you get two free PSS support incidents with the retail SKU. With the OEM SKU, the two incidents exist but the call is supported by the OEM's product support call center, not by Microsoft PSS. Note the SBS free support incidents are current as this writing and could change in future releases.

•Mission critical business down for registered partners. You can call into Microsoft PSS and, as a registered partner, plead your case that your client has a server down situation that is mission critical. If you're successful, you'll be granted a free PSS support incident. These requests are evaluated on a case-by-case basis.

•Microsoft Certified Solution Provider/Partner support five-pack. Simply stated, sign-up to become a Microsoft Certified Solution Provider/Partner and you are granted five PSS incidents per year. This value in-kind nearly equals the costs of the certified partner program (as of this writing it's $1,500 USD per year). Remember that this has many more benefits above and beyond paid incidents (such as over $25,000 of free software for its modest $1,500 USD annual fee), so be sure to think about that as well.

•$250 USD (approximately) per incident. For the rest of us, you can always call in and pay by the drink. That is, a PSS incident as of this writing is $250 USD. The good news is that it's well worth it as PSS will stay on the telephone with you for hours until the matter is solved.

BEST PRACTICE: This is a best practice in the truest sense: time management. You should endeavor to adhere to the one-hour rule if for no other reason than basic SMB consulting practice profitability. It works like this. A "standard" SMB consulting gig where you install a solution such as SBS can yield around $4,000 USD in today's market. Compare that to enterprise technology gigs that start around $400,000. Obviously the IT consulting talent on an enterprise gig can go "heads down" and break the one-hour rule while still allowing for overall engagement profitability. But darn it, if you break the one-hour rule on an SMB consulting gig, you're seriously threatening the profitability of that project. There's just not enough financial slack to cover for mistakes and missteps.

Go To Market

Microsoft's methodology resources are predicated on its current "Go To Market" (GTM) message. In this section, I explore the components of GTM and then send you to a site where you can attend GTM courses in the USA and Canada.

GTM is based on four broad headings: Learn About It, Build On It, Sell It, and Deploy It. Each of these is a separate sections below has respective methodology elements extracted from numerous partner and project guides (I discuss these guides below in the next major action).

> BEST PRACTICE: Microsoft has also color-coded its GTM methodology. This color coding is enforced in Microsoft partner communications. So when you view a Web page or printed guide, you'll want to know what GTM area the discussion topics relates to by using this list:
>
> - Learn About It = Rust, Orange/Red color
> - Sell It = Yellow
> - Build On It = Green
> - Deploy It = Blue

Learn About It

The Learn About It component, which emphasizes educating yourself, contains these items, depending on the specific topic at hand (for example, some items relate to security, communications, infrastructure, etc.):

- Business opportunities
- Campaign opportunities
- Sales readiness
- Technical readiness
- Sales training resources
- Technical learning path

- Market opportunity for security solutions

- Learning path with recommended tracks

- In-depth white papers

Build On It

The Build On It component, which emphasizes developing your solution (infrastructure or application), contains the following:

- Resources for system builders

- Application development tools

- Rich solution selling job aids

- Customer-ready presentations and demos

- Case studies and selling tips

Sell It

The Sell It component, which emphasizes the selling of your services and solution, contains the following:

- Marketing collateral

- Case studies

- Presentations

- Pricing and licensing

- Product information

- Preinstallation aids for OEM system builders

- Software development resources for ISVs

- Marketing templates

- Sales data sheets

- Demonstrations

- Application compatibility information

Deploy It

The Deploy It component, which emphasizes the "grinder" or delivery aspects of your consulting practice, features the following:

- Project guides

- Product information

- Technical support resources

- Microsoft Project 2000 templates for security solution projects

- Prescriptive guidance for successful deployments

- Tools and support

- Service opportunity guides

- White papers

Figure 11-1 displays standard GTM discussion on a Microsoft Web page.

Figure 11-1:
The Microsoft Small Business Server GTM message is shown here.

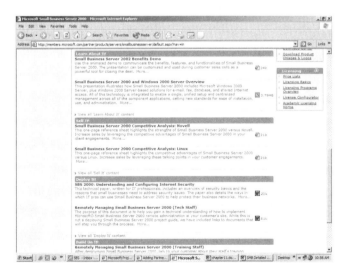

More Microsoft Resources

Not surprisingly, there are more Microsoft resources relating to technology consulting methodologies. In this section I present Microsoft resources including partner and project guides. As you read this section make sure you always compare these lists to the latest offerings at Microsoft's partner portal at www.microsoft.com/partner. Microsoft frequently adds to its partner-related resources.

Microsoft partner and project guides

Microsoft often communicates its technology consulting methodologies to its partners via its partner and project guides. The following gives you a sampling of both as of this writing, which I thought would be of interest to you. Note that both kits typically are discs with literature, slide decks, and technical resources.

Partner Guides

Partner guides tend to conform more to the strict GTM message from Microsoft. In general, partner guides emphasize marketing over technical topics. As of this writing in mid-2003, here are several of the partner guides available:

- Small Business Server 2000 Partner Guide (note this will be updated for SBS 2003).

- Go To Market Windows Server 2003

- Microsoft Windows Server 2003

- Secure, Connected Infrastructure Solutions: Sales, Marketing, and Technical Resources to Help Build Secure Solutions

- Desktop Mobility, Collaboration, and Communication

- Communications Infrastructure: Sales, Marketing, and Technical Resources to Help Build a Communications Infrastructure Solution

- Microsoft Customer Relationship Management

- Microsoft Office: Transforming Information Into Impact

- Intranets and Portals

- Desktop Security and Reliability

- Communications Infrastructure: Sales, Marketing, and Technical Resources to Help Build a Communications Infrastructure Solution

- Microsoft Mobility Solutions: Wireless Communication Anytime, Anywhere

- Drive Sales, Drive Profits

- Microsoft Volume Licensing

- Microsoft Windows XP / Microsoft Office XP: A Powerful Combination

- Microsoft Office XP: The Desktop Productivity Experience

- Microsoft Office XP: The Dependable Foundation for Businesses of All Sizes

Learn more about partner guides at: http://members.microsoft.com/partner/salesmarketing/partnermarket/partnerguides/default.aspx?nav=ln which is shown in Figure 11-2.

Figure 11-2:
Check here frequently for new partner guides to build and perfect your technology consulting methodologies.

Project Guides

Project guides tend to be more technical in nature and organize Microsoft software and solution information according to five specific organizational roles:

- Business decision makers

- Sales and marketing staff

- Technical staff

- Project manager

- Customer training staff

Microsoft designs project guides to help consultants build a methodology (underlined for emphasis!) for implementing Microsoft software and solutions. They consolidate and present the information necessary for successful customer engagements. Project guides, based on widely recognized best practices and procedures, identify a specific service offering that can be delivered successfully to customers.

- Assessing Information System Security in the Small and Medium Business

  This project guide describes the value of a security assessment, discusses security assessment methodology, and presents important areas that should be included in every security assessment. This project guide is shown in Figure 11-3 and can be found at: http://members.microsoft.com/partner/projectguides/system_security/ (I give the general project guide URL at the end of this section for the remaining guides).

Notes:

Figure 11-3:

The components of the Assessing Information System Security in the Small and Medium Business project guide are shown here.

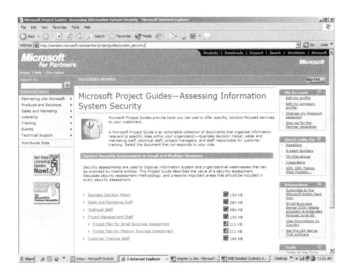

- Implementing Small Business Manager Project Guide

  All the information your staff needs to sell and deploy Small Business Manager can be found here. The Deploying SQL Server 2000 Project Guide is included.

- Upgrading Exchange 5.5 to Exchange 2000 Using the HP DAS-to-SAN Exchange 2000 Migration Solution

  This project guide shows how to sell and implement an Exchange 2000 SAN migration project. Specifically, it covers the migration of the small to medium-sized organization from Microsoft Exchange 5.5 with direct attached storage (DAS) to Microsoft Exchange 2000 with a storage area network (SAN) solution.

- Business Intelligence Project Guides

  These two project guides, the Business Intelligence Solutions guide, and the Interactive Reporting Solutions guide show how to use Microsoft Office XP (and other Microsoft products) to deliver scalable decision support solutions for medium-sized business customers and interactive reporting solutions for small business customers.

- Securing Windows 2000 with Internet Security and Acceleration Server 2000 Project Guide

  Comprehensive background information to help you plan your security implementation, along with step-by-step procedures needed for product installation.

- Deploying SharePoint Portal Server Project Guide

  This is the information your staff needs to sell and deploy SharePoint Portal Server to your medium-sized customers.

- Deploying SQL Server 2000—Technical Staff Only Project Guide

  Easy to follow, step-by-step preinstallation and installation instructions for your technical staff to use to install SQL Server 2000.

- General Project Guide

  Read this project guide for general information relevant to all projects presented in the project guide Series.

- Implementing Exchange 2000 Server Project Guide

  This guide covers new installations, upgrading from Exchange Server 5.5, and migrating from competitive products. Help for your project management and customer training staff is included.

- Desktop Project Guide

  The Deploying Secure Wireless Networks Project Guide, Deploying Windows XP Professional, Office XP—The Microsoft Desktop, and Deploying Windows XP Professional for Small Businesses Project Guides are all included on this page.

- Windows 2000 Server Project Guide

  This page includes multiple project guides relating to Windows 2000 Server, including: Securing Windows 2000 with Policies and Templates; Deploying Secure Wireless Networks; and Consolidating Microsoft Servers.

- Microsoft Business Solutions Customer Relationship Management Project Guides

  These project guides show how to sell, implement, and customize Microsoft Business Solutions Customer Relationship Management solutions.

All of these and more project guides can be found at the following URL: http://members.microsoft.com/partner/productssolutions/ projectguides.aspx?nav=ln

> BEST PRACTICE: I've found both the partner and project guides to be extremely valuable. When you subscribe to the Microsoft Action Pack or become a Microsoft Certified Partner, you will receive tons of both partner guides in the monthly/quarterly mailer with your membership. Partner guides may also be purchased for a nominal fee (typically $15) from the Microsoft Partner site (www.microsoft.com/partner).

> But I have even better news regarding project guides! As a general rule, project guides are free on the Microsoft Partner site and available for immediate download and use.

Microsoft consulting services

The good news is that Microsoft doesn't really compete against you, the SMB consultant! And the even better news is that you, the SMB consultant, can engage Microsoft Consulting Services (MCS) to assist you when you get in over your head. Imagine a situation where you've taken on a somewhat larger assignment than you are accustomed to. Then add technologies outside your technical niche. Instead of surrendering and accepting defeat, you reach out for assistance. I've seen it done before on a "Microsoft Solution for Internet Business" project, which I discuss in just a few pages.

Notes:

BEST PRACTICE: MCS could be just the mentor you need as you try to scale your SMB consulting practice to take on enterprise engagements (if that's what you want to do). Consider using MCS as a consulting partner for your first few large engagements so you can safely learn the new neighborhood. Granted, MCS has a very real cost to it and you might not profit greatly from your first few enterprise engagements, but you get the point.

Figure 11-4:
Microsoft Consulting Services is friend, not foe.

Learn more about MCS at: www.microsoft.com/business/services/mcs.asp.

Notes:

Microsoft solutions/operations framework

Microsoft has two consulting methodologies weaved into numerous white papers and Microsoft Press books. These are the Microsoft Solutions Framework (MSF) and the Microsoft Operations Framework (MOF). Both models are beyond the scope of SMB consulting, but are mentioned here for reference purposes. You are encouraged to visit the Web sites below for more information:

- The MSF provides "people and process" guidance to help teams and organizations become more successful delivering business-driven technology solutions to their customers. Read more about MSF at:

www.microsoft.com/technet/treeview/default.asp?url=/technet/itsolutions/tandp/innsol/default.asp

- MSF is about achieving mission-critical systems reliability, availability and manageability. Read more about MSF at:

  www.microsoft.com/technet/treeview/default.asp?url=/technet/itsolutions/tandp/opex/default.asp

Microsoft QuickStart Deployment Program

You might want to cherry pick from MCS's five step "QuickStart Deployment Program" as you define the service delivery aspects of your SMB consulting practice. There are five elements to the QuickStart Deployment Program, according to MCS:

1. **Evaluate.** The Microsoft QuickStart for Evaluating Windows 2000 Service provides workshops designed to cover the core features of the product, build consensus on the drivers for deployment, and make initial architectural decisions. Note that as of this writing, the Evaluate phase hade not been updated for Windows Server 2003.
2. **Plan.** The MCS QuickStart Planning Service provides fixed duration packaged services that rapidly produce a first pass architecture design and identify risks for the full deployment.
3. **Build.** Microsoft offers services to follow up on the risks identified in the plan phase; lab testing; completion of a detailed design document; creation of installation, operations, training, deployment, and communications plans; and a pilot implementation.

4. **Deploy.** At the conclusion of the build phase, all decisions have been made and tested so everything is ready for a rapid and trouble free deployment. Custom services are available to oversee and execute the deployment.

5. **Operate.** A complete operations plan is critical for successful deployments. Microsoft offers services to deliver top-quality operational best practices customized for your environment.

Learn more about the MCS QuickStart Deployment Program at: www.microsoft.com/business/services/quickstart.asp

Microsoft Solutions for Internet Businesses

Microsoft has a comprehensive well-known "bundle" of e-commerce programs that, when teamed with the hardware provided by preferred top tier providers and services from by Microsoft Certified Gold Partners, presents an all-in-one solution. The actual programs contained in Microsoft Solution for Internet Businesses (MSIB) are:

Microsoft Windows 2000 Server Family
- Core platform for e-commerce and line-of-business (LOB) applications (will be updated for Windows Server 2003)

Microsoft Commerce Server
- Rich catalog features, including XML-based catalog schema
- Flexible order processing
- Personalization and targeted merchandising
- E-business analytics for critical business-decision support
- Management user interface (UI)

Microsoft Content Management Server
- Content creation and publishing
- Content templating
- Content check-in/check-out
- Content versioning

- Publishing workflow

- Multichannel content delivery

- Dynamic content rendering

Microsoft Solution for Internet Business (MSIB) Accelerator

- Prescriptive Architecture Guidance (PAG)

- Solution sites and integration code

- Solution-based services and support

Microsoft SQL Server

- Reliable, scalable database and analysis system with built-in support for XML

Microsoft Internet Security and Acceleration Server

- Firewall

- Web caching

- Secure, fast Internet connection

Microsoft BizTalk Server

- Creation and management of dynamic business processes that span applications and organizations

- Internet and external data integration using 300+ prebuilt data system adapters

Microsoft SharePoint Portal Server

- Search

- Collaboration

- Document management

The idea behind MSIB was to bring a comprehensive solution involving software, hardware, and services in a "one-stop-shopping experience" to the enterprise customer seeking an e-commerce solution. In many ways, this is in alignment with what you're trying to do as an SMB consultant. Granted, not every SMB consultant is a system builder, but probably has a preferred hardware provider relationship as part of the SMB service delivery mix.

More information on MSIB can be found at: www.microsoft.com/solutions/ msib/default.asp .

Brelsford's Dozen: Methodology Samples

There's nothing like looking to the leaders when formulating your own SMB consulting practice. By that I mean you can cherry pick methodology examples from existing large, medium-sized, and small consulting practices to assist in the rapid development of your own methodologies. So in this Brelsford's Dozen segment, you will visit 12 Web sites from other consulting practices and draw out methodology elements that make the most sense to you. Consider using a search engine or specialized information sites, such as Kennedy Information's Top 50 Consulting Firm list (www.kennedyinfo.com), to find Web sites for other consulting firms and their respective methodology postings. Do it now!

SMB Methodology Tips and Tricks

This section offers some sage advice on practice methodology for both the budding and experienced SMB consultant. These are taken directly from the street and not the textbook.

> BEST PRACTICE: Revisit "SMB Consulting Proposal Framework" found early in Chapter 7 as one methodology component to guide your practice.

Franchising

I encourage SMB consultants to view their practices as franchises and take steps to ensure the consistently high-quality delivery of services. This includes incorporating franchise-like behavior, such as distributing satisfaction surveys (discussed earlier in the book in the Minder section) and eliminating the key man (also discussed previously in this book). The thought here is to develop a well-respected practice that could be duplicated by underlings you hire and train.

Evergreens

On the Spring 2003 Microsoft Go To Market (GTM) tour, one instructor with significant consulting experience gave the "evergreen" speech. He spoke towards the need for a technology consultant to have ongoing client relationships, not just project work. One suggestion he made focused on the business intelligence area using Microsoft tools such as Data Analyzer for Office (see www.microsoft.com/office/dataanalyzer/default.asp). This tool allows you to data mine business information in any size company. The instructor's point was that a tool like Data Analyzer might be a monthly engagement (say a four-hour visit) where the consultant runs reports and shares the findings with management. The true context of this discussion involved the enterprise where the consultant "sits" between the IT department and the management team and gets the two departments to work together. That is, the IT department houses the business data and the management team needs the information. By using Data Analyzer, the two departments are effectively linked by the consultant.

> BEST PRACTICE: I've seen this "man in the middle" approach to consulting in other places as well. I once had a consulting manager boss who thrived in political environments and billed many hours as a man in the middle. Typically Barry would be engaged by a school board to work with the IT department for a school district, necessitated by because the fact that the school board and IT department didn't talk to each other well and needed a mediator. Barry got the engagement. Good work if you can find it and want it!

Visio methodology templates

A hidden jewel in Microsoft Visio (which can be acquired cheaply in the Microsoft Action Pack subscription I mention numerous times in this book) is the built-in consulting methodology templates. In Visio you can use the following methodology templates as more tools in your SMB consulting practice. These templates might be a "deliverable" that you could offer clients as a service.

- Yourdon and Coad

- Booch OOD

- Total Quality Management

- Mind Mapping

- Gane-Sarson

- Jackson

- Jacobson Use Cases

- Nassi-Schneiderman

- Real-time Object Oriented Modeling (ROOM)

- Rumbaugh OMT

- Shlaer-Mellor

- Ssadm

- UML

Barriers to exit

Another consultant, a Canadian, spoke to me once about creating barriers to exit. I've discussed a similar concept earlier in this book under the heading of trust relationships. The idea here is to make yourself so valuable to a client that they'd let everyone else go before they'd part with you! You'll need to discover what types and levels of services make you invaluable to a client, but you get the point: focus on client retention as part of your SMB consulting methodology. I've tried to implement barriers to exit by appropriately introducing technologies such as SharePoint collaboration to my clients. Adding value by introducing welcome technologies is effectively a barrier to exit in SMB consulting.

SMB Case Study

Some time ago, I penned an SMB consulting column for the dearly departed journal, *IT Contractor* magazine. One month, I shared the story of an SMB consulting engagement I had at a lumber retailer on a small island outside Seattle. Long story short, the engagement had everything this chapter is about in the work methodology area. Point your browser to www.certmag.com/ itcissues/jul02/exp_brelsford.cfm?printversion=1 to read the entire story (as seen in Figure 11-5

Figure 11-5:

SMB Consulting case study at IT Contractor magazine (now part of CertMag).

Notes:

Brelsford's Mailbox

Time to reach into my Inbox and grab reader mail to share with you.

Hi Harry—

Thank you very much for a very information/productive seminar on Microsoft's Small Business Server.

I was wondering if you could e-mail me some additional information. My vertical market is Real Estate and I heard you say that you support a couple of clients in that area. I am interested in getting as much information about software/hardware and anything else that you think might be useful for me in selling and supporting this vertical market. I have purchased Goldmine, Act, Top Producer, as well as other mortgage and real estate software to put together a turn-key system that I can market to the mortgage and real estate industry. Any information or contacts you could give me would be greatly appreciated.

I am also interested in subscribing to your e-mail newsletter. Thank you again for your consideration.

Jose G.

Hey, Jose—Thanks for the note. I can offer you the following advice based on what you described above: develop a bullet-proof service delivery methodology. I say that because you've already got a great sense of what to focus on (both product and economic sector) and your enthusiasm is apparent for the field of consulting. I suspect you will do very well in landing clients using some of the approaches outlined in this book for sales and marketing (in the Finder section). So I want you to think about how you're going to consistently deliver high-quality services to your clients, allowing you to be profitable. Might I suggest it be as simple as starting with a mere checklist of steps for implementing each of the products you've described above? Keep me posted on your progress.

Your partner in crime…harrybbbbb

Summary

This chapter has tried to impress upon you that consulting methodologies aren't just for the enterprise. Rather, SMB consultants can benefit from having consulting methodologies that bring necessary structure and lead to profitability. This chapter recast the traditional consulting methodology discussion through SMB consulting lens including:

- Adhering to the one-hour rule

- Using the "Go To Market" methodology of learn about it, build on it, sell it, and deploy it to your advantage.

- Availing yourself of countless Microsoft methodology resources, including partner and project guides, Microsoft Operation Framework and Microsoft Solution for Internet Businesses.

- SMB methodology tips and tricks, such as franchising, evergreens, and exit barriers.

Chapter 12
SMB Consulting Niches

In This Chapter

- Selecting from different niches including Microsoft Office, collaboration solutions, e-commerce solutions, and customer relationship management (CRM) solutions

- Considering technology consulting niches, such as project management, training, etc.

- How to mentor power users at your client site

- Selecting additional SMB niches, such as selling and supporting Line of Business (LOB) applications, programming, infrastructure, and security

- Providing advisory and business consulting services

- Packaging yourself to reflect your niche

- Sage advice for the SMB nicher

This is the chapter where the pedal truly hits the metal. Few decisions you make will impact your professional success as an SMB consultant than the niche you elect to serve. This chapter focuses on a variety of SMB niches to select from, with the following chapter targeted specifically at Small Business Server (SBS).

Microsoft Office

One product that is omnipresent in nearly every SMB client organization, but doesn't get the respect it deserves, is Microsoft Office. This tried-and-true front desk workhorse actually represents a tremendous consulting opportunity for SMB consultants who are willing to look beyond Word as a simple word processor. In this section, I'll highlight Microsoft Data Analyzer, an impressive analytical tool, followed by what I call a fresh look at Outlook.

Microsoft Data Analyzer

Microsoft has tools you can use to put yourself in the "Business Intelligence" (BI) consulting business and help customers "mine" their data. One such tool is the Microsoft Data Analyzer, which can be purchased from Microsoft for under $200 USD and incorporated into Microsoft Office. This is shown in Figure 12-1 and can be found at www.microsoft.com/office/dataanalyzer/default.asp.

Figure 12-1:
Obtaining Microsoft Data Analyzer

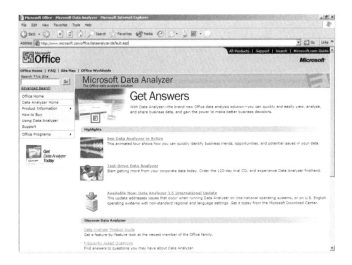

It's important that you understand the role of Microsoft Data Analyzer, which is trying by design to introduce BI to roughly 80 percent of the organization (meaning the majority of knowledge workers in the organization). Microsoft figures that, because Microsoft Office is pervasive on nearly every business desktop, why not deliver a BI solution for the masses? Microsoft freely admits for the most sophisticated forms of BI analysis, a business might deploy a partner's solution such as SAS or SPSS (high-end quantitative analysis software applications).

So if you accept that Microsoft Office is likely on your customer's desktop computers, then you would accept that your SMB customers already have most of the tools necessary to conduct BI! Figure 12-2 shows the sample data contained with Microsoft Data Analyzer and gives you a look at BI in action. What you are looking at is the fact the Western Europe on the right (colored green on the screen, but grayscale in this screenshot) has achieved 40 percent year-over-year growth for July 2001 (center of screen) versus July 2000. Australia achieved only 20 percent year-over-year growth.

Figure 12-2:

Viewing data with Microsoft Data Analyzer

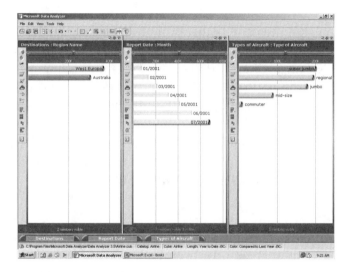

Fresh look: Outlook

Outlook could be called the most under-used tool in Microsoft Office. Although you likely utilize its powerful universal e-mail properties, its ability to manage your information, transfer it to a PDA device, and store information to public folders is where its real value shines through.

Managing information

One of the oldest tricks in SMB consulting is to have a handful of billable hours in your hip pocket ready to legitimately "bill" at a client site. One bucket of these readily available billable hours is to help your clients make better use of Outlook. Perhaps you will train the client's staff on organizing e-mails in Outlook folders. I've never seen a business person who didn't appreciate learning more about Outlook! It's likely your real-world usage of

Outlook is readily convertible to billable hours with your clients.

PDA synchronization

Another rabbit to pull out of your hat is to provide real value by assisting your clients in the purchase of a "personal digital assistant" (PDA), such as the Compaq IPAQ. Mailbox data in Outlook can easily be copied or synchronized to a PDA, allowing your customer to access e-mails, contacts, and appointments while away from the office. It's a nifty feature that can result in great billable hours for you at each client site.

> BEST PRACTICE: Remember that PDAs will synchronize information from a user's Mailbox. It will not synchronize information from the Exchange Global Address List (GAL). This is important to remember for a simple reason: Small Business Server 2003 creates a GAL entry for every user added, but doesn't create a mailbox-based contact record that can be synchronized to a PDA. Ergo, the boss can't see employee contact information on his PDA while driving. You can step in and remedy this situation by creating a contact record for every employee at your client sites!

Public folders

The Microsoft solution theme of "institutional knowledge retention" plays out with Outlook Public Folders. There are many ways SMB clients use public folders, including creating a common contact list (of company customers), creating common calendars (so everyone can be scheduled appropriately), and to receive e-mails (such as "Jobs"-related e-mail from company employment advertisements). Some firms make "posts" to public folders, such as human resources matters (e.g., employment manual). You can help facilitate this process as the SMB consultant.

But the example I really want to show off right here, right now, is the use of public folders to truly retain institutional knowledge: faxes! Small Business Server has shipped with the Shared Fax Service for a few releases. The Shared Fax Service is now part of the Windows Server 2003 operation system. When an inbound fax is received by the computer, it can be e-mailed to a public folder where it may be reviewed and permanently stored.

BEST PRACTICE: Storing faxes to a public folder solves a huge problem regarding lost faxes. In the past, I've had clients who couldn't find an important paper-based fax. The client was obviously angered. Enter computer-based faxing and storing the resultant fax TIF file image in a public folder. Presto! No more lost faxes and the safe preservation of institutional knowledge and business know how.

Figure 12-3:
Using Outlook public folders to receive faxes.

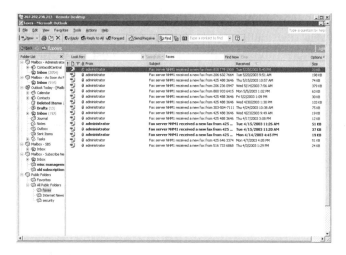

BEST PRACTICE: It's not necessarily what I intended when I set out to write this book, but along the way I found more than one SMB consultant who has niched on Outlook. That's all they do-all day long. Of course they do much more than I've outlined in this section. For example, I found one SMB consultant who engages in the advanced customization of Outlook. You'll find there are several great advanced Outlook texts on the market that are part of your path to SMB consulting riches if you so desire.

And now for some late breaking news. Right near the end of the book-writing process, Microsoft release more information on an Outlook 2003 add-on titled "Business Contact Manager," which is being billed as the CRM solution for SMB. No additional details available at press time, but be sure to monitor this development on the Office and Outlook sites at Microsoft.

Collaboration

First things first. Let's talk terminology. Microsoft is now encouraging its partners, as of this writing to refer to common baseline tasks, such as e-mail and messaging, as collaboration. Of course the term "collaboration" certainly involves more than e-mail and even includes SharePoint technologies, but the point about updating your "Microspeak" terminology is not to be missed. Depending on the professional field, collaboration means different things to professionals. For example, a therapist might consider the term "collaboration" to be some form of touchy-feely therapy.

> BEST PRACTICE: There are many terms in business and technology that have dual meanings. For example, "risk" in finance can have a totally different meaning than "risk" in real estate. Be sure to translate your terminology when moving between professional groups.

Collaboration is threatening to certain old school managers and business owners (even those found in SMB). Why? Because many business oldsters are what we call "solid-line organizational chart" people. They believe communication flows up and down the hierarchy. But collaboration tools tend to promote dashed-line or informal communications where employees might be speaking directly with stakeholders, such as large customers. Egads, that scares the devil out of some folks.

> BEST PRACTICE: Part of the SMB consulting opportunity in the collaboration area is what I'd call "management consulting." If you encounter a solid-line organizational business person and you have business therapy skills, you might counsel these people to embrace change, become dashed-line managers and so on. This could turn into lucrative billable hours for you.

SharePoint technologies

Certainly one of the main collaborative solutions being offered and promoted by Microsoft right now is the SharePoint group of technologies. SharePoint comes in two flavors: Windows SharePoint Services (WSS) and SharePoint Portal Server (SPS) as of this writing. The idea behind SharePoint technologies is many-fold, including:

• Acting as an Intranet to foster better internal communications

- Serving as a low-end document management system

- Acting as a workflow application for managing approvals

- Managing versioning

- Providing a collaborative environment with discussions

- Retention of organizational knowledge by minimizing rework

The primary interface is Digital Dashboard which can be customized in both appearance and functionality. Digital Dashboard is shown in Figure 12-4.

Figure 12-4:
Meet Digital Dashboard in SharePoint Portal Server.

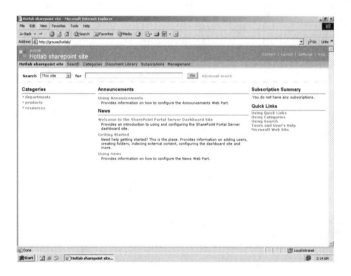

BEST PRACTICE: Digital Dashboard was once a standalone product at Microsoft and was well known for serving as an Executive Information System (EIS). An EIS is a business information system oriented toward business owners and executives. You could create an EIS in SharePoint's Digital Dashboard. For example, you could hook Great Plains Dynamics data stored in a Microsoft SQL Server database and use that data to display the DuPont Ratio Model as red, yellow, and green traffic lights. Imagine a satisfactory Current Ratio (Current Assets-Current Liabilities) being displayed favorably as a green light in the Digital Dashboard.

Much more information on Microsoft SharePoint technologies can be found at www.microsoft.com/sharepoint. You can also learn more about SharePoint in SMB by viewing the SharePoint-related services provided by Microsoft at www.bcentral.com.

Time for some straight talk. Microsoft's SharePoint technology area represents a tremendous opportunity for the SMB consultant on several levels.

First, the opportunity to be a business management consultant in defining the organization's information management needs. Here, you would interview company employees to discover how they store information. For example, do employees store data in the My Documents folder on the local C: drive? Do employees struggle to understand the difference in share names on the network (USERS, COMPANY) and what to store in each share location? The results of this interview process would be compiled into a report to the manager/executives/owners at your client site.

Second, defining the structure of SharePoint is rewarding work. What document categories should be created? What fields should be added to document profiles? The outcome of this planning process is displayed in Figure 12-5 where stored documents are displayed.

Figure 12-5:
The document library in SharePoint Portal Server.

Third, the implementation of a SharePoint solution will involve give-and-take dialog between the consultant and the client. This will include the appearance of the Intranet pages hosted by the Digital Dashboard component. It will also include the movement of existing documents into the SharePoint store repository.

Finally, there is a tremendous training opportunity for instructing end users (staff) on the proper use of SharePoint. Several students in recent Microsoft Hands On Training Labs I had the pleasure of delivering in 2003 saw this as being of tremendous benefit in delivering SharePoint to customers.

> BEST PRACTICE: To be honest, WSS will probably meet the need of most SMB clients and it's free as part of Small Business Server 2003. WSS is much more robust than its predecessor SharePoint Team Services (STS) and includes document management (check-in, check-out, and versioning). Start your SMB clients with WSS!

Outlook and Exchange Server workflow

Another collaborative offering from Microsoft is a workflow approach using Outlook and Exchange Server. Here the idea is to route e-mail based on criteria, such as matching keywords. For example, an e-mail that is denoted as a "bad idea" might be sent to the "round file" (that is American slang for the trash bin).

To deploy a workflow solution based on Outlook and Exchange Server, you'll first need to plan out what you're trying to accomplish. It might be that your workflow is really replicating a business process, such as approving new account applications. You will then need to acquire the Microsoft Development Environment tool. This tool allows you to create the workflow logic and apply it to the Exchange Server environment. A sample workflow project that routes e-mails based on good and bad ideas is shown in Figure 12-6.

Notes:

Figure 12-6:

When creating the workflow, it's critical to draw the arrow directions correctly to properly create the workflow logic.

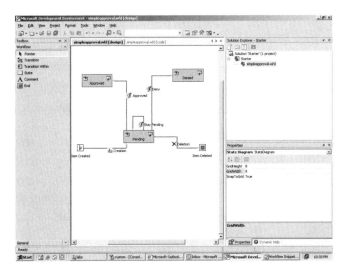

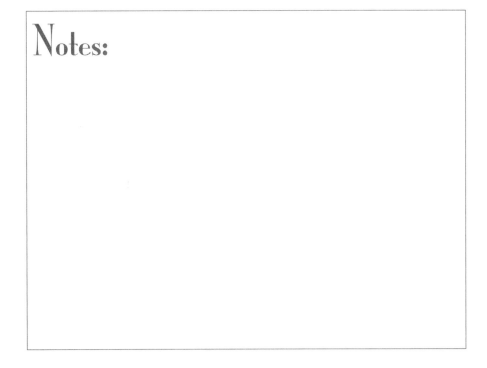

Notes:

Once the workflow is created, it routes and processes e-mail. For example, in Figure 12-7, the administrator is correctly advised of workflow processing for all items. This is by design.

Figure 12-7:

How you will see the workflow in action.

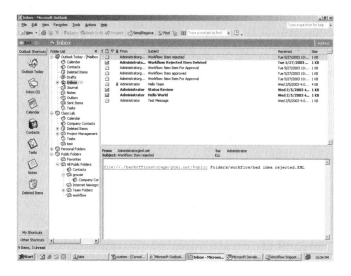

BEST PRACTICE: One of the problems with being successful as Microsoft is that some of its solutions compete with each other. For example, approval routing (the example shown in the above two figures) can also be handled by SharePoint-based solutions. So my opinion is that the Outlook/Exchange Server workflow combination, while becoming "legacy" in the eyes of bleeding-edge technologists, is suitable when directly replicating business processes. I can think of situations in paper-based offices, such as an insurance company, where this would work wonders.

E-Commerce

So your grandmother makes the best jam in the county. She wins the first place blue ribbon at the county fair each year. You've decided that her unique talents, creating prize-winning jams, should be exploited and marketed around the world. You propose to incorporate her and then create for her an Internet e-commerce presence. This is truly an SMB case study in the making.

You'll want to consider the following when pursing e-commerce work as an SMB consultant. Microsoft's baseline e-commerce solution, based on Commerce Server, will set your client back over $25,000 in software-related licensing fees before you sell your first jar of jam. You'll need the enterprise edition of Commerce Server to allow for Internet connectivity, etc. Pretty bleak, eh?

But fear not. Microsoft bCentral, acting in its SMB portal role, has an e-commerce solution starting at $25 USD per month, as seen in Figure 12-8.

Figure 12-8:
Start with Microsoft bCentral for your SMB e-commerce solution first to save time and money.

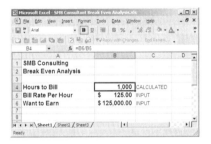

This isn't the "real" Microsoft Commerce Server solution at the enterprise-level but it will work for most SMB customers and at a fraction of the price compared to purchasing the real Commerce Server product. It's a great deal for SMB scenarios. In fact, I use the e-commerce service at bCentral myself to manage my SMB Nation conference registrations, etc. The interface for managing my e-commerce function is shown in Figure 12-9.

Notes:

Figure 12-9:

What you see is what you get. This is the real Microsoft Commerce Server solution being delivered as an affordable ASP-type service to SMB clients.

BEST PRACTICE: It's important to encapsulate for you what the SMB consulting opportunity here is. First, you can get the smallest of your SMB clients to sell products and services over the Internet and accept payment (credit cards, PayPal, etc.). You can bill hours for the setup and maintenance of their bCentral-based e-commerce site. Second, you can assist these same customers in transitioning to a bona fide e-commerce solution once it makes business sense. It's the old "start with us, grow with us" solution-selling message from Microsoft in the SMB sector. You get the point.

More information on Microsoft Commerce Server technologies can be found at www.microsoft.com/servers and select Commerce Server.

Microsoft Line of Business Applications

One of the more exciting Microsoft developments in the early 21st century is its entry into line of business applications. This completes its solution-selling message because it allows you to provide a business application on top of its infrastructure. That is, you could potentially deliver end-to-end Microsoft solutions to your customers. I profile Microsoft's customer relationship management and accounting solutions followed by a surprisingly long list of Microsoft's LOB family!

Microsoft Customer Relationship Management

Microsoft's Customer Relationship Management (CRM) solution, while initially oriented towards that enterprise and the large side of the medium space, has recently shown hope in the medium portion of SMB space. That's because Microsoft realizes that many of its enterprise-level solutions can be scaled to medium area in SMB. Microsoft's CRM solution, which I won't explore in great detail here, can be explored at www.microsoft.com/crm. The Microsoft CRM product page is shown in Figure 12-10.

Figure 12-10:
Microsoft's CRM solution is generating positive buzz in the channel.

Also, as mentioned above in this chapter, Microsoft is positioning the Outlook 2003 add-on called "Business Contact Manager" as a CRM for SMB (including the smallest of companies in this space). Be sure to educate yourself more on Business Contact Manager. (In a future revision of this book I'll highlight this tool much more.)

BEST PRACTICE: Every SMB consultant seems to be looking for the silver bullet and the magic elixir to boost their profitability. I join in these sentiments. Both you and I realize that we can't make it as simple network installers in this new era of mature operating systems and the like. Thus, we must provide more value to our clients. Embracing the CRM offering as a consulting service is one such vehicle to do more for our clients as SMB consultants. I also like the CRM offering as an avenue for additional work, because I don't need to be a CPA or accounting specialist as the next section on Great Plains might lead you to believe.

CRN magazine recently sent the SMB-version (really more medium-sized than small) of Microsoft CRM product through the ringer and found it was a feature-rich, acceptable CRM application for businesses under 500 users who are tolerant of an Outlook interface. More important, this CRN article reported that only 15 percent of businesses in the mid-tier marketplace have CRM solutions. This statistic got Microsoft excited about the potential of this underserved market segment and should get you excited as well as an SMB consultant potentially looking for a tribe! Read the CRN review of Microsoft's CRM solution at www.crn.com/sections/special/midmarket/midmarket.asp?ArticleID=42090.

Microsoft Great Plains

One of the defining moments in my SMB career was working for a Great Plains accounting software reseller in the mid-1990s. I was responsible for networking infrastructure and a co-worker named Vernon (a CPA) handled the Great Plains accounting practice. We were like bread and butter. I'd go in and implement the computer network infrastructure and Vernon followed with his Great Plains Dynamics accounting solution. It was a business model that worked very well.

This same business model works even better today because Microsoft has acquired Great Plains and rolled its accounting system offering into its SMB area. Ergo, you, the budding SMB consultant, could provide an end-to-end solution in the financial accounting area.

BEST PRACTICE: Be advised there is more to Great Plains than meets the eyes. It's not a simple installation of "click next" dialog boxes. Rather, important business decisions, such as the financial chart of account structure, need to be made upfront. To be honest, the best way to approach this SMB consulting space is with at least two consultants. One consultant handles infrastructure and the other handles Great Plains. This is, of course, the same Vernon and Harry tag team I defined in the opening paragraph of this section.

Great Plains basically comes in two flavors: jumbo and small. The jumbo size, oriented toward medium-sized firms, is known simply as Great Plains and contains the following modules:

- Bank Reconciliation
- Business Portal
- Cash Flow and Collections Management
- Customization Tools
- eBanking
- eExpense Automated Expense Management
- Fixed Asset Management
- Foundation
- General Ledger
- Great Plains Standard
- Multicurrency Management
- Payables Management
- Receivables Management

The small-sized Great Plains offering is known as Small Business Manager and offers financial management, sales, purchasing, inventory, payroll, and reporting capabilities. I've observed many infrastructure SMB consultants embrace Small Business Manager as a way to grow their consulting practice. For more information on Great Plains, visit www.microsoft.com/greatplains.

Note that Microsoft is also the proud owner of the respective Solomon accounting application family. Details at www.microsoft.com/businessSolutions/Solomon/default.mspx.

Additional Microsoft LOBs

As I was writing this book, what surprised me during my research phase was how many LOB applications Microsoft offers. It's very eye-opening! Here is a Microsoft LOB application area list as of mid-2003:

- Analytics and Reporting
- Field Service
- Financial Management (in addition to Great Plains and Solomon)
- Human Resource Management
- Inventory and Order Processing
- Manufacturing
- Online Business Services
- Project Management (this includes solutions from Microsoft's Navision product area and is discussed further in the next section)
- Supply Chain Management

Needless to say, Microsoft is frequently adding LOB application assets to its product family. You can read the latest at www.microsoft.com/BusinessSolutions/default.mspx.

BEST PRACTICE: The next time you're reading Business Week magazine in the lobby of your doctor's office as you wait for your appointment, be sure to scan to pages 72-73 of the April 21, 2003, edition to read the article titled "Small Biz — Microsoft's Next Big Thing?" This is one of the best combo business/technology articles I've read that clearly articulates Microsoft's new SMB LOB strategy. You could also search for it online at www.businessweek.com.

Project Management Consulting

Project management skills are readily transferable between industries. Perhaps you learned project management in a construction management course at a local college. Or maybe you learned project management in the field by just doing it. The project management techniques you learned (and I discussed in Chapter 8 of this book) can be turned into cash for you, the SMB consultant. Why? Because there are billable hour opportunities providing project management consulting services.

I'll temper my excitement from the last paragraph with the understanding that you probably didn't purchase and read this book with the idea that you'd be a strict business consultant providing project management services. Fair enough. The real point to this section is to encourage you to take a fresh look at Microsoft Project. Perhaps you looked at Microsoft Project a few years ago. Much like the little tykes on your block where you live, Microsoft Project has really grown up! It now has a client/server architecture to it. The client-side is the Microsoft Project desktop application that was explored in Chapter 8. The server-side is shown in Figure 12-11 and can be found at www.microsoft.com/projectserver.

Figure 12-11:
Pitched as an "enterprise" project management server solution, Microsoft Project Server offers profitable consulting opportunities for the SMB consultant.

BEST PRACTICE: So just how would an SMB consultant niche on an enterprise tool like Microsoft Project Server? Very carefully! You would want to understand the type of SMB client that could take advantage of this solution set, such as engineering and architecture firms. And if you can stomach it, perhaps you'd take on an enterprise-level project engagement for a while to go make the big bucks. Seriously, providing technology consulting services on a major project like a pipeline project might just be the way to set aside a financial nest egg you could use to better capitalize your fledgling SMB consulting practices. Ahhhh, the trade-offs we all must make on the way up!

There is another interesting twist on Microsoft project management solutions and it was a bullet point in the prior section on LOBs. Microsoft's Axapta acquisition provided it an immediate project management LOB application family. This is shown in Figure 12-12 and I recommend you explore the consultant module.

Figure 12-12:

Microsoft's project management LOB application might be an SMB consulting niche for you to consider.

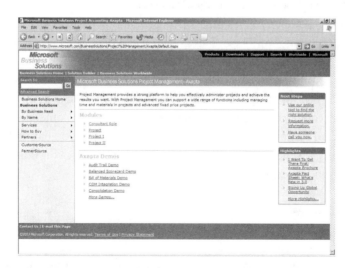

bCentral Consulting

Perhaps I like to swim against the tide of conventional wisdom even when it means confronting an internal Microsoft product team like the bCentral group. But I truly believe that bCentral isn't just an end-user consumer play, but also a small business consulting platform. Try the following thoughts on for size and see if you agree with me.

E-commerce revisited

Earlier in this chapter I presented the bCentral-based e-commerce capabilities as a low-cost way to start using the bona fide Microsoft Commerce Server product. It was sort a "start with us, grow with us" message centered around doing business on the Internet. Having used bCentral e-commerce capabilities, I can report to you that there is a true SMB consulting opportunity here. The hours that I spent learning how to hook the e-commerce component to my Web site, implement PayPal, and sign up as an approved credit card merchant are the same hours available to you for billing a small business customer. Why? Because you can add value in the process by freeing up the small business owner to focus on business operations and not mastering bCentral's e-commerce function. Remember, it's not like your small business clients have tons of free time to do this stuff.

Technology and small business

So if you spend some quality time surfing around Microsoft's bCentral site at www.bcentral.com, you'll see that it is not just Microsoft's small business portal, but much more. It's the merger point between business and technology. And that intersection is where you can thrive as an SMB consultant. You can have one role as a business advisor to a small business and another role as the technology advisor. You can help someone's grandma sell her award-winning jams and hams worldwide. And you can bill appropriately for the pleasure. I love bCentral and I think you'll love it as you learn more and more about it.

Finder, minder, grinder

Across the pages of this book, I've pumped bCentral as a tool for you to use in organizing an SMB consulting practice using the finder, minder, grinder paradigm. For example, in the early chapters, you learned that bCentral can assist your efforts in getting the business. Later you learned in the minder section that bCentral can help you manage your business activity. Finally, I'm presenting to you that bCentral can be the consulting work you perfom. That is, you can be an SMB consultant that consults to small businesses directly on bCentral matters. This view-one not held by the bCentral team in Building 30 at Microsoft's Redmond campus-is nevertheless legitimate.

> BEST PRACTICE: Go ahead and take the plunge. Identify yourself as a bCentral consultant who helps small businesses implement the suite of bCentral solutions. I'd be thrilled to hear from you on how it works out. Drop me a note at harryb@nethealthmon.com and let me know. Who knows? Perhaps I'll be able to profile your success story in the next release of this book.

More SMB Niches

So it's time to pile it on and list a buffet of SMB technology niches for you to evaluate. This is the section that will accomplish exactly that. Following this section will be discussion on "softer" skills such as training, mentoring and business consulting. Let's rock.

Infrastructure

You have by now correctly concluded that I have a bias toward the infrastructure in the technology consulting field. At one time, infrastructure alone was a great way to make a six-figure consulting income. But infrastructure became more mature and less complicated, allowing more technology consultants to enter the field and benefit from easier and simpler deployment scenarios.

Don't get me wrong. You can still make a living providing infrastructure-related services as an SMB consultant. I've spent a large part of the book, including the next chapter, convincing you of this. But the reality today is that you need to do more than just infrastructure. The following sections outline what you can put "on top" of the infrastructure.

Narrow Vertical Market Applications

Countless SMB consultants whom I've had the pleasure of meeting and corresponding with over the years have shared with me their business models, including being resellers and consultants for independent software vendors (ISVs) who sell narrow vertical market applications, such as legal, manufacturing, retail, and medical applications.

Legal

Beatrice Mulzer is as big of fan of SMB consulting as anyone. She successfully relocated from Michigan and to thrive in an "old boys" network of central Florida, where a woman probably has to prove herself more than a man. But Beatrice didn't do it on infrastructure alone. She realized early on as a new Floridian that her marketplace didn't have huge infrastructure needs and many client sites were happy with peer-to-peer networking. Nope, Beatrice made it happen by aligning herself as both reseller and consultant with a legal software application called "Sanction II," which is trial presentation software by Verdict Systems. So now Beatrice can both install an infrastructure solution such as SBS at a law firm, followed by the deployment of a trial presentation solution. It's the old "hot dog and bun" strategy of selling complementary products (a marketing concept in the view of the five Ps of marketing presented in Chapter 5 of this book). Beatrice's SMB consulting practice is demonstrated in Figure 12-13.

Figure 12-13:
EvidencePresentations provides both infrastructure and application-level consulting services.

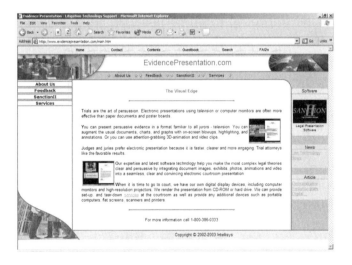

Manufacturing

A former coworker at a consulting firm where I once was employed had his technical niche focused on manufacturing. It allowed him to demonstrate his years of business expertise cultivated in the manufacturing area and combine it with technology solutions, such as manufacturing resource planning (MRP) and enterprise resource planning systems (ERP). There are countless programs focused on manufacturing for you to evaluate and consider adding to your consulting portfolio. Try searching on the terms "manufacturing software" using a search engine such as Google (www.google.com).

> BEST PRACTICE: Remember that manufacturing is one of the most capitalized industries alive. That translates into the following for you, the SMB consultant: Manufacturing clients aren't afraid to spend what it takes to maintain and improve operations. Many technology consultants have found the manufacturing area to be financially rewarding!

Retail

An underserved marketplace is the retail sector. You might recall in Figure 5-8 of Chapter 5 that retail presents tremendous opportunities for applying technology. One SMB consultant who is taking on the retail challenge is Amy Luby from Omaha, Nebraska. Amy has signed on as a Microsoft Authorized Reselling Partner for its retail management solution (listed earlier in this chapter in the Microsoft LOB discussion). This allows Amy's consulting practice, Mobitech (show in Figure 12-14), to implement both SBS (infrastructure) followed by retail-oriented business applications.

Notes:

Figure 12-14:
Mobitech has spanned the SMB technology field by adding retail technology consulting to its infrastructure work.

BEST PRACTICE: Don't forget to tell your retail clients that Microsoft has a site which presents its family of software products from a supporting retail professional's viewpoint. Visit www.microsoft.com/retail to learn more.

Medical

Numerous times, and in many different cities, I've met SMB consultants who have selected the medical area as a consulting focus. It has worked well for these folks, from several perspectives. First and most foreground as of this writing is the HIPPA compliance area in the USA. HIPPA is a set of rules and regulations that affects the medical profession on many levels. Regarding technology, HIPPA dictates how patient data must remain secure. An attendee at Microsoft's four day "Go To Market" workshop in Denver shared with me his business model that focused on HIPPA compliance. He likened it to a mini-Y2K boom and said his business was thriving. But in the next breath he also confided that he would need to develop new areas of expertise in the medical technology area, as HIPPA is a short-term boom that will have passed by mid-decade (2005).

Another area in which to provide medical technology services is practice management. Here I cite my friend who is an SMB consultant in Las Vegas, Nevada. He has paid a fee to a medical software ISV to "own" a territory. He then sells and implements a medical practice solution that he puts on top of SBS. An interesting twist in the licensing of the medical practice solution is that an annual fee is charged for each employee. This recurring revenue piece is a nice offset to my friend's project-oriented infrastructure consulting work.

> BEST PRACTICE: Be sure to see the insightful article on niching in health care technology consulting in a recent issue of CRN. The author, Jeff O'Heir, wrote in the May 30, 2003, article titled "VARs Rely on ROI to Stay Healthy" that health care markets are low-hanging fruit. Read about it at www.crn.com/sections/Features/Features.asp?RSID=CRN&ArticleID=42239.

Database

I've always been slightly envious of folks in the database consulting area, for a number of reasons. These reasons, listed herein, might effectively sell you on becoming a database administrator (DBA) or database consultant in your quest to build your SMB consulting practice.

Technology immaturity

Possibly you've drawn the following conclusion as a stakeholder in the technology community. Whereas infrastructure could be considered mature with its one gigabyte network transmission speeds, the "data" area feels particularly immature. There is a sense amongst business people and technology professionals alike that we've not even tapped the potential of databases. I don't know about you, but getting in on something early when it's immature, such as the management of data, is akin to buying low and selling high in the financial community. That's a good thing.

Ongoing relationships

Folks I've seen who present themselves as database consultants seem to sustain excellent long-term relationships if they're competent at their craft. This plays out in two ways. First, there is the "camping out" effect. I once served an insurance company as its infrastructure consultant. This particular account was in the medium-space, with just over 100 employees. By all accounts it was your run-of-the-mill engagement, with my services being engaged on an as-needed basis. But there was an interesting twist. The database developer, a consultant brought in to develop a comprehensive company-wide database solution, was always there when I was there. In talking with him I learned that he had been there 40 hours a week for the past two years building a custom Oracle database. He billed at his normal consulting rate for his time ($100/hour). Do the math and you'll see that he was raking it in from this SMB gig! Right then and there I had a new appreciation for databases.

Then there is the "evergreen" concept to databases. Often with database deployments routine reports are compiled along with the ever-present list of special reports. Clients are always thinking of new reports that they'd like to see from the database. This translates into great ongoing work for the SMB consultant that adds a database skill set to her practice.

Business acumen

Another reason that I like databases as a consulting area is that it explores the marriage between business and technology. You're creating databases that are typically full of business data. Database-related consulting is a home for people who truly have a business interest in computing and enjoy interacting with business people. It might be that if your college major was business and you have a technology skill set, you'll want to take a look at database-related consulting.

Cool analytics

Data provides the foundation for information and information is power. Ergo, the database is everything and infrastructure is a supporting actor. Because of the importance of data in business, Microsoft devotes one afternoon of its four-day GTM HOT labs to business intelligence using SQL Server. Specifically it was devoted to SQL Server Analysis Services, which extends the former OLAP Services component. Analysis Services introduces data mining, which can be used to discover information in OLAP cubes and relational databases. Figure 12-15 shows an analytical feature found in the data-mining capabilities of SQL Server Analytical Services.

Figure 12-15:

This is an example of using a decision tree to present data-mining information.

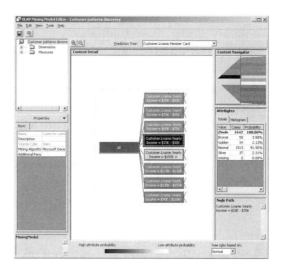

Programming

The good news is that the programming tools are much more efficient, more powerful, and easier than when I flunked out of C programming in the late 1980s. The bad news is that even on a good day, many SMB consultants aren't really great at programming. Nonetheless, some SMB consultants have found a niche in being programmers to SMB-sized organizations. One set of SMB consultants who literally live just up the street from me in my home town of Bainbridge Island, Washington, have found a way to make a living via programming. They primarily provide Visual Basic programming services for medium-sized clients. It works.

> BEST PRACTICE: If you think you might be interested in programming, please start with what I call "Bill in a box," which is better known as Visual Studio. Visual Studio is a bundle of programming tools akin to how BackOffice was a bundle of infrastructure tools. If you acquire Visual Studio and have a computer of sufficient power with a modern operating system from Microsoft, then there is nothing technically holding you back from being the next Bill Gates. Properly equipped with Visual Studio and assuming you're really

smart, you could well be on your way to developing the next killer application and becoming a billionaire! Learn more about Visual Studio at msdn.microsoft.com/vstudio/.

So another take on programming issues is the following: How does the whole darn .NET framework fit in SMB? I see the interaction of SMB clients and the .NET framework area occurring with LOBs. Think about when SMB businesses typically choose to upgrade their infrastructure-only when forced to. Such a "force" occurred in the late 1990s when Great Plains indicated it would no longer support the NetWare platform with the NLM version of its accounting system. That caused a major migration of Great Plains customers to Windows NT-based networks. As you can see in a recent customer letter from Timberline (an accounting ISV), it is leaving the NetWare platform as well.

Figure 12-16:
Timberline announces discontinued support for various operating systems in this letter causing the client to consider the strategic IT consequences.

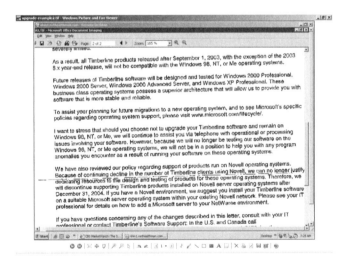

A more important part of the story not told in Figure 12-16 above speaks to the future. It's entirely likely that my client will receive a letter from Timberline one day proclaiming that a new release, based on the .NET development framework, delivers incredible new features never imagined.

Clients, seeing the value in the new accounting software version, will stampede to upgrade. And that's where you, the SMB consultant, come in. You'll be invited to upgrade the networking infrastructure to support the latest version of the .NET framework (e.g., to upgrade the network to Windows Server 2003).

Security

I hardly have to sell you on security. It's a great niche that has proved profitable for SMB consultants over the past several years. This is unlikely to change, as security is what we call in accounting an "ongoing concern."

Internet Security and Acceleration Server

One security application to master in the Microsoft community is Internet Security and Acceleration (ISA) Server. This is the five-pronged security defense tool from Microsoft that provides:

- Firewall. ISA Server is a three-layer firewall providing protection at the low-level packet layer, protocol/session layer, and application layer (e.g., Simple Mail Transport Protocol application filter). This multilayer firewall capability is important to organizations of all sizes.

- Caching. Frequently accessed Web pages can be cached to allow for faster retrievals at LAN speed. To be honest, this is more important at the enterprise level than the SMB level. I've had an enterprise friend tell me this was the entire reason that they purchased ISA Server (this friend used a hardware-based firewall for the firewall function). Enough said.

- Integrated VPN. ISA can manage the VPN process in a more secure way than the native routing and remote access in the Windows Server operating system (version from NT forward). The VPN architecture that is supported includes (1) ISA Server-to-ISA Server office-to-office full-time connectivity and (2) remote users who create a dial-on-demand VPN connection from their home office or hotel room.

- Integrated Policy. An audience member at the GTM hands-on lab workshops taught me a thing about integrated policy. This particular gentleman was the IT director for a police department in the Denver,

Colorado, area. He reported that the ability to manage user access to the Internet was the key reason they selected ISA Server. This police department actually used a hardware-based firewall, and their interest in ISA Server was its integration with Active Directory. At face value, this speaks more toward enterprise scenarios than SMB.

• Extensible Open Platform. To me this is the key to Microsoft's ISA Server platform and fits well with the SMB consultant seeking to develop a security niche. Part of the ISA Server paradigm was to develop an open development platform for partners to build better mousetraps that sit on top of ISA Server. Consequently, you have partners like Trend Micro developing comprehensive security suites that "hook" ISA Server.

BEST PRACTICE: I find Microsoft's attitude about ISA Server being an extensible open platform for partners to develop upon to be refreshing. By its very nature, the security area is multi-vendor. It's not possible for one company, even those with the sharpest minds like Microsoft, to know it all in security. Rather, a collective community effort is required to battle the black hats out there (The black hats are bad guys!).

Note that ISA Server presents an interesting proposition in the SMB space. As of this writing, it's part of the SBS suite (which makes it quite a bargain). This is clearly the cheapest and most efficient way to acquire ISA Server. Its baseline price of $1,499 USD is the exact same price as the baseline SBS product (as of June 2003). Purchasing ISA Server outside of SBS would require the ISA Server purchase price outlay plus a Windows Server operating system to run it.

BEST PRACTICE: The ISA Server opportunity for SMB consultants is obviously security, but also selecting, mastering, and supporting a few third-party products that sit atop ISA Server. For example, you might become a Trend Micro consultant and learn how to integrate the Trend Micro products with ISA Server. This will assist your efforts to become a more well-rounded SMB consultant with a security niche.

Be your own black hat

In my Advanced SBS Workshop, I have attendees perform "black hat" actions against themselves to show what the world can see. Try it and you'll find it to be a humbling exercise, because you might see some things you didn't want to. That is, a few of your SBS client sites might not be as secure as you believed they were. The good news is that it's you running the black hat activity, not an evil-doer who could truly wreak havoc on your client systems. You would then fix your network based on your "black hat" findings.

The network scanning tool I use in the workshop and in the field is GFI's LanGUARD Security Scanner (www.gfi.com). There are many such tools and I encourage you select your favorite. In Figure 12-17, I show the results of an external scan performed against an SBS network. Notice the results reflect the ports that were opened by SBS's Internet Connection Wizard. More on this procedure in Chapter 13.

Figure 12-17:
GFI's LanGUARD is a great tool to black hat yourself.

BEST PRACTICE: When you black hat your client sites, be sure to bill them for the pleasure. I consider that part of my security hardening services, and my clients have gladly paid for this work. Also, I found it's a really cool comparison to run GFI's LanGUARD on the inside local area network, and then black hat from the outside and compare the reports for the same client. The reports should be dramatically different, with the inside report displaying much information and the outside report displaying little information.

Beyond security: Spam, virus protection, and backups

Finally, on this topic, realize that security is more than just firewall-type protection. I believe security also encompasses spam fighting, virus protection, and even tape backup/restore services. An SMB consultant can deliver a variety of services under the "security" heading and add real value in the consulting relationship. Visit sites such as CDW (www.cdw.com) for a listing of spam fighters, anti-virus applications, and backup products.

BEST PRACTICE: I've always said that, God forbid, should I lose my ability to make a living in the SBS product area, I'd immediately run up my credit card and attend training at GFI on spam fighting, Trend Micro on virus protection, and Veritas on Backup Exec disaster recovery. I'd become a "911" kinda guy who boards flights, flies all over the country, and assists businesses in distress that have either been attacked via virus or lost their data and need to recover it. It's a living, and I'm sure a darn good one.

Being a Trainer

Perhaps you've heard the old phrase that everyone subconsciously wants to be a trainer. That is, human nature is good, and we seek to help out others. That might well be the case, but training is also the road to great client service and billable hours. Remember, there are several ways to both skin a cat and reach your annual billable hour goals. It just might be that training will help get you to the promised land of over 1,000 billable hours per year as an SMB consultant.

BEST PRACTICE: Let's take a moment to debunk the widely believed myth that trainers are people who can't do the work. Some people centuries ago started a nasty rumor that trainers are technology professionals who have failed and washed out of the day-to-day hands-on consulting community. You are encouraged to take a different viewpoint. First, training is a high honor a là the popular "top gun," where the best pilots were used to train new and inexperience pilots. Second, a good consultant can benefit from training assignments, as the act of training sharpens your public presentation skills and makes you a better communicator (and more of an extrovert!).

Let me drive home the point. If you work for me in my consulting practice, I'll expect you to have some billable hours each year as a trainer (note I don't hire full-time trainers, but rather I hire consultants with the ability to do some training). That's because, in addition to the points made immediately above about extrovertism and honor, there is a leadership dimension to being a trainer. Our society holds teachers in high esteem. When political leaders look for someone to appoint to a commission, they often look for someone who: is an industry leader, holds a master's degree (which could be a certification in our community), has work that's been published, and possesses teaching experience (such as being an adjunct instructor at the local college). I'm only interested in hiring consultants who are willing to develop leadership skills, train, and ascend to the top 10 percent of their respective peer group. And that's why being a trainer is a best practice as an SMB consultant!

Training can take three forms: sage on stage, guide by side, and mentoring.

Sage on the stage

This is the classic Microsoft Certified Trainer (MCT) approach of stand and deliver-an approach considered effective since Aristotle. The nice thing about this approach is it allows for a one-to-many relationship and is an efficient and effective way to deliver information. This approach typically works best with a canned curriculum, such as a course from Microsoft (the Microsoft Official Curriculum courses) or a third-party provider. The "sage on the stage" approach is considered "old school" when it comes to teaching technology, but don't knock it, as it works well.

BEST PRACTICE: You might try the old "in for a penny, in for a pound strategy" with respect to training. Perhaps you want to make training-related revenue a significant part of your SMB consulting existence. Fair enough and God bless you. If such is the case, then you need to consider becoming an MCT trainer (details at: www.microsoft.com/traincert/mcp/mct/default.asp). There is an especially compelling reason to become an MCT: SMB is getting special attention from the Microsoft training and certification group right now! As discussed in prior chapters about managing your consulting practice, Microsoft has developed an SMB course and SMB certification exam. It is believed that this is only a first step with future SMB courses and exams planned for the certification community. So an SMB consultant would be making a timely decision to become an MCT!

Guide by the side

Another training paradigm is "guide by the side." Lord knows there have been countless academic studies that compare the effectiveness of sage on the stage to guide by the side and some of those studies are specific to technology training! But let's not go there right now. Rather, I'd like to define guide by the side training and discuss how you might make money at it as an SMB consultant.

With technology training, you can clearly see there is an active learning element that might not be present in softer subjects like psychology. You "do" computers and you learn by doing. Microsoft recognized this in its rollout of HOT Labs where the instructor, after making a few introductory comments (30 minutes or less) fades to the background and assumes the role of lab assistant. The approach has been well-received. Students really enjoy the opportunity to just "do it" and perform the clicks when working with a technology. If you're not familiar with the HOT Lab concept, visit www.handsonlab.com. At this site, you'll complete some real HOT Labs that have been released for public consumption.

So you can provide one-on-one training to clients as a guide by the side. You'll instruct the user on how to perform tasks, etc., using technology. It may well be that you'll still deliver your training in a classroom environment, but you'll engage in what a classic business book titled In Search of

Excellence called "management by walking around" or MBWA. That is, you'll wonder around and act as a guide by the side in the classroom.

> BEST PRACTICE: Still not convinced to add training to your portfolio of SMB consulting services? Then try this on for size: no pager or cellular telephone calls after hours! That's right. Something a few of us have discovered in the SMB consulting space is that training is a discrete activity and ends at a fixed time. Sure, you might get a follow-up e-mail or two from students, but, in general, when training is over-it's OVER! It's a very pleasant outcome and one way to bring order back to your professional life if you're feeling stressed as a successful SMB consultant.

Mentoring services

I've had some great engagements in SMB consulting land where I didn't perform the technical work. Rather, I simply mentored or guided someone. In these situations, I used to joke that I was acting as a technology therapist! Seriously, I've had three of these engagements and I would typically show up once per week to train and mentor a specific individual into becoming a technology professional. In one case, I helped a registered health care nurse transition into her new role as the health care clinic's network administrator. She was also earning her MCSE designation at the same time. Another engagement involved assisting a new college graduate in her first IT professional position. This engagement involved both business and technology consulting. Finally, there was the senior IT professional with a UNIX background who needed a helping hand in becoming more confident with Windows-based networking. All good work and I'd encourage you to weave this form of service delivery into your SMB consulting practice.

> BEST PRACTICE: So you want an easy way to build your home theater, eh? Then be a trainer! Seriously, this strategy works for justifying the purchase of a DLP projector that is 2,000 lumens of brightness or higher and makes for a kick-ass home theater after hours. By day, I use such a project to lead workshops and training sessions. But come darkness, I morph into a DVD-addicted couch potato watching the best and worst of Hollywood.

Training areas

I've listed just a few possible training areas in which I've worked as an SMB consultant. You can certainly add to this list additional areas such as:

- Outlook

- Inbound/Outlbound Faxing

- Microsoft Office

- LOB Applications

The LOB application area warrants special mention. Here you will endeavor to learn a client's specific mission critical business application and then turn around and teach its usage to staff. This is good work for SMB consultants, but just be sure to bill for your learning time. The client shouldn't expect you to absorb a lot of learning hours for a task (teaching a specific LOB) that isn't easily replicable. In other words, it's fine to do custom work, but that client has to be willing at pay for it.

> BEST PRACTICE: It's been said a trainer needs to stretch himself occasionally and you should consider that as you prepare your list of training areas. Heck, I've lectured on C# programming and Microsoft Content Management Server (two areas hardly in the SMB consulting domain). And there are limits as to how far you should stretch. Some training centers are known to be sleazy and will throw you in to deliver a course you know nothing about. This is the old "warm body" school of training and should be avoided.

Finally, it's been said that if you really want to learn a subject, then teach it! I often learn as much from my students as I teach them. It's a two-way flow of information that is mutually beneficial. When I deliver my workshops, I typically leave the city at the end of the week having extracted a gold nugget or two from students' war stories on SMB consulting I can use to become a better SMB consultant-or at least incorporate in a future book!

Advisory Services

Remember that there is an entire consulting industry out there built on the "advisory services" business model. That is, management consultants and even some technology consultants view their role as advisory in nature much like an attorney. This type of work is typically performed at the medium-sized organization or larger, but there are possibilities for small companies as well. This section outlines advisory services opportunities in the SMB area.

As-built drawings

Some time ago I enjoyed strong SMB consulting sales (and billable hours) by using an early edition of Visio to walk into client sites and completely document their network. I referred to this as "as-built drawing," to borrow a term from the construction industry where an architect will sketch the drawings and floor plans of a building to document everything. I'd like to tell you I thought of this great client service, but such is not the case. Rather, I observed a similar service being offered by a competing consulting practice called "Super Docs" which essentially documented a network. Hey, didn't someone say imitation is the most sincere form of flattery?

> BEST PRACTICE: Remember that you can acquire Visio as part of the Action Pack subscription program I've outlined in this book (learn more about Action Pack at www.microsoft.com/partner). Visio also has built-in sample templates to kick-start your efforts to as-built a client's network. More specific information on Visio can be found at www.microsoft.com/visio.

By the way, if the term "as-built" doesn't sit well with you, you're welcome to use a different analogy, such as "set of x-rays" or something similar to make your point with clients.

Technology audits

The term "technology audit" refers to several different services, depending on who is doing the talking. An SMB consulting firm near my home in Washington State would refer to this in the context of a security audit (which would be more appropriately discussed in the prior section). A consultant with whom I once raced sailboats named Floyd told me that where he worked-Digital Equipment Corporation-a technology audit was thought of as a annual check-up or physical fitness exam of the technology infrastructure.

The point is you can go to a client site, conduct an assessment of what the current state of their technology is, and then conclude such a report with recommendations.

Planning

Perhaps you swore up and down as a young technology-bit tweeker that you'd never ever be reduced to being a consultant who stood in front of a white board drawing out planning models. Guess what? You need to sincerely put that option back on the table as an SMB consultant looking for your just financial rewards. Admittedly this is more likely to bear billable hours in the medium, not small company space, but the work is good. You'll be acting as part management consultant as you assist your client in defining a technology strategy and how to capitalize on it for business purposes.

Many of the technology planning books out there are oriented toward enterprise-level engagements, and I don't intend to reproduce those works here. Suffice it to say that there are probably some good, billable hours awaiting you for your value-added planning services for your clients.

> BEST PRACTICE: Please tolerate a mild case of repetition here. In the SMB consulting game, make sure you're not giving away planning under the guise of your sales effort. Clients should pay for planning and respect your capabilities. Don't give away the milk and cow just to land an SMB consulting gig. I discussed this sales effort versus paid planning issue in Chapter 6 of this book in the section on the one-hour SMB sales effort.

Business consulting

No doubt you've picked up on my attempts to make you part management consultant in addition to technology guru as you've read this book. I'm guilty as charged. Today's solution-selling paradigm requires you to provide counsel to your clients on both the bits and the biz issues of the day in the world of technology. Those who do extremely well as SMB consultants will have the dual skill set of business and technology.

BEST PRACTICE: And why not go to night school and get your MBA? Not only will you then be the consultant with the master's degree, but you'll have developed some strong business skills. And remember, even if you go broke at some point, they can't repossess your MBA!

To jump-start your business consulting side, read Ten Reports That Small Businesses Need, a 24-page white paper from NetIQ. It's located at netiq.com/f/form/whitepaperrequest.asp?id=2277&origin=ONiesbn_10rsolo, where you'll need to complete a short registration form. Enjoy!

Packaging Revisited

Time to weave in a little more marketing talk that was explored in Chapter 5 of this book. This concerns packaging you and your services in the context of developing a consulting practice niche.

Leasing and financing

Once on a trip through Phoenix, Arizona, I met an aggressive SMB consultant who told me about his successful business model. This included his use of leasing to make himself the complete package for his clients. Here's how it worked. James, the SMB consultant, had a leasing arrangement that included the software (SBS, Microsoft Office, etc.), hardware, and consulting services. So for a single monthly lease payment, James could deliver his total SMB solution to his customers. Very attractive!

BEST PRACTICE: Arranging a leasing package isn't as difficult as you might think. Simply look in your telephone book and contact leasing firms that handle business leases. Another leasing avenue would be your local lender.

Microsoft also has a leasing program that might be the best program for you and your SMB consulting package. It's called "Total Solution Financing" and is provided by Microsoft Capital Corporation. You would work through a Microsoft Business Solutions Partner to structure the lease arrangements that will be presented to your clients. This is exciting stuff and you can learn more at www.microsoft.com/BusinessSolutions/highlights/financing_feature.mspx or by calling 1-888-477-7989 (USA) or 1-701-281-6500 (international). As you read this, Microsoft Capital Corporation should be operating in international markets.

BEST PRACTICE: Remember that your leasing arrangement might become an unexpected profit center beyond your core operations of SMB consulting. This is akin to how Kodak (the film manufacturer) has made more of its profit in some years by trading silver metal futures than its core operations of selling film. That's the good news. The bad news is that your business banker won't like to see too much of your profit generation from non-core operations, as she will then question your basic business model and ask questions, such as "What business did you say you're in?" Of course this last point would only be a concern if you have a business banking relationship, such as a commercial line of credit, etc.

Be the temp agency!

Earlier in this book I spoke about finding your first clients by working for a temporary agency or contract house. But have you considered becoming a temp agency as part of your packaging? Hear me out on this one. Having seen the internal operations of an international temp agency, I can report to you that the margins are surprisingly high (upwards of 60 percent) and the management mechanics are relatively simple (playing matchmaker between the talent and the business needing that talent).

Notes:

There is a franchise in the SMB space that allows you to effectively bring consultant and client together. It is Soft-Temps (www.stfranchise.com), and more about this opportunity is shown in Figure 12-18.

Figure 12-18:
Soft-Temps provides a turn-key consulting franchise for you to create your SMB consulting practice.

So I called te Soft-Temps at 1-800-221-2880 and asked for the information packet as part of the research in writing this book. You pay an initial franchise fee of $2,985 to get the ball rolling and in return receive training, business operations support, and many more benefits expected by a franchisee from the franchisor.

> BEST PRACTICE: The notion of being a temp agency or franchise is what I call the "Barry Method" of SMB consulting. Barry, a former boss, loved to scheme service delivery business models where he could make all the money and not have to do the work. If the accounting term "passive income" was named after someone, it was Barry. So if you're reading this Barry, Soft-Temps is for you!

Technology service providers

Another interesting twist on SMB consulting is the business model employed by Winterlink out of Berkeley, California (www.winterlink.net). This firm calls itself a technology service provider and provides outsourced support for SMB clients. They correctly identified the key characteristic of SMB organizations to be they typically don't have in-house technology expertise. Winterlink provides a big league outsourcing arrangement much like you'd see in the newspaper when EDS (an enterprise-level consulting firm) receives a contract for managing the US Navy's entire IT infrastructure. On the one hand, Winterlink is saying all the right things with respect to its core message about being a partner. On the other hand, the part of the message that is more draconian centers on replacing your existing SMB consultant with them (that is, Winterlink is growing via a displacement strategy).

Aligning with channel partners

Maybe you want to sign on with numerous channel partners that frequently make the news at CRN (www.crn.com). For example, you might like to join the SMB consultant in Cleveland who is a TechSelect Partner as part of the TechData's channel program (www.techdata.com). HP has SMBOne. Early in the book I discussed Dell and Gateway's channel partner programs. The list is long and ever-changing as existing programs are revamped and new programs introduced.

Underserved Areas

There are some underserved areas in the SMB marketplace that are just there for the begging. Consider the following:

- Advanced Outlook Customization. Indeed Outlook was presented earlier in this chapter and you should really go out and purchase one of the advanced Outlook customization books on the market. Two books stand out: Building Applications with Microsoft Outlook Version 2002 (Randy Byrne, Microsoft Press) and Microsoft Outlook Version 2002 Inside-Out (Jim Boyce, Microsoft Press).

- Digital Dashboard in SharePoint. Previously, Digital Dashboard was a standalone product, but today it is incorporated into Microsoft's SharePoint technologies. Digital Dashboard could be the basis for developing Executive Information System (EIS) applications that report financial information in simple-to-view graphics (such as the traffic light metaphor of red, yellow, and green lights). Specifically, a Digital Dashboard solution might display the DuPont ratio model from the world of finance. The financial information used to calculate the components of the DuPont ratio model could be extracted from the SQL Server tables holding Great Plains Dynamics accounting data.

- SBS. Yes, you are reading correctly. One of the great underserved areas in SMB is SBS itself. But that is changing, as Microsoft refines it message to promote the product, so that's a good thing. The next chapter is dedicated to SBS.

Sage Advice for Niche Pickers

So, as this important chapter on selecting your technology consulting niche winds down, here are some random thoughts on working smart.

What color is my parachute?

Earlier in this book I presented the Myers Briggs Personality Assessment test as a way to really learn about yourself and your clients. Please revisit that discussion in Chapter 8 if it's slipped your mind. Myers Briggs could help you determine what type of technology niche you might pursue based on your personality type (e.g., an introvert might want to consider programming). Another resource to review is the infamous book What Color Is My Parachute, by Richard Nelson Bolles (Ten Speed Press). This book is the gold standard for answering the proverbial "What do I want to do with my life" question. While primarily focused on job hunting, What Color Is My Parachute can offer some value to the SMB consultant. Don't forget there is an oft-repeated common perception out there that all consultants are really just job hunters in disguise!

Assured outcome

Mark this as the last time I was truly spanked. I was called in by the president of the consulting firm I worked for in the late-1990s on a Saturday to be "taken to the woodshed." His anger came from his perception that I was growing my SBS practice too fast! He said that rapid, unmanaged growth spells the downfall of many a consulting practice, and his wasn't going there. His point was that too-rapid growth results in anything but assured outcomes in client engagements. Client engagements should be like rigid military engagements with the following elements: command, control, and communication. Client engagements should be like a CP's deliverables to clients: assured outcomes.

When a consulting practice gets ahead of itself, it is doomed to failure. The growth must occur at a pace where a positive assured outcome occurs at each customer site.

> BEST PRACTICE: And yes, part of the consulting firm president's message to me was to pick a technology niche where you can have an assured outcome that is positive. In the SBS 4.x era, it's difficult to say that an assured outcome of a positive nature was even possible. That, of course, changed with SBS 2000 and beyond, where the product reached important maturity milestones. Bottom line is that you should select a stable and mature technology niche if having a positive assured outcome is your goal.

Hearing Microsoft's Go To Market message

The genius behind the four-day Microsoft GTMHOT Lab (spring 2003) message was that you could sample six technologies in a "captain's plate" fashion and then select which technology you wanted to learn more in-depth to carve your niche. This was a way, to use New Age touchy-feely language, to find your "tribe" in the world of technology consulting. So you might attend Microsoft Hands-On-Training Labs that travel around and discover your tribe in the process. Another part of the current GTM message is "solution selling" and the fact that you can't make it as a "bits" person anymore in this field. (I've shared this message with you in several parts of the book including earlier in this chapter.) Continue to monitor the Microsoft Partner site (www.microsoft.com/partner) for more on the GTM message.

Niching by economic sector

In an earlier section of this chapter I spoke to narrow vertical markets, such as legal, medical, and manufacturing. That was in the context of supporting an industry application. Now I want you to consider economics sectors, such as legal, medical, manufacturing, local governments, and the like from a general SMB consulting view. Perhaps you don't want to support LOB applications for one specific community. Maybe you want to restrict your craft to infrastructure topics, such as network deployments and administration. Fair enough. There's nothing holding you back from saying "I only do networks for medical offices." Niching by economic sector is a very powerful consulting strategy and might be the outcome of having read this chapter. Forward in good health, mate!

Brelsford's Dozen: Create Your Top-12 Niche List!

No chapter is complete without a Brelsford's Dozen thrown in. I want you to take a break and make a list of the top dozen niches, ranked in order of desirability, in which you'd like to consider performing as an SMB consultant. Just do it:

1.
2.
3.
4.
5.
6.
7.
8.
9.
10.
11.
12.

Notes:

Brelsford's Mailbox

Hi Harry...

Thank you very much for a very informative/productive seminar on Microsoft's Small Business Server.

I was wondering if you could e-mail me some additional information. My vertical market is real estate and I heard you say that you support a couple of clients in that area. I am interested in getting as much information about software/hardware and anything else that you think might be useful for me in selling and supporting this vertical market. I have purchased Goldmine, Act, Top Producer, as well as other mortgage and real estate software to put together a turn-key system that I can market to the mortgage and real estate industry. Any information or contacts you could give me would be greatly appreciated.

I am also interested in subscribing to your e-mail newsletter. Thank you again for your consideration.

José C.

B-S-P

Howdy, José, and thanks for the e-mail message. I think you're on the right track by bundling a solution for a target niche, such as real estate and mortgage professionals. This will certainly make your marketing more focused and, I suspect, the quality of your consulting services higher. Good focus, my man. Be sure to bookmark a few important real estate and mortgage sites so you can learn more about the industry. The National Association of Realtors is once such site at www.realtor.com. Another interesting site is CBS's MarketWatch (select the Personal Finance, Real Estate page) at www.marketwatch.com. Finally, it should not be lost on you that the real estate industry has weathered the recent economic downturn very nicely because low interest rates generated significant real estate transactions and mortgage financing/refinancing activity. It's always good to focus on an economically health industry, mate!

All the best to you...harrybbbb

Summary

This chapter is one of the most important chapters in this book as it presents the "grinder" mind-set of doing the actual work. What is critical is that you select the best-suited work for you. We're all different and one person's coal lump is another person's diamond. This chapter specifically addressed:

- Having you consider technology consulting niches, such as project management, training, etc.

- Encouraging you to mentor power users at your client site

- Presenting sufficient information to help you select SMB niches, such as selling and supporting Line of Business (LOB) applications, programming, infrastructure, and security

- Discussing the notion of providing advisory and business consulting services

- Sharing important information on "packaging" yourself and your niche

- Giving sage advice for the SMB nicher

Chapter 13
Small Business Server 2003

In This Chapter

- Small Business Server defined

- Understanding Small Business Server in the SMB space

- Building your SMB consulting practice around Small Business Server

- Small Business Server 2003 installation and deployment sguidance

- Adding value in SMB engagements with Small Business Server

- Tools to build better client relationships within Small Business Server 2003

We arrive at the final and perhaps most technically applicable chapter in this entire SMB consulting tome. This is the chapter about making Small Business Server 2003 (SBS) work for you in your SMB consulting practice. Thankfully, the release candidate for SBS 2003 was available late in the writing of this book and I received permission from Microsoft to present it here (thanks, Redmond!). Let's get started.

> BEST PRACTICE: This chapter isn't meant to serve as an entire book on SBS. Rather, I paint SBS in the context of being a niche service deliverable in your SMB consulting practice. Please refer to my SBS specific books for intensive technical detail on SBS, including Small Business Server 2003 Best Practices.

Defining Small Business Server

At it's core, SBS is a bundle of server-side applications and features optimized for the small business. It comes in two versions: standard and premium. The components included in SBS are:

- Windows Server 2003 operating system. This is the standard operating system SKU that has been optimized for two processor support only (instead of the typically four processor support).

- Exchange Server 2003. This is the e-mail messaging application.

- Windows SharePoint Services (WSS). This application provides intranet collaborative capabilities and basic document management capabilities.

- Shared Fax Service. This is the computer-based faxing application.

- Outlook 2003. This is the latest version of the world's most popular messaging client.

- Remote Web Workplace. This is a Web-page based portal that allows a mobile or at-home worker to check e-mail securely via Outlook Web Access (OWA), connect to his own desktop computer at work, or establish a connection to the internal SharePoint site.

- Security. Security is of course a complex matrix and includes logon, folder/file-level, and Internet-related security measures (and even employees who don't lie, cheat, or steal). All of these measures (except employee behavior) are present in SBS 2003. Internet intrusion protection is provided by Routing and Remote Access Service (RRAS) in the standard SBS edition and ISA Server 2000 in the premium.

- Consoles. The internal management consoles use MMC 2.0 technology and present an updated look and feel, with the tasks now broken into core SBS items and other server applications.

The premium edition of SBS 2003 will also include the SQL Server 2000 database and the ISA Server 2000 security application.

So all feature talk behind us, the SBS definition can also be viewed from three different business and deployment philosophies.

- Bargain in a box. Many folks purchase SBS for simple economics: It's cheap. The bundled costs of SBS are significantly cheaper than the standalone price of the individual components purchased separately. In fact, the pricing model for SBS has been cheaper than any two separate components purchased separately. That is, SBS is cheaper than purchasing Windows Server 2003 and Exchange 2003 Server alone. This pricing paradigm holds for both the standard and premium editions of SBS 2003.

- Consulting practice in a box. SMB consultants have deployed SBS at client sites because its structured setup and deployment approach is, in effect, a repeatable methodology. That's music to the ears of a mature SMB consultant who is looking for a positive assured outcome at each client site.

- BackOffice in a box. This is the feature creature argument. Many people purchase SBS because of the sheer number of applications it offers. These applications can make a small business with a modest technology budget appear larger than life in the eyes of the business community. That is, a small business can look and feel like a large business with SBS.

Installation and Deployment

Again, to manage your expectations, this chapter isn't intended to constitute an SBS book (my opening comments early in the chapter point you to my full-fledged SBS books). Rather, I want to send you forth as an SMB consultant thinking about what work you might perform for clients (that is, in fact, the intent of the whole Grinder section of this book). Ergo, you'll get a technical sampler of SBS 2003 starting with this overview of the installation and deployment process.

To be honest, the installation and deployment process has become less and less time-consuming in the past two SBS releases. In fact, today with the OEM SKU, it's possible to install SBS in as little as 15 minutes, whereby the SMB consultant only provides personalization information and agrees to the license! I'll highlight the SBS installation and deployment process here, but don't get too hung up on it. At this point it's only a small part of the overall SBS experience.

The installation and deployment process can be broken out into the four phases:

1. Character-based operating system (OS) installation
2. GUI-based OS installation
3. SBS installation
4. SBS post-installation tasks

Each of these points is further discussed below. Note that the SBS 2003 version being demonstrated here is the standard edition without SQL Server or ISA Server.

> BEST PRACTICE: There are three upgrade scenarios in SBS 2003. These include:
>
> • Windows 2000 Server to SBS 2003
>
> • Windows Server 2003 to SBS 2003
>
> • SBS 2000 to SBS 2003
>
> Microsoft will also release different sophisiticated migration scenarios at a future date (no further details at press time).

Character-based OS installation

This stage is the same as your typical Windows Server 2003 installation and is otherwise uneventful. You may need to provide mass storage device drivers early in the character-based phases. I had to do this when I installed SBS 2003 RC under VMWare 4.0. Here I needed to provide the VMWare SCSI mass storage driver in order for the installation to complete correctly.

An important decision you'll need to make in this stage will be the size of your partitions. There are truly a few ways to proceed here. You could have an enormous C: drive or divide the hard disk into C:, D:, and E: drive partitions to house the operating system, SBS applications, and data respectively. The choice is yours. In Figure 13-1, you'll see that on my "sample" installation under VMWare 4.0 on my laptop for demonstration purposes, I elected to have only a 6GB partition for C: drive. In the real world, C: drive would be significantly larger under any scenario (say 10GB minimum).

Figure 13-1:
The disk partition is being formatted in the character-based setup phase.

BEST PRACTICE: Be sure to format your partitions as NTFS under SBS 2003. Correct me if I'm wrong, but in this day and age there isn't a justifiable reason for formatting a server disk partition as anything but NTFS with a new SBS 2003 installation.

The server machine reboots after the end of the character-based setup and launches into the GUI-based setup phase.

GUI-based OS installation

The GUI-based setup phase completes the installation of the underlying Windows Server 2003 operation system and is basically on "auto-pilot." This phase doesn't require much interaction from the SMB consultant except to respond to some personalization and licensing screens. The Your Product Key screen is shown in Figure 13-2.

Notes:

Figure 13-2:

You'll provide your license information on the Your Product Key screen.

The end of the GUI setup is followed by a reboot and the Welcome notice for SBS 2003 appears.

SBS installation

The SBS 2003 installation phase is very similar to past SBS installation phases. You'll make decisions regarding the following:

- Blocking/warning messages. If you're not sufficiently equipped for your SBS installation, you'll receive a blocking message that must be corrected before you can proceed. An example of this type of message would be "insufficient RAM memory." If you're not optimally equipped to proceed with the SBS installation, you'll receive a warning message that allows you to proceed after acknowledgement. A warning message is shown in Figure 13-3.

Notes:

Figure 13-3:

This warning message advises you that two network adapter cards are optimal as a security best practice (even though its wording is more generic than that).

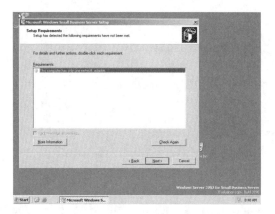

- Company information. The company information screen, shown in Figure 13-4, gathers meta data, which is used elsewhere in SBS 2003. An example of this is how the information is used in creating a Global Address List (GAL) record for each network user in Microsoft Exchange. However, this information isn't used to create employee Outlook Contact record-as I have repeatedly asked the SBS development team to do-so you could see all your coworkers appear as Outlook Contacts (and be easily synchronized to your personal digital assistant (PDA)).

Notes:

Figure 13-4:

Company information is entered in the SBS 2003 setup phase.

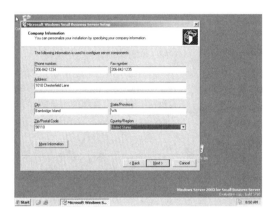

- Internal domain information. Much like SBS 2000, you'll create the
  internal domain name that ends with the "local" suffix. I don't have
  space to go into the entire theory here on why you wouldn't use
  "com," but suffice it to say it's a security best practice to shield your
  internal domain from the outside world. The Internal domain information screen is displayed in Figure 13-5.

Figure 13-5:

*Creating your internal domain name screen is a point of no return in the
naming schema of your client network. The name you select here is committed in a few screens.*

BEST PRACTICE: There is a readily accessible DNS domain naming primer by clicking the More Information button on the Internal Domain Information screen. You'll read a doctoral thesis on this topic on the information screen that appears.

- Local area network (LAN) IP subnet addressing. By default, the LAN IP subnet address is 192.168.16.2. It can be changed to your own custom IP subnet address range, but I'd recommend you accept the default. It's part of making all of your SBS client sites exactly the same! This screen is shown in Figure 13-6.

Figure 13-6:

Make your IP addressing decisions here. Unless there are compelling reasons to do otherwise, accept the default 192.168.16.2 addressing.

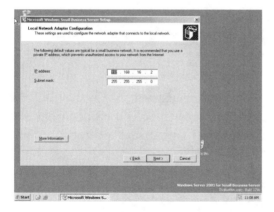

- Automatic logon. You'll provide the administrator's password in order to allow an automatic logon at the two reboots that take place when installing SBS 2003.

- Windows configuration stage. The Windows Configuration screen in SBS 2003 replaces the Scenario Baseline stage from SBS 2000. But the behavior is essentially the same. The DNS naming/IP addressing will be committed and Active Directory is installed and configured. The server machine is made the root of the Active Directory forest. Core networking components, such as DNS, DHCP, WINS, and Terminal Services are configured. You will receive a notice that the Windows Configuration step can take up to 30 minutes, although I found this to be closer to 15 minutes. A progress screen from the Windows Configuration stage is shown in Figure 13-7.

Figure 13-7:
In many ways, the Windows Configuration stage makes many irreversible changes that can't be modified again in the SBS 2003 setup.

A reboot follows and you are presented with the Component Selection screen as shown in Figure 13-8. Here you will make decisions about which applications to install and where to install said applications (storage location).

Figure 13-8:
The second part of the SBS 2003 setup phase starts with the Component Selection screen.

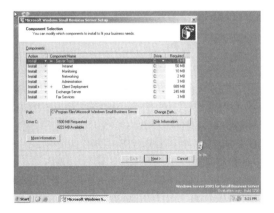

BEST PRACTICE: To be honest, my preference here (Component Selection screen in Figure 13-8) is to have you accept the default installation settings by clicking Next unless there is a compelling reason to do otherwise. Under this thinking, you'd just click Next on the successive setup screens as well.

- Data folder redirection. One the final setup decisions you make concerns the Data Folders screen. Here you will direct the data to the storage location of your choosing. For example, you might install the User Shared Folders on a drive other than the system drive (which is typically C: drive). This is shown in Figure 13-9.

Figure 13-9:
This screen tells SBS where important files and folders will be located.

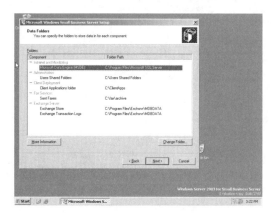

A final Next click at the Component Summary screen (it's nearly identical to Figure 13-8) launches one to two hours of SBS setup activity under a traditional (not OEM) installation, depending on the speed of your machine and the selections that you've made. Upon the next reboot, you move to the next section on post-installation deployment.

SBS post-installation tasks

Old habits are hard to break. The To Do List from SBS 2000 is also now called the "Complete the configuration" screen shown in Figure 13-10. However, in the Server Management console discussion in the next section, it's still referred to as the "To Do List" (which is my favorite).

A couple of key post-installation points should be made here. First, the engineering that went into the tasks on this list is incredible and might not be apparent to you at first blush. The intention of the list is to go through it from top (starting with View Security Best Practices) to bottom (Configuring Monitoring) and complete each task in order. The idea here is the "SMB consulting practice in a box" paradigm. In other words, the SBS 2003 setup and deployment steps are really a desirable SMB consulting methodology.

Figure 13-10:
The Complete the configuration screen replaces that old To Do List. This screen is broken into two functional areas: Network Tasks and Management Tasks.

BEST PRACTICE: As you read the following narrative on the Complete the configuration screen, understand that you might well elect to complete some tasks and not others. That's fine as long as you honor the methodology and start at the top and work your way to the bottom. What I'm saying is that every site might not need remote access (task three in Network Tasks) or faxing (task three in Management Tasks). But at least you did it the "SBS way" by working your way down the list and selecting the tasks that make sense to you.

With the Complete the configuration screen, you'll essentially secure the SBS server machine and then connect it to the Internet. You will then provide for remote connectivity and activate the server. You'll need to activate your newly deployed SBS 2003 site upon completing the installation for it to be fully functional after the initial 14-day grace period expires. The activation process starts with the fourth selection in the Network Tasks area on the Complete the configuration screen. Next you would add your client access licenses (CALs) followed by adding your printers, users, and computers. This is followed by configuring fax, backup, and monitoring. It's really as simple as that.

> BEST PRACTICE: It's still possible to find ways to be unsuccessful with SBS, which is something I'm trying to prevent. Hear me out on this one. In Seattle, we have a very large enterprise company familiar to all of you who've ever flown the friendly skies-Boeing. Members of the Boeing information technology department have been known to volunteer to install SBS at their church on a week-end. However, these well-intentioned Boeing folks often make the mistake of disregarding the SBS setup wizards and the Complete the configuration screen, then end up having an unsatisfactory experience because of it. Better to follow the SBS way and have an assured successful outcome.

This ends the section on SBS setup and deployment, which is basically a one-time event undertaken at the start of the SBS 2003 life cycle. You then move into the ongoing maintenance phase.

Ongoing Maintenance

Early in this book we explored the idea of using different SMB consulting business models regarding time and billing, maintenance contracts and the like. This section is more granular and explores performing the maintenance work surrounding an SBS site. I'll explore the Server Management console and provide a Brelsford's Dozen of common maintenance tasks.

Server Management console

This is your command and control console that is central to your ongoing success with SBS 2003. It lists functional technology areas under Standard Management. Specific application-level tools are listed under Advanced Management. This is shown in Figure 13-11.

Figure 13-11:
Make this, the Server Management console, your main interface with SBS 2003. Period.

BEST PRACTICE: Unless you can prove otherwise, you should always attempt to perform all server-related tasks from the Server Management console. That's because in keep in the spirit of the SBS way, you want to use the native SBS tools before looking under the hood and using the traditional Windows Server 2003 tools.

A tool that might cause you to look under the hood (and not be found on the Server Management console) would be Certification Authority from Start, All Programs, Administrative Tools. This tool, installed by default in SBS 2003 (but not SBS 2000) provides the secure socket layer (SLL) capabilities when using features such as Outlook Web Access or the Remote Web Workplace in SBS 2003. More later in this chapter on Outlook Web Access and Remote Web Workplace.

I'll now explore the finer points of the SBS 2003 Server Management console, starting with the Standard Management area and followed by the Advanced Management area.

BEST PRACTICE: Far be it from you to lose a hot and heavy game of SBS trivia one evening. Make a mental note that the SBS 2003 Server Management console is based on Microsoft Management Console (MMC) 2.0 technology, not SharePoint technologies. That's important because for a while, many believed the SBS consoles in the SBS 2003 would be based on SharePoint. Such is not the case.

Standard Management

Presented by functional tasks, these are the components found under Standard Management.

- To Do List. This was presented in the prior section as the Complete the configuration screen.

- Information Center. This is actually pretty cool in SBS 2003. You have links to download the latest SBS 2003 updates, view the online documentation, hop and skip over to the SBS 2003 Community Web site, and seek technical support.

BEST PRACTICE: Starting in mid-2003 forward, Microsoft is supporting the nurturing and development of "communities" for its various technologies. This includes user groups, peer-to-peer forums, newsgroups, and Most Valuable Professional (MVP) support. SBS 2003 is no exception and the SBS 2003 Community Website link is where it all begins. The hyperlink takes you to http://go.microsoft.com/fwlink/?Linkid=16919 which then redirects you to http://microsoft.com/windowsserver2003/sbs/default.mspx as seen in Figure 13-12.

As a successful SMB consultant, you'll want to tap into the Microsoft global "communities" effort in the way that best meets your needs. For example, you might want to attend an SBS user group meeting or participate in an online Microsoft newsgroup.

Figure 13-12:

Microsoft's SBS 2003 Community Website.

- Internal Web Site. Explore this link as SBS 2003 now provides an out-of-the-box internal Web site to be used at your client site. The tools include changing the Web site name, importing files, adding links, controlling access, configuring alerts and so on. A great addition and shown in Figure 13-13.

Figure 13-13:

Be sure to take advantage of the built-in internal Website in SBS 2003 at your client sites.

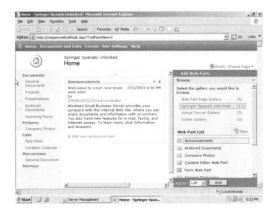

- Fax (Local). This is a one-stop location to configure and manage the fax process. Note you can right-click the Fax (Local) icon in the left pane and select Properties to directly access the Shared Fax Service Property sheet, which is the way many SMB consultants managed the fax capability in the SBS 2000 time frame. You will see that the Shared Fax Service in SBS 2003 hasn't changed much from the prior SBS release. Faxing is discussed more later on in the chapter.

- Monitoring and Reporting. A cornerstone to your success as an SMB consultant with SBS 2003, this link allows you to configure the server monitoring and reporting capability. More on this later in the chapter.

- Internet and E-mail. This basically provides (and extends) the functionality of the Internet Connection Wizard from the SBS 2000 days. In SBS 2003, it's called the Configure E-mail and Internet Connection Wizard.

- Shares. This allows you to observe and manage the default shared folders in SBS 2003. Note some of these are hidden administrative shares, such as IPC$.

- Backup. You really want to click through the Backup link. Backup is much improved in SBS 2003. Trust me.

- Licenses. This is where you manage licenses in SBS 2003, including the ability to add, backup, restore, transfer, and even purchase licenses. Yes, you read correctly! You can purchase additional licenses online in the SBS 2003 time frame.

- Users. Manage users from this link. Three cool capabilities amongst many are the (1) Configure Password Policies, (2) Configure My Documents Redirection, and (3) Change Mailbox and Disk Quota Limits selections.

- Client Computers. Manage client computers from this link. One neato capability is the Create Remote Connection Disk selection for enabling remote workers to easily connect to the SBS network.

- Server Computers. Manage server computers from this link.

- Printers. Manage printers from this link.

- Distribution Groups. Manage distribution links from this link.

- Security Groups. Manage security groups from this link.

- User Templates. Create and manage user templates from this link. This is a powerful capability in SBS 2003 and allows you to create users based on a template. For example, the accounting template you might create would have the exact settings you want on the computer network for bookkeepers. Future users who are bookkeepers would be set up using the accounting template.

Advanced Management

The Advanced Management template exposes the native application tools and has a much more application-centric viewpoint. Elements include the following:

- Active Directory Users and Computers. This is the MMC that exposes Active Directory in the SBS network. This is the native Active Directory tool in the Windows Server 2003 operating system.

- Group Policy Management. Microsoft is emphasizing Group Policy in the SBS 2003 time frame. This Group Policy is elevated in status in the Server Management console in this version of SBS. It effectively replaces the Define Applications link from the legacy SBS 2000 To Do List.

- Computer Management (Local). This is the same Computer Management MMC found under the Administrative Tools folder.

- First Organization (Exchange). This is System Manager for Exchange Server 2003.

- POP3 Connector Manager. This is an SBS-specific tool for configuring POP3 e-mail support within Exchange Server 2003.

- Terminal Services Configuration. This link allows you to configure Terminal Services server-side settings.

- Internet Information Services. This is the IIS management tool, which, in the day-to-day management of SBS, is utilized more than you might imagine.

- Migrate Server Settings. You've heard that the best is always saved for last. Such is the case with the Migrate Server Settings link. It's here that the SBS development team demonstrates it really listened to feedback in the last development cycle. For example, the Health Monitor configuration you perfect on your test server can be exported to another SBS 2003 server machine. You can also migrate e-mail and Internet connection settings. Very cool!

So much for that feature review of the Server Management console. What is important to glean from the above discussion is that you will perform much of your ongoing SBS 2003 maintenance tasks from the above links.

Brelsford's Dozen: Ongoing maintenance tasks

So here is a list of ongoing maintenance tasks that are SBS deliverables for you, the SMB consultant.

1. Updating virus definition data files. Assuming you've selected a capable client/server anti-virus protection application, such as Trend Micro's OfficeScan suite, it's now incumbent upon you to keep current. You'll want to consider updating the virus definition data files hourly so that your SBS client is not exposed to evil and destructive viruses.

2. Verifying backup jobs. Perhaps only second to virus detection would be data backups. You'll read in the next major section of this chapter how the Server Status Report can be very beneficial in sending the tape backup log to you each morning. But even more important than performing and receiving notice of a backup is the ability to conduct a test restore. Test restores are typically performed once a month or even more frequently.

3. Black hatting yourself. You can never let your guard down when it comes to security. Security is truly an ongoing maintenance task, a function that you will never "complete." So one way to determine the security fitness of your SBS client sites is to run a security scanning tool against the SBS server machine. This method also allows you to confirm the security settings you believe you've configured and implemented correctly.

BEST PRACTICE: I can recommend the GFI LANguard Network Security Scanner tool for the above task. You will want to run this tool on the internal LAN and then run it across the Internet. The reports should look very different. Figure 13-14 displays the results from running this on the LAN. Figure 13-15 displays the results when run against the server across the Internet. It's okay for the internal report to display much more information than the external report. It's the external report that should report minimal information and be a reflection of your sound security practices at your SBS client sites!

Figure 13-14:

Running a tool such as LANguard Network Security Scanner on the inside of your LAN is a sobering experience! Lots of details on what you should know are being reported.

Figure 13-15:

This displays the results of LANguard Network Security Scanner being run on the same server machine across the Internet. The results reflect few port openings and match what was configured via the E-mail and Internet Connection Wizard.

4. Updating the SBS client site. Keeping the server and desktop machines up to date with security bulletins, patches, and service packs takes a lot of effort on the part of the SMB consultant. Microsoft has numerous tools to aid in this process, including its periodic security bulletins (subscribe at www.microsoft.com/security), the use of the Microsoft Security Baseline Analyzer (view more information at www.microsoft.com/technet), and built-in Automatic Update capabilities found on both the server machine and desktop machines (see the Automatic Update icon at the lower right of the server desktop near the time display). And as an SMB consultant, you want to be sure to educate yourself on the power of the Software Update Service (SUS) for keeping your client sites automatically current with Microsoft system updates you have personally approved for distribution. Details on SUS at www.microsoft.com/security.

5. Supporting end users. Try as you might, you can't get away from supporting end users at your SBS client sites. Everything from "I can't print" to "I can't log on" to "The network is running slowly" will come your way. You might view these calls as work orders from

your client sites. And what the heck, in the name of end user support, go ahead and educate yourself on how to utilize Windows Server 2003's Shadow Copy Restore capability to better protect user data between backups.

6. Checking system health. This includes viewing Server Status Reports daily for each client site, configuring Health Monitor to fire alerts, and periodically logging on and looking at the Performance tab on the Task Manager tool.

7. Installing line of business (LOB) applications. Here again, you can't get away from support for small businesses applications. As an SMB consultant, I've found myself being called into action to assist with Great Plains Dynamics, Timberline Accounting, Oracle, and others.

8. Disk Space Management. You should monitor storage consumption and consider imposing disk quotas (see the Users link under Standard Management in the Server Management console). Don't forget to defragment the disks periodically by using Disk Defragmenter found in the System Tools folder (Start, All Programs, Accessories).

9. Auditing. In the world of SMB, I've observed two primary auditing needs. First, there is the small business owner who wants to know who is logging on. The configuration steps for this can be found in a Microsoft KBase article Q300549. The second auditing need is to determine who might have deleted a file or folder. Start the configuration of file and folder auditing by right-clicking a hard disk drive (such as Local Disk) from My Computer, selecting Properties, Security tab, click the Advanced button and then select the Auditing tab on the Advanced Security Settings dialog box that appears. Whew!

10. Adding hardware. In the dark days of Windows NT era of SBS 4.x, adding hardware was, shall we say, hard. Now it is much easier. That remains the case today with the underlying Windows Server 2003 operating system that is the foundation for SBS 2003. Select Add Hardware from Control Panel to add hardware.

11. Reboots. Okay, reboots are nearly—but not completely—a thing of the past. Microsoft has strived to reduce reboots, but you'll occasionally perform one because you've added an application or an operating system patch. Figure 13-16 displays a slide from the Spring 2003 Go To Market HOT Lab that traveled the USA that breaks down reboots between planned and unplanned.

Figure 13-16:

The underlying Windows Server 2003 represents the highest degree of operating system reliability to date. The planned and unplanned reboot categories list forms of reboots and recent improvements that have decreased the need for such reboots.

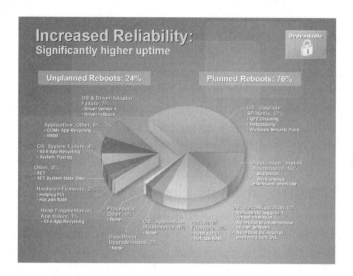

12. Documentation. An ongoing maintenance task is to fully document the client's network via a notebook. This allows the client to understand what work has been performed and, God forbid something should happen to you, the next SMB consultant can hit the ground running. The SBS development team has made a subtle improvement in SBS 2003 with respect to creating your network notebook and documenting your activities. When you reach the last screen of a wizard, say the Add User Wizard, you are presented with summary information on a "Completing" page. In the prior release of SBS (SBS 2000), you had to manually highlight the text and copy/paste it into a document that became your network notebook. In SBS 2003, this end of wizard summary information has a print, save and e-mail option!

BEST PRACTICE: Earlier in the book (Minder section) you learned the importance of writing a site report for your client after each visit. Here you tell the client about the work you performed and the time that you billed. If you take these site reports in printed form and place them in a notebook, you've gone a long way towards creating the best damn network notebook in Texas and that's no bull! Seriously-the history captured by site reports is very valuable over the life of an SBS network.

13. Client Status Meeting. Good golly Miss Molly! Let's make this one a "baker's dozen." So finally-and not to belittle the importance of this task be placing is last-are client status meetings. Here you must make it part of your ongoing SBS maintenance as an SMB consultant to periodically sit down and chat with your clients. Case closed!

Adding Value in SBS Engagements

One of the great opportunities with SBS 2003 is the ability to add value long after the initial installation and deployment have been completed. This plays very well into successful SMB consulting best practices that encourage long-term client relationships. Your clients want to, over the course of time, take advantage of the many features found in SBS 2003. This section presents additional features that will add value for both you and your clients.

BEST PRACTICE: Time for a mid-point mea culpa. This chapter, while presenting SBS 2003 from an SMB consulting point of view, isn't designed to be a book unto itself. For that, I direct your attention to my forthcoming Small Business Server 2003 Best Practices book (November 2003) that is thicker, flies faster and further, gets better gas mileage, has more horsepower, and IS TOTALLY DEDICATED TO THE TECHNICAL ASPECTS OF SBS 2003! Whew! Just wanted to manage your expectations that this book is about becoming a successful SMB consultant and my other books are not only more technical in nature, but written to be your next step.

Remote Web Workplace

This is probably the number one cool feature in SBS 2003 that will get your clients excited about this product release. It's one of the "killer applications," as we like to say in technology. So the storyline starts with an employee on the road or seeking to work from home. They direct their Web browser to the company's fully qualified domain name (FQDN) or however you setup the DNS. A resource record at your ISP routes such incoming traffic from the Internet to your SBS server. When presented with the initial Welcome Web page, you will select Remote Web Workplace. Click OK or Yes when presented with any security alert messages. Complete the logon at the Remote Web Workplace logon dialog box. After a successful logon, you'll arrive at the Remote Web Workplace, as seen in Figure 13-17.

Figure 13-17:

The Remote Web Workplace and its capabilities represent one of the great opportunities for SMB consultants to show clients something really cool and new in SBS 2003.

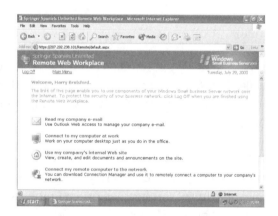

Once you've arrived at the Remote Web Workplace, you have some options to read e-mail, connect to your own desktop back at the firm, work with the company Web site, or add your remote computer as a client to the company network. I'll show off one feature that is especially cool: connecting to your desktop computer at work. Do this by clicking Connect to my computer at work. Click Yes after reading the security warning relating to the Remote Desktop ActiveX Control. A screen will appear listing computers to connect to and options for connecting to each computer. I show that in Figure 13-18. Click Connect. Click OK at the Remote Desktop Connection Security Warning dialog box.

Figure 13-18:
Check out the options for connecting to your own desktop computers. These include transferring files back and forth between your remote location and work.

The session that follows is effectively a Terminal Services session that facilitates complete control of the local desktop computer at work. Clients really enjoy being able to access their very own desktop computers when working remotely. Don't forget it!

Windows SharePoint Services

It's time to mix the bits and business. I've discussed Windows SharePoint Services (WSS) in different parts of this book and want to reiterate a few things here. WSS can be used by the SMB consultant for:

- Management consulting opportunities. You can assist your client in undertaking a company-wide survey about how information is managed. Employees can be interviewed to see whether they store information locally on their desktop computer or a network share. The outcome of these interviews and the survey process can be an effective information management policy.

- Intranet portal. WSS is way more cool than you might first appreciate-and really much more than a mere internal Web site. In reality, you can link important information to a WSS page from Excel that can be updated in real time, allowing you to create something of an

Executive Information System (EIS) for your SBS client. Note that default home page for the small business setup in SBS is the WSS Intranet portal. This was displayed earlier in the chapter in Figure 13-13.

- Document management. Yes, WSS has document management capabilities, including the ability to check documents in and out, maintain document versions, and even support document routing. Because it ships with SBS 2003, WSS might be thought of as a poor man's document management solution that will more than meet the document management needs for many small businesses. For other small businesses, WSS will only be a sampler and wet their appetite for a bona fide document management program (such as Document Locator - Small Business Server edition from ColumbiaSoft at www.documentlocator.com). Regardless, there are great SMB consulting opportunities in the document management area. The basic document management capability is displayed in Figure 13-19 for you where I've created a client category to store SMB consulting documents.

Figure 13-19:

The out-of-the-box experience with WSS is one of rapid deployment. You can easily create document categories and add documents to the repository, as seen here.

BEST PRACTICE: For much more information on SharePointtechnologies, including WSS, visit with my partner in crime, Bill English, at his excellent SharePoint site: www.sharepointknowledge.com. Bill is a fellow author and has made SharePoint his niche. He'll take you to the next level in this specific area like few others can. Tell him Harryb sent ya!

Security hardening

You can add value as the SMB consultant for your SBS client by engaging in security hardening efforts. I'll present one example and then hand you off to two great security authors for further tutelage.

Fire ISA intrusion alerts

ISA Server has a built-in intrusion detection capability that can be by viewed via the Intrusion Detection tab sheet on the property sheet for the IP Packet Filters as seen in Figure 13-20. Remember that ISA Server 2000 will ship in the premium edition of SBS 2003.

Figure 13-20:
Configure the intrusion detection capabilities in ISA Server.

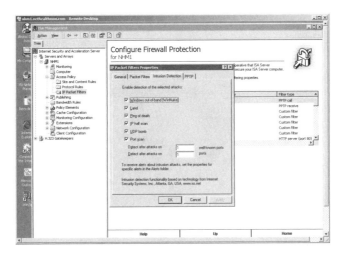

You would then configure an ISA alert to fire an e-mail when an intrusion detection attempt occurs. This configuration is shown in Figure 13-21 and occurs via the Alerts folder.

BEST PRACTICE: I recommend somewhere along here that you create a public folder in Exchange called "Security." This folder, which will be SMTP e-mail enabled by default, will allow you to send ISA Server intrusion detection alerts to it for viewing by everyone at your client site (because everyone has Outlook on their desktop computer).

Figure 13-21:
Configuring the intrusion detection alert to fire to a public folder titled "Security."

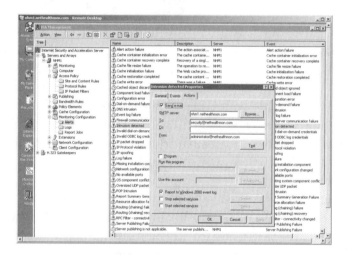

So finally, we get to the point where you add value in the client's eyes via securiy hardening. Many clients with an eye to the outflow of cash will periodically pose the questions "Why is the SMB consultant here?" and "Will you explain again just how value is added in this consulting relationship?" These same small businesses often feel invincible because they believe that no one is out to get them on the Internet or even knows that they exist! This is your cue to dispel any and all invincibility myths. Assuming you've followed my intrusion detection alert sample here and left it in place for a day or more, simply walk over to the client's desktop and expand the Security public folder. The results should look similar to Figure 13-22, which is very sobering indeed! The client has newfound respect for you, the SMB consultant, and your security hardening skills!

Figure 13-22:

It's a real eye-opener for clients to see how many intrusion detection attacks are launched on their site.

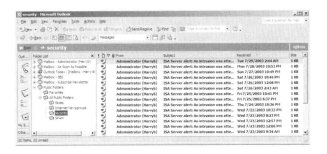

> BEST PRACTICE: Such a dramatic demonstration will also help you build better SMB consultant/client communication. This one exercise, so visible in nature, provides an outstanding opportunity to engage in valuable communication with your client. From that conversation, you may be asked to perform additional work in the security area. And don't forget that additional work is a good thing!

Author! Author!

Two fellow authors can take you to the next security level. Roberta Bragg is a big supporter of SMB and was even a leading presenter at SMB Nation! Roberta has a number of ISA and security books on the market that are continuously updated. You'll find her excellent books by searching on her name (Roberta Bragg) at Amazon (www.amazon.com). Another well-respected security author, Dr. Thomas Shinder, has excellent knowledge about SBS and how to implement the very best security you can. To say that Dr. Tom has some strong feelings about SBS and security is an understatement (you can read one of his op-ed pieces at www.w2knews.com/index.cfm?id=434). Most important, bookmark Dr. Tom's excellent ISA Server site at www.isaserver.org.

Outlook 2003

Clients love Outlook. It's one of the most underexploited tools on an SBS network and it represents a bushel of billable hours just waiting for the SMB consultant to add value at the client site. Many end users probably use about 50 percent of its capabilities and that's because they likely taught themselves (e.g., how to send and receive e-mail). Consider the following Outlook 2003 opportunities at your client site:

Training

An old trick that many SMB consultants know is to bring in the DLP/LCD projector from their home theater and herd everyone at an SBS client site into the conference room for Outlook training. When I've done this in the past, the training duration was anywhere from one hour to a full day, depending on the client's needs and interest level.

I'd encourage you to schedule training at each of your SBS 2003 client sites to show off the new features in Outlook 2003. These features include better mail management with colored priority tabs (Quick Flags), the ability to preview an e-mail in the far left vertical pane, and the ability to arrange e-mails by conversation thread. Complete Outlook 2003 features can be found at www.microsoft.com/outlook.

> BEST PRACTICE: One of the best ways to organize your new Outlook 2003 training session is to simply print the Welcome to Microsoft Office Outlook 2003 e-mail that appears in your Inbox when you first launch Outlook at a client PC. It lists 11 new Outlook 2003 capabilities that you could spend at least an hour explaining and demonstrating to end users.

Improving business operations

Outlook offers an opportunity for a dose of business consulting as well. For example, in SBS 2003, there is now a public folder and contact list automatically created based on the company name you entered during the SBS setup phase. The idea is that you, the SMB consultant, will work with your client to create a centralized company contact list for your client sites. This would be in lieu of maintaining multiple contact lists and business cards in Rolodex spindles around the firm. Imagine the delight of a small business owner when he has the true sense that he's got his company-wide contacts (clients, vendors, staff) under control! And he'll be even happier when you create a company-wide calendar under the public folder as well, to coordinate everyone and workflow! The company-related public folder is shown in Figure 13-23.

Figure 13-23:

SBS 2003 automatically creates a company public folder to encourage centralized information management and workflow management.

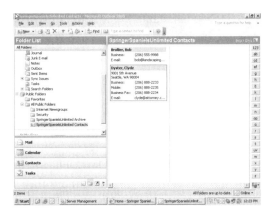

BEST PRACTICE: I've already said it once earlier in the chapter, but I'll say it again because the shoe fits here. It is sad but true that when you enter a user in SBS 2003, say an employee for the small business, a contact record isn't automatically created (only a GAL record, as described in the setup section above). So as the SMB consultant, you will want to add value by adding each employee in the company public folder (similar to Figure 13-23). And don't forget to add yourself with full contact information so the client knows whom to call immediately when SBS work needs to be completed.

Outlook Web Access

As you might expect, there is a generational improvement to Outlook Web Access (OWA) in the SBS 2003 release. It's faster and certainly more attractive than its predecessor. I found that it can help overcome an objection expressed by many clients that OWA in the past didn't feel like real Outlook and it ran sluggishly. The new OWA is displayed in Figure 13-24 and Figure 13-25.

Figure 13-24:
OWA access can be optimized at logon, where the user elects a premium client or the basic, faster client. Security levels can also be set as observed in the figure.

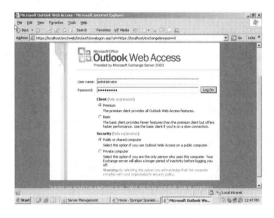

Figure 13-25:
All users who want to access e-mail remotely will appreciate the new OWA version in SBS 2003.

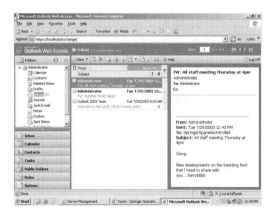

BEST PRACTICE: In the past, I was guilty of installing the real Outlook client on the actual SBS server machine (along with other SMB consultants, I might add!). There are reasons not to do this, centered around MAPI operations. In fact, in SBS 2003, you now

13-34

Harry Brelsford *SMB Consulting Best Practices*

receive the warning message shown in Figure 13-26 when you attempt to install the real Outlook program on the server machine (this is a great warning notification!). So what's a poor SMB consultant to do who wants to read and send e-mails while working on the SBS server machine itself? Easy answer in SBS 2003: Use OWA! Figure 13-25 shows the correct URL to accomplish this as http://localhost/exchange. And hey, another neat thing is that a local OWA session isn't automatically authenticated (even on the local host, you had to provide use logon credentials) which is an improvement over the legacy SBS 2000 product (where local OWA sessions where automatically authenticated).

Figure 13-26:
Do not attempt to install the real Outlook client on the SBS 2003 server machine itself.

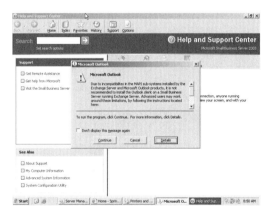

BEST PRACTICE: The SBS 2003 online HOT Lab in mid-2003 had you ignore the error in Figure 13-26 when you worked with Outlook on the actual server machine. That was a no-no to both introduce that approach and then have you ignore the resulting error message!

Visit www.smbnation.com for additional SMB and SBS book, newsletter and conference resources.

Outlook Express and IMAP

Don't forget the fussbudgets at your client sites who simply don't like OWA. Granted, with the new OWA version there should be fewer of these stick-in-the-muds, but you can always use Outlook Express with IMAP to give these folks a satisfactory e-mail experience. I suggest this because Outlook Express is found on nearly every computer at any Internet café as a feature of Internet Explorer. The use of IMAP is appealing to business people because only e-mail headers are downloaded (the entire e-mail isn't downloaded until opened). Make this one of your SBS network tricks for your remote users.

Additional servers

You'll recall the SBS product map in Figure 5-2 earlier in this book where SBS was presented in the context of four tiers or levels. The third level related to adding more servers on an existing SBS network. This is great additional work for the SMB consultant and is often driven by the need to support a robust line of business application (LOB), such as a manufacturing package, that can benefit by running on a member server. Other opportunities include adding a member server running Terminal Services in Application Sharing Mode to support many remote workers.

> BEST PRACTICE: As the SMB consultant, you might revisit your assumptions about having a member server running Terminal Services in Application Sharing Mode as the only way to support your flock of remote workers. The new Remote Web Workplace approach encourages users to tunnel into their own desktop PC to work remotely. Can you say "paradigm shift"?

Don't forget the opportunity expressed in Figure 5-2 as Level IV to take your clients beyond SBS with additional servers. Here the client has outgrown the SBS licensing limitations and moved into the full Microsoft Servers product SKUs. This type of migration makes use of the SBS migration kit and will involve both planning and deployment hours on your behalf as the SMB consultant.

Miscellaneous tasks

In this final section on adding value, I point you towards some quick hitters to add value at your client site. Some of these are background benefits that might make the SMB consultant's life better, but overall the tasks still add value to the SBS 2003 network.

- Time Synchronization. Educate yourself on how to synchronize your server and workstations to Internet-based nuclear time. One client I knew expressed frustration that not only did the computer network have the wrong time, each individual workstation had a different time! Start with KBase articles: Q323621 and Q120944.

- Licensing. Talk about a niche! I'm not suggesting you master Microsoft licensing, but you should at least stay current with licensing matters so you can advise your clients. Each product page, such as the SBS product page at Microsoft, has licensing information. Additionally, suppliers like TechData have online licensing tools that are pretty darn cool.

- Paging Files. Consider optimizing your SBS site by moving the paging file to another hard disk to improve performance. Make the upper and lower limits of the paging file the same size to minimize fragmentation.

- Printer Events. I'd recommend you eliminate all of those pesky printer event log entries from Start, Printers and Faxes, File, Server Properties, Advanced. Turn off the check box for the printer information, warning, and error events as seen in Figure 13-27. Believe me, your customer will call with a proverbial "I can't print" when printing isn't functioning. You hardly need pesky event log entries to notify you of such.

Notes:

Figure 13-27:

Who needs 'em? Turn off the printer event log entries to keep your System event log more readable.

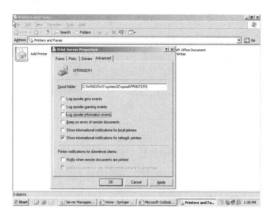

- Exchange Tasks. Time for a data dump. I'm just gonna list some Exchange-related tasks you need to consider performing at your client sites:

  1. Moving Exchange stores. Educate yourself on how to move Exchange stores to another hard disk when you run out of space.
  2. Recover deleted mail. You might know this tool as the hero button which allows you to quickly restore a single piece of e-mail from the Tools menu in Outlook. In SBS 2003, the deletion settings are turned on by default for 30 days (you had to manually implement this in SBS 2000). This is shown in Figure 13-28 below. Consider increasing the day count to 120 days for even greater safety.
  3. Managing terminated employees. Consider disabling and not deleting the accounts of the dearly departed. If you do so, you'll need to hide the disabled employee from the Global Address List so the user name doesn't appear when people send internal e-mails. This is accomplished on the property sheet for a user under Active Directory Users and Computers when the Advanced Tasks view is enabled.
  4. Second MX record and mail-bagging. Educate yourself on how to have SMTP mail reroute to a second server off-site if your SBS

server is down. This starts with a second, lower priority MX record entry in the DNS at your ISP. You would then use the POP3 Connector in SBS 2003 to go gather the redirected e-mail after such an incident. Go forth and learn more about this.

5. Multiple SMTP e-mail domains. So here the deal is that you can support clients with subtenants, such as in an executive suites scenario. This approach also works well where you have shared office space. Hint: Start your education on this by creating multiple recipient policies in Exchange.

Figure 13-28:
You can make an immediate difference and add instant value by becoming familiar with the recover deleted mail feature in Exchange. This will allow you to recover a client's errantly deleted e-mail in less than one minute!

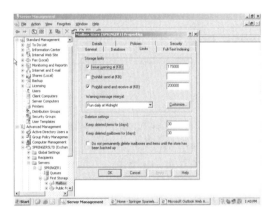

Premium edition matters

The wisdom imparted over the past several pages about SBS 2003 is based on the standard edition I've been working with. The premium edition, not available for my testing as I wrote this chapter, will feature ISA Server 2000 and SQL Server 2000. Here's what I've got to say about that.

ISA Server 2000

Hopefully, I've been clever and woven sufficient ISA Server 2000 discussion into the above sections. That's been my intent. For example, the security hardening topic suggested that you fire ISA Server 2000 alerts to a public folder for viewing. To be honest, perhaps your best guide in the premium edition for ISA Server 2000 will be your own working knowledge of this product in the SBS 2000 time frame. My forthcoming Small Business Server 2003 Best Practices book (due November 2003) will have extensive discussion of ISA Server 2000 and beyond!

SQL Server 2000

The hidden jewel of the SBS 2003 premium edition, SQL Server is also the forgotten child. Historically, only 10 percent of SBS clients even use SQL Server. That's unfortunate because, as a relational database, it's one of the most powerful applications in the SBS product suite. I've seen SQL Server used three ways in the SMB space with SBS:

- Supporting line of business applications. SQL Server supports many LOBs as the engine. For example, Great Plains Dynamics uses it.

- Importing Microsoft Access data. Using the flat file Microsoft Access program, some firms import their data in SQL Server to improve performance and increase database use and functionality.

- Development. Once in a blue moon, you'll see a small business that is developing a custom database with SQL Server.

BEST PRACTICE: One of the most powerful SMB consulting opportunities with SBS is to deploy and exploit SQL Server at your client sites. I'd recommend taking a few of the five-day Microsoft Official Curriculum courses on SQL Server to really learn this product if you intend to offer such services. You can find details at www.microsoft.com/sql. And don't forget that your client might be interested in knowing that SQL Server is the most expensive component in the SBS 2003 premium edition, which might be inducement alone to use it. Clients will feel they're getting a real bargain!

And again, this section only teased you about the possibilities of SBS 2003 without going deep into any one solution.

Building Better Client Relationships

It's always a good feeling to know that you've been heard. During the life of SBS 2000, I and other SMB consultants who use SBS found the Server Status Report (SSR) to be a great tool for building strong client relationships. Some of the improvements that we recommended have now appeared in SBS 2003 for the out-of-the-box benefit of all SBM consultants. So now for my last SMB consulting secret in this book for you: the proper use of the SSR!

The drill is this: Each morning at roughly 7:00 am, just prior to business opening, you want each of your client sites running SBS 2003 to send a complete SSR to your attention. Over morning coffee, you read and reply to each of the reports. For example, you might tell Jeanette, the office manager at the property management firm, that they received a good backup last night (based on your reading of the backup log), the virus definition file was updated (because you read the attached update log), and the disk space, processor utilization rate, and memory consumption all look fine. A sample SSR is shown in Figure 13-29.

You would configure the SSR from the Configure Monitoring link on the Complete the configuration screen (aka To Do List). You will complete the Monitoring Configuration Wizard. Click Next at the Welcome screen. Make the selections to receive the Performance Report and the Usage Report on the Reporting Options screen and click Next. Put in your e-mail address on the E-mail Options page so you, the SMB consultant, will receive the SSR. Select which client staff members will be able to review the usage report. Typically you allow executive, managers, and owners to review usage reports to monitor how the SBS network is being used. Supply your e-mail address again on the Alerts screen to receive e-mail alerts. Click Finish on the completion screen after reading the detailed configuration. Note that the report will indeed be shipped at 7:00 am each day. After this initial configuration is complete, a reboot is requested (one of the few requested reboots in SBS 2003).

Figure 13-29:

The holy grail of SBS is the SSR!

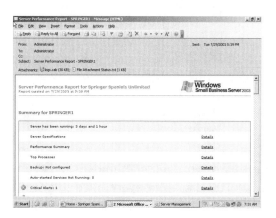

Note that I've configured the SSR to send attachments. You will want to do this for the tape backup log, virus definition update log, and other computer logs that you want to monitor. Such modifications are made from the Change Server Status Report Settings link under Monitoring and Report under Standard Management in the Server Management console. Kindly note the native backup program's backup logs are a selection you can easily make from a list of other log files (it is not a custom log addition like it was during the SBS 2000 era).

> BEST PRACTICE: A few best practices to recite here. First and foremost, the SSR gives you a vehicle for creating daily positive communication with the key stakeholders at each of your client sites. That's something every SMB consultant should continually strive for and is the essence of successful SMB consulting with SBS 2003. This will result in a greater number of referrals from existing clients and, as such, can be the cornerstone from which to build your SMB consulting practice.
>
> Second, to even receive the report means about a dozen things are working correctly. For example, the power is on at the client site and your site. The server is operating as well as Exchange e-mail. What I'm getting at is that if you don't receive the report,

you know something is wrong and you can call the client first thing in the morning when they open for business. And it shouldn't be lost on you why the 7:00 am send time is so advantageous. Imagine if the send time were 1:00 am and the tape backup wasn't complete. The tape backup log you would receive wouldn't tell you whether the tape backup was successful or not. And what if the report arrived at 1:00 am, but a wind storm knocked out your client site at 5:00 am (true story)? You'd probably feel silly replying everything was fine when indeed the client doesn't think the same that morning as she sits in the dark!

Third, the reports allow you to communicate that everything is all right on 99 out of 100 days. But every once in a while, the tape backup doesn't complete and so on. When such is the case, you'll at least know problem spots exist and you can quickly bring such matters to your client's attention. Clients can handle the truth and will appreciate the communication.

BEST PRACTICE: A final advance area of further study for you would be to learn the finer points of Health Monitor. I breezed over it just above when I had you select the alerts to fire to your e-mail address for your SBS client site. There is much more to Health Monitor. The best guide is to print and read the online help for Health Monitor (which is basically the only Health Monitor book in the world).

Important Note

I'm honor-bound to repeat a disclaimer from the first part of this chapter. The information in this chapter is based on Microsoft Windows Small Business Server 2003 Release Candidate in mid-2003. Some of the features, functionality, and user interface (as shown in the screenshots) may well change by the time the final product is released in October 2003. Microsoft was kind enough to grant me permission to write this chapter based on the release candidate, for which I'm very grateful. Your cooperation in this matter is appreciated.

Brelsford's Mailbox

Harry,

I need to establish a relationship with someone familiar with SBS and Microsoft SQL. I do web site integration and typically subcontract the dynamics. My experience to date is with a group doing Linux, PHP, PostgreSQL. My current thrust is dealing with people recommending and installing SBS who want to use Microsoft products. How can you help me?

Myron
Narragansett, RI

Hi, Myron!

Thanks for the e-mail. Your e-mail is of particular interest because there are many SMB consultants out there who have niched on SBS and would love to team with someone such as you. I'm impressed that you've stepped up and asked for help with network infrastructures in the SMB space. Plus, I think many SMB consultants could really benefit from seeing how you add value with an SBS installation with databases and additional operating systems.

So a next step for you would be to post your request to the small business technology consulting group at Yahoo! Many of the readers of this book are members there and will gladly assist you. The Yahoo! group I mention can be found at: http://groups.yahoo.com/group/smallbizIT.

Keep in touch and let me know how it goes!

best to you...harrybbbbb

Summary

This chapter was the capstone for the entire book. You've learned how to plan for your SMB consulting practice, you then proceeded to understand how to gain new clients, manage those clients, and provide different services to those clients. This chapter strongly promoted SBS 2003 as a niche you should master. Specific topics covered in this chapter include:

- Small Business Server defined

- Understanding Small Business Server in the SMB space

- Building your SMB consulting practice around Small Business Server

- Small Business Server 2003 installation and deployment guidance

- Adding value in SMB engagements with Small Business Server

- Tools to build better client relationships within Small Business Server 2003

Appendix A

SMB RESOURCES

This appendix lists SMB resources that will be useful in starting and growing your SMB consulting practice. All of these resources have previously been listed in the book, but this appendix displays these resources in one easy, at-a-glance location.

Microsoft Partners Sites

- Main Microsoft Partner site: www.microsoft.com/partner

- Microsoft SBS Partner Locator Tool: sbslocator.cohesioninc.com/apartnerlocator.asp

- Microsoft Certified Partner Resource Directory (how to find a Certified Partner): directory.microsoft.com/resourcedirectory/solutions.aspx

- Action Pack: members.microsoft.com/partner/salesmarketing/partnermarket/actionpack/default.aspx

Microsoft Windows Small Business Server (SBS) Sites

- www.microsoft.com/sbserver

- www.microsoft.com/sbs

- www.microsoft.com/partner/sbs

Additional Microsoft or Microsoft-related Sites

- Main Microsoft site: www.microsoft.com

- Microsoft Office templates: officeupdate.microsoft.com/templategallery/

- bCentral small business portal: www.bcentral.com

- bCentral Technology Consulting Directory: directory.bcentral.com/ITConsultant/

- Great Plains: www.microsoft.com/greatplains

- Microsoft Visio: www.microsoft.com/visio

- Asentus: www.asentus.net

- Hands On Lab: www.handsonlab.com

- Granite Pillar: microsoft.granitepillar.com/partners/

- Entirenet: www.entirenet.net/registration

- Directions on Microsoft: www.directionsonmicrosoft.com

- Microsoft Solution Selling: www.solutionselling.com/mspartners/ fusion.html

- Dr. Thomas Shinder's ISA Server Web site: www.isaserver.org

- Bill English's SharePoint Web site: www.sharepointknowledge.com

Third-party SBS-related Sites

- Small Biz Server Links: http://www.sbslinks.com/

- Wayne Small's SBS Web site: www.sbsfaq.com

- Another SBS FAQ site: http://www.smallbizserver.net/

- Susan Bradley's SBS Web site: www.sbslinks.com/

- Grey Lancaster's SBS Web site (one of the original SBS site): www.smallbizserver.com/

Newslists, User Groups, Trade Associations, Organizations

- Small BizIT "Small Business IT Consultants" newslist at Yahoo: groups.yahoo.com/groups/smallbizIT

- SBS – Microsoft Small Business Server Support: http:// groups.yahoo.com/group/sbs2k/

- San Diego SBS User Group: www.sdsbsug.org

- CompTIA: www.comptia.com

- Network Professional Association: www.npa.org

- Adelaide Australia SBS User Group. For information, contact Dean Calvert: dean@calvert.net.au

- Boston, MA, USA SBS User Group. For more information, contact Eliot Sennett: eliot@esient.com

- Cincinnati, OH, USA SBS User Group. This SBS group is a SIG that is part of a larger general user group. For more information, contact Kevin Royalty: kevin_royalty@yahoo.com

- Cleveland, OH, USA SBS User Group. For more information, visit http://www.gcpcug.org/ or contract Fredrick Johnson: fjohnson@rosstek.com

- Denver CO, USA SBS User Group. For more information, contact Lilly C. Banks: lilly@iSolutionsUnlimited.com.

- Omaha, NB, USA SBS User Group. For more information, contact Amy Luby: aluby@tconl.com. has started a user group in the Omaha, Nebraska area, 10 users

- Portland, OR, USA SBS User Group. For more information, visit http://pdxsbs.fpwest.com or contact Patrick West: patrick@west.net

- San Francisco/Bay Area, CA, USA SBS User Group. For more information, contact Ed Correia: ecorreia@sagacent.com

- Seattle, WA, USA SBS User Group. For more information, contact Steven Banks steve@banksnw.com

- Southern CA, USA SBS User Group. For more information, contact Donna Obdyke: DObdyke@prodigy.net

- Sydney, NSW, Australia SBS User Group. For more information, contact Wayne Small [wayne@correct.com.au] and visit http://www.sbsfaq.com/Sydney%20SBS%20UG/

- Black Data Processing Association (BDPA): www.bdpa.org

- West Sound Technology Professional Association: www.wstpa.org

Seminars, Workshops, Conferences

- SMB Nation: www.smbnation.com

- Microsoft TS2 events: www.msts2.com

- Microsoft Big Day/Business Solution Series: www.msbigday.com

- Microsoft Momentum Conference: http://www.microsoft.com/partner/events/wwpartnerconference/

- ITEC: www.goitec.com

- Guerrilla marketing and sales seminars: www.guerrillabusiness.com

- Who Moved My Cheese seminars: www.whomovedmycheese.com

- Myers-Briggs Type Indicator: www.apcentral.org

- Millionaire Mind / T. Harv Eker: www.peakpotentials.com

- TechMentor: www.techmentorevents.com

- SuperConference (accounting/technology): www.pencorllc.com

Business Resources

- US Small Business Administration: www.sba.gov

- Palo Alto Software for business planning: www.paloaltosoftware.com

- PlanWare: www.planware.org

- Outsourced accounting: www.cfo2go-wa.com

- US Federal Reserve Web site: www.federalreserve.gov

- Presentations: www.presentations.com

- CardScan: www.cardscan.com

- Plaxo: www.plaxo.com

Media

- Small Business Best Practices newsletter: www.nethealthmon.com/newsletter.htm

- CRN: www.crn.com

- SBS Maven Andy Goodman posts SBS-related articles at http://www.12c4pc.com.

- Small Business Computing: www.smallbusinesscomputing.com

- PC Magazine Small Business Super Site (www.pcmag.com/category2/0,4148,13806,00.asp)

- Mary Jo Foley's Microsoft-Watch: www.microsoft-watch.com

- NetworkWorldFusion SMB portal: www.nwfusion.com/net.worker/index.html

- Microsoft Certified Professional Magazine: www.mcpmag.com

- Certified Magazine: www.certmag.com

- Windows and .NET Magazine: www.winnetmag.com

- CRMDaily: www.crmdaily.com

- TechRepublic: www.techrepublic.com

- VAR Business: www.varbusiness.com

- Small Business Technology Report: www.smallbiztechnology.com

- Win2K News: www.w2knews.com

- SmallBizTechTalk: www.smallbiztechtalk.com

- Eweek: www.eweek.com

- ComputerWorld: www.computerworld.com

- Kim Komando Show: www.komando.com

- WinInformit: http://www.wininformant.com/

- Entrepreneur Magazine: www.entrepreneur.com

- INC Magazine: www.inc.com

- Fortune: www.fortune.com

- Bizjournals: www.bizjournals.com

- CNN: www.cnn.com

- Business Week: www.businessweek.com

- CBS MarketWatch: www.marketwatch.com

- USA Today: www.usatoday.com

- Money Magazine: www.money.cnn.com

- Bruce Williams (financial radio): www.brucewilliams.com

- Suzy Orman on CNBC: http://moneycentral.msn.com/content/ CNBCTV/TV_Info/Anchors&Reporters/P5519.asp

SMB Hardware & Software Companies

- HP/Compaq: www.hp.com

- Gateway: www.gateway.com

- IBM: www.ibm.com

- Dell: www.dell.com

- ConnectWise: www.connectwise.com

- Document Locator – Small Business Server edition: www.documentlocator.com

- TimeSlips: www.timeslips.com

- QuickBooks: www.quickbooks.com

- Shavlik patch management program for SBS: www.shavlik.com

Miscellaneous

- Google search engine: www.google.com

- NPower, not-for-profit technology agency: www.npower.org

- eBay: www.ebay.com

- GeekSquad: www.geeksquad.com

- Geeks On Call: www.geeksoncall.com

- Soft-Temps: www.soft-temps.com

- REI: www.rei.com

- Brooks Brothers: www.brooksbrothers.com

- Insurance for technology professionals: www.techinsurance.com

- Robert Half International salary survey: www.rhii.com

- AOL for Small Business: aolsvc.aol.com/small_biz

- eProject: www.eproject.com

Appendix B

BRELSFORD'S DOZEN

CUMULATIVE COLLECTION

This appendix places all of Brelsford's Dozen advisories in one place for easy reference.

Brelsford's Dozen *chapter references:*

Chapter 3

Introducing Brelsford's Dozen

Chapter 4

Brelsford's Dozen: Have 12 Months' Cash on Hand

Brelsford's Dozen: Client Rejection Ratio

Chapter 5

Brelsford's Dozen: Better Business Research

Brelsford's Dozen: Competitive Survey

Brelsford's Dozen: Giveth Business Cards

Brelsford's Dozen: Receiveth Business Cards

Brelsford's Dozen: Attend a Dozen Marketing Events per Quarter

Chapter 6

Brelsford's Dozen: Great Expectations

Chapter 7

Brelsford's Dozen: Scope a 12 Percent Fudge Factor

Brelsford's Dozen: Nine out of 12 New Clients Must be Referrals

Brelsford's Dozen: Partnerships!

Brelsford's Dozen: Finder's Fee

Brelsford's Dozen: Scanning Contemporary Texts

Chapter 8

Brelsford's Dozen: Communications

Brelsford's Dozen: Analyze This!

And Analyze That!

Brelsford's Dozen: Client Treatment

Chapter 9

Brelsford's Dozen: Daily Limits

Brelsford's Dozen: Annual Departures

Chapter 10

Brelsford's Dozen: Bill 1,200 Hours per Year!

Brelsford's Dozen: 12 Percent Profit Margin

Brelsford's Dozen: Calculating True Costs

Brelsford's Dozen: Assume a 12 Percent Write-off Rate

Chapter 11

Brelsford's Dozen: 12-to-1 Odds

Brelsford's Dozen: Methodology Samples

Chapter 12

Brelsford's Dozen: Create Your Top-12 Niche List!

Chapter 13

Ongoing Maintenance Tasks

Introducing Brelsford's Dozen

This chapter presents the foundation for your consulting career. But it's not the last you will hear about foundation-level issues in this book. In each chapter, I'll present pragmatic and practical SMB consulting rules, titled "Brelsford's Dozen," that layer right on top of the foundation you've built in this chapter. For example, in the Finder section of the book, I share with you some Brelsford's Dozen rules for getting more business. And it should not be lost on you that the following rules, presented as the body of this chapter, were your first exposure to Brelsford's Dozen:

1. GainTrust

2. Practice Expectation Management

3. Overcommunicate

4. Be Willing to Wear Many Hats

5. Become a Business Advisor

6. Take a Long-term View

7. Act as a Client Advocate

8. Mentor Your Clients

9. Provide Pro Bono Services

10. Live By Referrals

11. Always Operate Under NDA

12. First, Do No Harm

Have 12 Months' Cash on Hand

All professionals and small business people, yourself included as an SMB consultant, need starting capital. Think about this. Maybe you've witnessed the following scenarios. Perhaps a friend or family member is in some type of commission-based professional capacity and started with a year of cash to initially cover living expenses. Or perhaps you saw a middle-aged, middle-management dude leave his corporate capacity and borrow against his retirement funds to open a hobby shop. Maybe you witnessed the housewife of a dentist start a fabrics store, bankrolled by her husband for the first year of operations. No matter what new business you might jump into, the first year is a total financial bearcat and you need some cash to carry you through!

This area of sufficient start-up capital is so important that I'll state the obvious again: Starting out with enough money is an essential fact of being in business for commission-based salespeople, small business owners, and SMB consultants alike. When you break out on your own, you need a reserve of cash on which to survive until your business efforts yield sustainable cash flow. In real estate sales career seminars, you're advised to have a year of cash for living expenses-although new real estate agents are notorious for running up credit card debt, or begging from family and friends, or otherwise borrowing from Peter to pay Paul to survive the first year. This real estate career advice applies equally well to SMB consultants just starting out.

But I can hear some of you asking why you should have one-year's cash on hand to launch as an SMB consultant. The billing cycle that follows the initial contract, which follows the initial sales cycle, is way out there! Plus I need to preintroduce a concept that I'll explore more in the Minder section of this book: accounting write-downs. Long story short, you'll have some billing write-downs in the SMB consulting field. Write-downs are charges against your billing revenues when a client will not pay your consulting invoice. Accounting rules dictate that you write down doubtful accounts receivable balances after a reasonable period of time. Figure 4-1 displays the 12-month initial cash-on-hand cycle for you.

Figure 4-1:
Proof positive the 12-month supply of cash at launch theorem holds true.

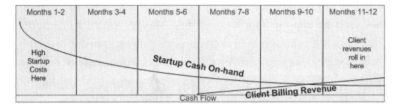

Betcha didn't know that the 12-month rule can even apply to established SMB consulting practices. From the first sales call to the first satisfied invoice (which is cash in hand to you), it's not uncommon for nearly 12 months to have passed. These stark facts about cash-flow timing are only stronger for the newbie SMB consultant.

Bottom line: Your new SMB consulting practice is a startup. It's risky and some of you, bless your hearts, might not be around in a year or two. This sobering reality is all the more reason to have sufficient cash to launch! You'll greatly appreciate having enough money at the ready, let me tell you.

Client Rejection Ratio

I discovered I needed an SMB consulting guideline to help me stay focused on selecting good clients. When I operated under no such rule, client selection decisions tended to be emotional and political, if not made in occasional desperation. Later, as a successful SMB consultant and after looking over my business development practices, I determined that I was rejecting about half the potential clients that asked for my services. So I devised the following rule for myself:

On average, reject six out of twelve clients.

Let me shed some light on how this rule works:

- **The long run** — When you first open your doors for business as an SMB consultant, it's probably not practical to say "no" to nearly anyone who wants to hire you. Sometimes you just have to take what you can get. Perhaps you'll reject only the most offensive prospects. To be honest, it took me years to get my practice to where I could comfortably turn away half the business.

- **Natural laws** — To some extent, the marketplace is already performing this winnowing for you. If you count how many sales calls never go past discussing your rate or how many client meetings you've attended where both you and your client discover that the service you provide is different than the one required by the client, then you're probably close to a 50 percent client rejection ratio without even knowing it.

- **Comfort zone** — If you have the confidence that leads will flow to you and being selective is critical to your success, you'll also have the confidence to say "no" when it doesn't feel right between you and a prospective client.

Better Business Research

For many pages, I've shared economic wisdom, studies, and statistics. But these business factoids are only as current, in many cases, as the day I wrote them. You must now march forth to the Internet and find and read a dozen updated articles on the SMB economic sector. Some Web sites to consider looking at are:

- *Entrepreneur.* Visit this Web site to learn more about SMB start up matters (www.entrepreneur.com).

- *INC.* Certainly a favorite and a source of many citations in this book: www.inc.com.

- CNN. After surfing over to www.cnn.com, click the **Business button** at **CNNMONEY** link on the left and then read the business news. Hint: Drill further into the technology and Business 2.0 links here.

- *Fortune.* As seen in Figure 5-10, *Fortune* has a dedicated small business portal (and also a magazine called *Fortune Small Business*). Visit www.fortune.com and click the **Small Business** link.

Figure 5-10:
Fortune Small Business portal

BEST PRACTICE: Consider that many SMB consultants only use the SMB space as a launching pad for enterprise engagements. IKON, the office supplies company, tried to use SBS in the SMB space to build up a list of consulting referrals so it could pursue enterprise work. Last I heard IKON was no longer in the consulting business. However, the SMB-to-enterprise strategy was sound and is often repeated. Some of you reading this book may well view your time as SMB consultants in that context. You'll be in good company down the road as many enterprise-level consultants started in the SMB space.

Notes:

Competitive Survey

Before you get too far into this SMB consulting lifestyle and bet the family farm, please do me and yourself a favor. Undertake a survey of a dozen SMB consulting competitors in your area. This doesn't have to be as sinister as it sounds (although I'll get to that in a moment). To conduct a rate survey, simply browse (and bookmark for future reference) the Web sites of your competitors. Many post their bill rates openly. Now for the sinister part. First, you can call your competitors and ask what their bill rates are, the implicit belief being that you are a customer. To be honest, I've probably received these calls unknowingly in the past and haven't worried too much about telling all. I figure my rates are what they are and I'm confident in my role as an SMB consultant not to be threatened by competition.

Next up and farther down on the sinister bar is trade show floor walking. One of the greatest all-time tricks for surveying competitors is to attend trade shows and talk directly to your competitors in their booths. You'd be amazed at what you can learn about their business models (including bill rates).

Giveth Business Cards

Set a goal of giving out 12 of your business cards per quarter (every 90 days) from this point forward, which amounts to one business card per week, a modest and achievable goal. Over time, this becomes a very powerful tool, as you're name will spread exponentially in your community.

> BEST PRACTICE: The above point of "modest and achievable" shouldn't be overlooked. It's been said time and time again from the school of life to the hallowed halls of the Harvard MBA program that a successful business person doesn't do one thing great but does lots of little things well. That is, you don't need to have the wisdom of Solomon to invent new marketing models to be successful. Rather, just give away one of your business cards per week.

Consider some of the group listed in the last section (chamber of commerce, Rotary, etc.) as avenues for you to attend events, participate in meetings, AND give away that weekly business card.

BEST PRACTICE: You can also do what Dorothy did. (No, I don't mean click your heels and say "There's no place like home!") I used to work with a seasoned professional named Dorothy a while back at a national contracting firm called 1-800-NETWORK. At the time, being full of pride, I probably didn't learn as much from Dorothy as I could have. However, reflecting back and having made amends, I think Dorothy really had a great practice when it came to giving away business cards. Dorothy's technique was to hand out two business cards at once with the phrase "...one for you and one to pass on to a friend." Needless to say, it was easy for Dorothy to meet and exceed her card giveaway quota.

To Dorothy -> you go girl!

Receiveth Business Cards

Not surprisingly, you now want to endeavor to obtain a dozen business cards per quarter (again, one per week). This is a fundamental SMB consulting marketing activity—and how you build your book of contacts. My premise here is simple enough. In Chapter 7, you'll learn more about being a rainmaker as I expand on the "building the book" concept.

Attend a Dozen Marketing Events per Quarter

Now for one of my favorite activities: eating hotel donuts and drinking coffee at marketing functions. Seriously, your goal is to be an SMB consultant on the fast track. You need to be seen everywhere, much like a rising star in Hollywood. You're job here isn't as difficult as the cast of NBC's top-rated show *Friends*, who necessarily need to be seen at the trendiest LA restaurants. Rather, it's to find some marketing venue to attend each week and "been seen." A couple of ideas:

- Host a table at a Microsoft Big Day/Business Solutions Seminar in the USA. I followed the Big Day circuit for over a year in the Pacific Northwest and had my table with other technology professionals in the back of the presentation room. The idea here was that local technology professionals could register to host a table for the day and speak to attendees (primarily business people) during the breaks and lunch hour. The table sign-up process is shown in Figure 5-16 and is found from the main Microsoft Business Solutions Seminar Web site (www.msbigday.com) by clicking the **Technology Providers** link on the left side.

Figure 5-16:

Microsoft's Big Day/Business Solutions Seminar is a great free marketing method for SMB consultants seeking exposure. You must register for a table to present your brochure and other marketing materials.

BEST PRACTICE: Expanding on the marketing versus sales discussion centering around Microsoft Big Day/Business Solutions Seminars, I can offer the following. When I hosted a table at these events, I found it to be true marketing. Introductions were made and it was incumbent on me to follow up on the lead I obtained. I never consummated a sales transaction at my table, thus I didn't view it as strongly as a sales event. Go ahead, host your own table, and make your own judgment. One thing is for sure—the price was right: FREE!

• Join a trade group. Earlier I spoke about the WSTPA trade group I belong to. I consider my monthly meeting to be one of my required marketing meetings. That's because the WSTPA has a real social element to it where "networking" (the human interaction form, not the multi-layer OSI model approach) is strongly encouraged. Another example shown in Figure 5-17, is the monthly chamber of commerce mixer (typically called "After Hours"). Nearly every chamber hosts such an event and, once you've paid your membership, attendance is usually free (or costs little). When you think about it, it really doesn't cost anything to stand around and talk to the membership, eh? Salute!

Figure 5-17:
As an example, here is the Bainbridge Island Chamber's announcement for the after hours event and monthly luncheon.

- Make-ups. So what if you miss a weekly marketing venue? What to do? Like the Rotary club, you need to endeavor to do a "make-up" meeting. You're not relieved of this responsibility. Like taking antibiotics for a health malady, you can double-up after missing.

Notes:

Great Expectations

A key element to success as an SMB consultant is to avoid making mistakes along the way. The world of advertising is littered with great mistakes, and by acknowledging and appreciating these mistakes, you can avoid repeating them. So as an SMB consulting/Brelsford's Dozen exercise, let's compile a list of advertising approaches you might want to avoid. Consider this the "Brelsford's Dozen of Great Advertising, Sales, and Marketing Mistakes to be Avoided." I'll provide the first two and then send you on your way to research another ten to complete the list as part of this SMB consulting assignment.

1. Coke Classic. Every business student studies this faux pas, where Coke broke something that was fixed when it changed the positioning of its mainstay cola beverage by introducing a "new and improved" version. Ouch!
2. Nike's Olympic Chain Saw Massacre. In the 2000 Summer Olympics (Australia), Phil Knight, CEO of Nike, Inc., came up with the idea of recreating a scene from a popular horror movie: A killer wielding a chain saw chases Olympian Suzy Favor in a television advertisement. Suzy makes a clean getaway, supposedly making the point that Nike shoes allow you to outrun killers, etc. However, the ad was taken the wrong way by the public and reflected an abusive and violent tone towards women.
3.
4.
5.
6.
7.
8.
9.
10.
11.
12.

Scope a 12 Percent Fudge Factor

All of your proposals should include at least 12 percent padding or inflated cost estimates to account for unknowns and mistakes. In actuality, this 12 percent value is pretty lean, because it doesn't take much of a mistake to cut through 12 percent padding. In your niche area of SMB consulting, you can probably get away with 12 percent padding. However, if you are bidding outside of your niche, consider 30 percent padding to cushion your lack of experience and to account for the unknowns and the unpredictable.

Nine out of 12 New Clients Must be Referrals

In the long run, nine out of 12 new clients (three-quarters) must be referrals or else you are facing an uphill battle to be truly profitable as an SMB consultant. "The long run" means different things to different people. Stock market day-traders view the long run as holding a stock overnight. Real estate investors view the long run as 30 years until a property is free and clear. For an SMB consultant, the definition of "the long run" lies somewhere between these two extremes. I've been an SMB consultant in the same market for over a decade and it's just in the past couple of years that I've actually had referrals coming in on e-mail, by voicemail, and through face-to-face conversations over lattés. You, too, will build your ability to gain referrals in your own time.

So just what tree do you shake to get all these inbound referrals to drop in your lap? Being a competent technical professional with great customer service skills is the first step. Look around right now and see if there's just one tiny thing you could do better. Have you answered that client's e-mail sitting in your Inbox? No? Then right here, right now, put this book down, double-click on the client's e-mail, and hit "Reply." I'm betting in less than ten minutes you can complete a customer service task that'll make your client feel good. Still sitting here? Go do it. The SMB consulting book will be here when you return.

> BEST PRACTICE: If you really want to impress your clients, call them up and ask how things are going since your last visit. Tell your client you just wanted to check in and make sure the fix you implemented is working as planned. Few people in the SMB consulting industry do this and you'll stand out in a very positive way.

A great way to boost the number of referrals you get is to look closely at the industries you are serving. Some industries and sectors of the economy lend themselves to being better referral sources than others. For example, excellent referrals are freely given in the not-for-profit sector, where the organizations keep in close contact with each other and are known to gossip! You might be serving the wrong type of business if you're seeking to grow by referrals and the businesses in that industry don't talk to each other via lunches, trade associations, etc. A friend of mine in the not-for-profit niche as a Chicago-based SMB consultant pointed out that many small businesses are so busy working 18-hour days that they literally don't talk to each other. His level of referrals and his success as an SMB consultant increased when he focused on the not-for-profit sector.

> BEST PRACTICE: Remember that these same referral sources in your various channels can turn against you if you disappoint any of them. Do a poor job at one not-for-profit organization and you can be blackballed from all the rest.

Don't forget I discussed a similar topic, the client rejection ratio that specifies how many leads you should reject as a healthy business best practice, in the early part of Chapter 4 of this book.

Partnerships!

If you thought Enron, with its financial wizardry and web of complex partnerships, was too much, consider this piece of advice: I suggest your rainmaking efforts might heavily focus on entering into and managing partnerships to drive your SMB consulting business. Could you imagine, over time, building up a dozen marketing relationship where you partner with different accounting firms? It's not beyond the realm of possibility and might just be the right fit for your marketing efforts.

Finder's Fee

When you consider the explicit and implicit cost to secure a client, it's surprisingly expensive (especially if you consider the time you devote to the sales process). So go ahead, try putting out the word that you'll pay a finder's fee for bona fide customers that are delivered "as advertised" and secured under an engagement letter. Tell the "finder" that you'll pay a 12 percent finder fee on the first 12 months of business. This should be fair, as the "finder" earns a commission that should be a source of motivation. And often, in SMB consulting, some of your best client billing opportunities occur within the first year of the relationship when the workload is highest.

Scanning Contemporary Texts

The next time you're traveling and you check in and clear security at the airport, spend some time (at least 12 minutes or more) and scan the business book section at the airport bookstore. I'd like you to discover at least a dozen contemporary business book titles that might help you develop your SMB consulting practice. No need to purchase all these books; you'll just get a handle on what current business best practices are being communicated, such as Guerrillas and Cheese!

Communications

Communicate with your clients frequently on a clear and consistent basis. For clients with whom you have an ongoing relationship, communicate every dozen business days. I selected this number as it fits with my style of checking in with my portfolio a couple of times per month. I've found that not adhering to this rule of communications results in the following outcomes:

- **Crises-based negative communications** — If you don't proactively communicate a couple of times per month with your active clients, the communication channel can take on a consistently negative tone. That is, the only time you communicate with your client is when there is a problem. Perhaps you've had those clients who call only when something is broken! This is not the firm foundation of communication you're seeking as an SMB consultant. I, for one, got tired of the "911" emergency mentality that can bedevil less experienced and less knowing consultants.

- **Manufactured information** — I've also found that if I don't proactively initiate communications a couple of times per month with my clients that, with the passage of time, clients will start to manufacture information, resulting in an unintentional fabrication. In order words, a lack of clear and consistent communications from you will create a void in the client communication model that will be filled by your clients. That sounds risky to me! I'll never forget a time when I was breaking my own rule and not being communicative with my client. Having not heard from me and having misinterpreted my parting comment one visit about performing surgery on a server, the business owner called one day to find out if I was out of the hospital yet. He had confused my surgery comments in his own mind and, when he didn't hear from me again, assumed I'd gone into the hospital. We enjoyed a good chuckle when we found out that information had been manufactured, but it sure illustrated the power of imaginary information. You should strive to prevent this with constant communication-because the outcome might not always be so humorous. In other words, if they don't hear anything from you about what you're doing and how their system is running, the client will interpret for himself how you and the system are performing. This is an EXTREMELY DANGEROUS WAY to operate, as most manufactured information is NEGATIVE (e.g., "That •@?#!$+% darn computer system isn't working again!")

By saying that you should communicate with clients a couple of times per month, I don't mean to suggest you need to sit at a telephone and "power call" for several hours straight. Mix it up. Some weeks call a few clients. Other weeks e-mail a note to different clients. The communications can often just be a quick: "How is it going?" I've found clients appreciate the gesture, and such behavior has resulted in additional work for me.

Analyze This!

Pop therapy meets SMB consulting reality. Consider that out of a dozen failed engagements (God forbid you never have so many failed engagements), you'll find the vast majority of engagements didn't fail for technical reasons, but rather because there was a communication breakdown with the client. If you're shown the door because of a "blue screen" on a misbehaved server, you were probably in trouble for months over poor communications. So, stand up and look at yourself in the mirror. Are you doing the best job you can to communicate with your clients currently? Can you improve your communication skills? Probably so. Read the next section on analyzing personality types and understanding where people are coming from.

Stated another way, may I propose for your consideration that an engagement is 12 times more likely to fail as a result of poor client communications rather than technical failure — a sobering thought when you think about it.

And AnalyzeThat!

Another take on the engagement management topic comes with assessing your own shortcomings, trips to the therapist's office included. Back when I worked for the consulting division of the accounting practice (mid- to late 1990s), the managing partner's advice about long-term success as a professional service provider (including SMB consultants) requiring great management skills was well-taken. I discovered that when it came to management tasks and roles, resistance is futile, and you'll either accept the management role with open arms or be dragged into it kicking and screaming. But if you want to last more than a fortnight as an SMB consultant, you've got to demonstrate at least basic engagement management skills.

On a more hopeful note, it's been said that of the three main areas of professional service delivery (and the broad outline of this book) — finder, minder, and grinder — that you can only master two out of three. Take your pick! Some people focus on management and technical services, leaving the marketing to others. Other folks like to get the work (finder) and then perform the tasks with little interest in management functions. It's okay to have strengths in two out of three key consulting areas, but you can't completely ignore any of the finder, minder, grinder functions as an SMB consultant.

Client Treatment

This proverb is simple to state. Treat your clients a dozen times better than you treat yourself, because an unhappy client will tell a dozen people about his unhappiness with you. Thus, it's in your interest to bend over backwards to have happy clients.

Daily Limits

Taking a page right from the airlines and railroads labor agreements, I want you to consider imposing a daily limit on your business activities. That limit is a maximum of 12 hours per day. Let me explain.

Airline pilots and railroad engineers have daily work limits in order to insure the safety of passengers. A fatigued pilot is a dangerous pilot. The same can be said for SMB consultants who overwork themselves and "get stupid" out on a client site. I've done it and perhaps you've done it as well! Granted, it's one thing to have an especially long day on a "911" emergency call and work the hours of a gifted surgeon. That's not my primary concern. It's about working too many long days in a row where the cumulative fatigue not only causes you to think unclearly but to burn out on being an SMB consultant. Too many back-to-back days, weeks, months, years of outrageously long work days will drive you from this line of work, which would be unfortunate.

Now exactly how do you measure 12 hours? Clearly I'm not talking about 12 billable hours. That's because, as you'll learn in the next chapter, a solid SMB consultant has a 50 percent utilization rate and 12 billable hours would translate into a 24 hour work day. Ouch! Rather, I'm talking about a maximum of 12 hours per day away from other activities, such as family and fun (although, of course, SMB consulting is fun). Translation: Count your drive time, telephone time, think time, and so on and you'll quickly hit 12 hours in a busy work day. Then I'm asking you to back off and not even do this too often. Ideally you're billing four to five hours per day and working, in aggregate, eight to 10 hours.

Annual Departures

No matter how wonderful you are, your firm is, and the salary is, you will lose some SMB consultants in your practice. It has been my experience that four out of 12 employees will leave per year in high technology consulting. That's the complex paradox of managing human beings. Some are unhappy with their career choices. Others are unhappy with you, but not their career choices. I've observed the following reasons for departures:

- Better offers

- Family matters (divorce and so on)

- Relocation

- Job not being a good fit

Bill 1,200 Hours per Year!

Armed with the understanding that a great SMB consultant has a 50 percent utilization rate, I challenge you to attempt to bill 1,200 hours per year, which would be at the extreme upper range of billable hour possibilities as an SMB consultant. This challenge assumes you are working 2,400 hours per year. Did you know that translates into 50 hours per week (each and every week)? That, my friend, is a busy week.

Fortunately—or unfortunately, depending on your viewpoint—you may occasionally work 80-hour weeks; however, few do this for extended periods of time. It's these 80-hour work weeks that can skew (not screw!) your average up. But remember that, in the long run, for every 80-hour work week in SMB consulting, there is a shortened week of 10 work hours lurking out there. The law of consulting that states "For every peak, there is a valley" holds true for SMB consultants. The key point is that the hours tend to balance out to a 50 percent utilization rate. You should keep short-term long hour aberrations in proper perspective.

12 Percent Profit Margin

For the sake of argument, use a simple 12 percent profit margin rate in the world of SMB consulting. This number is actually close to true, once you do the math for a large sample size of professional services firms. Consider that large accounting firms, after everyone is paid, are darn lucky to have a 12 percent profit margin (something they'd freely admit to you). And this profit margin calculation accounts for the compensation paid to the employees and partners of the law firm. It also accounts for the depreciation expense over three years to recover the costs of the state-of-the-art network that the hardworking SMB consultant implemented (that's you!). So if accountants will accept a 12 percent profit margin, then you should happily accept it too!

For SMB consultants, understanding that profits are truly the bottom line is critical. After you have paid yourself a salary and have paid all of your taxes and expenses, you need to have about 12 percent of the gross revenue left (this is your 12 percent profit). Profit is the reward above and beyond just making a living as a consultant, the reward for taking a risk to start your own firm. It's also the money used to pay for capital additions and acquisitions.

> BEST PRACTICE: If you're not making a 12 percent profit margin in the long run, consider packing up your SMB consulting shingle and becoming someone else's employee. Why bother with the headache and frustration of running your own consulting practice when for nearly the same compensation you could work as an employee? This is a strict financial argument that doesn't account for the freedom you have as an SMB consultant, but you get the point. And perhaps you are really happy as an SMB consultant and don't want to assign a financial measurement to everything. But my point here should at least be taken under advisement.

Calculating True Costs

If you assume a 12 percent profit margin, you now need to understand how expensive your marginal costs are. That personal digital assistant (PDA) you've been eyeing to keep track of your tasks, address book, and calendar is more expensive in reality than it first appears to be. Getting certified, such as earning the MCSE or the Certified Cisco Internetwork Expert (CCIE), can be surprisingly expensive.

Something like a PDA is useful to the SMB consultant (I have one myself). A good PDA, for the sake of argument, costs $500. Assuming a 12 percent profit margin in SMB consulting, it takes just under $4,200 in revenue to earn a $500 profit. That PDA you want to purchase for $500 will suck the profit out of $4,200 of billable time. If you didn't buy the PDA, your profit would be $500 higher. Addressing the $4,200 in billable time, if your bill rate is $100 per hour, you would need to bill at least 42 hours to generate the profit needed to pay for the PDA (actually slightly more hours when you account for write-offs, which are discussed next).

> BEST PRACTICE: Perhaps you're a certification addict. Many SMB consultants are. You're satisfied with your life as an SMB consultant and now you want something more. You want to validate your professional technical qualifications with an MCSE. Your hard costs for an advanced certification, such as the MCSE, may exceed $10,000. This is a staggering number when you consider that $10K just ate all of the profit out of $83,000 in SMB consulting revenue—very possibly all of your profit for one year's worth of work. Don't forget your SMB consulting utilization rate is going to take a hit for the hundreds of preparation hours you'll incur to pass the intensive MCSE exams. You really have to ask yourself whether or not such an expensive technical certification designation will truly pay off for you as an SMB consultant.

Assume a 12 Percent Write-off Rate

Another Brelsford's Dozen in the world of SMB consulting concerns write-off rates. All SMB consultants should and do take write-offs. Believe it or not, it's good SMB consulting practice management.

Dissatisfied clients

Some time or another, you will have one or more dissatisfied clients. You may not know it from their communication with you, which might be very pleasant when held face-to-face. Rather, you'll know it by observing your accounts receivable balance. When a client's account ages 30, 60, or 90 days, they are typically showing with their pocketbooks how dissatisfied they are with your services.

Client dissatisfaction results for many reasons, such as technical incompetence and poor communications, which are explored in various parts of this book. The specific reason for the client dissatisfaction is not the point here; rather, be aware that unhappy clients will shrink your consulting revenues as an SMB consultant.

Learning curve analysis

You have picked a niche, have mastered client relations, and are making money. Do you really need to recognize this 12 percent write-off rate? Yes. For example, suppose you are an SMB consultant in the networking niche who started in the Windows NT 4.0 days. Over the years, you mastered Windows NT 4.0 and enjoyed client respect. Then Windows 2000 was released, and you ran head-on into Active Directory. Billing adjustments are made to account for time you spend learning Active Directory at the client site. This is time you can't reasonably expect the client to pay. So, you've got a legitimate write-off on your hands. Such write-offs are an acceptable part of being an SMB consultant. You need to factor in learning curve analysis for product upgrades and new releases. It's all part of your budgeting model.

Trying new niches

Professional services firms are often looking for new opportunities. One reason is that niches, while well-defined and lucrative, can also mature and dry up. For example, suppose you're a SBS nicher in the SMB consulting game and Microsoft decides to release no future SBS upgrades. Over a couple of years, your SBS niche can be expected to dry up.

Be thinking about and developing new niches. Such professional development is just good SMB consulting management. The drawback is that, in developing new niches, you often have to take significant write-offs (which some SMB consultants call "write-downs") as you refine your consultant methodology and technical expertise. Many times such development comes through an implicit understanding with clients that you'll work for half-price on their job in order to break into that niche.

> BEST PRACTICE: A good consulting manager knows to expect reasonable write-offs. In fact, if such write-offs are absent, the consultant manager knows that either the SMB consultants on staff are hiding mistakes, loafing on the job, or not expanding their professional and technical boundaries. A small number of mistakes go with the SMB consulting territory. And if you are developing a new consulting niche, your propensity for making mistakes is higher while you are learning and mastering a new area.

One-Hour Rule

This section addresses something so obvious, its one of the great mysteries as to why SMB consultants don't do it: seek help when they can't solve a problem. It's easy enough to commit yourself to better business practices and promise to work more efficiently and effectively. However, a combination of human nature and Murphy's Law can highjack our best behaviors, and we find ourselves engaging in what is known in the recovery movement as "insanity." We repeat the same behaviors over and over again expecting a different outcome. We simply don't admit our powerlessness on occasion and ask for help.

Been there and done that. But I did learn the value of the one-hour rule—where you call for help after one hour of troubleshooting—after I hired employees and took on consulting manager responsibilities. Here I witnessed firsthand, as sometimes only a person removed from the problem on the outside looking in can do, the phenomenon called "heads down." I've seen an individual put in nearly twenty billable hours on a dot matrix printing problem (of course the client could have purchased several dot matrix printers for the equivalent cost). I've seen a person accrue ten billable hours on an "I can't log on" workstation problem (again, you could have purchased a new workstation for that amount). This concept leads us into the following Brelsford's Dozen.

12-to-1 Odds

I propose the following SMB consulting theorem for your approval. If you don't adhere to the one-hour rule, you run significant risk of going heads down and putting in a dozen hours before you look up again and, enlightened by your defeat, finally ask for help. Prove me wrong on this but I believe, based on my own observations, that I'm on target here.

Here are the seven steps for successfully implementing the one-hour rule.

1. **Keep time.** You must glance at your time piece when you start a specific task, such as trying to resolve an "I can't print," so know when an hour would have passed. It's easy to forget that you've even committed an hour to the problem if you don't know what time you started.

2. **Wear the extrovert hat.** Don't sink into introverted mode, as it'll be especially difficult to look up after an hour and make an outbound plea for help.

3. **One hour.** At the one-hour mark, call your consulting manager or a peer in the industry. Granted, if you work for yourself as an SMB consultant, you are the consulting manager, so you'll need to call a peer to describe the situation and brainstorm some ideas to solve the problem.

BEST PRACTICE: So you don't have any friends in the industry, eh? Then be sure to either join or start an SMB-related user group in your area. Information on starting a user group was presented in Chapter 9 in the "Managing Yourself" section.

4. **Newsgroup postings.** Minutes later, if after speaking to someone in step #3 above and the problem is still unresolved, immediately post

your troubleshooting scenario to a couple of newsgroups. This can include the Microsoft newsgroups accessed from the support link on any Microsoft product page or the Yahoo! third-party newsgroups. Be the extrovert and post to newsgroups after one hour. These links are found in appendix A.

5. **Walk away.** Go take an early lunch to clear your head out. Walk away from the problem and take a fresh look at it when you come back. It works wonders to see the sunshine and then return to the server room refreshed.

6. **White board**. If the problem escapes a solution, do as I say and as I try to do: Use a white board in a conference room to "map it all out." I once was bedeviled by a complex server upgrade from NetWare to NT for a 500+ user site. Long story short—problems were encountered using the NT-based NetWare emulation feature as part of the migration process. The situation became so confusing—not to mention stressful—it took a few hours in the conference room to draw out where we'd been, what we'd done, and where we were headed to get it all straight! Use the white board as a tool in your methodical approach to SMB consulting.

7. **Call Microsoft Product Support Service (PSS).** When all else fails, call for bona fide Microsoft support earlier rather than later. There are at least four ways to engage PSS:
   • Small Business Server free support incidents. Specific to the world of SMB consulting and the SBS product, you get two free PSS support incidents with the retail SKU. With the OEM SKU, the two incidents exist but the call is supported by the OEM's product support call center, not by Microsoft PSS. Note the SBS free support incidents are current as this writing and could change in future releases.

   • Mission critical business down for registered partners. You can call into Microsoft PSS and, as a registered partner, plead your case that your client has a server down situation that is mission critical. If you're successful, you'll be granted a free PSS support incident. These requests are evaluated on a case-by-case basis.

• Microsoft Certified Solution Provider/Partner support five-pack. Simply stated, sign-up to become a Microsoft Certified Solution Provider/Partner and you are granted five PSS incidents per year. This value in-kind nearly equals the costs of the certified partner program (as of this writing it's $1,500 USD per year). Remember that this has many more benefits above and beyond paid incidents (such as over $25,000 of free software for its modest $1,500 USD annual fee), so be sure to think about that as well.

• $250 USD (approximately) per incident. For the rest of us, you can always call in and pay by the drink. That is, a PSS incident as of this writing is $250 USD. The good news is that it's well worth it as PSS will stay on the telephone with you for hours until the matter is solved.

BEST PRACTICE: This is a best practice in the truest sense: time management. You should endeavor to adhere to the one-hour rule if for no other reason than basic SMB consulting practice profitability. It works like this. A "standard" SMB consulting gig where you install a solution such as SBS can yield around $4,000 USD in today's market. Compare that to enterprise technology gigs that start around $400,000. Obviously the IT consulting talent on an enterprise gig can go "heads down" and break the one-hour rule while still allowing for overall engagement profitability. But darn it, if you break the one-hour rule on an SMB consulting gig, you're seriously threatening the profitability of that project. There's just not enough financial slack to cover for mistakes and missteps.

Methodology Samples

There's nothing like looking to the leaders when formulating your own SMB consulting practice. By that I mean you can cherry pick methodology examples from existing large, medium-sized, and small consulting practices to assist in the rapid development of your own methodologies. So in this Brelsford's Dozen segment, you will visit 12 Web sites from other consulting practices and draw out methodology elements that make the most sense to you. Consider using a search engine or specialized information sites, such as

Kennedy Information's Top 50 Consulting Firm list (www.kennedyinfo.com), to find Web sites for other consulting firms and their respective methodology postings. Do it now!

Create Your Top-12 Niche List!

No chapter is complete without a Brelsford's Dozen thrown in. I want you to take a break and make a list of the top dozen niches, ranked in order of desirability, in which you'd like to consider performing as an SMB consultant. Just do it:

1.

2.

3.

4.

5.

6.

7.

8.

9.

10.

11.

12.

Ongoing Maintenance Tasks

So here is a list of ongoing maintenance tasks that are SBS deliverables for you, the SMB consultant.

1. Updating virus definition data files. Assuming you've selected a capable client/server anti-virus protection application, such as Trend Micro's OfficeScan suite, it's now incumbent upon you to keep current. You'll want to consider updating the virus definition data files hourly so that your SBS client is not exposed to evil and destructive viruses.

2. Verifying backup jobs. Perhaps only second to virus detection would be data backups. You'll read in the next major section of this chapter how the Server Status Report can be very beneficial in sending the tape backup log to you each morning. But even more important than performing and receiving notice of a backup is the ability to conduct a test restore. Test restores are typically performed once a month or even more frequently.

3. Black hatting yourself. You can never let your guard down when it comes to security. Security is truly an ongoing maintenance task, a function that you will never "complete." So one way to determine the security fitness of your SBS client sites is to run a security scanning tool against the SBS server machine. This method also allows you to confirm the security settings you believe you've configured and implemented correctly.

Appendix C

SMB SUCCESS KIT

This is a loose collection of SMB succcess strategies in an easy to read, at a glance format called "Bits and Bytes." It is followed by an SMB consulting toolkit and a list of ten things your should not forget about small businesses.

Bits and Bytes

- Show up! 80 percent of success is just showing up, according to Woody Allen, the famous. It's true.

- Minimize mistakes. A huge part of business success is simply avoiding mistakes.

- Communicate. Your words will serve you well as an SMB consultant and set you apart from others when serving clients.

- Master a technical niche. Find something that you're both competent and interested in and go for it. The rewards will follow.

- Savor the moment: working for yourself. Take five, walk outside on the desk, feel the warmth of the sun and give out an enormous Wahoo! You're making it as a self-employed SMB consultant.

- Grow with each opportunity. Some engagements will stretch your technical skills. Some engagements will stretch your business skills. Grow and learn something from each engagement. Be able to say "I learned something new today!"

- Don't overbook yourself. Hopefully you didn't get into this business to be so busy you become forgetful and stressed. This is another way of saying don't forget the names of your spouse and children.

- Watch your finances. Enough said!

- Don't sweat the small stuff. The professional relationship between a client and an SMB consultant is a marriage. Choose your battles carefully.

- Pay your taxes. Enough said!

- Mentor others. Here's your chance to easily earn Karma Dollars! Help someone out how is new to the technology consulting field.

- Thrive and survive under any conditions: A great consultant can do well in any economy based on mastering the following skills:

(1) having a technical niche in demand, (2) strong communication skills, and (3) above average client management skills.

- Be in the top 10 percent of your peer group. You'll know it when you get there. You'll start to show up on "Who's Who" lists in your local business papers.

- Take Next Steps! Ponder the future. Read futuristic viewpoints about the technology area such as "Future of Technology Is Hardly Ever What Anyone Has Predicted" (Portals column, Lee Gomes, Wall Street Journal, 4-14-03). Also subscribe to Directions on Microsoft newsletter (www.directionsonmicrosoft.com).

- Take Next Steps #2: Attend SMB Nation conference once a year (www.smbnation.com)

- Take Next Steps #3: Subscribe to Small Business Best Practices newsletter (free at www.nethealthmon.com)

SMB Consultant Toolkit

Here are some items for your SMB consulting tool kit that you carry to your client sites:

- Action Pack Subscription

- TechNet Subscription (Premium DVD version)

- Resource kits and other tattered books. There's nothing like having a resource kit or two, along with your favorite books, spread out in front of you when performing server surgery. Consider carrying both Small Business Server 2000 Best Practices and Small Business Server 2003 Best Practices

- Catalogs. Like you, I receive the monthly catalog mailings from the national hardware/software resellers. Surprisingly, these catalogs come in handy when discussing technology solutions with clients, particularly when I need to draw a few prices out of thin air.

- Monthly newspapers for computer users. In Seattle, each January issue of the Puget Sound Computer User (http://www.pscu.com/) lists a potpourri of local reseller, consulting, labor, and publishing resources for the technology community. It's called the Business Directory issue. This type of publication is also available in many other North American areas. The January issue helps me refer my clients to competent professionals in technical areas that I don't serve (such as UNIX).

- Handheld tape recorder. There's nothing like having a recorded journal of the steps you took to troubleshoot a problem or build a server. It's an invaluable item to carry.

- Laptop computer. You'll need a computer with the ability to access the Internet and download drivers and search Microsoft's knowledge base (http://www.microsoft.com/). And let's face it; you just need a laptop computer with you as an SMB consultant for tons of other reasons.

- External modem with modem cable (serial 9 to 25 pin out). Sometimes the client's Internet connection (say broadband) or modem just won't function correctly and work needs to get done. Because of my experience with Small Business Server, I now carry an external US Robotics 56K Sportster modem just in case, and it always works.

- A long telephone line and an analog telephone. The long telephone line is for reaching the Telco wall jack that's always across the room. The analog telephone is to plug into that wall jack to test the telephone service thoroughly.

- A cellular telephone. Enough said.

- Telephone numbers of peers to call for advice. There's nothing like calling a BackOffice buddy to help you out of a jam.

- A portable file cabinet. This can help you maintain working client files with office layout drawings, field notes, and billable-hour charge sheets. A well-organized SMB consultant is a happy SMB consultant. Trust me.

- A portable tape deck/radio. When the cat's away, why shouldn't the mice have just a little play?

- Kneepads. No, these aren't for receiving a client delivered spanking. I carry them to protect my old skier's knees when I'm fishing cable around a crowded server room.

- Working clothes. One moment you're selling your SMB consulting services in a glass tower. The next minute you're implementing SBS in a dusty warehouse. It's best to carry a change of clothes, including a working suit, pullovers, and tennis shoes, and be prepared to change in the water closet.

- Good old fashioned junk food. It's funny how many amazing feats you can accomplish with an elevated blood sugar level.

Ten Things Not to Forget About Small Businesses

1. **They have no computer strategies and no IT budgets.**

    Small businesses do not have separate budgets for separate things. Nor separate strategies for separate areas of the business. Every dollar they have might go to dozens of different places—wages, stationary, marketing, computing, and paying off loans. They spend their money based on what they absolutely have to spend it on now. And if there is 'spare money' then it goes on aggressive activities like getting more customers. They do not plan their computer purchases. They buy something new when they have to—when the old one breaks or they've grown so much they need the additional capacity.

2. **They depend upon free advice.**

    They rely upon an informal network of computer advisors. Friends, family, business acquaintances, guys at the computer store, even computer professionals until the money meter starts running. They are hungry for this advice and they really value someone who can give an authoritative answer to a technology question in clear, simple, and easy to understand English.

3. They aren't interested in growth for it's own sake.

For the most part they didn't start the business in order to become millionaires. They did it so they can carry on the job they love in an environment they can control. So they have really mixed feelings about growth. Some will acknowledge that survival demands growth but most would rather stay as they are—assuming they can guarantee sufficient income to keep going. The ideal is growing revenues with no additional outlay—of time and resources.

4. They get no kick from admin.

They started the business in order to be a lawyer, or a baker, or a tree surgeon or a photographer. Not to be a CEO or Office Manager or administrative assistant. They resent then amount of time they have to spend managing people and resources, filling in forms, doing invoicing, finding replacements for absent employees. This sort of stuff is the reason many of them left corporate life in the first place. For most of them dealing with computers sits on this crappy side of the business.

5. They don't know that much about computers.

Small business people are not computer experts. They are less informed than BDMs in large companies. Unlike BDMs they don't have an IT department to educate them or a board to demand an effective IT strategy. Many small business people are unable to tell you the difference between an operating system and an application. Or what RAM is. Or what sort of computer they have at the moment. They tend to know only what they need to know— enough to perform the specific functions they got the thing for. Thus, when it comes to buying a new one or upgrading they feel under-informed and defensive.

6. They have long memories.

Most small businesses have been around a few years. And they're likely to be run by the same people now, as they were when they were started. They don't have the regular flow of people that your average large corporation does. So they have long corporate memories. They remember all the problems they've had with their computers very vividly. And their risk aversion means they move pretty slowly. To quote one small business owner "New version of Windows? We've only just got over installing Windows 3.1"

7. They are extremely risk averse.

They have no safety net. If their business fails their income disappears—and their dreams. They therefore think long and hard before they do anything that might change the way things are working. If they make a mistake with the software there's no IT director to carry the can. This is why they prefer software that's been around a while—preferably for a couple of versions. But, they keep costs low by keeping staffing low—which means they're always short of time. So they tent to react to problems rather than foresee them. They therefore react badly to people asking them to think ahead and plan for the future of their businesses. They'd rather deal with the future of their businesses. They'd rather deal with the future when it gets here. Key small business motto—If It Ain't Broke Don't Fix It.

8. They like to make their own decisions.

These are independent people. That's one of the reasons they're doing this. They don't like to be told what to do. They get a real sense of satisfaction from making business decisions—they exhibit less of the concern about decision-making sometimes seen with IT guys or BDMs. They do their research and they take as much free advice as they can but then they make their own decisions and they stick with them.

9. Their businesses are unique.

They don't think of themselves as small business people. They think of themselves as butchers or bakers or candles-stick makers. And they tend to believe that their business is unlike any other. They assume that any general "small business solution" will be inapplicable to them. They assume that anyone who wants to sell anything to them will have to get to know their business first.

10. They rely upon their computers.

Many small businesses could not exist without their computers. But this does not mean they are into the idea of "computing." They may have a crucial customer database on an old 386 running DOS. It's probably incredibly cumbersome to work with and a little buggy but it's absolutely essential to their business. So they'll put up with the bugs rather than risk losing the whole thing by moving to a new machine or new software. (And they are used to how that old machine works. They don't want to waste time learning how to deal with some new system.)

Index

T

Time management, 1-8 to 1-11, 4-6, 5-58, 9-7, 10-2, 10-10

Tactics, sales tactics, 2-7, 6-5, 6-30

Trust, 3-1, 7-41

Training, 5-36, 9-26, 9-32, 10-11, 12-32, 13-31

Trade groups, 9-34

Terminal Services, 6-17, 6-22

Trade-outs, 10-16, 10-29

TS2 events, Microsoft, 9-35, 6-43

Telemarketing, telephone calls, 8-28, 6-48

Trade shows, 6-53

Telephone book advertising, 6-55

U

User Group, 9-34

UNIX, 6-24

Upgrades, 6-26, 6-27

Underserved areas of opportunity, 12-43

V

Variety of work, 1-7

Volunteering, 4-14

Virtual private networking (VPN), 6-22

Value, adding value, 12-24

Visio, Microsoft, 8-23, 8-24, 9-12, 11-26, 12-37

Visual Studio, Microsoft, 8-39, 12-27

W

Writing, 2-4, 5-49, 7-19, 7-31

Work, 5-6, 7-42, 9-9

Workshops, 5-51, 6-55

Workstations, Windows-based, 6-19

Windows SharePoint Services, 8-23, 8-25, 9-10, 12-6, 13-26

X

XML, 11-23, 11-24

Y

Yourdon and Coad template, 11-26

Z

Zero-based budgeting, 2-11, 10-20